BONE
ANTLER
IVORY
& HORN

**The Technology of
Skeletal Materials
Since the Roman
Period**

BONE ANTLER IVORY & HORN

The Technology of Skeletal Materials Since the Roman Period

ARTHUR MacGREGOR

CROOM HELM London & Sydney
BARNES & NOBLE BOOKS Totowa, New Jersey

© 1985 Arthur MacGregor
Croom Helm Ltd, Provident House, Burrell Row,
Beckenham, Kent BR3 1AT
Croom Helm Australia Pty Ltd, First Floor, 139 King Street,
Sydney, NSW 2001, Australia

British Library Cataloguing in Publication Data
MacGregor, Arthur
Bone, antler, ivory and horn.
1. Man — Tools
2. Bone implements
I. Title
621.9'08'0901   GN799.T6

ISBN 0-7099-3242-1

First published in the USA 1985 by
Barnes & Noble Books
81 Adams Drive, Totowa, New Jersey, 07512

Library of Congress Cataloging in Publication Data
MacGregor, Arthur, 1941-
    Bone, antler, ivory, and horn.

    Bibliography: p.
    Includes index.
    1. Bone carving–History. 2. Horn carving–History.
    3. Ivory carving–History. 4. Implements, utensils, etc.
    –History. I. Title.
TT288.M3   1985   736'.6   84-18535
ISBN 0-389-20531-1

Typeset by Columns of Reading
Printed and bound in Great Britain
Produced by Bookchase (UK) Ltd

Contents

Figures and Tables

Tables

Acknowledgements

In compiling this study I have enjoyed the co-operation of a number of institutions and the friendly collaboration of many colleagues. In the initial period of my research Mr James Rackham's zoological advice and his discussion of the whole range of the enquiry was of enormous value. Professor John Currey made it possible for me to attempt a scientific assessment of the materials concerned by his liberal provision of expertise and laboratory facilities. Several colleagues working on related topics have commented on my draft texts and have generously shared the results of their own research with me: amongst those I would particularly like to mention are Dr Kristina Ambrosiani, for access to and discussion of the material from Birka and other Swedish sites; Dr Philip Armitage for references to medieval and later horn and bone industries; Dr Stephen Greep for discussion of Roman bone working; and Dr Ingrid Ulbricht for access to and information on the material from Hedeby. My own research benefited from the guidance of Professor Rosemary Cramp and from the scrutiny of Mrs Leslie Webster and Mr Christopher Morris.

A number of excavators have kindly allowed me to mention their finds in advance of their final publication: these include Mr P.V. Addyman, Mr G. Beresford, Mr N.Q. Bogdan, Mr P.D.C. Brown, Mr. A. Carter, Mrs. N. Crummy and Mr D. Phillips.

I would also like to extend my thanks to those colleagues whose illustrations have been reproduced with their specific consent, and also to those from whom agreement has had to be assumed. In either case the primary source of illustrations is acknowledged in the captions.

My wife has lived with proliferating drafts of this book over several years and has provided some critical appraisal of them. The final version was typed with great care by Mrs F. Holt.

Preface

In recent years, which have seen a variety of sophisticated methods and techniques applied to the analysis of certain categories of archaeological material, the study of items made from skeletal materials has remained resolutely neglected. Useful accounts have appeared of some groups of objects related typologically or stratigraphically, but their impact has been limited by the lack of an overall context in which they could be set.

The object of this survey is to provide a general background against which individual finds, specifically those of northern Europe since the Roman period, may be viewed in their proper perspective. Several factors exercising varying — sometimes crucial — degrees of control over the final products are considered, and their inter-relationships examined. The principal materials, bone, antler, ivory and horn, are reviewed in terms of their structure, morphology and availability; their mechanical properties are compared and quantified in objective scientific terms; and the working methods applicable to them are considered, drawing on the evidence of manufacturing techniques visible on the objects themselves, and that of tools recovered from archaeological deposits. There follows a review of objects made from skeletal materials since the Roman period, acknowledging where appropriate the considerations outlined above, together with other evidence from archaeological, historical and ethnological sources.

By treating together the disparate objects considered here and the evidence of varying kinds which can be brought to bear on them, it is hoped at once to provide a useful body of reference material and, perhaps, the basis for a more comprehensive and integrated approach in the future to the examination of artefacts made from skeletal materials.

1. Raw Materials

The element of objectivity gained by examination of each of the raw materials considered here is a necessary prerequisite for the proper study of the artefacts which were made from them. In some instances their distinguishing characteristics came to be acutely appreciated by those who utilised them, both as the result of personal observation and of generations of inherited knowledge. This was the manner in which any craftsman learned his trade in the days before a theoretical grounding was added to the otherwise practical curriculum of the trainee technician. By the time he had finished his apprenticeship, such a craftsman would have acquired a 'feel' for his materials based on the experience he had gained for himself and had absorbed from his masters: he might well find difficulty in expressing precisely why one piece of raw material was particularly suitable for one purpose or another, but his judgement would be no less valid and accurate for all that. In our attempts to reconstruct the factors which led to the evolution of particular craft practices in antiquity we are, in the case of skeletal materials, denied access to any body of accumulated knowledge, since nearly all use of these materials ceased long ago and written records relating to them are few. Instead we must substitute scientifically-obtained data through which objective valuations can be made and from which we can attempt to infer the qualities which led to the consistent adoption of specific materials for specific purposes.

The overall picture which emerges from this exercise places skeletal materials in a new light: whereas there has in the past been a tendency to regard bone, antler and horn as inferior substitutes for metal or even ivory, the respective mechanical properties which each of these possesses are in many ways truly remarkable, and often render them supremely suitable for particular tasks.

A further important consideration is the manner in which the gross characteristics of particular materials, especially whole bones, directly conditioned the evolution of typologies. In the past these typologies have all too often been studied with no reference whatever to such factors, but in many cases it can be shown that the morphology of the raw materials had a crucial influence and, in some instances, even led to the conditioning of forms subsequently executed in other materials in which these primary controls were absent.

An initial problem encountered in this study is one of suitable terminology. Osseous skeletons, while consisting of many diverse components, are structurally distinct from teeth; neither of these in turn has anything in common with the keratinous material of which horns are composed. In an attempt to produce an appropriate portmanteau word which would encompass all animal substances used in the production of tools and implements, the term 'osteodontokeratic materials' has been adopted by some archaeologists (e.g. Dart 1957) while Halstead (1974) has settled for the more prosaic 'vertebrate hard tissues'. While each of these alternatives possesses a higher degree of biological precision than that adopted here, the term 'skeletal materials' is preferred, as it conveys to the non-specialist a more comprehensible (if strictly less accurate) impression of the scope of this enquiry.

Since a good deal of emphasis is to be laid here on the conditioning exerted on the evolution of artefacts by the raw materials from which each of them was formed, it will be necessary to begin with an account of each category of material in turn; in this way, the nature of each can be assessed, mutual comparisons can be made, a working terminology established and the characteristics by which each can be identified made known.

Bone

The archaeologist with an interest in bones is already well served by a number of publications, among which those of Brothwell (1972), Chaplin (1971), Cornwall (1974), Ryder

(1968a) and Schmid (1972) deserve particular mention. In each of these works, however, particular emphasis is placed on the morphology of bones, the problems of identifying them and their distribution and function within the living skeleton. Although these factors are of some importance in the present context, they are secondary to the main theme. As the materials reviewed here are considered outside the environment for which they were originally evolved, their fitness for their original function is not of direct importance, although the qualities which recommend them for utilisation in a particular way are often interconnected with their original skeletal function.

Formation

According to the manner in which it develops at the foetal stage, a broad distinction is drawn between membrane (or dermal) bone, which originates in fibrous membrane, and cartilage bone, whose origins lie in pre-existing foetal cartilage. Both types develop through a process of ossification, in which soft tissue is progressively replaced by bone through the action of specialised osteoblast (bone-producing) cells, although details of the process differ for the two varieties. Ossification continues after birth at the growing zones until the definitive size is reached. Cartilage bones are formed by gradual replacement with bone tissue of embryonic cartilage models. They are extended (Figure 1)

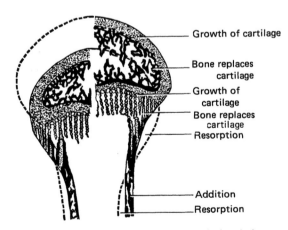

Growth of cartilage

Bone replaces cartilage

Growth of cartilage

Bone replaces cartilage

Resorption

Addition

Resorption

Figure 1: Extension of long-bones by endochondral ossification (after Ham). While new cartilage is added to and ossified at the growing ends, a complimentary process of resorption maintains the original form of the bone

by progressive ossification of the proliferating epiphyseal cartilage which separates the diaphysis or shaft from the articular ends or epiphyses (endochondral ossification), the process being completed with maturity. In the case of membrane bones growth takes place around the peripheries (intra-membraneous ossification), the junctions or sutures between certain bones again becoming fused in maturity (Freeman and Bracegirdle 1967; Ham 1965; Weinmann and Sicher 1955).

The distinction here is therefore between the types of tissue being replaced by the developing bone: the resulting bones are indistinguishable except perhaps for some difference in the coarseness of the initial fibres (Pritchard 1972), and this primary tissue is in any case quickly replaced under normal processes (p. 7). Further evidence for the close links existing between the two types of bone lies in the fact that elements of both types are involved in the development of some bones: the clavicle and mandible, for example, are classified among the membrane bones, even though a large proportion of each has its origin in cartilage, while the long bones, which are counted among the cartilage bones, have much of their shafts formed in membrane (Pritchard 1956).

An important bone-forming membrane, the periosteum, sheathes the external surfaces, while the interior cavities of certain cartilage bones are lined with a corresponding membrane, the endosteum. In addition to its normal osteogenic functions during growth, the periosteum may be stimulated to produce new bone in order to repair damage, or in response to demands from the muscles or tendons for more secure anchorages (McLean and Urist 1961; Ham 1965).[1]

Structure

Bone tissue consists of an organic and an inorganic fraction, intimately combined. The organic matrix accounts for a considerable part of the weight (variously estimated at between 25 per cent and 60 per cent of the total) and volume (between 40 per cent and 60 per cent of the total) of adult bone (Frost 1967; Sissons 1953; Wainwright *et al.* 1976). It consists of about 95 per cent of the fibrous protein collagen (which is also a major constituent of tendon and skin), along with other forms of

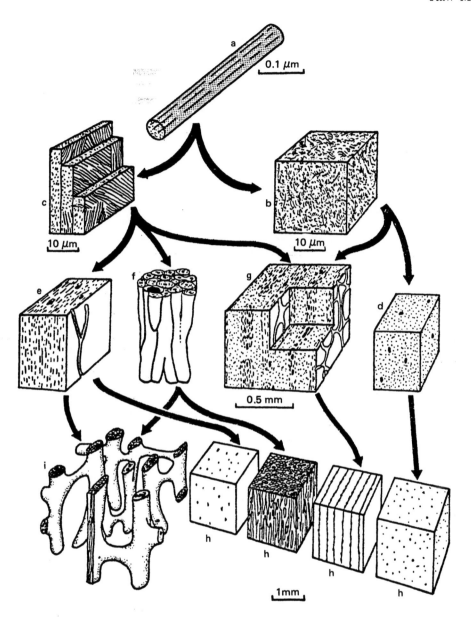

Figure 2: Structure of mammalian bone at different levels of organisation (after Currey) (The arrows indicate which types may contribute to higher levels of structure.)

Key
a   Collagen fibril with associated mineral crystals.
b   Woven bone. The collagen fibrils are arranged in random fashion.
c   Lamellar bone. There are separate lamellae, and the collagen fibrils are arranged in domains of preferred orientation in each lamella.
d   Woven bone. Blood channels are shown as large black spots. At this level woven bone is shown by light stippling.

e   Primary lamellar bone. Lamellae are indicated by light dashes.
f   Haversian bone. A collection of Haversian systems, each with concentric lamellae around a central blood channel.
g   Laminar bone. Two blood channel networks are exposed. Note how layers of woven and lamellar bone alternate.
h   Compact bone, of the types shown at lower levels.
i   Cancellous bone.

proteins and polysaccharide complexes. Typical collagen has a structure of rope-like fibrils arranged in close proximity to one another and frequently interlinked (Currey 1970a), forming a basic scaffolding for the bone structure.

In the natural process of ossification, mineral crystals — generally agreed to be hydroxy-apatite, a complex of tricalcium phosphate and calcium hydroxide — surround the collagen fibres.[2] There is some dispute (summarised in Wainwright *et al.* 1976) concerning the shape of these apatite crystals: the commonly-held opinion is that they have the form of needles, but some authorities have claimed that these are in reality plates viewed end on. Whatever their form, the apatite crystals, which are aligned with and bonded to the collagen fibrils, are distinguishable only with high-resolution equipment, their thickness being in the order of 4nm, so that they are quite invisible under the conventional optical microscope. A certain amount of amorphous (non-crystalline) apatite is also present in the inorganic fraction.

With these basic ingredients organised in various ways, bone is produced in a number of forms. Following Currey (in Wainwright *et al.* 1976), the different bone structures encountered in the mammalian skeleton may be classified as follows (Figure 2).

A primary distinction can be made between woven and lamellar bone. Woven bone (Figure 2b) is characterised by an absence of marked orientation in its structure, both in terms of the collagen fibres, which proliferate in all directions in coarse bundles varying in diameter up to 30µm, and of the apatite crystals which frequently do not adopt the orientation of the fibrils. Compared with lamellar bone, it displays a higher proportion of amorphous mineral, and a higher mineral/organic ratio.

By contrast, the collagen fibrils in lamellar bone (Figure 2c) are grouped in finer bundles of about 2-4µm diameter and are arranged in distinct layers or lamellae. Within each of these the fibrils are generally aligned in the plane of the lamella and are grouped into distinct 'domains'. The fibrils within each domain display a preference for a particular orientation, although adjoining domains may vary from each other in their preferred alignment: in successive lamellae, variations of up to 90° in orientation of the fibrils occurs. Some variation in the dimensions of lamellae is also distin-guishable, but typically they are about 5µm thick while the width of the average domain is about 30-100µm. Most (but not all) authorities believe adjoining lamellae to be separated from one another by a perforated sheet of 'interlamellar bone', pierced here and there by occasional fibrils passing from one lamella to another.

Running through bone tissue of either of the above types small cavities or lacunae can be seen. These interconnect with one another and with neighbouring blood-vessels, by means of small channels named canaliculi. Within the lacunae lie osteocytes (bone cells),[3] generally sub-spherical, irregular and randomly distri-buted in the case of woven bone and oblate spheroid, more regularly spaced and more evenly sized in lamellar bone. The processes of these cells ramify through the above-mentioned channels.

At the next highest order of structure, Currey distinguishes four principal types of bone (Figure 2d-g). Woven bone may be found proliferating in any direction for several milli-metres in extent, pierced randomly by blood-vessels (Figure 2d). Primary lamellar bone found at this level of magnitude has the lamellae aligned with the local surface of the whole bone and is permeated by blood vessels with the same general orientation (Figure 2e). Either of these types can be modified after their initial formation into a third type characterised by so-called Haversian systems (Figure 2f). These are formed by resorption of bone around blood vessels by osteoclast cells, the resulting circular or ovoid channels (which generally follow the long axis of the bone) subsequently becoming filled with newly deposited lamellar bone oriented with the channel walls (Figure 4). The collagen fibrils within each lamella generally run spirally to the axis of the channel, the direction of the fibrils changing between successive lamellae (McLean and Urist 1961). The size and complexity of these Haversian systems varies considerably: Weinmann and Sicher (1955) estimate 5-20 lamellae per system, while Ham (1965) gives the usual number as 'less than half a dozen'. Haversian systems may form around vessels within the thickness of the bone (Figure 3) or at the peripheries (Ham 1965). The outer limit of the Haversian system is delineated by a 'cement line' of calcified mucopolysaccharide through which pass only very few canaliculi, those in the outermost lamellae generally looping back on themselves. The blood vessels lying at the heart of the Haversian system are therefore largely isolated from adjacent systems, except where they interconnect through the so-called canals of Volkmann, which also connect with the periosteal and endosteal blood supply (Figure 4). Because Haversian systems and the blood vessels they contain frequently branch and divide, however, their isolation as seen in cross section is more apparent than real. Fourthly, at this level of structure laminar bone may be encountered (Figure 2g). The laminae in question result from a particular method of bone formation incorporating both woven and lamellar bone (Figure 5). Each increment is formed by the growth of a scaffolding of woven bone around the network of blood vessels distributed on the surface of the bone. Woven bone quickly engulfs the vessels, which are left lying in a series of cavities. While further

laminae are being formed on the new outer surface by continuation of this process, lamellar bone gradually forms on the insides of the cavities, filling them in and adding strength and rigidity to the whole bone. The resulting structure, therefore, consists of alternating layers of woven and lamellar bone.

Moving to the final level of structure, two categories are distinguishable: compact and cancellous bone. Compact (or cortical) bone (Figure 2h) may be formed from any one or more of the middle order types described above. As the term implies, there are no gaps in the structure of compact bone, other than those occupied by blood vessels. By contrast, cancellous (or trabecular, or spongy) bone has an open structure of trabeculae formed of lamellar or Haversian bone (Figure 2i), in which the aggregate volume of the vascular spaces may equal or exceed that of the bone matrix (Hancox 1972). It is at this last level that bone will generally be treated here. Although

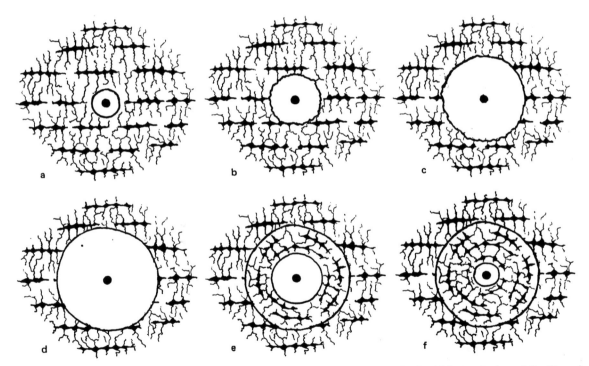

Figure 3: Diagrammatic cross-section of the formation of a Haversian system within the thickness of a bone (after Currey)

Key
a   Blood vessel within a channel in the bone.
b   An erosion cavity forms around it.
c   The cavity increases in size.

d   The surface is smoothed off.
e   New bone is laid down on the surface.
f   The Haversian system is complete.

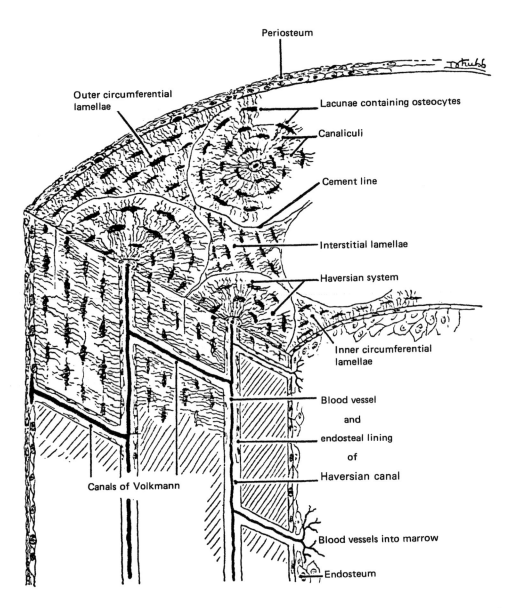

Periosteum

Outer circumferential lamellae

Lacunae containing osteocytes

Canaliculi

Cement line

Interstitial lamellae

Haversian system

Inner circumferential lamellae

Blood vessel

and

endosteal lining

of

Haversian canal

Canals of Volkmann

Blood vessels into marrow

Endosteum

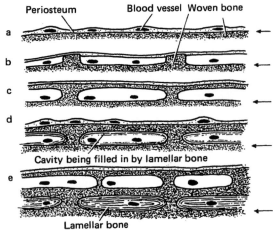

Periosteum   Blood vessel   Woven bone

a

b

c

d

Cavity being filled in by lamellar bone

e

Lamellar bone

Figure 4: Three-dimensional diagram showing structural components of a long-bone shaft (after Ham). In reality, many more Haversian systems would occupy the area indicated

Figure 5: Growth of laminar bone (after Currey)

Key
a   Resting surface. Periosteum has blood vessels between it and woven bone at surface.
b-c Scaffolding of woven bone with cavities.
d   Cavities filled with lamellar bone.
e   Process repeated. The position of original surface indicated by arrows.

compact and cancellous bone are immediately distinguishable from one another with the naked eye, their identical structure at a microscopic level should, however, be borne in mind: their essential similarity is underlined by the fact that cancellous bone can be converted into cortical bone by the deposition of lamellar tissue while, under other circumstances, cortical bone may be resorbed to a cancellous form.

Indeed the entire bone structure undergoes continual change and renewal throughout life, old tissue being resorbed by bone-destroying osteoclast cells and new bone being deposited in its place. Woven bone, which makes up most of the embryonic skeleton and which is also deposited at the margins of growing bones and at fracture sites, fulfils the skeleton's needs for rapid supplies of tissue. Once established, however, it undergoes gradual conversion to mechanically superior lamellar bone which eventually makes up a large proportion of the adult skeleton. Naturally, therefore, intermediate or mixed types of tissue are commonly found within a single bone.

In old age the rate of renewal slows down, so that an increasing proportion of the bone is made up of old tissue, resulting in an increase in brittleness. Even in youth the quality of bone may fluctuate considerably, since the skeleton is in a state of constant metabolic exchange with the rest of the body, acting as a mineral reservoir and releasing its reserves into the

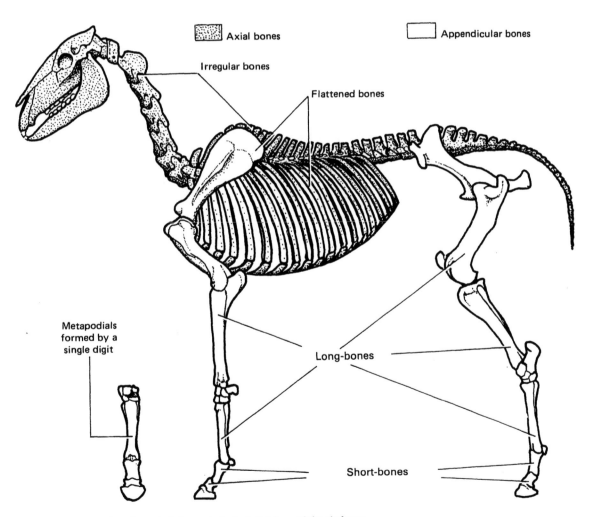

Figure 6: Mammalian (horse) skeleton: principal divisions of the skeleton

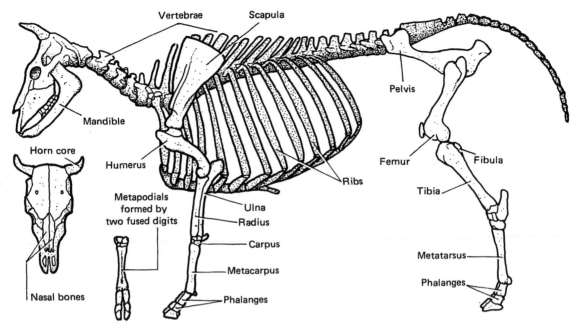

Figure 7:   Mammalian (cattle) skeleton: principal bones mentioned in text

blood stream in response to demands from other bodily systems. Extended periods of malnutrition will give rise to changes of this nature as will other more natural events. During pregnancy and lactation, for example, calcium and other minerals may be resorbed from the skeleton in this way, while the trabeculae of so-called 'medullary bone', found in the long bones of laying fowls, form a reservoir of calcium which is readily resorbed for the production of egg-shells (Hancox 1972).

Morphology: the Mammalian Skeleton

A major division into two parts can be made of the mammalian skeleton (Figures 6-7). The first comprises axial bones which either lie along the medial line of the torso (in which case they are each symmetrically shaped, as in the sternum and vertebrae) or else they are ranged in bilateral symmetry on either side of the median, as with the ribs. Appendicular bones, which form the second major group, include the limbs and their respective girdles. A third group, the visceral bones, which develop in various soft tissues, will not concern us here.

The axial skeleton includes both flattened bones, such as the ribs, which help in the support and protection of the organs, and also irregular bones, principally the vertebrae, which form a strong but flexible channel for the spinal cord and are also provided with complex processes for the attachment of muscles. In the appendicular skeleton, most important from the point of view of utilisation are the long bones, basically elongated hollow cylinders with expanded articular ends, which act as supporting columns for the limbs and provide a system of levers on which the muscles and tendons may act. There are also a number of compact or short bones concentrated in the area of the wrists and ankles, the dimensions of which are more closely comparable in all axes. In their definitive forms, bones of either group comprise a certain amount of internal cancellous tissue and an external envelope of compact tissue, the relative abundance of each varying widely according to the form and function of the particular bone.

As well as providing support and protection, as mentioned above, living bones are bound up with various other physiological systems which directly condition their detailed form. Various foramena exist for the passage of nerves and nutritive blood-vessels (e.g. Figure 72b) and, for example, to allow inter-connection with the

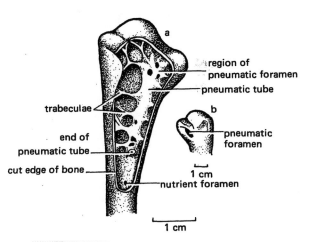

Figure 8: Cutaway view of pneumatic humerus of an adult fowl (*Gallus domesticus*) (after Bellairs and Jenkin)

Note: In most aerated bones the pneumatic foramen opens directly into the bone but in this instance it leads into a pneumatic tube.

blood-forming red marrow found within the flat bones of the skull, sternum and ribs and in the cancellous extremities of long bones. Yellow marrow, mostly fat, occupies the interiors of the long bone diaphyses of mammals (medullary cavity). In birds the long bone marrow is absent and the hollow cavities or sinuses so formed give rise to so-called pneumatic bones (Figure 8). In some species almost every bone becomes pneumatised in the course of development, being invaded by air sacks connecting with the bronchial system, nasal chamber or auditory passages (Bellairs and Jenkin 1960).

Clearly there is a great deal of variation between the bones of different species: for details of these variations, reference should be made to the standard works mentioned on pp. 1-2. A knowledge of their distinguishing features is invaluable in the study of bone artefacts and, even when the gross form of the bone cannot be used as a guide, the trained eye can detect clues which may permit identification of the type of bone used or even the species concerned. A few examples may usefully be quoted.

The sandwich-like structure of cancellous bone between two thin layers of compact tissue which is characteristic of some discoid playing pieces (Figure 72b) distinguishes them from others of similar general appearance but which are solid (Figure 72a). The former category can be shown to derive from the mandibles of horse or cattle, which exhibit this same structure, while the nutrient foramen which pierces the cancellous tissue on some examples locates the precise spot on the jawbone from which they were cut (Figure 36). The solid counters are generally of antler, such cancellous tissue as may be present usually (but not invariably) running axially within them.

A glance at the expanded-headed pin shown in Figure 64, no. 37 might suggest that it was one of the series of pig fibula pins which naturally display this form (Figure 64, no. 39); a closer look, however, reveals that it is pierced by a nutrient foramen, demonstrating that it has been cut from the shaft of a long-bone from a cattle or horse-sized animal, so that the raw material can have had no conditioning effect on the shape in this instance. The source of raw material for certain long-toothed combs can be established in the same way (Figure 102). As a final example, the side-plates of composite combs (p. 82) or the flat decorative strips identified below as casket mounts (p. 197) have few features to distinguish them from one another or to relate them to any particular source on the obverse (decorated) surface, but when the reverse is examined, some display a cancellous structure which indicates that they are made from the ribs of cattle-sized animals, while others are identifiable as antler (cf. Figure 9a, b); a third group of casket mounts, which is made up of large plates of thin and flat material, occasionally displays a stripe of cancellous bone which confirms that they have been cut from scapulae, the spongy stripe marking the area from which the *spina scapula* has been removed (cf. Figure 96). Other examples of similar clues will be quoted as they are encountered in the section on artefacts.

Antler

Paired antlers, like horns, are restricted to the *Artiodactyla*, or even-toed ungulates. The similarity ends there, however, for unlike horn (a modified, non-deciduous skin tissue) antlers are outgrowths of bone.[4] They are carried by most members of the deer family (*Cervidae*) and, with the exception of reindeer and

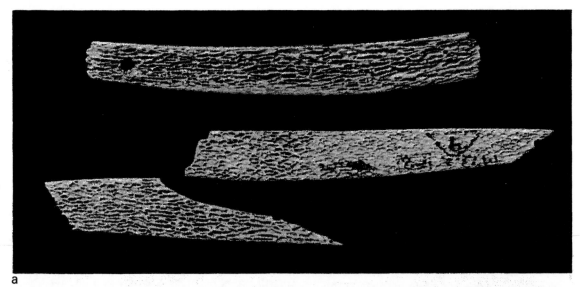

a

b

Figure 9:   Comparison of cancellous structures in bone and antler: (a) comb case fragments made from rib bones (reverse) (b) offcuts of red deer antler (reverse)

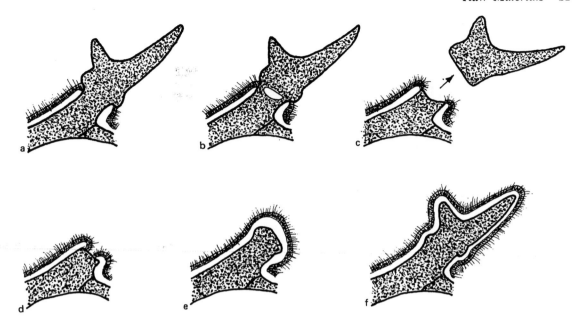

Figure 10: Growth cycle of antler (from Schmid, after Weber)

Key

a Mature antler.
b Resorption sinus forms between pedicle and basal burr.
c Antler shed.

d Skin covers scar on pedicle.
e Regeneration of antler begins.
f Antler fully grown and velvet ready to shed.

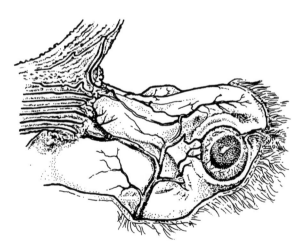

Figure 11: External blood supply to velvet in growing antler (after Bubenik)

caribou, are limited to the stags only. Their principal function is to impress and they are important as objects of display as well as combat: stags without antlers (hummels) do nonetheless lead normal lives in the herd (Chapman 1975; Darling 1937) and may even enjoy certain biological advantages.

Formation

Antlers grow each year on small permanent protuberances of the frontal bones named pedicles, which usually develop in the animal's first year (Figure 10). In the past there has been considerable disagreement surrounding the nature of the ossification process in antlers (summarised in Chapman 1975), but it now appears that a form of endochondral ossification takes place at the growing tips, while a certain amount of tissue is added intramembranously to the surface of the antler. The rate of growth may be as much as 2cm per day, promoted by immense numbers of osteoblasts which quickly become engulfed in tissue to form bone cells. Blood is supplied internally

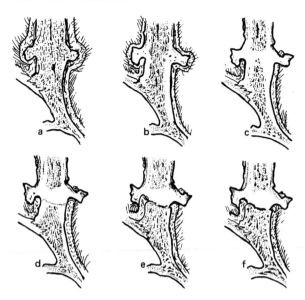

Figure 12:   Cross-section through antler base and pedicle showing progressive changes during growth and shedding (after Bubenik)

Key
a   Period of intensive growth.
b   Ossification of burr begins, restricting internal nutrition.
c   Ossification complete, isolating antler from blood supply via pedicle.
d   Demarcation line appears.
e-f   Resorption sinus forms.

of the antler of a bony coronet around the burr, whose processes engulf and eventually strangle the larger vessels and which, by continuing to press against the velvet, restrict the passage of further blood, causing the skin to wither. More recently, however, others have claimed that the process is controlled by hormonal activity (Chapman 1975). The period taken for full development of the antlers varies according to species and prevailing conditions: sample growing times of approximately three months for roe deer and four months for fallow deer in captivity have been recorded, while wild red deer in Russia are said to take from about four-and-a-half to six months to complete the growing cycle, including the shedding of the velvet (quoted in Chapman 1975). Further information on the growth and development of antlers in various species in differing habitats is given by the same author.

The cycle is completed by shedding of the antlers. Numerous osteoclast cells ranged along the distal end of the pedicle gradually erode the tissue along the junction with the antler burr until a resorption sinus is formed (Figures 10, 12). This cavity expands eliptically until finally the antler detaches itself at the pedicle junction which, after only minimal bleeding, is covered first of all by a scab and later by new skin tissue.

Structure

Antler tissue consists primarily of coarsely-bundled woven bone, which is particularly suited to the rapid growth requirement of antlers (cf. p. 7). In cross-section (Figure 9b) the compact outer tissue is seen to enclose a spongy core which permeates the length of the beam and each of the tines, the tips of the latter being capped with compact tissue. (There is no blood-forming tissue within this cancellous core). The unbroken canals which characterise the cancellous tissue of antler are immediately distinguishable from the more discrete formations found in certain skeletal bones (Figure 9a). The proportion of cancellous to cortical tissue varies during the growing cycle, according to the level of blood being supplied internally at that particular stage (Figure 12). In the region of the burr, in particular, extra tissue is progressively deposited until flow stops. Sections through the pedicle and burr of mature

to the growing antler by way of the frontal bones and the pedicles, which are highly vascular at the beginning of the cycle, while the soft, hairy skin known as velvet which covers the antler during the growing period carries an external blood supply within its numerous vessels (Figure 11). The formation of tissue around this network of arteries leaves the surface of the antler characteristically channelled or 'guttered'. As the base of the antler gradually ossifies (Figure 12) the internal blood supply diminishes to such an extent that ligation of the velvet results in the death of the antler (Chapman 1975).[5] As the antler reaches its definitive size and becomes fully ossified the blood supply to the velvet too begins naturally to dry up, so that it eventually shrivels and falls away, beginning at the tips of the tines. It has been suggested (Macewen 1920; Matthews 1952) that occlusion of the blood vessels is brought about by the development at the base

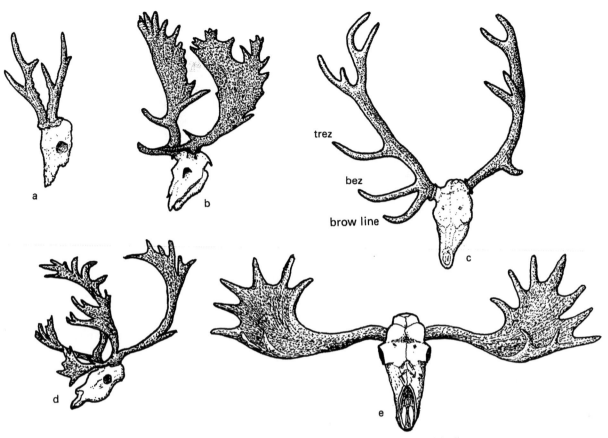

Figure 13: Antler morphology: (a) roe deer (b) fallow deer (c) red deer (d) reindeer (e) elk

antlers just before shedding show dense bone tissue completely sealing off the antler at the burr, with the blood trapped in the antler now congealing and disintegrating (Macewen 1920). Some Haversian systems develop, either as a result of direct deposition of bone mineral or through replacement of the outermost spongy tissue by compact bone, after the definitive size has been reached. This activity ceases soon after the period of growth and calcification has expired and from then on the antler is effectively dead.[6]

The density and the ratio of mineral to organic matter in antler is comparable with skeletal bone. To some extent, the enormous mineral requirement for the annual production of antlers is met at the expense of the internal skeleton: a certain amount of mineral resorption from the skeleton takes place during the growing period (see pp. 7-8), the degree probably becoming greater in the event of available diet being mineral-deficient (Chapman 1975).

Morphology

According to Morris (1965) there are forty-one living species of deer, but the antlers of only those likely to be recovered from archaeological contexts in northern Europe need be considered here. Hence, five species are examined, the antlers of which have a common micro-structure[7] conforming to the description given above but which vary considerably in morphology (Figure 13).

As deer develop in maturity their antlers tend to increase in complexity as well as size. The variations between species are discussed in general terms below, but in each case detailed development is conditioned by a number of factors, among which diet and health are important in addition to age. Hence, in a year of poor weather, scarce fodder or ill health, first antlers may fail to develop in young deer, while in older animals elaboration of the antlers may be curtailed. Furthermore, once maturity has been reached no further elaboration takes place in succeeding years and, indeed, regression sets in as the beast continues to age.

Within single species quite marked differences in size can occur according to habitat. Hence the present-day population of red deer in the British Isles is considerably smaller on average than its central European counterpart (Ward 1928) and within the continental mainland there is a significant shift in size from east to west (Reichstein 1969). Ecological changes in the course of time may have a similar effect: red deer from early medieval Wales, for example, have been found to be very large by comparison with modern specimens, approaching in size those of the Pleistocene period and reflecting the primeval state of the forest cover (Noddle 1975).

The simplest antlers are those of roe deer (*Capreolus capreolus* L.), which have relatively straight slender beams and rise almost vertically from the head (Figure 13a). They lack a true brow tine, but fork regularly about two-thirds of the way along their length, the posterior tine again subdividing to make a normal maximum of six points per head (Ward 1928). Malformed antlers showing abnormal elaboration are, however, not uncommon among roe deer (Tegner 1951; Bubenik 1966). Whitehead (1964) quotes lengths of just over 30cm and a circumference around the coronet of 12.5cm among the best recently-shot heads from the British Isles. The surface of the antler is normally markedly gnarled and guttered.

Fallow deer (*Dama dama* L.) have antlers which are larger and smoother than those of the roe and are distinguished by their palmate upper parts (Figure 13b). At the rear of the palmation a number of projections or 'spellers' are normally formed, the lowest of them sometimes projecting to form a well-developed tine. Forward-facing and upcurving bez and trez tines also develop. Lengths of over 70cm are considered good by Whitehead (1972).

Red deer (*Cervus elaphus* L.) have somewhat more complex antlers, sub-cylindrical in section and with a normal maximum in the British Isles of twelve or fourteen points per pair for prime

animals in the wild and a length of about 90cm (Figure 13c). Specimens from central and eastern Europe are more heavily built and commonly produce twenty or more points on antlers over 120cm in length (Whitehead 1972). The surface can be quite heavily guttered or it may be fairly smooth; in any case, the tines normally have a smooth surface, sometimes enhanced by the effect of wear occasioned by the stag abrading them on vegetation or on the ground.

Antlers are carried by both sexes of reindeer (*Rangifer tarandus* L.), those of the bulls being heavier. The upper points are often palmate and the bulls frequently display a forward-facing 'shovel' close to the base of one or both antlers (Figure 13d). A back tine may project from halfway up the beam. Whitehead (1964) records good average dimensions for the antlers of modern Scandinavian reindeer of 127cm length and 12cm circumference for the beam, with 28 points per head. Ulbricht (1978) notes that the brow tine projects immediately above the burr: the consequent oval-shaped burr and the characteristically granular surface, together with well-defined and elongated cancellous pores allow even fragmentary pieces of reindeer antler to be distinguished from those of red deer.

Among elk (*Alces alces* L.), the largest members of the deer tribe, the bulls carry enormous palmated antlers, set at right angles to the face and terminating in a broad denticulated shovel (Figure 13e). The antlers spring from pedicles growing from the side (rather than the top) of the head, rendering them easily recognisable when the pedicle is intact. In addition, the burr takes the form of a wide heavily-beaded disc and the porous internal structure of the antler is coarser than that of red deer (Ulbricht 1978). Ambrosiani (1981) notes a more easily visible network of blood-vessels in elk antlers. The antlers may have a spread of over 120cm and up to 18 or 20 points (Whitehead 1972).

Ivory (Teeth)

Mammalian teeth are formed in the soft tissues of the jaw, an enamel crown being laid down initially, followed by the body of the tooth in the form of dentine. As the crown erupts through the gum, roots are developed which anchor it firmly in place. In most mammals the majority of the teeth present in adult dentition are preceded in infancy by a set of deciduous (milk) teeth.

Formation

The cells involved in the formation of enamel, the ameloblasts, are distinct from the osteoblasts responsible for bone manufacture. An enamel matrix in the form of an amorphous gel is secreted by the ameloblasts, taking on a honeycomb appearance with the development of mineral crystals (Wainwright *et al.* 1976). Distinct groups of secretory vessels develop into elongated processes (the Tomes processes) which become incorporated into the honeycomb structure, where they deposit filaments of apatite. These filaments develop into crystal-

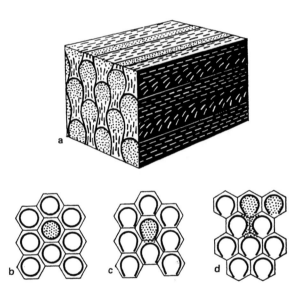

Figure 14: Enamel formation (from Halstead, after Boyde)

Key
a   Block diagram of arrangement of enamel crystallites in prisms from human enamel.
b-d Diagrams of cross-sections of enamel prisms (hexagons) to illustrate contributions of a single ameloblast (stippled). Heavy circles or horseshoes represent organic inclusions. (b) Single ameloblast contributes the crystallites for a single prism, as in whales. (c) Crystallites contribute to two ameloblasts, as in ungulates. (d) Each prism receives contributions from four ameloblasts, as in man, carnivores and elephants.

lites of relatively large dimensions compared with those of bone and dentine, reaching sizes of 160 x 40 x 25nm (Halstead 1974). As the apatite crystals increase in size and become more closely packed, the organic matrix is gradually squeezed out to the external border, so that in mature enamel it declines to negligible proportions (about 1 per cent) (Weidmann 1967).

Seen in cross-section under the electron microscope, the cellular honeycomb structure is dominated by a series of horse-shoe-shaped features whose interfaces are accentuated by the differing orientations of the crystals laid down by the Tomes processes and by an interposed sheath of organic matrix (Figure 14). In certain groups of species the secretions of individual Tomes processes affect adjacent 'cells' in the honeycomb structure, resulting in the partial breakdown of the basic prismatic appearance (Halstead 1974).

In mammalian enamel the prisms are arranged in zones running radially from the dentine junction to the periphery of the tooth. Within each zone the prisms follow a somewhat wavy path, the direction being constant for alternate zones. Under reflected light these zones appear alternately dark and light, producing characteristic 'Hunter-Schrager bands'. Incremental rings, the so-called 'striæ of Retzius', are also distinguishable in some mammalian enamel.

Dentine is also formed by specialised cells, the odontoblasts. In the initial stages of formation, however, another group of cells arranged in a subodontoblast tissue layer secrete an organic matrix of predentine, consisting largely of collagenous fibres, and the same cells are responsible for the initial calcification of this matrix. Subsequently the odontoblasts take over this process and, as the secretion of further matrix continues, the odontoblasts withdraw, leaving characteristic 'dentinal tubules' along which extend the principal cell processes. Unlike bone, therefore, the cells are not trapped within the matrix as it forms (Figure 15). As development continues, the odontoblasts become more closely packed and take on a columnar appearance (Halstead 1974); the synchronous action of the odontoblasts, advancing in ribbon-like formation ahead of the dentine edge, contrasts with the independent movement of osteoblasts. Mineral

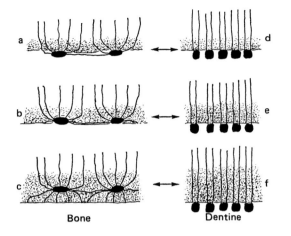

Figure 15: Comparison of growth in bone and dentine (after Currey)

Note: In bone (a-c) the cells are engulfed in advancing tissue, maintaining contact with one another and with the free surface by canaliculi. In dentine (d-f), the cells, which are more closely packed but which are independent of one another, advance with the tissue surface leaving processes behind them. (The level of the initial surface is indicated in the figure by arrows.)

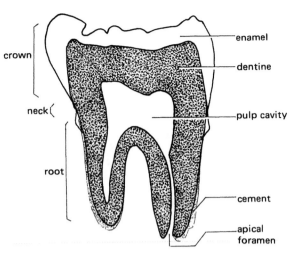

Figure 16: Diagrammatic cross-section of a human tooth showing the constituent parts (after Freeman and Bracegirdle)

salts are deposited in the form of spheres (calcospherites), interspersed with non-mineralised tissue. Depending on the degree of calcification which takes place, one of three types of dentine may ensue: if no further activity follows, so that the calcospherites are interspersed with numerous non-mineralised areas, it is known as interglobular dentine; full calcification, when the calcospherites fuse together and exclude all non-mineralised tissue, produces fully mineralised dentine; at an intermediate stage, when small non-mineralised areas survive, marbled dentine is produced.

A third form of mineralised tissue, termed cement, is also to be found in teeth. Structurally it compares more closely with bone than with dentine or enamel.

Structure

Three major elements are distinguishable in the structure of teeth (Figure 16): the crown protudes from the gum and forms the cutting or grinding surface; the root is buried in the tissues of the jaw; the neck connects these two extremities. In section the tooth displays a central cavity filled with dental pulp, extending from the crown to the tips of the roots where it connects through canals with the central nervous and nutrient systems. With the exceptions mentioned below, these canals narrow as growth declines with maturity. The bulk of the crown is made up of dentine, capped over its exposed area by an envelope of enamel. Generally speaking, the enamel has a maximum thickness over the cusps on the grinding surfaces and tapers away towards the roots. On the outer surface of the roots is a thin, hard coating of cement, which may also invade the folds of the enamel of the crown. Following initial deposition of the enamel cap, growth takes place as a result of the action of odontoblasts lining the pulp cavity. Usually, growth will cease when a definitive size has been reached in maturity.

In the case of specialised teeth in certain species, such as the incisors of rodents, the pulp cavity remains widely open at the root and growth is constant throughout life; elephant and walrus tusks are also continuously incremented in this way, though in later years production is limited to maintaining equilibrium as material is worn away from the tips.

Morphology

Teeth have evolved differently in different species according to feeding habits. A fully diversified set of mammalian dentition includes four distinct classes of teeth: incisors, used for cutting or tearing food; canines for seizing prey or for rooting in the ground; molars for crushing or grinding food; and premolars, which are intermediate in location between the incisors and the molars and may be adapted to assist in the functions of either, according to species. The full complement of teeth on each side of the jaw, upper and lower, is three incisors, one canine, four premolars and three molars, all adding up to forty-four teeth and normally expressed by the following formula: $I\frac{3}{3} C\frac{1}{1} P\frac{4}{4} M\frac{3}{3} x2 = 44$. Only a few mammals with relatively unspecialised dentition, such as the pig, have all these teeth fully represented. Most have less, but a few (notably some of the toothed whales) have more. An analysis of mammal and other dentition, species by species, is given by Cornwall (1974). Special mention will be made here only of some of the teeth of larger mammals which feature in the production of artefacts.

Foremost among these are the walrus and the elephant, each of which is equipped with a pair of teeth of such enormous size that they are distinguished with the name of tusks. In both instances the tusks are composed almost entirely of dentine,[8] with little more than a cap of enamel. In walrus the teeth in question are the upper canines, while in elephant the tusks are highly developed upper incisors.

Although they are limited to males in the Asiatic elephant (*Elephas maximus*), both male and female African elephants (*Loxodonta africana*) carry tusks.[9] As well as these massive incisors, which can grow to over 3m in length (Ward 1928), and weigh some 85 kg or more, elephants do have other teeth, which are all molars (Figure 17a): the formula for elephant dentition is thus: $I\frac{1}{0} C\frac{0}{0} P\frac{0}{0} M\frac{3}{3} x 2$. The molars seem never to have been prized by craftsmen, however, for although they are of prodigious size they are not at all homogeneous in construction and are heavily sheathed in enamel (Penniman 1952).

The large adult tusks of the elephant are preceded in the normal way by two deciduous incisors, which reach only about 5cm in length before they are shed. A pulp cavity extends part-way along the length of the adult tusk: since this continues to grow throughout the life of the elephant, the cavity remains wide open in the manner described above (p. 16). In transverse section the ivory is seen to be permeated by characteristic dentinal tubules which radiate from the pulp cavity and incline obliquely towards the tip (Figure 18). The regular gyrations performed by these tubules produce, in the words of Sir Richard Owen (1856), 'striæ proceeding in the arc of a circle from the centre to the circumference in opposite directions, and forming by their decussations curvilinear lozenges'. Miles and Boyde (1961) have shown that in longitudinal sections cut radially to the centre of the tusk the tubules pass across the thickness of the ivory in regular sinuous curves, while tangential sections show that the tubules are arranged in domains within which the curvatures adopted are all in the same phase but which are in reverse phase to those in adjacent columns. Viewed in section, ivory has a tendency to split along these lines, producing a characteristic 'cone-within-cone' effect (Gaborit-Chopin 1978; Penniman 1952), although this may only appear with antiquity or excessive drying.

The unique modification of dentine structure seen in elephant ivory was thought by Owen (1856) to have been developed to produce a tougher and more elastic material, in response to the unusual degree of stress imposed on it by the enormous weight of the tusks and by the manner in which they are used by the elephant. A certain amount of cement covers the base of the tusk.

One extinct member of the elephant family may be mentioned here: this is the mammoth (*Mammuthus primigenius*), whose remains survive in sufficient quantity in certain regions (p. 40) for their tusks to have become an article of commerce. In cross-section these tusks exhibit the intersecting arc structure described above for modern elephants. Penniman (1952) claims that freshly preserved mammoth ivory can be distinguished from that of our contemporary elephants by its finer striæ which intersect at more acute angles. Tomes (1923) and Sowerby (1934) recognise no such easy distinctions, however, even among the best-preserved specimens, and Sanford (1973) has stressed more recently the practical difficulties of

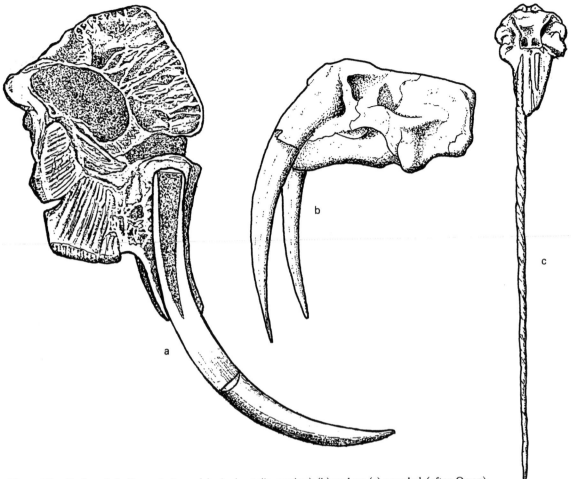

Figure 17:   Tusk and skull morphology: (a) elephant (in section) (b) walrus (c) narwhal (after Owen)

separating one from the other when the ivory survives under less than ideal conditions.[10]

Walrus tusks (Figure 17b) which can grow up to 1m in length, are found both in males and females, those of the male tending to be more massive and curved (King 1964). The dentine is laid down in two distinct layers: the outer coating is homogeneous in structure, although coarser than elephant ivory and with a yellow tinge, while the innermost layer, which builds up in the former pulp cavity, is of marbled dentine and is translucent and crystalline in appearance (Figure 19). Walrus ivory lacks the intersecting arc structure typical of elephant ivory: in walrus tusks the dentinal tubules are straight and parallel, interrupted occasionally by globular areas of secondary dentine. Towards the roots of the tusk there are cavities

in the marbled dentine. The tusks are specially developed for grubbing up hard-shelled molluscs on which the walrus mainly subsists, crushing them easily between its well-developed cheek teeth (Cobb 1933; King 1972), and for manoeuvring on the ice.

Among other marine mammals, certain of the toothed whales (the *Odontoceti*, as opposed to the *Mystacoceti* or whalebone whales) have teeth which are remarkable for their number as much as their size, up to fifty being found in each side of the jaw in some species; other species, however, have only a single pair (L.H. Matthews 1952). Whale teeth are relatively undifferentiated, being adapted for seizing prey under water but not for masticating it. Most of them have a simple conical shape, with the microcospic dentinal tubules running very

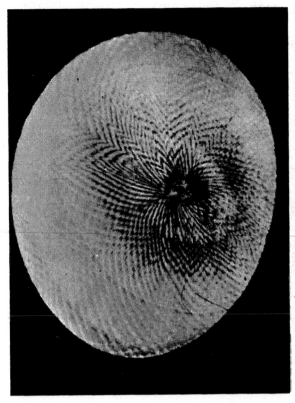

Figure 18: Transverse and longitudinal sections of African elephant tusk (scale *c.* 2.5:1). Source: Pitt Rivers Museum

straight (Penniman 1952).

Finally, the teeth of the narwhal (*Monodon monoceros*), one of the Arctic whales, may be brought to notice. In the male of the species are found two tusks of which the right hand one is normally vestigial, hardly protuding beyond the maxillary bone, while that on the left side is deeply embedded in the skull and extends forward in line with the body axis, reaching a length of up to 3m and a diameter of about 8cm (Figure 17c). The pulp cavity extends for virtually the whole length of the tusk, while on the exterior surface a spiral groove winds all the way to the tip. At a microscopic level the structure of narwhal ivory is relatively coarse, with random clustering of the dentinal tubules (Penniman 1952; Sanford 1973).

Keratinous Hard Tissues

By definition, keratinous tissues are not derived from the bony skeleton; they occur rather on the body surface and function as exoskeletal elements. Amongst the hard keratins (which also occur in the form of claws, hooves, hair and feathers), horn and baleen in particular have formed the bases of manufacturing industries which are briefly considered below and, since the uses to which they were put sometimes overlap with those relating to skeletal materials, an account of their respective structures is included here.

Formation

In each case the keratin, which has a rigid fibrillar structure, is synthesised in the epidermis. Cells gradually migrate from the innermost (Malpighian) layer into a cornifying layer in which three strata are distinguishable (J.Z. Young 1957): the *stratum granulosum*, characterised by granules of keratohyalin (the origin of which is obscure, but which seems to be involved in the formation of soft keratin); the *stratum lucidum* (a clear translucent layer in

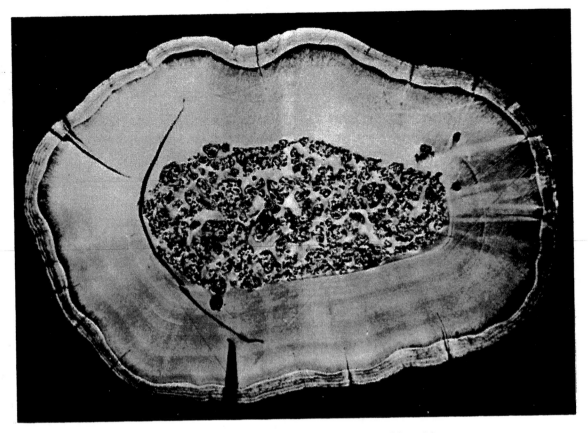

Figure 19: Transverse section from a walrus tusk (scale *c.* 2.5:1). Source: Pitt Rivers Museum

which the cells become closely packed and cease to be distinguishable as separate entities); finally, the *stratum corneum*, which itself consists of many layers, is made up entirely of fully keratinised dead cells.

By contrast to the forms of extracellular deposition described above for skeletal tissues, keratin is laid down within the actual cell, which eventually becomes so overloaded that it dies. Whereas in soft keratinous tissues (such as skin), dead cells are continually being sloughed off, in hard keratins they are retained permanently, being continually added to from the underlying generative zone and, to some extent, becoming calcified (Halstead 1974).

Morphology

Horn

The horns carried by certain mammals,[11] such as cattle, sheep, goats and antelopes, consist of a non-deciduous cuticle composed of keratin and laid down in the form of a sheath surrounding a bony horn-core (the *os cornu*) projecting from the frontal bones at either side of the skull (Figure 20). The surface of the horn, characterised by a structure of fine parallel lines, is immediately distinguishable from bone, antler and ivory. A great range of sizes and shapes is exhibited according to species and a wide variety of colour according to breed (Hartley 1939). New tissue is added in a periodic manner at the base of the horn, resulting in varying degrees of ridging. This ridging, which is more marked in some species (e.g., sheep) than in others (e.g., cattle), may increase with age (being sometimes used as a measure of such) or with other considerations (Thompson 1942). In all instances the horn displays a non-nucleated structure throughout.

The keratinous structure of horn has, therefore, nothing in common with the material of

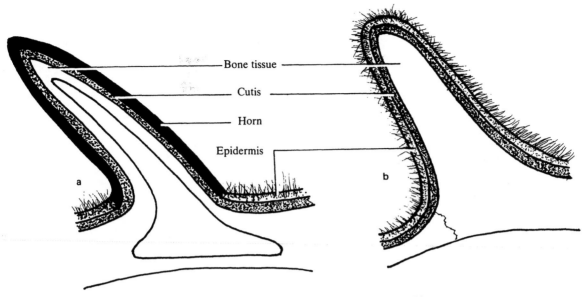

Figure 20: Diagrammatic cross-sectional comparison of horn (a) with growing antler (b)

deer antler which, as has been emphasised, is a form of bone. Hence the terms horn and antler should never be used interchangeably.

Baleen
Baleen, popularly referred to as 'whalebone', is derived from the keratinous brush-like plates which take the place of teeth in the *Mystacoceti* (p. 18) and which function as huge sieves, filtering from seawater the shrimp-like krill which form the basis of the whales' diet. The baleen is suspended in numerous sheets from either side of the upper jaw: some species have several hundred plates, which may develop to over 3m in length (Matthews 1968). Each plate is constructed in the form of a sandwich a few millimetres in thickness (Figure 21), with a medial stratum of tubules arranged in a matrix of cementing tissue and flanked on either side by horny covering plates. Each element in the sandwich consists of a different kind of keratin, of which only the tissues of the tubules become partly mineralised, apatite crystals being laid down in concentric formation to add strength to the structure. In use the covering plate and the cementing matrix are progressively worn away by the action of the tongue towards the distal end of the lingual surface; the fringes of tubes exposed in this way form the basis of the filtration system (Halstead 1974).

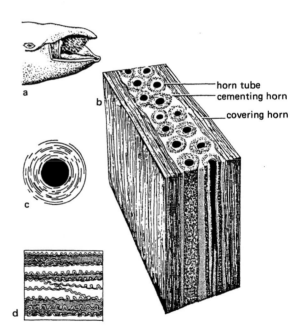

Figure 21: Baleen (after Halstead)

Key
a Location in roof of whale's mouth.
b Block diagram of baleen.
c Section of horn tube with areas of calcification indicated.
d Drawing based on electron micrograph of keratinised epidermal cells, those shaded being mineralised.

Notes

1. Interesting illustrations of this process at work may be seen among the Patagonians, who develop spiral grooves on their humeri from continually hunting with the *bolas* (Halstead and Middleton 1972) and the Balearic slingers of the Roman army, whose humeri developed similar features (Wells 1964).

2. Halstead and Middleton (1972) mention that when collagen is introduced into a solution of calcium phosphate the mineral readily precipitates: they describe collagen as 'the ideal seed bed on which crystals of apatite can form'.

3. Osteocytes often start their existence as bone-forming osteoblasts, later becoming surrounded by calcified substance and embedded in the bone matrix.

4. While the disitinction is of convenience and some importance to us, no lengthy history can be claimed for it. The *Oxford English Dictionary* (1933) explains that the term antler was originally reserved for the brow tine of a stag's horn (Old French *antoillier*, earlier *antoglier*; cf. Latin *ant(e)ocularum* and German *Augensprosze*, the tine in front of the eyes) and later was applied to all tines. Discussing the elk in 1738, John Ray says that 'the horns have no brow antlers', and as late as 1864, reference is made to 'the brow antler of a stag's horn'. Its current application to the entire structure is, therefore, of no great antiquity.

5. Wislocki (1942) has observed that the internal blood supply via the pedicles is at best negligible in comparison with that derived from the velvet.

6. These variations are common to all species of deer. For this reason, species identification on the basis of the texture of the cancellous tissue and its abundance relative to the surrounding cortical tissue, as proposed by Bouchud (1974), seems a little unwise.

7. Some success has been achieved, however, in distinguishing elk from red deer antler at a microscopic level (Ambrosiani 1981): the difference between the two species claimed on the basis of gross cross-sections may be at least partly conditioned by the precise location of the sections in relation to the burr (see p. 12).

8. According to Tomes (1923) the dentine in elephant ivory contains up to twice as much organic matter as that found in human teeth.

9. Following Tomes (1923), W.E. Cox (1946) contrasts the warm translucency of African ivory with the denser white colour and more open grain of Indian ivory, which is also softer in its fresh state. Considerable variations can occur within African tusks, however, which are categorised commercially as either 'hard' or 'soft', the latter usually coming from the eastern part of the continent (Ward 1975). For this reason, attempts to distinguish the country of origin of ancient ivories are seldom made.

10. Tomes (1923) claimed that it took the eye of an expert to distinguish elephant ivory from that of mammoth which, he suspected, was sometimes substituted for modern ivory by unscrupulous dealers in England and elsewhere. On a visit to the docks in 1899 he found about ten tons of mammoth ivory recently imported and awaiting distribution. Sowerby (1934) mentions large consignments of mammoth tusks sent from eastern Siberia to Shanghai in recent years, and confirms that it is hard to distinguish from elephant ivory.

11. Not all members of the families listed carry horns: some varieties of cattle and sheep, at least, are polled (hornless). On the evidence for medieval horned and polled sheep, see Armitage and Goodall (1977).

2. Bone and Antler as Materials

From the histological descriptions already given, it will be clear that two elements, one organic, the other inorganic, are combined in the make-up of all skeletal tissue. Individually, these elements have quite distinct mechanical properties and their combination makes skeletal tissues most impressive as structural materials.[1] As with other materials of composite structure, some qualities are contributed by one element and some by the other, the combination being greater than the sum of the constituent parts. The principles behind this phenomenon have been exploited since bricks were first made with straw, but it is only in comparatively recent years that they have been fully comprehended; the development of synthesised composite materials such as fibreglass and filled rubber,[2] which embody the same principles, is counted among the most important advances in materials science in the twentieth century (Gordon 1976).

In the case of mammalian skeletons, the organic collagen may be said to provide tensile strength while stiffness and compressive strength are contributed by the mineral crystals. It must immediately be admitted, however, that this is an oversimplified statement which fails to acknowledge the intimate and complementary behaviour of the two materials. For example, although the collagenous matrix is capable of more elastic behaviour than the apatite crystals with which it is permeated, the mineral crystals would become cracked and broken if the tensile load exceeded their ultimate stress. In practice, bone displays a modulus of elasticity (see p. 26), which is intermediate to that of its two components. Fibreglass and similar 'two-phase' materials exhibit the same characteristics, having a modulus of elasticity midway between that of the two components, but a greater strength than is possessed by either one (Halstead 1974).

A further illustration of the advantages gained by skeletal materials from this composite structure is provided by an examination of the behaviour of cracks. All solids exhibit tiny surface or internal irregularities in the form of notches or holes which, from a structural point of view, present hazards, since they have the effect of concentrating stresses around them (Gordon 1978). Figure 22a illustrates the manner in which lines of force acting on a single crystal run in regular fashion from one end to the other, while in Figure 22b the stress-concentrating effect of a notch can be seen. If whole bones were constructed of solid mineral, such stress concentrations would be highly dangerous, since cracks would tend to run through the entire structure without impediment. As has been shown, however (p. 4), bone mineral in the form of apatite needles is arranged in closely-packed but discrete units clothed in a collagenous matrix, with the result that the likelihood of cracks running from crystal to crystal is diminished each time an interface is encountered, by means of the so-called 'Cook-Gordon crack stopper' effect (Figure 23). This results in the force generated by a crack opening up a second crack at right angles to its original direction, further spreading being blocked in this way (Gordon 1976). The effectiveness of this arrangement is maximised by two factors: firstly, if the long axes of the crystals are aligned with the direction of the principal loads encountered, as tends to occur in stress-bearing laminar bone and, secondly, if a sheath of pliant material can be introduced between the crystals, a specification fulfilled in bone tissue by the collagenous matrix. At a higher level of structural organisation, similar defence mechanisms can be observed, comparable weak interfaces being encountered between laminae, between lamellae and around Haversian systems (p. 4). The normal alignments of osteocyte lacunae and of blood channels tend also to be with the main axis of the bone, ensuring that the stress-concentrating effects are minimised, and providing further potential crack-stoppers.[3]

The form of structure just described is desirable only when the direction of stress is fairly predictable, since the high degree of

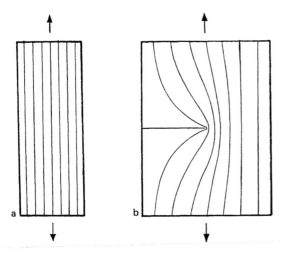

Figure 22: Diagram of the stress-concentrating effect of a narrow slit in a material (after Currey)

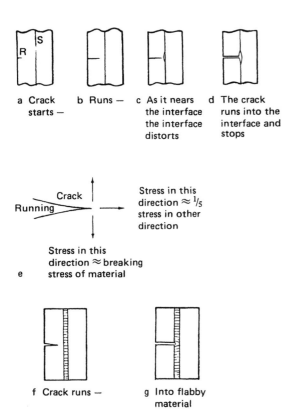

Figure 23: Diagram of the blunting effects of interfaces in brittle materials (after Currey)

orientation which makes the bone stronger in one direction inevitably makes it correspondingly weaker in others. The advantage of this anisotropic (directionally oriented) arrangement is that greater unit strengths can be achieved in directions normally subject to maximum loads than would be possible with a similar volume of isotropic (non-aligned) material. Hence woven bone, with its relatively non-aligned structure, may have a lower ultimate strength than laminar bone but will be more consistent in performance when stresses are encountered in more than one direction. This feature renders woven bone suitable for growing bones in which maximum stresses can change direction with development.

The ratios of organic and mineral matter in skeletal bone are finely balanced to produce optimum mechanical performance. The effect of deviation from this may be seen in certain highly specialised bones: for example, in the tympanic bullae of the ear, which are not expected to bear any degree of stress, an abnormally high level of mineralisation brings about a marked decline in elasticity and impact strength, while in antlers some of the ability to resist the impact loads to which they are subjected during combat is achieved by an adjustment downwards of the 'normal' mineral content (Currey 1979).

Further instances have been noted of ways in which structural features of bone can be considered as analogous to those found by scientists and engineers to be highly efficient in synthesised materials. Halstead (1974), for example, has likened the alternating alignment of collagen fibrils in successive lamellae of Haversian systems (p. 4) to man-made ply structures, the advantages of which are well known. There is no doubt that the whole bone gains in strength from the effect of this microscopic feature. At a higher order of magnitude, Gordon (1978) has pointed out that the sandwich structure of certain flattened bones (p. 8), in which the space between the dense outer surfaces is filled with spongy cancellous tissue, is one which, over the past fifty years, has been widely adopted for the construction of strong lightweight panels; in these, the outer skins are formed of wood or plastic and the interiors of paper honeycomb, or more recently, foamed resins. The excellence of this type of structure in resisting bending or buckling loads is obviously as important in the design of skeletons as it is, for example, in aircraft construction, where man-made versions were first used.

Mechanical Properties

A brief examination of the mechanical properties of bone and antler provides not only a better understanding of their respective qualities but also a body of factual data through which objective comparisons of their performance can be made. Furthermore, once armed with this information we are equipped to demonstrate a number of conditioning factors which clearly determined the consistent choice of some skeletal materials in preference to certain others.

Although the principles embraced by the twentieth-century study of materials science have been elucidated for the most part only in comparatively recent times (see, for example, Gordon 1976, 1978), they have applied no less inexorably to every physical artefact ever produced by the hand of man: in other words, their existence has not been dependent on our comprehension of them. This is not to say that their effects may not have been observed, and due allowance made for them: a craftsman's 'intuitive' knowledge of the potential and limitations of his material is in reality the result of close observation of its performance under everyday and extraordinary circumstances. Intuition of this kind may be the result of a lifetime of attention, enhanced perhaps by the inherited experience of many previous generations.

The objective definition of the properties of our materials will not serve as a substitute for the hard-won skills of the craftsman, but will make it possible for us to apprehend, perhaps more clearly than any lengthy practical apprenticeship, some of the controlling factors which lay behind the traditions and practices current among those whose wares form the basis of the discussion below.

Definitions

The clarity of the discussion which follows may be enhanced by a few brief explanations of the terminology used. These have been drawn from a number of sources: further reference may be made to Currey (1970b) and Frost (1967).

Stress
The stress acting upon a solid is an expression of the load or force applied to the material divided by the cross-sectional area. At any point in the material, therefore, Stress $= \frac{load}{area}$, the equation being equally true for compressive and tensile stress. The SI (System International) unit for stress is the Meganewton per square metre (MN/m^2). (1 Newton = 0.102kg force; 1 Meganewton = 1 million Newtons, almost exactly 100 tons force).

Strain
Strain is an expression of the proportion by which a material is extended (or compressed) under stress, represented by the formula, Strain $= \frac{increase\ in\ length}{original\ length}$. The product is usually represented as a percentage.

Stress-strain Diagram
The relationship between stress and strain for any given material can be expressed in the form of a graph (Figure 24), which is constant for the material. In the stress-strain curve given in Figure 24a, OA is a straight line portion, in which an increase in stress produces a proportional increase in strain. This is the so-called region of elastic strain where, if the stress is removed, the strain will return to zero. If the stress is increased beyond point A where the curve begins to bend over, the material continues to behave elastically, although the stress is no longer proportional to the strain. Beyond point B, known as the elastic limit, elastic behaviour ceases (i.e., the strain fails to return to zero when the stress is removed and the material remains deformed to some extent). In the example given in Figure 24a, if the stress is increased to point B, the material remains deformed to the extent $0-0^1$. This permanent change is known as plastic strain. Beyond the elastic limit the curve gets progressively flatter until at point C the material finally breaks. The value CD is the ultimate stress of the material which may, for our purposes, be considered to represent its 'strength'. The area contained within the stress-strain curve at the breaking stress is a measure of the work per unit volume which had to be expended in order to break the specimen; in other words, it is approximately

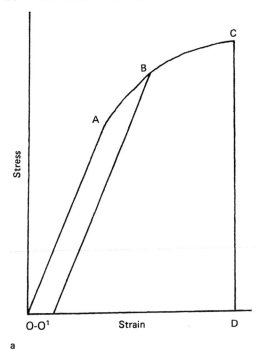

a

b

Figure 24:   Stress-strain curves (after Currey)

In curve (a), in the region OA the strain is directly proportional to the stress, and in this region if the stress is removed the strain will return to zero (elastic strain). Beyond point A, the material does not lose all its strain: if the stress is removed at point B the material remains deformed by the extent $O\text{-}O^1$. With increasing strain the material finally breaks at C, the value CD representing the ultimate stress of the material. The area under the curve,

up to any particular stress, is a measure of the work per unit volume that has to be performed on the material in order to achieve that stress. The highest amount of energy is not necessarily absorbed by the material with the highest ultimate stress: this is shown by the curves in (b), in which the ultimate stress in OEF is the greater while a larger area is contained within OGH.

proportional to the amount of energy which was absorbed before breaking. This expression we shall call 'toughness'. It is important to appreciate the distinction between strength and toughness: by reference to Figure 24b, it will be seen that the material represented by the curve OGH, while having a lower ultimate stress (strength) than that represented by OEF, contains a greater area within the curve and hence is tougher.

Modulus of Elasticity
Many solids produce a stress-strain diagram of the kind given in Figure 24, in which part of the curve is occupied by a straight line, indicating that an increase in stress within certain limits produces a proportional increase in strain. Under these circumstances, the ratio of stress to strain, as expressed by the slope of the

straight line, is a constant, known as the elastic modulus or Young's modulus of elasticity.[4] Hence elastic modulus = $\frac{\text{stress}}{\text{strain}}$. Young's modulus, measured in GN/m^2 (1 Giganewton = 1,000,000,000 Newtons) is effectively a measure of stiffness; the less the deformation for a given load the stiffer the material. This is not the same thing as 'strength', however: cf. values for stiffness (E) and ultimate tensile strength for collagen and keratin, in Currey (1970a).

Bending strength (modulus of rupture)
Measurement of the bending strength provides a further useful index of the properties of materials and has the advantage of being fairly easily established. The degree of accuracy necessary in the production of test specimens is also markedly less for the bending test (Currey 1970b). The value is gained by the formula

Maximum stress $= \frac{\text{bending moment x deflection}}{\text{moment of inertia of section}}$. Because the forces operating on the specimen are more complex than those involved in a straight-forward tensile or compressive test, however, the product cannot be regarded as identical with the ultimate stress and is referred to as the modulus of rupture. Currey (1970b) suggests a division of the value for the modulus of rupture by 1.5 to produce a more accurate figure for ultimate stress.

Comparative Values and Applications

Although a considerable amount of research has been expended in determining the mechanical properties of bone (see Currey 1970b for a review), the results which have been sought and achieved relate mostly to living skeletons in which the bone functions in a wet environment, whereas artefacts made from this material were used (and, at least in some instances, manufactured) while dry. Although few figures for dry tissues have been published, Currey (1979) made use of such figures as there were to discuss mechanical differences between certain specialised tissues.

Table 2.1 lists such figures as have been gained for bone and antler.[5] The results were obtained by machining test specimens of raw material to a size of about 30 x 3 x 2mm and loading them in three-point bending in an Instron 1122 table testing machine with a head speed of 2mm per minute. Several important factors emerge from these figures. The values for bending strength gained for each material under wet and dry conditions respectively are

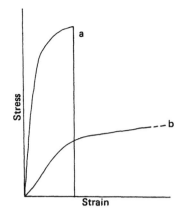

Figure 25: Stress-strain curves showing the effects of soaking antler: (a) dry specimen (b) wet specimen

particularly striking: in each case, wetting them reduces their bending strengths in the long axis by a factor of one third or more (see also Figure 25).[6] The importance of making determinations in relation to archaeological material under appropriately dry conditions, in contrast with the normal practice for biological purposes, will be self-evident. It will be seen that the effect of soaking alone induces changes in the stiffness of the material which could be capitalised upon in moulding processes. (These figures have no direct bearing on any reduction in *hardness* by soaking, which may have been used as a preliminary to cutting — see pp. 63-4).

Of more immediate practical importance are the differences in bending strength detected

Table 2.1: Comparisons of bending strength and modulus of elasticity in skeletal materials

	Bending strength (MN/m^2)				Modulus of Elasticity (GN/m^2)			
	Longitudinal		Transverse		Longitudinal		Transverse	
	Wet	Dry	Wet	Dry	Wet	Dry	Wet	Dry
Bone (cattle tibia)	199	299	98	96	13	25	9.9	20
Antler (red deer)	178	343	82	123	10.7	21	4	8
Ivory (elephant)	155		72.5		6.8		2.6	
Horn (sheep)					3.8			

between the longitudinal and transverse axes. These differences are certainly of an order which could have been apprehended in everyday use of these materials, and an examination of one type of artefact, the composite comb, demonstrates that this was indeed the case. (This topic is discussed more fully in MacGregor and Currey 1983). Dealing first with the method of assembly, an examination of the surface structure of the antler used for the majority of these combs reveals that it is invariably aligned in the horizontal plane (i.e., in the long axis) in the case of the side plates, and vertically in the case of the tooth plates (Figure 43). Whereas many bones of larger animals and many of the more sizeable red deer antlers are capable of producing plates in which large numbers of teeth could be cut at right angles to the 'grain' of the tissue, the fact that the teeth in composite combs are cut with the 'grain' means that the tooth plates are necessarily restricted in length (as defined in Figure 43), and hence it was only by riveting numbers of them side-by-side that long combs of the types favoured from the late Roman period until about the thirteenth century could be produced. The reason why comb makers chose to cut tooth plates in the vertical plane can be demonstrated by reference to the bending strengths shown in Table 2.2: in each case the dry material is stronger by about three times in the long axis than across the grain — 343 as against 123 for antler, and 299 as against 96 for bone. Immediately it becomes obvious that the apparently cumbersome and 'primitive' method of comb manufacturing was in fact cleverly devised to maximise the properties here revealed.[7]

By a further step the reason can be demonstrated for antler being widely preferred to bone, both in the manufacture of composite combs and indeed for a great many other purposes. The values for bending strength of dry bone given in Table 2.1 are lower in each axis than those for dry antler, but the differences are too slight to be of much significance. More significant are the properties revealed in Figure 26. Here the similar values obtained for the modulus of rupture of the two materials are reflected in the almost equal heights achieved by the curves before the breaking point was reached, but a more telling comparison can be made by examining the area contained within the curves which gives a measure in each case of the work done on the specimen before it finally broke. It is clear from the graphs that a greater amount of work was needed to break the antler, and, by reference to Table 2.2, we can see that the difference is in the region of three times in the longitudinal axis — 117

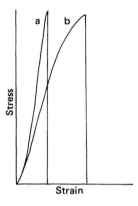

Figure 26:   Stress-strain curves for: (a) bone and (b) antler

Table 2.2:   Comparisons of bending strength and work of fracture in bone and antler

	A		B	
	Bending strength (MN/m^2)		Work per unit area (arbitrary units)	
	Longitudinal	Transverse	Longitudinal	Transverse
Bone	299	96	39	7
Antler	343	123	117	16

compared with 39; the transverse values again show a significant difference in favour of antler, this time in the region of two and a half times.[8]

In practical terms, these figures mean that antler is a significantly tougher material than bone, with a markedly better capacity to absorb shocks and sudden impact loads such as those the teeth of composite combs might suffer while being dragged through tangled hair, or which might befall any number of the other implements commonly made from antler. These results are clearly of fundamental importance to the understanding of these materials, and, ultimately, to the explanation of the rise of the antler industry during the period under review.

Notes

1. For comparisons with other materials see Gordon (1978).

2. Halstead (1974) considers filled rubber to be closely analogous to bone.

3. On the importance of the angle of the nutrient foramen, for example, see Wainwright *et al.* (1976).

4. Young's modulus may be regarded as an expression of the stress which would double the length of the material if it did not break first: that is, the stress at 100 per cent strain.

5. These compare closely with figures from a further series of tests published by MacGregor and Currey (1983). I am indebted to Professor Currey for his kindness in making available his time, advice and laboratory facilities for the initial work reported here.

6. The initial series of tests for this project were all carried out using wet material, before it emerged that dry conditions would be more appropriate for archaeological considerations. By the time this conclusion was reached, my stocks of ivory had been exhausted and hence figures for dry tissue were not obtained. Wet bone was found to have a bending strength in the longitudinal axis of 199 and wet antler of 178.

7. In a further series of tests (MacGregor and Currey 1983), in which the 'work to break' was accurately calculated, the difference in performance between the longitudinal and transverse axes was even more striking, amounting to a factor of six times.

8. See also note 7.

3. Availability

The factors controlling availability varied in kind for each category of raw material in antiquity. Bones from butchered animals would presumably have been freely available to all and sundry throughout the period; horn, on the other hand, at least by the medieval period, was largely monopolised by the powerful horners' guilds and hence would seldom have found its way into unprofessional hands; the reservation of the deer as a 'beast of the forest' (p. 32) in the early medieval period would again have ensured that few antlered carcasses would have come within the reach of the general public but, as will be shown, the antler-working industry depended primarily for its sources on shed antlers and hence was subject to other sorts of control; and finally, with the possible exception of fossil material (p. 40), ivory arrived in Britain only through very long-distance trade routes whose fortunes fluctuated widely over the centuries under consideration. No statement can, therefore, be made concerning general availability, each material having to be considered in turn.

Bone

Easy availability must have been a major factor in encouraging the utilisation of bone; certainly there can seldom have been any shortage of raw material to satisfy the needs of the professional and casual user alike. For the most part, the species involved were identical with those generally exploited for food or motive power and no evidence has been found of particular animals having been sought out exclusively for their skeletons. Every midden was a potential source of raw material for the manufacturer, although we may assume that where organised workshops were concerned, specified bones would have been reserved by butchers or slaughterers for sale to the trade, thereby eliminating the need for scavenging. Skinners may also have played an important part as suppliers of raw material: the fact that the lower limb bones of certain beasts are often removed with the skin from the carcass and are separated from the hide at a later stage may have encouraged such a relationship. Metapodials, which have little meat on them and have only minor nutritional value, are among the more commonly utilised bones, adding further weight to this tentative suggestion.[1] Furthermore, Noddle (1975) mentions that from one area of Norfolk in the eighteenth century there is evidence that the trade in animals was controlled by the tanners, and finds evidence from elsewhere to confirm the relatively greater importance formerly attached to skins and horns compared with meat.

The fact that the mechanical properties of bone may be adversely affected by prolonged heating would rule out the use of cooked bones for some purposes at least; Ulbricht (1980a), however, has suggested that cattle mandibles utilised at Schleswig had been separated first from the skull, probably after cooking. The masses of unutilised bones recovered from every settlement excavation would suggest, however, that supply far exceeded demand. On the other hand, it has already been stressed that bone is by no means a uniform material and that utilisation was never a random process: even if there were a well-developed bone-working industry in operation in the vicinity, we can be sure that the majority of bones would have been scorned as unsuitable by craftsmen. The consistent utilisation of specific bones is a theme on which increasing evidence will be brought to bear here. As information about more large groups of excavated animal bones is published in a comprehensive manner, it will be interesting to see whether certain species are consistently under-represented by particular bones, as this may form evidence for this process at work. Such a suggestion has already been made on the basis of a disproportionate lack of the distal ends of metacarpi from excavations of various dates in Exeter, Devon (Maltby 1979). Evidence from rubbish pits such as those found in Roman Augst, Switzerland

(Schmid 1968) and at Saxon Southampton (Holdsworth 1976) demonstrates the deliberate selection of long-bones for certain purposes. Other evidence provided by the artefacts themselves is presented below.

One domestic animal whose bones were commonly utilised but which would not normally have been slaughtered was the horse. There still seems to be some doubt as to whether horse flesh was eaten in post-Roman Europe. Theodore of Tarsus, Archbishop of Canterbury (669-90), is said to have encouraged the orthodox Greek view which discouraged the practice (Levison 1946). Its consumption was specifically prohibited by Pope Gregory III (*c.* 732) (Dümmler 1892) and again by the English Legatine synod of 786 (Liebermann 1912), but in the intervening period the Confessional of Archbishop Egbert of York (732-66) records that horse flesh could be eaten, although it was shunned by many people (Thorpe 1840). In time the prohibitionist view was carried to the Continent by English missionaries and by those of the Irish church, and the eighth century saw a revival of the Mosaic concept of clean and unclean flesh, horse meat being assigned to the latter category (Levison 1946). A number of complete carcasses found buried in medieval levels at York suggest that horses were not eaten at this time, although conceivably these particular horses could have been diseased and hence unfit for consumption. It may be significant, for the reasons suggested above (p. 30), that the great majority of utilised horse bones are metapodials, perhaps reflecting a common trade in skins.

Northern Europe never spawned a bone-based carving industry of the type known in Greco-Roman Egypt (Marangou 1976) or in northern Italy, where the vigorous and successful school of the Embriachi flourished in the fifteenth century (Dalton 1909), even though the raw material for both schools was provided by the same long-bones of horses and cattle which were put to more prosaic purposes in the north. Only in the case of certain cetacean bone carvings did bone-working reach the level of an art north of the Alps. Although there were undoubtedly variations in the density of different species of animals in different areas, only one group may be singled out as having a significantly limited distribution in the British Isles, namely large cetaceans. Although

isolated individuals do stray southwards, they are certainly more at home in the more northerly latitudes: this is reflected in the widespread utilisation of cetacean bone in the north and west of Scotland, where it was used to produce a range of implements which are unknown or which occur in other materials elsewhere (see, for example, p. 189). The latter circumstance may result partly from the development of specialised tool kits in the more northerly environment (as for example, the so-called blubber-mattocks on p. 178), but may also be due to their counterparts elsewhere being made in wood which has not survived.

Although a number of artefacts of cetacean bone are found in southern Britain before the Scandinavian incursions and subsequent settlement, their occurrence increases significantly during the Viking period, persumably as a result of their being diffused southwards by a culture in which cetacean bone was an important native raw material.

It is unclear to what extent whales were actively hunted before the Arctic-based industry developed in the seventeenth century, but inshore pursuit of some species seems very likely. Clark (1947) reviews the most accessible species and the methods of catching which preceded the invention of the harpoon gun, concluding that some inshore whaling was probably practised from as early as the Neolithic period in Scandinavia. It has been argued elsewhere that a steady flow of raw material beyond that afforded by casual strandings would have been necessary for the development of certain standardised types of cetacean bone tools in the Late Iron Age of the north of Scotland (MacGregor 1974). Sjøvold (1971) comes to the same conclusion concerning cetacean bone implements of the sixth to tenth centuries from Norway: the absence of earlier finds of the same kind may, he suggests, indicate that whaling did not begin until about the sixth century, but he stresses the unsatisfactory nature of the earlier negative evidence.

Although whaling must have been an uncommon pursuit in Anglo-Saxon England,[2] evidence that it was followed is contained in Ælfric's *Colloquy* (lines 116-20) (Garmonsway 1947):

Forþam leofre ys me zefon fisc þæne ic mæz ofslean, þonne fisc, þe na þæt an me ac eac spylce mine zeferan mid anum sleze he mæz besencean oþþe zecpylman. 7 þeah mænize zefoþ hpælas, 7 ætberstaþ frecnysse, 7 micelne sceat þanon bezytaþ.

Miss Susan Hitch has prepared the following translation:

> Because I prefer to catch fish that I can kill, rather than fish which at one blow can sink or destroy not just me but my companions too.
>   And yet many do catch whales and escape the danger, and make a great deal of profit from it.

Clark (1947) reproduces claims that the Basque whale fishery was already active by the tenth century, reached its height in the twelfth and thirteenth and by the fifteenth had penetrated as far afield as Ireland, Iceland and Norway in search of Atlantic Right Whales. There was no such enterprise in medieval England, however, where the rarity value of whales is reflected in the fact that the ownership of stranded specimens was carefully established, their worth being assessed at as much as £100. By this time, however, the bones had ceased to have any commercial value, except in the bleakest northern areas where, on the evidence of Olaus Magnus (1555), the large ones were sought after for house building and the smaller ones for fuel.

Antler

From the late Roman period onwards it was antler rather than bone which provided the bulk of raw material. Until the advent of increasingly strict forest laws in the medieval period, it seems likely that the general availability of antler varied little. Thirty-one parks, spread over nine English counties, were already established '*ferarum silvaticarum*' by the time *Domesday Book* was compiled, however, so that deer were certainly not free for all before the Conquest. The ultimate decline of the antler industry may nonetheless be attributed, at least in part, to the increased protection extended to deer during the medieval period or to their reservation for the king's purposes (see below).[3] The development of a controlled hunting season, when stags could only be taken between April and September (O. Rackham 1980), would further have limited supplies of antler. A striking example of the shift from antler to bone can be seen in the contrast between the overwhelming predominance of antler used at Hedeby (Ulbricht 1978) and the 13:1 superiority of bone over antler at Schleswig (Ulbricht 1980a), the settlement which superseded Hedeby in the eleventh century.

On the other hand, the naturally-shed antlers which account for the bulk of the utilised material (p. 35) are clearly not dependent on deer being slaughtered. Apart from two thirteenth-century references to the collection of antlers from royal forests for the production of crossbow nuts (pp. 160-1), no evidence has been found concerning the legal status of shed antlers in England. A sixteenth-century record from Sweden shows that they were then considered the property of the finder, but by that time utilisation had dwindled to insignificant levels: the reference occurs in the *Historia* of Olaus Magnus (1555), where he mentions that elk, red deer and roe deer may be hunted only by the nobility and other privileged persons but that the antlers they shed in the forest can be taken by those who find them.

Roe deer have formed a permanent element in the fauna of the British Isles since the last glaciation, although their distribution in the wild has become progressively more limited during the present millennium. Armitage (1977) notes the disappearance of their bones from archaeological deposits in London dated later than the thirteenth century. According to Turner (1899), the roe suffered the greatest single blow to its continuing survival by being demoted in the fourteenth century from its status as a beast of the chase: in his *Select Pleas of the Forest*, Turner records that in 1339-40 the Court of the King's Bench ruled that the roe was to be considered thenceforth as a 'beast of the warren' and not of the forest. In losing the protection which had hitherto limited its enemies to the upper echelons of society, the roe would have become subject to widespread extermination from game forests throughout England. Other evidence can be found, however, to suggest that this ruling was not generally applied, and was limited to the peculiar case of the Manor of Seamer which occasioned the decision (J.C. Cox 1905). As far north as southern Scotland the roe deer population suffered further from the spread of

Figure 27: Current distributions of deer populations (after Whitehead): (a) roe deer (b) red deer (c) fallow deer (d) elk (e) reindeer

farming and the consequent contraction of forest cover. Today it survives within the south from Sussex to Dorset, in Norfolk, and sporadically to the extreme north of England, and it is found throughout much of Scotland (Whitehead 1964). On the Continent it extends from Scandinavia to the Mediterranean and as far west as Portugal (Figure 27a).

Red deer are also indigenous to the British Isles and formerly enjoyed a much more widespread distribution than currently, wild stock now being limited to Devon, Somerset, and East Anglia in the south, and to the mountains and moorlands of the Lake District and central and northern Scotland, together with isolated parts of Ireland (Whitehead 1964). With the exception of some isolated communities in western Norway, the northerly continental limit lies in Skåne in southern Sweden. From there southwards it is distributed in appropriate habitats over much of the mainland (Figure 27b).

The red deer was the supreme animal of the hunt and, as such, enjoyed protection in medieval England from all but the King and favoured nobility throughout the vast acreage of royal forests which were a major feature of the English countryside from the Conquest until the early Tudor period. The royal privilege was not to be lightly violated, for illegal taking of the King's deer was punishable by death, mutilation or blinding until the time of Edward I, when corporal punishment was replaced by heavy fines. Nevertheless, considerable stocks of deer were lost to poachers: in 1251 the Earl of Derby and four companions were charged with taking no less than two thousand deer over a period of six years from the royal park of Peak Forest, while on a single day in 1334 a party of forty-two men slew forty-three (in some accounts sixty-three) red deer in Pickering Forest. More important depredations were made as a result of the gradual spread of agriculture into areas which had previously been given over to forest, and the turmoil of the Civil War dealt a final blow to many of the surviving herds (Whitehead 1964).

Unlike roe and red deer, fallow deer were artificially introduced to the British Isles.[4] The date of introduction has been much disputed: Whitehead (1964) quotes a number of opinions which have been expressed on the subject, none of them with any demonstrable basis in fact, variously crediting the Romans, the Gauls and even the Phoenicians with their importation. Jennison (1937) concluded that by the third century the species was well established for, towards the end of the reign of Severus, Gordian (later Emperor Gordian I) was said to have imported to Rome a large number of stags of fallow deer (*cervi palmati*), including some from Britain. In this assertion Jennison appears to be mistaken: a recent edition of the source (Magie 1960) translates the passage *cervi palmati ducenti mixtis Britannis* as 'two hundred stags with antlers shaped like the palm of the hand, together with stags of Britain. . .' Fallow remains have been reported from a number of Roman period sites, but conclusive evidence of either identity or date has been lacking in each case (Chapman and Chapman 1975). While it is possible, therefore, that there was some small-scale Roman introduction of fallow deer into Britain, they did not become permanently established. Even on the continent, the paucity of fallow remains of Roman date is striking (Luff 1982). The first documentary evidence of their presence in Britain occurs in Ælfric's *Colloquy*, where hunting of *rann* (glossed *dammas*) with hounds and nets is mentioned (Garmonsway 1947). By the twelfth century, FitzStephen's *Description of London* describes the forests lying around the city as well-stocked with stags and fallow deer (Douglas and Greenaway 1953). The earliest archaeological indication of their presence seems to be a pendant made from the palmate end of an antler, found at the Lloyds Bank site in York, where settlement spans a period from about the ninth to the eleventh centuries (MacGregor 1982a). The eleventh century would, both on archaeological and historical grounds, therefore, be the most likely last possible date for the introduction of the fallow deer. An introduction by the Normans, either from their territories in France, Sicily or southern Italy, where fallow could have persisted (possibly in parks) since the Roman period (Chapman and Chapman 1975), or from the Levant, seems most likely. As well as providing sport, fallow, like the rabbits and pheasants also introduced by the Normans, would have provided an economically attractive source of meat from poor agricultural land (O. Rackham 1980). Such was its subsequent success as a park animal in the medieval period that by the seventeenth century, when stocks were held in over seven hundred parks in England, it was claimed that there were more fallow deer in a single English county than in the whole of the rest of Europe (Whitehead 1964). During the Civil War these stocks were again greatly depleted and many of the surviving feral herds may have been established in the wild at this time. Fallow occurs today in Europe in widely scattered, though isolated, communities (Figure 27c), in continued contrast to its widespread distribution in England.

Elk antlers of the last two millennia have not figured numerously in archaeological excavations outside Scandinavia. The date of its disappearance from post-Pleistocene Britain is uncertain: remains have been noted from a number of Romano-British sites including Newstead, Borders Region (J. Curle 1911) and from Tudor London (Armitage 1977). Whitehead (1972) has suggested that the elk survived until at least the ninth century in the British Isles but the more generally held opinion is that it disappeared during the Mesolithic (e.g. Armitage 1977). The later finds are all of antler only (cf. p. 37). Today it is widely distributed in the swamps and woodlands of Norway and Sweden and eastwards to Siberia north of about latitude 57°N (Figure 27d), although formerly it extended south to the Ukraine and the northern Caucasus (Whitehead 1972).

Reindeer have had a markedly northern distribution since the last glaciation, being limited today to Norway, northern Sweden and Finland, with a variant (*R. tarandus tarandus*) extending eastwards into north Russia (Figure 27e).

Since the natural distribution in Great Britain of red and roe deer in the period considered here is likely to have included a very large part of the country, no special significance can be attached to the mere fact of the occurrence of their respective remains in archaeological contexts. The bones of deer form a fairly normal element among food refuse, although the numbers of individuals represented is seldom very high.[5] By contrast, remains of antlers, particularly those of red deer, are very numerous in early medieval urban manufacturing centres, leading to the conclusion that the antlers themselves were brought into the towns and were not simply utilised as waste material from butchered animals. This conclusion is further reinforced by the fact that antler bases displaying natural ruptures at the burr (indicating that they were shed in the wild; see p. 12), far outnumber those in which the burr and pedicle are intact and which would, therefore, have been removed from dead carcasses. This situation has been noted wherever large-scale antler working has been established, as at York (MacGregor 1978a) and Dublin (B. Ó Ríordáin 1971) and at several continental settlements including Århus in Denmark (Andersen *et al.* 1971) and Hedeby, Schleswig-Holstein (Reichstein 1969). At Ribe shed antlers outnumbered those sawn from carcasses by a factor of 4:1 (Ambrosiani 1981) and at Wolin in northern Poland the proportion was 3:1 (Müller-Using 1953). Among remains from early medieval Lund, Sweden, red deer were again represented overwhelmingly by antler fragments; among the few deer bones identified, several were fragments of calvaria, presumably brought in attached to the antlers of slaughtered deer (Bergquist and Lepiksaar 1957; Ekman 1973).

Clearly, therefore, shed antlers were being collected from forests and hillsides to supply this industry, which no doubt paid a going rate for its material.[6] While it seems likely that crafts such as comb-making were practised all the year round (pp. 49–50), the supply of shed antlers would have been highly seasonal, although varying in timing from area to area. Red deer generally cast their antlers over a two-month period in late winter or spring and fallow deer follow a similar pattern. Roe deer, on the other hand, shed from about October to December, but the small size of their antlers meant that they were never used interchangeably with those of the other two species. Reindeer shed, according to sex and age, between November and May. Ambrosiani (1981) has noted that the season when elk antlers are cast (around January) corresponds to that when squirrels' furs are at their thickest and most valuable, adding the suggestion that fur trappers could have collected and sold antlers along with furs at seasonal markets. This idea accords with Christophersen's observation that a considerable knowledge of local terrain and game would have been necessary in order to find antlers in quantity (Christophersen 1980b), and with Olaus Magnus's

(1555) comment that it was no easier to find antlers than to see hinds calve.

The fact that shed antlers are subject to deterioration if uncollected re-affirms the suggestion that this must have been an intensive, seasonal operation: those which escape the attentions of rodents and of the deer themselves, which frequently gnaw antlers[7] and other bones (Sutcliffe 1974, 1977), eventually degrade under the action of weathering and particularly of frost. We must therefore envisage some degree of stockpiling of raw material by comb makers and, perhaps, by suppliers anticipating better prices during the months of scarcity. A system of exchange (presumably of finished articles for raw materials) between urban craftsmen and the population of the surrounding countryside has been suggested as a common means of acquisition of antlers in Poland (Cnotliwy 1956).

Attempting to gauge the extent of the catchment areas on which manufacturing centres could draw for their raw materials is an exercise in which conclusive answers cannot yet be reached. Given the former country-wide distributions of our native British species, it seems impossible for the moment to distinguish the antlers of any one region from another[8] and, as yet, no remains of exotic deer have been distinguished from stratified archaeological sites in Britain (but see pp. 37-8). On the Continent, however, some imaginative studies have produced results indicating that a degree of long-distance trading in antlers did develop.

Although red deer are widely distributed on the Continent (Figure 27b), examination of their northern periphery has produced a detailed picture in which their presence or absence in specific areas can be shown (Figure 28). Finding examples of red deer antler burrs at Birka, which lies outside the distribution area, Ambrosiani (1981) has justifiably concluded that they must have been imported for utilisation. Even within the area of distribution, some success has been achieved in distinguishing locally-shed from other red deer antlers. Encouraged by the fact that a shift occurs in the average size of deer between eastern and western Germany, Reichstein (1969) set out to establish the level of importation (if any) to Hedeby by detailed comparison of burr sizes between slaughtered — and hence probably local — animals and antlers which had been

shed in the wild. The results showed no marked disparity in size between the two groups, suggesting that all the material was collected fairly locally, but comparison of the Hedeby figures with those from Wolin, some 350km to the east, gave a distinct separation which proved the usefulness of the method. It was then applied by Christophersen (1980b) to two groups of material from Lund, with interesting results: examining the shed antlers from a late eleventh-century context at St Botulf and comparing them with twelfth-century burrs from slaughtered animals found on the neighbouring Stortorget site, Christophersen found a close agreement in size distribution between the two populations, suggesting that the shed antlers had been gathered locally. When the shed antlers from Stortorget were plotted, however, their distribution varied markedly both from that of the antlers derived from dead animals on the same site and from the shed antlers from St Botulf. While stressing the small size of the samples involved, Christophersen is justifiably optimistic in claiming that the stat-

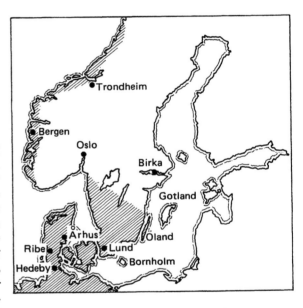

Figure 28: Detailed distribution of red deer in Scandinavia during the later prehistoric period (after Ahlén)

Note: The principal sites producing evidence of red deer antler working in the Viking and early medieval period are marked. Note that in Scandinavian terms the Viking age marks the end of the prehistoric period.

istics suggest some degree of importation of non-local antler by the twelfth century, perhaps reflecting increased demand, or a decline in local supply due to environmental changes, or both.

Other indications of trading in red deer antlers have been noted among excavated material from Wolin, where Müller-Using (1953) has taken the virtual absence of paired antlers from slaughtered deer as an indication that they may have been killed at some distance from the settlement: for convenience of transport, he suggests, the antlers could have been separated from the skull on the spot and bundled up with others, with the inevitable result that the original pairs would often have become separated by the time they reached the manufacturer.

A few skeletal fragments as well as antlers of elk were recovered from Hedeby, suggesting the possibility of local derivation (Ulbricht 1978). Ambrosiani (1981) has cast doubt on this claim, however, finding no historical evidence for the occurrence of elk west of the Oder and interpreting these remains and elk antler found at Ribe as more probably of Scandinavian origin. It may yet be premature to dismiss the elk from the north-western Continental mainland in view of finds recorded from the Netherlands: these include an antler from Dorestad (Prummel 1978), which could admittedly have been imported; an elk mandible from the same site is, however, less easy to explain (Prummel 1982). Part of a metapodial from early medieval Rijnsberg was judged to have been utilised as a 'glider' (Clason 1967), and other remains of elk have been found in medieval layers overlying the Roman fort at Valkenburg (Prummel 1975).

The presence of four reindeer burrs at Stortorget (Christophersen 1980b) and of numerous fragments of antler elsewhere in Lund, Lödöse and other settlements (Ekman 1973; Lepiksaar 1975) lying beyond the southern distribution of the reindeer (Figure 27e), confirm the existence of a long-distance trade in their antlers. Ulbricht (1978) notes small quantities of reindeer antler among manufacturing waste from Hedeby, but Ambrosiani (1981) suggests that minor amounts of material of this kind, as with the elk fragments mentioned above, could have been diffused as the stock-in-trade of itinerant craftsmen.

Although there is every indication that reindeer have been absent from the British Isles in post-Pleistocene times, evidence is produced periodically which purports to deny this undoubted fact. It comes in three forms: archaeological, literary and representational.

The first concerns physical remains of reindeer found on a number of northern habitation sites, for which the evidence is summarised by J.A. Smith (1870). He mentions finds from the brochs of Cinn Trolla, Keiss, Kintradwell and Yarhouse, and from the vicinity of some hut circles at Tain (all in Highland Region), as well as others recovered from geological rather than archaeological strata. In addition, Munro (1879) describes two antler fragments from Lochlee Crannog, Strathclyde, which he considers derive from reindeer. One important fact not previously commented upon but of crucial significance here is that all these remains are of antlers. No skeletal fragments have been recorded.[9]

Two possibilities suggest themselves: the first is that the antlers mentioned were imported as raw material for manufacture; the second is that the fragments in question represent fossil remains recovered from waterlogged peat bogs or clay beds, brought into the settlements for use. Viking period interest in former brochs is well documented and it would be perfectly possible for imported material to find its way to those sites at this time for local utilisation, although the stratigraphic origins of the pieces mentioned are too imprecise to allow close dating.[10] More concrete evidence of early importation of antlers comes from a radio-carbon date recently obtained from the well-known Abbots Bromley 'horns': the so-called 'horns' are in fact reindeer antlers mounted on head-dresses and still worn by village dancers in an annual circuit of their parish in Staffordshire (Alford 1933); recently they have produced a C_{14} date of AD 1065 ± 80 (Buckland 1980) which, unless ancient antlers were imported at a later period (which seems even more unlikely), must mean that they were shipped to England around the eleventh century. The possibility that the above-mentioned fragments from archaeological contexts were also imported cannot, therefore, be excluded.

Considering the second possibility, that the Scottish antlers represent fossil material dug out of the peat, it may be noted that reindeer antlers of Pleistocene date are certainly found from time to time embedded in bogs: examples from Orkney and Strathclyde are illustrated by J.A. Smith (1870) and others from Dumfries and Galloway are described elsewhere by the same author (1879b). The fragments mentioned above could also have been found in this way, perhaps during peat cutting, and, since the dampness of the peat would have preserved a good deal of the original appearance and mechanical properties of the antler, they would quite naturally have been saved for utilisation. (At least one fragment from Keiss Broch, Highland Region (J.A. Smith 1879a) showed signs of working). This is the explanation which seems to have most to recommend it, but the question can finally be resolved only with the aid of scientific dating methods: perhaps when improvements in technique bring down the minimum sample size required for radiocarbon dating it will be possible to settle the matter once and for all.

In the meantime, before reindeer can be excluded from the list of species available in Britain for everyday utilisation, one literary reference must be taken into account. The following passage occurs in *Orkneyinga Saga* (Guðmundsson 1965):

Pat var siðr jarla nær hvert sumar at fara yfir a Katanes ok par upp a merkr at veica rauodyri eca hreina.

A literal translation may be given as follows:[11]

It was the earls' custom to go over to Caithness nearly every summer and up into the woods there to hunt red deer or reindeer.

In the absence of corroborative evidence for the currency of reindeer in Scotland at that time, the accuracy of the sagaman's statement must be open to doubt. Two considerations must be borne in mind. The first is that the saga was written by an Icelander who, although he had visited Orkney (and, almost certainly, Norway), is not known to have set foot in Caithness; he is unlikely, therefore, to be speaking from first-hand experience of the country or indeed of the animal, for the reindeer was unknown in Iceland at that time. The second is that, bearing in mind his likely unfamiliarity with the species, he may not have meant to imply that reindeer were hunted as an alternative to red deer but used the terms synonymously or indiscriminately (see E. Magnusson, quoted in Harting 1880). Both these contentions find favour with present-day scholars of Icelandic literature.[12]

Finally, one representation on a Pictish slab from Grantown-on-Spey, Highland Region, must be considered. The stone has incised on it a representation of a deer which, it has been suggested (J.A. Smith 1870), bears a certain likeness to a reindeer. The morphology of the antlers is much closer to red deer, however, and quite unlike that of reindeer, as illustrated in Figure 13. Smith's tentative identification may therefore be dismissed and with it all notion of reindeer surviving to this date in the British Isles.

Ivory

The excellent working properties of ivory have long recommended it as a raw material for carving into ornaments and objects of utility. Here only the species most likely to be encountered in northern Europe are discussed: for others, such as hippopotamus, see W.E. Cox (1946) and Penniman (1952).

Elephant

During the Roman period Britain lay at the north-west frontier of an empire whose south-eastern fringes bordered on the oriental world and which, for all its size, possessed a communications network which was impressive by any standard. Hence, goods and materials from the east and the far south could easily be diffused over the entire Roman world, and among them was ivory.

A great deal of ivory reached the Roman empire through trading posts founded on the Red Sea coast. The original function of these stations, several of which had been planted in the third century BC, was to acquire live elephants from Ethiopia and the eastern Sudan for military purposes. Following the rout of Ptolemy IV's African elephants by a similar force of Seleucid Indian beasts at the Battle of Raphia (217 BC), their military significance declined, but the Red sea ports were maintained, partly to carry on the now established trade in ivory (Jennison 1937). Although the

Syrian elephant was by now extinct, a diminishing population survived in north-west Africa (Scullard 1974). Indian ivory was also imported on a considerable scale through Egypt, particularly after its annexation by Rome. Little of this material seems to have reached the far north, however, and of the four carved ivories from Roman Britain listed by Toynbee (1964) all are judged to be imports. Of the small items manufactured from ivory, the fan handles and parasol ribs found in York are of special interest (Richmond 1947). No evidence of manufacturing or carving waste is known from Britain at this time.

In the immediately post-Roman world, the disruption of former commercial trade routes resulted in little ivory reaching northern Europe. The Islamic expansion of the seventh and eighth centuries also took its toll. When ivory began to appear again in northern Europe it was almost exclusively in what may broadly be termed ecclesiastical contexts, in the form of croziers, reliquaries and 'liturgical' combs (pp. 78-81). Under the impetus of the Carolingian renaissance, the volume of ivory working resumed something of its former importance (Volbach 1952), although for another three centuries or more the overwhelming consumer (and, perhaps, importer) of the raw material remained the church and the royal households. Beckwith (1972) lists a few ivories from eighth and early ninth-century England which demonstrate some small degree of production. In the earlier part of this period, the evidence of re-cut ivories demonstrates some continuing scarcity of raw material (Longhurst 1927), although by the middle of the ninth century the size and thickness of the carved plaques testifies to a more plentiful supply on the Continent (Gaborit-Chopin 1978). By the ninth or tenth century art historians recognise at least three important schools of ivory carving in north-east France, in the middle Rheinland and in the lower Rheinland respectively (Longhurst 1927). Even so, this plenitude was more marked in the Ottonian courts with their close relations with Italy than elsewhere in northern Europe, where ivory remained scarce for a further four centuries or so. Beckwith's (1972) catalogue, although selective, ascribes no single Anglo-Saxon ivory to the period between the early ninth and the late tenth century. In this context the two elephant ivory fragments interpreted as

manufacturing waste and recovered from an Anglo-Scandinavian or Norman context in York (Radley 1971) are a rare find.

The agencies by which ivory reached the European market in the post-Roman period were primarily Byzantine. Lombard (1952) notes that until the fourteenth century no reference can be found among Arab geographers' writings (which form the principal source of information on matters of this kind) to ivory originating in west Africa and reaching the Mediterranean across the Sahara. The Byzantine demand was met for the most part by the Islamic markets in Iraq and Egypt, through which passed ivory from India and from East Africa. Zanzibar, Madagascar, Ethiopia and Upper Egypt or the Sudan are mentioned as important sources of African ivory for the Egyptian markets,[13] while a certain amount of Indian material arrived there via Ceylon (Labib 1965). By way of the important fairs of Pavia and elsewhere, this ivory eventually found its way into the workshops of northern Europe. Beckwith (1972) identifies a few Anglo-Saxon ivories from the period between the late tenth and the late twelfth centuries, but only in the later thirteenth and fourteenth centuries did the flow of material increase substantially, when French and Flemish ports began to play a significant role in its direct importation (Gaborit-Chopin 1978).

In the renewed affluence of the medieval period ivory began to reach a much wider market, in the form of handles, pommels, gaming pieces, mirror-cases and a range of further wholly secular objects. The continuing development of international trade ensured the supply of raw materials on an appropriate scale, to the extent that by 1258, in Paris, the principal medieval production centre, no fewer than three different degrees were recognised among the ivory carvers of the city (Cust 1902). The extent to which the carvers worked closely with craftsmen in precious metals and enamels and were essentially involved in the same artistic movements during the medieval period is stressed by Gaborit-Chopin; indeed, the ivory sculpture of the period may have been executed by artists who also worked in other media, while a variety of specialists produced buttons, gaming pieces, buckles and the like (Gaborit-Chopin 1978).

Special mention must be made here of one

group of objects which fails to conform to the view of the course of the ivory trade outlined above. In a number of pagan Saxon graves dating from the fifth and sixth centuries have been found a series of large ivory rings, interpreted as bag rings (pp. 110-12). The graves in question show no other sign of particular affluence, nor are other exotic imports much in evidence. Considering the absence of ivory from the more noble Frankish graves of the period, its comparatively common appearance in rural cemeteries in England and on the Continent is all the more puzzling.

One possible explanation suggests itself: it may be that the ivory in question derives not from contemporary elephants but from the fossil tusks of long-extinct mammoths. This possibility has previously been considered by Green (Myres and Green 1973), who rejected it on the grounds that fossil material from England invariably fractures within a short time of being uncovered. While this may well be true of tusks coming from well-drained gravel deposits, it does not hold good for all mammoth sources in this country. Dawkins (1869) mentions a tusk from Clifton Hall, between Edinburgh and Falkirk, which was found 'in such preservation that it was sold to an ivory turner for £2. Before it was rescued . . . it had been sawn asunder for the manufacture of chessmen.' Sir Richard Owen (1846) describes another tusk from Dungeness, Kent, as yielding ivory fit for manufacture and a further specimen from the Yorkshire coast as hard enough to be used by ivory turners. Indeed, the tendency of ivory to split in the 'cone-within-cone' fashion already mentioned (p. 17) might even have encouraged its utilisation in the manufacture of rings, since these are merely cross-sections of cones or cylinders, while positively discouraging the development of other types of artefact. The bronze binding strips found on certain rings (Figure 62b) may have been designed to prevent further delamination rather than to repair accidental fractures.

The fact that only the outermost periphery of the tusk is used for these rings makes the positive identification of species difficult. As already described (p. 17) the angle of intersection of the radiating striæ is said by Penniman (1952) to be distinctive for elephant and mammoth respectively, but this distinction is clearly seen only in the central area of the solid tusk, which is inevitably missing from the rings, and is less marked at the periphery. Other writers have, in any case, been more circumspect in consideration of the differences, and the surviving surfaces on many rings are often too eroded for this detail to be distinguished. The problem could immediately be resolved with the aid of a few radiocarbon determinations, since mammoth ivory could hardly be younger than about 10,000 years. As yet, however, radiocarbon sample sizes are unacceptably large for application to this problem, the minimum weight being in excess of that of many of the ring fragments themselves.[14]

As well as native British sources, origins in Germany, where similar rings are also known (R. Koch 1967; Roeren 1960; Vogt 1960), and from Siberia might also be considered. An account of the Siberian sources is given by Digby (1926). In one year he saw about 1,000 pairs of mammoth tusks, some of them in perfect condition and entirely suitable for the production of billiard balls, piano keys, combs and the like. It must be admitted, however, that the possibility of direct importation of this material to Anglo-Saxon England seems even more remote than an African or Asiatic origin.

Walrus

The increasing popularity of walrus ivory from the late tenth to the twelfth or thirteenth centuries, as a raw material for working into secular and devotional objects, can be related to the expanding commercial and political relations which developed with Scandinavia during this period and indeed to an increasing interest in this material manifested in the Viking homelands (Kielland 1930). As a result of the activities of Scandinavian merchants, walrus ivory came to be traded down the Volga to the Middle and Far East, where it was held to have considerable prophylactic powers, probably being taken (along with narwhal tusk) for unicorn horn (W.E. Cox 1946; Olaus Magnus 1555). Its popularity in England is reflected in the overwhelming number of carvings in this material listed by Beckwith (1972).

The natural distribution of the Atlantic walrus today extends little south of 65°N, although formerly it may have been somewhat more widespread (King 1964). Foote and Wilson (1970) mention Greenland and northern Norway as important sources until the thirteenth century. Historical references mention isolated sightings as far south as the Thames, where William Caxton recorded one in 1456; between 1815 and 1954 a total of twenty-one sightings were noted, all but two of them off the Scottish coast (King 1964). While a certain amount of material may, therefore, have been collected locally, it is unlikely that the market could have been satisfied from this source. The status of a walrus skull from twelfth-century levels at Lund (Bergquist and Lepiksaar 1957) is again unclear.

A passage of some importance in the discussion of this topic appears in the account of Ohthere's voyages contained in the Old English *Orosius*; its precise significance, however, has in the past been disputed (cf. Foote and Wilson 1970; Skeat 1888). The passage (f.8ᵛ line 30- f.10ᵛ line 6) runs as follows (Bately 1980):

Swiþost he for ðider, toeacan þæs landes sceawunge, for þæm horshwælum, for ðæm hie habbað swiþe æþele ban on hiora toþum — þa teð hie brohton sume þæm cyninge — 7 hiora hyd | bið swiðe god to sciprapum. Se hwæl bið micle læssa þonne oðre hwalas: ne bið he lengra ðonne syfan elna lang; ac on his agnum lande is se betsta hwælhuntað: þa beoð eahta and feowertiges elna lange, 7 þa mæstan fiftiges elna lange; þara he sæde þæt he syxa sum ofsloge syxtig on twam dagum.

The passage has been newly translated by Susan Hitch as follows:[15]

Besides surveying the country he went there principally for the walruses, because they have very valuable bone in their teeth — they had brought some of these teeth to the king — and their hide is very useful for ship ropes. This walrus is much smaller than other whales: it is no more than seven ells long; but the best whale-hunting is in his own country: those are forty-eight ells long and the biggest fifty ells long; he said that he as one man in six or seven (boat loads) had killed sixty of them in two days.

Narwhal

Narwhal tusks were highly prized during the later medieval period, when they were believed to be unicorn horns and to possess fabulous powers (Humphreys 1953). Their northerly distribution (generally north of about 65°N) put them beyond easy reach and although certain complete tusks are recorded in royal treasuries, examples of utilisation are rare.[16]

Beaver

The teeth of one further species deserve special mention. Reference is made below (p. 110) to several finds of the incisor teeth of beaver (*Castor fiber*), an animal long since extinct in the British Isles. Its former presence in England is, however, recalled in a number of place names of Anglo-Saxon or Old English origin, such as Beverley, Beavercotes and others (Ekwal 1960; A.H. Smith 1956). No written or archaeological evidence can be found to suggest that it survived into the medieval period in England, but its presence in Wales can be verified up to at least the twelfth century (Harting 1880; Corbet 1964). In addition to a number of Welsh place names commemorating the beaver, such as Beaver Pool, Beaver Dam, Vale of the Beavers, etc., Harting records two direct references to the animal. In the Laws of Howel Dha (940) the King was named the sole beneficiary of all beavers, martens and ermines killed for the manufacture of garment borders; since, however, their skins were valued at 120 pence (compared with 24 pence for marten and 8 pence for wolf, fox and other furs), they were evidently already scarce in Wales by that time. Over two centuries later, Giraldus Cambrensis mentions in his *Itinerary* of 1188 (II, 49), that beaver was then to be found in Wales only on the River Teifi in (modern) Dyfed. Giraldus states that the animal also survived on a river in Scotland in his day. Two sixteenth-century references to beaver surviving in sufficient numbers on Loch Ness in the previous century to have formed the basis of an export trade are open to suspicion in view of the fact that the animal is absent from a list of native fur-bearing animals included in an Act of Parliament of 1424 (Harting 1880).

While the continuing survival of the beaver cannot, therefore, be demonstrated beyond the end of the twelfth century, the teeth which were prized as amulets in the Anglo-Saxon period (p. 110) could certainly have come from native animals.

Horn

As explained elsewhere (pp. 66-7), the processes involved in horn working were such that it was necessarily a sedentary occupation. An organised long-distance trade in animals is not verified archaeologically or historically, so that all early horn working would have relied on comparatively locally bred beasts. It was not until the seventeenth century that this localised pattern began to break down under the development of large-scale cattle droving and the introduction of foreign horns, notably those of American bison and Indian water buffalo (Armitage 1980, 1982).

The horns of aurochs (*Bos primigenius*) may be mentioned briefly, although the likeliood of their being encountered during the period considered here is extremely slight. The latest recorded specimen from Britain has been radiocarbon dated to the fourth millennium BC, athough the species survived on the Continent well into our era, and aurochs bones have been noted on a number of Roman period sites in Germany (Luff 1982). The drinking horns found at Sutton Hoo (pp. 151-2) have been identified as deriving in all probability from aurochs and hence must have been imported under the exceptional circumstances surrounding this extraordinary burial.

Under normal circumstances there are likely to have been close links between skinners and tanners on the one hand and horners on the other.[17] Archaeological evidence for such relationships is only just beginning to emerge, and in this context the large numbers of horn cores recovered from a late medieval tannery at 's-Hertogenbosch-Gertru in the Netherlands is particularly significant (Prummel 1982).

Notes

1. Although concentrations of foot bones (phalanges etc.) found on excavations may result from trimming the exremities of hides at the tanning stage, the metapodials are never left in the skin at present-day abbatoirs: Considering the additional weight and inconvenience which would have been incurred, it seems unlikely that they ever would have been. On the trading of horns with skins, however, see p. 30.

2. For discussion of a reference to whaling in the Alfredian *Orosius* see p. 41.

3. Conversely, the development of 'court schools' of antler workers in Poland has been connected with their privileged access to antler in this way by Kurnatowska (1977), who mentions several such workshops found in the vicinity of feudal seats. For some further discussion of factors affecting the presence or absence of antler from excavated sites see Grant (1981).

4. There were, however, native Pleistocene varieties which did not survive the last glaciation.

5. At Hedeby (Ulbricht 1978) and Ribe (Ambrosiani 1981), for example, the paucity of red deer bones suggests that venison was not normally eaten.

6. In the earlier stages of economic development (p. 50) some customers may have supplied their own antlers. It is also possible, of course, that some collecting was done by the craftsmen themselves.

7. Darling (1937) notes variations in this tendency among red deer, according to the mineral and other resources of their environment.

8. Dr D.R. Brothwell has suggested to me that trace element analysis might be used to distinguish between antlers from different ecological zones, but so far I have not had the opportunity of testing this possibility. Some preliminary work in this field was carried out in Sweden but had to be abandoned due to lack of funds before firm results were achieved (Kristina Ambrosiani, personal communication).

9. The presence of a fragment of reindeer antler, said to have been found under a Roman altar at Chester (Harting 1880), may be explained in the same way as the others discussed here.

10. No evidence of Scandinavian settlement in Scotland can be found before the early years of the ninth century (Klindt-Jensen 1969).

11. Dr Ruth Ellison has kindly studied the passage at my request and has provided the translation given here.

12. I am grateful to Dr Ellison for this information.

13. Mas'oudi (quoted in Lombard 1952) records in the tenth century that tusks of 230kg and more were obtained from Zanzibar.

14. I have been fortunate in gaining the tentative agreement of a laboratory currently developing new methods of dating small samples of material to apply itself to this problem when the process has been perfected.

15. I am grateful to Miss Hitch for undertaking this translation and that reproduced on pp. 31-2.

16. Perhaps the most impressive object to incorporate narwhal tusks is the seventeenth-century royal throne of Denmark, now in Rosenborg Castle, Copenhagen, and illustrated by Bencard and Hein (1982). In the sixteenth and seventeenth centuries vessels made from narwhal ivory were prized for their supposed property of being proof against poison.

17. Grancsay (1945) notes the importance of tanners as suppliers of horns to the British army in the eighteenth century, for the manufacture of powder horns.

4. Handicraft or Industry?

Throughout the period under review some types of object are, by their simple and utilitarian nature, unlikely to have been manufactured as items of trade, but would have been made by the user as required. Among those considered below, items such as bone skates (Figure 76) and scapula scoops (Figure 96) may be assigned to this category. Other classes of material display a wide range of skills in their production techniques: the more elaborate bone pins (Figure 64), for example, would certainly have had some retail value, but few would have paid for a crude dress-pin hacked from the fibula of a pig when pork was (metaphorically) on everyone's menu. Evidence for the use of certain tool types, such as lathes or the fine saws used in cutting comb teeth, in itself indicates ownership of a somewhat specialised toolkit, quite apart from any skill displayed in its use. Yet other items may be identified as entirely 'professional' on the quality of workmanship alone, or possibly in combination with the use of costly raw materials (Figure 74).

Qualitative judgements of this kind are of limited value, however, and fail to combine to produce a comprehensive picture of the character and scale of the 'industry' dependent on skeletal materials. For this purpose more is to be gained from examination of concentrations of manufacturing waste or of items abandoned in the course of production because of breakage or some other factor. There are too few finds of this nature to throw any useful light on ivory working, and even for bone, antler and horn, adequately recorded and published finds provide a precarious basis for a systematic reconstruction.

Bone and Antler

Evidence of bone-working has been found on a number of Roman excavations, but the scale is usually small and the nature of the products unspecified: hence 'a small heap of bone chippings' from Springhead, Kent, was identified as waste from the manufacture of bone objects (E. Tilley in Penn 1957), and 'workshops' similarly occupied have been noted at Puckeridge, Hertfordshire (*Britannia* 4, 299), and at Kelvedon, Essex (*Britannia* 10, 311). Boon (1974) mentions scapulae found at Silchester, Hampshire, from which 'eyelets' had been systematically drilled. Scattered finds of unfinished pins from Roman sites such as Latimer, Buckinghamshire (Branigan 1971) and Winterton, Lincolnshire (Stead 1976), are impossible to distinguish as other than the products of individual enterprise, but concentrations of bone blanks, partly-shaped and finished pins indicate the presence of a specialist. Finds of this nature have been made at York (RCHM 1962), at Cambridge (*Britannia* 7, 341) and during more recent work at Springhead, Kent (*Britannia* 9, 472), but in no instance is it possible to gauge the volume and duration of production. Spoons, which form one of the other major categories of bone utensils of the Roman period, have been found on two occasions in circumstances indicating on-the-spot manufacture. Excavations during the nineteenth century at Woodcuts, Dorset, produced one completed spoon and sixteen rough-outs (Figure 29): eight of them came from the shaft of a well and the others lay scattered about the site, but they must, surely, represent the output of a single producer, if not the remnants of a single 'hoard' (Pitt Rivers 1887). A more recent find of manufacturing waste from Winchester, Hampshire, includes two roughed-out spoon bowls similar to those from Woodcuts (Figure 29), and over two hundred other fragments, at least a third of which were judged to be spoon handle fragments (N. Crummy 1983). The entire deposit came from an area of some six square metres in the fill of a ditch, and is probably to be dated to the mid second century.

An important find of over 1,700 bone casket or furniture-mounts from a fourth or fifth-century layer at the Market Hall, Gloucester,

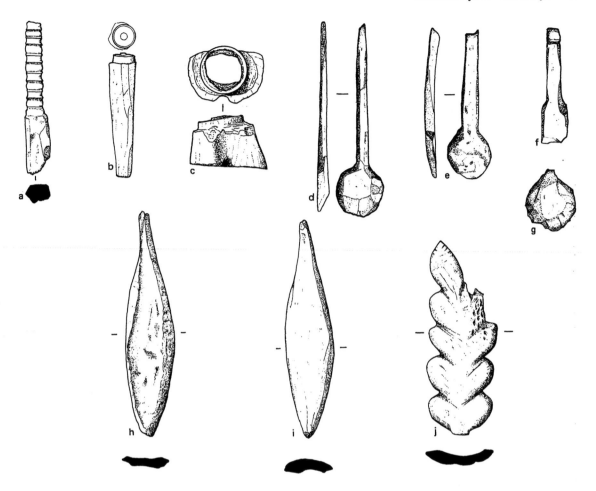

Figure 29: Unfinished and waste pieces (scale 1:2) from Roman bone-working industries: turned pieces from Colchester (a) and Exeter (b); turning waste from London (c); spoon blanks from Woodcuts (d, e) and Winchester (f, g); coffin fittings from Colchester (h-j)

provides strong evidence for the activities of a user, if not a producer, of these items at this period (Hassal and Rhodes 1974). From Colchester, Essex, unequivocal evidence for on-site manufacture of more elaborate mounts has been demonstrated by N. Crummy (1981): a deposit consisting of twenty-one rough-outs and unfinished mounts in various foliate shapes (Figure 29h-j) was found along with mounts of other forms, fixing pegs and further items, in a context dated to the early part of the fourth century. The mounts provide a rich source of evidence not only in the form of traces of working with various tools but also of the nearby presence of a production site; the absence of shavings and offcuts which might be expected to form the major part of the waste from manufacturing was particularly noted, however, and hence it was impossible to establish what other items, if any, may have been produced in the vicinity.

The making of composite combs, which had achieved considerable popularity by the end of the fourth century (pp. 82-3), is demonstrated in very few places during this period. The most helpful find comes from Quenstedt, Südharz, where some fifty pieces of antler, ranging from unworked fragments to prepared tooth-plates, side-plates and a completed comb, were discovered, along with a late Roman brooch (Grimm 1930). Smaller collections of third or fourth-century material come from Grossjena,

Saale (Bicker 1936) and from Gröbitz, some 15km distant (B. Schmidt 1967).

For all these Roman period production sites supporting evidence which might help identify the status of the bone and antler workers is lacking. Were they employed full-time in their craft? Did they work in other materials? Were they sedentary or itinerant? It seems that for this period primary evidence to help answer these questions is yet to be found.[1] On the basis of evidence gathered from later finds (pp. 48-51), it may be suggested that the craftsmen concerned were professionally engaged in their work, but that many of them would have been condemned to an itinerant existence, fulfilling the needs of the largely rural population with a small stock-in-trade and by manufacture on demand. The larger urban centres, however, may already have supported small numbers of such craftsmen on a sedentary basis: in administrative centres such as York and London the resident population would have been swelled by a continual flow of visitors with business to settle and money to spend. Among the peddlars and tradesmen thronging the commercial quarters of these civil centres, bone and antler-workers must certainly have been represented. Evidence for the use of certain techniques such as lathe-turning (pp. 58-9) enhance this suggestion, although the rudimentary lathes of the period would have been easily transportable.

In addition to these civilian pursuits, there appears to have been an element of production for, and by, the military. Among the activities which could be identified in an extensive armourers' workshop at Caerleon, Gwent, for example, were the production of bone scabbard chapes (p. 163) and splints for composite bows (pp. 155-8), the latter numbering over forty (Nash Williams 1932; Boon 1972).[2] Items such as sword hilts may also have been produced under similar circumstances: at Augst, northern Switzerland, for example, Schmid (1968) has noted the systematic utilisation of long-bone shafts for the production of handles, in addition to non-service material such as hinges and pins.

The social upheaval attendant upon the collapse of Roman rule would certainly have robbed most sedentary craftsmen of their ready markets and it seems likely that the bone and antler industry, which continued to function throughout the succeeding centuries, was carried on at that time largely by itinerant workers. The fact that composite combs (which, we may assume, were almost invariably professionally produced) commonly accompany the dead as, presumably, they did the living population in most of northern Europe, implies that there was no shortage of demand at this time, though the market was necessarily scattered. Consistencies of style notable in widely-distributed combs tend to encourage this view and this very mobility may have been an important factor in determining the paucity of production sites so far recognised, without which more definite conclusions are impossible to reach.

Some small-scale activity consistent with this hypothesis has been noted in the fifth or sixth century at Helgö on Lake Mälar, Sweden, in the form of sawn antler fragments and unfinished components for composite combs (Ambrosiani 1981). From the seventh century important evidence comes from a settlement on the Meuse at Huy, Belgium: here unsawn tooth-plates and other elements from antler combs, together with quantities of waste, were found associated with two *Grubenhäuser* identified by the excavator as 'bone workshops' (Willems 1973). The degree of permanence implied by the finds is, however, unclear.

In the fifth to seventh-century settlement at West Stow, Suffolk, some eighty-five composite combs were found, some of them concentrated in groups of five or six from certain huts; evidence in the form of rough-outs of red deer antler from the same site indicate that some types at least were being manufactured on the spot (West 1969).

By the eighth and ninth centuries the beginnings of the revival of urban life led to the reappearance of evidence for bone and antler workers in major settlements. Southampton, Hampshire, has produced traces of antler comb-making (Addyman and Hill 1969) and other, as yet unspecified, activities, in the form of seven rubbish pits full of sawn-off articular ends from long-bones (Figure 30) (Holdsworth 1976).[3] Similar discoveries (though on a smaller scale) have been made at Dorestad in the Netherlands (Clason 1978), where there is also evidence for the production of combs and other objects in bone and antler (Holwerda 1930; Clason 1980). Although a great deal of the rich repertoire of bone and antler objects from the

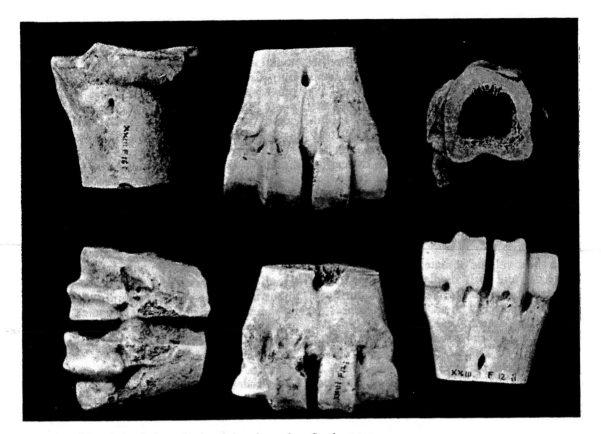

Figure 30: Discarded articular ends of cattle long-bones from Southampton

Frisian terps (Boeles 1951; Roes 1963) belongs to this period, information on manufacturing has not been forthcoming. Yet more sawn-off articular ends have been found at Münster, Nordrhein-Westfalen, where they were accompanied by clear evidence of the craft activity which utilised them: here in an eighth-century horizon, in a quarter where various industrial processes were pursued, comb making dependent on horse bone rather than antler was carried out. Many blanks and rough-outs as well as finished combs were found, clearly demonstrating to the excavator the presence of a professional workshop (Winkelmann 1977). The large number of sawn ends, of which over three hundred were found, certainly points to some measure of settled activity.

Until recently antler-working in Poland from the sixth to the eighth centuries was attested only by finished products, notably combs, but now unfinished rough-outs and other antler fragments are known from seventh-century Cekanów, from eighth-century Ujście and from seventh to ninth-century Nowa Huta (Kurnatowska 1977). This industry is designated by Kurnatowska 'semi-artisan', and is thought by her to have been carried on by itinerant craftsmen.

Contemporary Slavic settlements in Moravia have produced a range of utensils and implements in antler and a wide variety of bones, occasionally accompanied by concentrations of manufacturing waste: Staré Město, Czechoslovakia, in particular, has been prolific in this kind of evidence (Hrubý 1957).

At the easternmost point of this survey, comb manufacture has been recognised in the form of a 'large quantity of production remains' at Staraja Ladoga in Russia, where the influence (if not the actual presence) of Frisian craftsmen has been postulated from the eighth century (Davidan 1970 and 1977; Hilczerówna 1966). Evidence of bone working on the site was particularly concentrated in four log houses, each with a hearth in one corner, interpreted as combined workshops and dwellings (Davidan 1977).

The period from the ninth to the twelfth centuries is perhaps the golden age of the bone and, more particularly, the antler worker. At this same time the quality and quantity of the evidence relating to the craft increases to a point where more meaningful assessments of it can be made and against which the validity of our more speculative conclusions for the earlier periods can be measured. This is not to say that universal agreement is to be found among those who have applied themselves to these questions, and indeed far-reaching reappraisals are currently being prompted by new research in Scandinavia.

The sheer volume of material recovered from Viking age and early medieval sites has in the past given excavators a comforting security in the interpretation of their finds. References to 'workshops' appear everywhere, with the implicit or explicit assumption of sedentary production. In Dublin, for example, comb-making workshops have been postulated in certain areas of the High Street and Christ Church Place excavations, on the evidence of characteristic antler waste fragments and unfinished component parts (National Museum of Ireland 1973; B. Ó Ríordáin 1976). To the 'bone-carver's workshop' suggested by earlier finds from Clifford Street, York (Ward Perkins 1949) recent excavation reports have added others, including one seemingly making extensive use of bone as well as antler (MacGregor 1978a, 1982a).[4] Some signs of similar activities have been found at Northampton, where casket mounts and beads were made in addition to composite combs (G. Oakley in Williams 1979).

On the Continent a series of settlements along the southern coast of the Baltic have produced evidence of intensive antler-working at this time. Among four buildings identified as workshops at Menzlin, Mecklenburg, two were certainly engaged during the ninth or tenth centuries in the production of bone and antler goods, principally combs, but also spindle-whorls and pins; many uncompleted items and much waste was also recovered from them (Schoknecht 1977). Several other smaller production sites in Mecklenburg are mentioned by Schoknecht and also by Schuldt (1980).

Large-scale evidence for antler-working is recorded from a number of Pommeranian settlements, notably at Kołobrzeg where some 1,700 waste and partly-worked fragments were found in and around a late ninth-century wattle hut (Cnotliwy 1956). The same author has published finds from Wolin, where over 9,000 waste fragments and many rough-outs for combs were found, again in association with actual workshop buildings (Cnotliwy 1958, 1970). Prolonged production in the same premises could be demonstrated at Wolin, suggesting to the excavator succession from father to son (Cnotliwy 1958). In an attempt to gauge the scale of production of one eleventh-century workshop there, Cnotliwy (1956) estimated an output of some 820-1250 combs for the century, representing a consumption of about 64,000 metres of antler. Although the figures are impressive, they represent only about ten combs per year, hardly the fruits of full-time activity and a salutary reminder of the inadequacy of most finds as a basis for reasonable speculation about craft organisation. These unexpectedly low figures might be explained by the alternative activities which some writers have postulated for those engaged in antler-working, on the basis of evidence for other crafts found in the same areas or even in the same buildings which housed their workshops. On this basis, amber-working has been suggested as a parallel activity at Menzlin (Schoknecht 1977), where beads, pendants and gaming pieces in this material were found, as well as at Kołobrzeg (Cnotliwy 1956) and Wolin (Cnotliwy 1958), while stone-working was judged to have taken place, though perhaps exceptionally, along with bone and antler-working at Kalisz (Kurnatowska 1977). At Staraja Ladoga, south of the Russo-Finnish border, it was suggested that jewellery-making, amber-carving and iron-working were all practised by craftsmen who also worked in bone (Davidan 1977).

Secondary activities of this kind are also postulated for antler workers at the most productive site for this material which has yet been excavated, namely the Viking period settlement at Hedeby, Schleswig-Holstein, occupied from the late eighth or early ninth century to the end of the first quarter of the eleventh century. Here an estimated 6 per cent of the site so far investigated has produced over a quarter of a million fragments and a wide range of finished items. On the basis of this very favourable sample, several conclusions have been drawn concerning the status and scale of the industry (Ulbricht 1978). There was, for example, no specific area of the settlement dedicated to antler-working: finished items and manufacturing debris were found widely distributed, such concentrations as there were suggesting that production was divided between a number of individuals or groups in various locations. This was taken to indicate that the work was carried out in the dwellings of the craftsmen (which is not to say in every household), rather than in a particular manufacturing quarter; furthermore the volume of output represented by waste fragments, viewed in the perspective of over two centuries of occupation of the site, suggested that the producers could not have been exclusively occupied in antler-working throughout the year and hence could not have been entirely dependent on this activity for their livelihood. The consistent working routines, the exhaustive utilisation of raw material by combining several lines of production, the consumption of large quantities of antlers — usually shed and occasionally imported — together with the skill displayed in many of the products, nonetheless point to largely 'professional' technicians. To the possibility that amber-working might have been practised at Hedeby as elsewhere, Ulbricht adds the suggestion that agricultural activities might have been pursued during the summer by the same people who dedicated their time to producing combs in the winter, these months also being appropriate for hunting and the collection of antlers. Other possibilities she considers are that older men retired from heavy labour, older children or women might have carried on the trade.

In recent years challenges have been made to the common assumption, whether tacit or explicitly stated, that finds of the kind of material described above necessarily demonstrate permanent (if not full-time) production centres. Kurnatowska (1977), for example, has speculated that the comparative scarcity of discoveries suggesting long-established workshops, taken together with the widespread distribution of common decorative motifs, might indicate that the craftsmen concerned were itinerant rather than settled. In the absence of viable evidence this question has

been difficult to resolve, but now two Scandinavian researchers have independently reached a common conclusion which provides a persuasive framework for the development of the bone and antler industry during the crucial period when major urban centres were beginning to appear.

In the more broadly-based of these investigations, Ambrosiani (1981) comes out firmly in favour of itinerant comb production throughout the Viking and early medieval period. Rejecting the suggestion that comb-makers spent part of their time engaged in other craft activities, she attributes the comparatively low annual outputs recognisable at many production sites not to part-time working but to the 'itinerant combmaker's temporary (or periodical) exploitation of the local urban market'. Seasonal factors such as warm weather (and, no doubt, better light) would have encouraged outside working in the summer months, while the indoor work noted at Staraja Ladoga might reflect a presence in winter. The findings from Hedeby, Wolin and elsewhere are reinterpreted by Ambrosiani on this basis, and the craft organization at Birka on Lake Mälar, Sweden, and at Ribe in Jutland, is explained in the same terms. The reasons for the increasingly widespread uniformity of form and style in the combs of the Viking period 'from Staraja Ladoga in the east to Dublin in the west' are similarly presented, not in terms of the prevalent fashion in any one area being disseminated elsewhere by travellers, but by the activities of manufacturers moving from place to place, leaving evidence of their presence in almost every settlement of the period, but most particularly in major market places. In this thesis certain varieties of comb accorded regional epithets such as 'Frisian' by earlier writers and, when found outside their normal area of distribution, interpreted as imports, are seen rather as the locally-made products of itinerant workers. While craftsmen operating at opposite ends of the zone described are unlikely to have had direct contact with one another, a degree of overlap between neighbouring territories would have been sufficient to ensure a constant exchange of ideas and practices which would have become widely diffused. Only with progressive urban development in the early medieval period does Ambrosiani find signs that the craft became sedentary.

The opportunity for detailed study of this process in operation was provided by excavated material from Lund, a city with a record of carefully-recorded investigations on well-stratified sites. It was grasped by Christophersen (1980a, 1980b) who produced from it an economic outline for the period from 1000 to 1350. A production model in three phases is postulated for Lund by Christophersen (1980a): initially he sees a 'homecraft phase' in which each household's needs are met by its own production, supplemented when necessary by purchases from itinerant craftsmen; this is followed by an intermediate 'customer production phase', in which the balance has changed so that the majority of items are commissioned directly from itinerant workers; in the third stage, designated the 'market production phase', local production is continuous and in the hands of settled craftsmen who produce their wares for the general market and not to individual demands. Each of these phases, which are linked to and dependent on the size of the community, should, according to Christophersen's theory, be recognisable by mutually distinct criteria as follows. Home craft production should produce mostly localised concentrations of waste linked to dwellings, quantitatively limited and heterogeneous in character. Waste concentrations from the activities of itinerant craftsmen should be individually somewhat heavier but chronologically limited in extent, showing no particular long-term connection with individual dwellings and being generally scattered within the central settlement area; individual designs may be recognised, but specialisation should be limited. In the final market production phase waste deposits should be characteristically of greater density and of longer duration, and should be concentrated around well-defined workshop premises: the products should be specialised and production methods standardised; evidence may be found for the supplementing of local resources with imported raw materials.

Comparing the actual finds from Lund with this theoretical model, Christophersen finds a good measure of correspondence, although the successive categories are mutually less exclusive than had been postulated. In the embryonic settlement (*c.* 1000-1020), production was indeed found to have been essentially on a home craft basis, although already some element of 'professional' involvement in the specialised production of combs could be detected: the emergence of professional craftsmen was, therefore, not dependent on urban settlement. These skilled technicians could have helped form the nucleus of the more sedentary (though not yet necessarily permanent) bone and antler workers who made their appearance during the principal period of expansion of the town, from about 1020 to 1150, concentrated in so-called 'production enclaves' in the town centre and represented by concentrations (some quite sizeable) of manufacturing waste. At this time other forms of production were not entirely displaced, both home production and itinerant workers apparently continuing to supply some of the community's needs. During the *floruit* of medieval Lund, *c.* 1150-1350, a new character to the industry was detected: production was concentrated in the area around the market place and was carried out in specialised premises, several such centres existing contemporaneously over several generations. The advent of these permanent workshops, each of which is thought to have employed some semi-skilled or unskilled labour in addition to the master craftsman, finally displaced for good the itinerant workers.

Christophersen finds evidence to corroborate his market-based model in parallel studies carried out on metal-working in medieval Lund. If the controlling economic factors carry the weight he attributes to them, then they may be expected to operate on an extended, and possibly universal, basis. Some support for their validity can be found in the concurrent emergence of differentiated activities within the workshops of Lund: after the middle of the twelfth century, specialisation on some four or five products per workshop could be detected, usually with one line predominating; at the same time there was a rationalisation of the output in greater standardisation of forms, and less elaborate decoration, representing early moves towards mass production and increased profit margins.

The introduction of these concepts will help to prevent over-simplistic interpretation of the evidence from this and earlier periods and, in future, considerations of new finds will be unable to ignore them. For later periods, however, their application will be of limited value since the industry seems no sooner to have found a settled basis than it went into a decline which ended in its extinction. The elaborate but cumbersome composite combs which formed the basis of the antler industry were gradually replaced from about the twelfth century with one-piece combs of bone, wood and cattle horn. The change was not synchronous everywhere: it was the fourteenth century before the final impact came in Poland (Kurnatowska 1977), and composite combs were still being produced in large numbers at this time in Scandinavia, for example at Trondheim in western Norway (Long 1975). By the time that the crafts of the medieval cities came to be documented and formalised into guilds, however, the industries based on antler had already been overtaken by those using horn[5] and from then on there is little evidence for utilisation on any but a casual and occasional basis.

Horn

Horn being more prone to decay and disintegration in the ground, archaeological evidence in the form of workshop debris or even finished objects provides a scant framework on which to base an overall survey of its utilisation, and while documentary records survive to illuminate the history of medieval horners their 'prehistory' is very shadowy indeed. The evidence which does survive, however, indicates that the craft enjoyed several centuries of development before emerging into the historical record from about the twelfth century onwards.

Although little is known of horn-working in the Roman period, a few finds of concentrations of horn cores[6] attest to the establishment of workshops which, by the very nature of the preparative methods involved in horn-working (p. 66), must have had some degree of permanence. One of these discoveries took place in a structure (interpreted as a cellar) at Augst in Switzerland, where 135 cattle horn cores were found heaped-up in a corner, augmented by a further 73 scattered in the overlying fill (Schmid 1968). The cores showed signs of having been hacked and broken from the skull in a manner still used among present-day slaughterers, and of subsequent removal of

the horn sheath.[7] Schmid had no hesitation in identifying these, together with numerous other sawn horn cores of cattle, sheep and goat found elsewhere at Augst, as the waste from a horn industry, particularly as several of the scattered finds had been cut into sections in a manner suggesting that the horn itself had been cut on the core before the latter had been discarded. These discoveries encouraged Schmid to support a Roman date for a similar find from Lauriacum (Lorch), in Austria, whose early origins had hitherto been in some doubt (Kloiber 1957): here an area of over fifty metres was strewn with horn cores (Figure 31), in some places seemingly laid next to one another forming a thick layer overlying a series of late Roman graves. Although cut-marks were observed on only a few cores, they may well represent the waste from a well-established workshop nearby.

At Exeter, Devon, a horn industry has been postulated on the basis of a marked underrepresentation of horn cores from levels dating from the second and fourth centuries: Maltby (1979) has suggested that the horns were reserved for utilisation elsewhere and has found corroborative evidence in the form of cut-marks around the bases of those cores which did survive. Cattle, sheep and goat horn cores all displayed this feature.

Another concentration of forty-six horn cores, from the site of a probable fourth-century Roman farm or villa at Kingston Hill Farm, Oxfordshire, was marked by a lack of

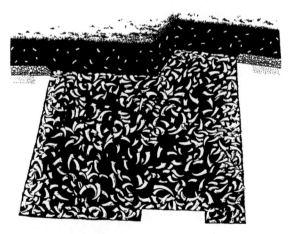

Figure 31: Perspective view of the 'horn core layer' at Lauriacum, Austria (after Kloiber) (The exposed section in the rear stands 1.10m high)

evidence in the form of cuts relating to removal of the horn sheath (R. Wilson in Parrington 1976), although the method of separating the horn cores from the skulls showed a systematic approach which is paralleled with cores more certainly connected with the horn industry from medieval Coventry (see below).

A recent find from London added to this small but persuasive body of evidence for Roman horn-working, when excavations at Angel Court produced ninety-eight cattle horn cores from a single late fourth-century layer: the presence nearby of a horner's workshop was strongly implied by this concentration, although quantities of postcranial bones from the same layer suggested too the pursuit of other, possibly related, activites (J. Clutton-Brock and P. Armitage in Blurton 1977).

In the immediately-succeeding centuries only occasional finds such as the Benty Grange helmet (Figure 80), the Cumberland sword hilt (Figure 87f) and entire horns such as those buried at Sutton Hoo and Taplow (pp. 151-2) serve as primary evidence that the horner's craft to some degree survived. Further inference may be drawn from the metal mounts found from blast or drinking horns (pp. 151-2) and from horn-shaped glass vessels which imitate them. Again the scale of production may have been larger then these few completed objects suggest. At Menzlin detached horn cores appear to have been found in some numbers, occasionally showing signs of sawing (Schoknecht 1977), and Dorestad was judged from finds of sheep, goat and cattle horn cores to have supported 'an intensive horn industry' (Clason 1980). Ribe too has produced considerable numbers of horn cores, outweighing other skeletal elements from the same species: some were certainly worked, but others may be waste from tanning (cf. note 6) rather than horn-working (Ambrosiani 1981).

Saxon Southampton, Hampshire, has yielded similar finds from cattle, sheep and goats in a range of sizes, and showing some variation in workshop practice, particularly noticeable in the case of goat horn cores which show no signs of cutting to remove the horn sheath. This factor is tentatively explained by the possibility that the trade was supported by imported horns hacked from the carcass at some distance from the town; under these circumstances the bond between horn core and sheath would have

partially rotted before arrival at the horner's, so that they could easily be separated by hand (Bourdillon and Coy 1980).

The recovery of several twelfth-century horn combs from Dublin (Dunlevy 1969) and others of probably similar date from elsewhere (pp. 95-6) provides tangible evidence of the activities of medieval horners. More particularly, their presence in York is advertised by a shallow pit, lined with clay and wood, which was found to contain horn cores of cattle and goats and was interpreted as a horner's soaking pit (Ryder 1970; Wenham 1964). Most of the cores were complete but some had been sawn through and others displayed various chopping marks from the processes of removing the horn sheath or working it *in situ*. The excavation (in a street known since at least the thirteenth century as Hornpot, or Hornpit Lane) also produced a large hearth which may have served in working the horns (p. 66). Dates from the twelfth to the fourteenth century have been suggested for these finds.

Further excavations at St Mary's Hospital at Ospringe, Kent, occupied between 1230 and 1470, produced numbers of sheep horn cores with part of the frontal bones attached, clearly intended to minimise damage to the horns themselves, and implying that they were destined for utilisation (Wall 1980). A single medieval layer at Angel Court, London, provided similar evidence in the form of over fifty horn cores of cattle and fifteen of sheep, some of them sawn into sections (J. Clutton-Brock and P. Armitage in Blurton 1977). Other medieval horn works have been attested by excavation of numerous horn cores of cattle and goats from Kingston upon Thames, Surrey (Armitage 1980), Bristol, King's Lynn, Norfolk, and Hereford (Noddle 1975). R. Wilson (in Palmer 1980) presents evidence for horning in the form of cattle horn cores from twelfth to fourteenth century levels at Oxford and provides some thoughtful comments on the manner in which skeletons became divided up in horning, butchery and skinning.

The significance of cattle, sheep and goat horn cores from Tudor levels at Baynard's Castle in London is discussed by Armitage (1977). There too there was evidence that the horns had been cut into sections on the core. At Coventry, West Midlands, three deposits of cattle horn cores, all dated to the fourteenth or fifteenth centuries, were found at Well Street; thirty-seven of these were largely intact and still attached to the frontal bones, these being separated from the skull at a natural suture (R.E. Chaplin in Gooder *et al.* 1964). The same author has commented on 'a confused mass of ox horn cores' found with late seventeenth-century pottery at Waltham Abbey, Essex, judged to be from similar breeds of cattle and to have been used for the same purposes as those from Coventry (R.E. Chaplin in Huggins 1969).

Two finds producing evidence of horning in a curious secondary form may be mentioned. At Cutler Street in London, a series of thirteen late seventeenth or early eighteenth-century pits was found, varying in area from about one to sixteen square metres, each solidly lined with carefully-stacked horn cores. Although the pits themselves were not necessarily connected with this industry, it is clear that horning was being carried out nearby (Armitage 1982). Similarly, two hundred horn cores were found lining a nineteenth-century pit at Greyfriars, Oxford (Armitage 1980).[8]

From the archaeological evidence alone it would have been quite impossible to postulate the well organised horn industry historically documented for many medieval and later towns. This encourages caution against underestimating the earlier importance which it may have held. It seems likely, however, that only settlements of a reasonable size could have supported such an industry from the animals slaughtered for the day-to-day needs of the population or at periodic fairs and markets, and that the lengthy pre-treatment involved in horn-working (p. 66) would seem to rule out any possibility of an itinerant phase in its development.

Notes

1. Dr Stephen Greep is currently working on a comprehensive analysis of the organisation of the Roman bone-working industry in which varying degrees of centralisation are postulated for the production of different items. I am grateful to Dr Greep for discussion of my own suggestions as made here.

2. Splints of this type were also found in concentrations at Carnuntum in Austria, although they were not necessarily manufactured there. There are thirty-two examples; see von Groller (1901). At Vindonissa (Windisch) in Switzerland, there are 10 examples; see Eckinger (1933). The certainty of manufacture at Caerleon too has been questioned by Stephen Greep (personal communication).

3. Compare the similar finds from Augst in Switzerland (Schmid 1968). The Augst finds have been taken as evidence of glue making, however, and not of manufacturing: Schmid suggests that since the adhesive properties of animal glue would be impaired by the inclusion of gristle, the articular ends of the bones may have been sawn off before boiling. Similar evidence from Tudor levels at Baynard's Castle, London, on the other hand, is thought to be connected with the manufacture of knife handles and other items (Armitage 1982).

4. On the possible significance of a former street in York named Hartergate, see MacGregor (1978a).

5. The joint guild for comb-makers and lantern-makers recorded in Lübeck, Schleswig-Holstein, and mentioned by Ambrosiani (1981), would almost certainly have been for horn workers, since this is the material used for lantern windows (p. 67).

6. Horn cores roughly hacked from the skull but showing no signs of further working may represent waste from tanning rather than horn-working. Schmid (1972) describes an accumulation of medieval goat horn cores found in association with layers of bark waste from a tannery in Basel, Switzerland. She suggests that goat hides were supplied to the tanners with the horns still attached and that they were discarded after separation, a practice still common in Switzerland. Evidence for greater antiquity of this method of handling comes from Augst, where a series of tanning pits was found surrounded by horn cores, together with sheep and goat foot bones, elements which are normally left in the hide until tanning, according to Schmid. Only when cut marks indicating removal of the horn from the core can be found is it possible for local utilisation to be postulated with some degree of certainty (but see the observations of Bourdillon and Coy quoted on p. 52).

7. See, however, note 6.

8. Dr Philip Armitage is currently preparing

a paper on the utilisation of animal bones as building materials, showing that the practice became quite widespread in the seventeenth and eighteenth centuries, some being incorporated into walling and others used for flooring, hard-core for roads, and lining for ditches and soakaways. I am grateful to Dr Armitage for information concerning these uses of skeletal materials.

5. Working Methods and Tools

Few tools have been found in circumstances which relate them directly to the working of skeletal materials. We may attempt, however, by reviewing the known range of implements available to the craftsmen of the period and by examining traces of working observed on certain artefacts, particularly those which remained unfinished, to establish the range of the craftsman's tool kit and the methods he employed in working his materials.

Cutting and Splitting

Saws were certainly among the most important implements used in the working of skeletal materials. Much more control can be exercised in their use than in the percussive methods of cutting discussed below. Traces of sawing can be seen, for example, on many discarded antler burrs where they have been separated from the beam (Figure 32). The saw marks show clearly how the material was rotated periodically so that the blade never became too deeply embedded; final separation was usually by breaking. Saws for this type of work must have been comparatively robust: unfinished cuts of 2.6mm width have been observed on certain pieces of waste while, at the other end of the range, the saw cuts may be as narrow as 0.1mm (Ulbricht 1978). Bourdillon and Coy (1980) comment on the absence of saw marks from butchered bones in Anglo-Saxon Southampton, concluding that traces of sawing are, therefore, in themselves an indication of utilisation. Dr Philip Armitage (personal communication) finds no evidence for the use of saws in butchery before the late eighteenth century.

In addition to their use in cutting up material and in shaping certain categories of artefact, saws were also used in applying surface decoration. Close examination of the cuts in schemes of incised decoration shows that they are either V-shaped in section, indicating that they were cut with a knife, or else they are square, in which case they have been saw-cut. Careful measurement of saw-cut decoration has revealed that double saws were sometimes used for this purpose, two blades being mounted side-by-side to produce double cuts which were always inevitably parallel to one another and a fixed distance apart: observations of this feature have been made at Staraja Ladoga (Davidan 1962), Hedeby (Ulbricht 1978) and York (MacGregor 1982a), and the prevalence of decorative motifs based on double lines suggests that double saws were widely used. Salaman (1975) and Rougier (in Wenham 1964) record that among recent comb-makers a double saw or stadda was normally used in cutting the teeth to ensure even spacing (Figure 33). Two short blades were wedged into a wooden back, an interposed metal strip known as a languid (or languet) keeping the separation constant; one blade projected slightly further than the other and acted as a guide when fitted into the slot of the previously cut tooth.

Saws of the Roman period in a variety of shapes and forms have been published (Gaitzsch 1980), but so far only two fragments have been found in Anglo-Saxon contexts, from Thetford, Norfolk and Icklingham, Suffolk, respectively (Wilson 1968, 1976). The Icklingham blade is single-edged and was evidently held in a rigid backing of folded sheet metal; the teeth are quite fine, averaging some 4.6 teeth per cm over 13cm. The blade from Thetford, which is incomplete, has teeth on both sides with frequencies of about 3.7 and 6.1 teeth per cm respectively. In addition, fragments from an iron saw blade found at Lochlee Crannog, Strathclyde (Munro 1879), should be noted.

Berg (1955) has published a fine Viking-age saw with a one-piece bow from Mästermyr, Gotland, while W.L. Goodman (1964), Hrubý (1957) and Kolchin (1956) illustrate alternative knife-like forms resembling modern keyhole saws.

Traces characteristic of axe cutting are common in certain groups of artefacts. At Hedeby it has been noted that the antlers of

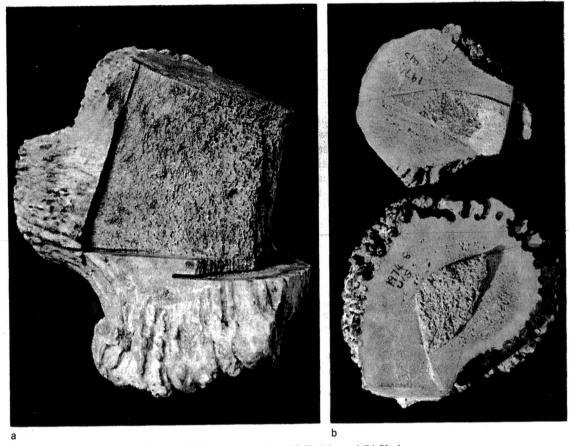

a   b

Figure 32: Discarded antler burrs exhibiting saw cuts: from (a) Hedeby and (b) York

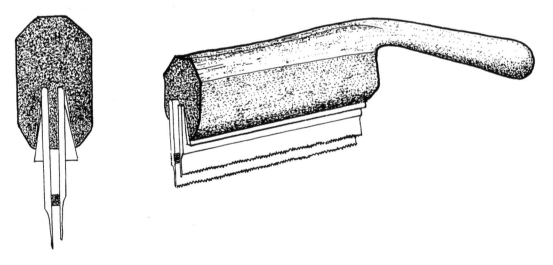

Figure 33: Double-bladed saw or stadda (after Salaman)

slaughtered deer were detached with a number of axe blows to the frontal bones of the skull (Ulbricht 1978); it was clear that the axes in question (which were presumably used by huntsmen or, perhaps, butchers) were much larger than the finer implements which were subsequently used by the antler workers themselves. Horners too made use of axes, recognisable chopping marks having been noted on the bases of discarded horn-cores resulting from the detaching of the horn itself (D.J. Rackham, forthcoming). At the production stage, axes seem commonly to have been used in shaping such items as skates (Figure 76) and socketed points (Figure 93). Axes of varying sizes have been found on numerous sites of the Roman period and later (Gaitzsch 1980; D.M. Waterman 1959; Wilson 1976). Wilson notes that some axes have butts showing signs of having been hammered, suggesting that they were carefully positioned before the cutting blow was delivered by striking the back of the axe. The process of splitting off thin slips of antler for the manufacture of comb tooth-plates must have required precise control of the kind which could have been achieved in this way. Broad chisels, which would have been equally appropriate for this task, are known in the Roman period (Gaitzsch 1980) but are uncommon in later levels: Wilson (1976) notes only one certain Anglo-Saxon example, from Southampton.

Wedges of iron which, along with those of wood, were important items in the carpenter's tool kit (being used to split timbers along the grain) would have been less useful in working more homogeneous skeletal materials. A recent find from Hedeby has, however, given a unique insight into the use of antler wedges in splitting up the thick beams of antlers for use; one such beam section was found with a wedge cut from a tine driven into the cancellous core at one end of the beam (Figure 34), the longitudinal outlines of the desired strips already having been marked out by deep grooves gouged into the compact tissue (Ulbricht 1978).[1] A similar function has been proposed for a series of angular wedges found at Menzlin (Schoknecht 1977). Practical tests have confirmed the efficacy of this technique (Ambrosiani 1981).

Some shaping operations seem to have been carried out with the aid of knives. Traces of their use, in the form of small depressions where chips of material have been sliced off, can be detected on utilised antler tines (Figure 93) and elsewhere. No doubt much of the incised free-hand decoration seen on bone objects — panels of interlace and the like — was executed with knives. The most likely alternatives, fine gravers or chisels, are unknown, although one example of a bone weaving comb of Iron Age date decorated in 'rolled graver technique' is known from Meare lake

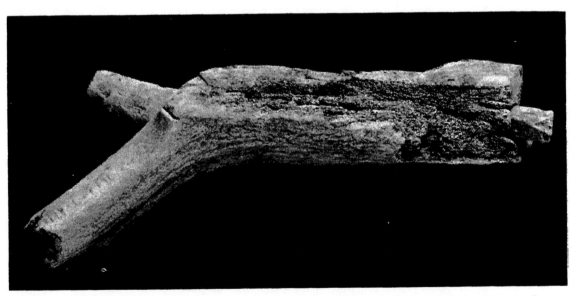

Figure 34: Viking age antler beam from Hedeby, with an antler wedge driven into the cancellous tissue at one end

village, Somerset (Penney 1975). Knives are among the best-attested implement types from all periods and include a variety of blade sizes appropriate to a range of tasks, from intricate carving to heavy chopping duties. One decorative example from Canterbury, Kent (Figure 88n) has been interpreted as a bone worker's knife on account of the care lavished on its ornamentation (Graham-Campbell 1978).

Although they survive only very rarely, draw-knives seem to have played an important part in the working of bone and antler. Flattened facets indicating their use can occasionally be seen on finished objects and concentrations of shavings of antler from Hedeby also provide an indication of their use. Draw knives seem the most likely implements to have been used in shaving down tooth plates for the manufacture of composite combs. Roman examples are illustrated by Gaitzsch (1980) and Anglo-Saxon versions by Wilson (1976).

Smoothing and Polishing

Gaitzsch (1980) reproduces files in a range of shapes and degrees of coarseness from the Roman period, and traces of their use can be detected on items such as bow-splints (Figure 83) and unfinished mounts found at Colchester (Figure 29).

A number of files have been recovered from excavations in Viking age and early medieval Novgorod (Kolchin 1956). Early examples are, as yet, unknown in Britain. Judging from the series of transverse parallel lines which may occasionally be detected on bone objects, some smoothing was done with the aid of a knife blade held cross-wise and pulled along the surface, producing characteristic 'chatter marks'. Otherwise, in the absence of suitable implements, various mineral and organic substances were most probably used for smoothing and polishing. It has already been suggested (MacGregor 1974) that fragments of pumice collected from shorelines in the northern isles may have been used in bone-working. A fragment found in an early tool box from Orkney (Cursiter 1886) may similarly have been used as an abrasive in woodworking. The use of a form of sandpaper, consisting perhaps of a piece of leather, together with quantities of fine sea sand has been suggested

on the basis of circumferential striations left on a late Slavic antler awl from Olsborg, Schleswig-Holstein (Hucke 1952). Other minerals which have been used in recent years for working skeletal materials include rottenstone (a decomposed siliceous limestone) and crushed chalk (Andés 1925). Organic alternatives recorded by the same author include powdered charcoal, ashes of bones or antlers, and shave-grass. Hard stems of shavegrass (*Equisetum*) were apparently chopped into finger-length pieces, thirty or forty of which were bound together, softened in water for half an hour, then used for scouring out blemishes in prepared horn. Another possible alternative was coarse fish skin, which was certainly used for smoothing ivory in the Roman period (Barnett 1954); the practice could conceivably have been followed in northern Europe. Present-day horn workers use a succession of increasingly fine polishing media, culminating in swansdown (Griffin, nd). The high degree of polish commonly imparted to such items as the side-plates of composite combs results in all traces of the coarser smoothing stages being obliterated.

Turning

The regular outlines of certain circular-section objects clearly demonstrate that they were lathe-turned. Some of the well-attested series of Roman knife handles with sinuous outlines or with relief mouldings (p. 169) were mass-produced in this way as were cylindrical hinges (pp. 203-5) and mounts. Schmid (1968) mentions also Roman containers (*Buchsen*) and rings produced in this way, and spindle whorls may be added to this list. A waste fragment from Exeter displaying a turned end is dated to the first century (Bidwell 1979). From Colchester, Essex, come two waste fragments with lathe stock centre-marks on the ends, and two lengths of bone turned with spool-and-bead moulding, one of them with an intact un-turned end (Figure 29); both are probably Roman though found in post-Roman contexts (N. Crummy 1981). From the Anglo-Saxon period, the common plano-convex gaming pieces which have been likened to slices cut from billiard balls on account of their symmetry are often said to be lathe-turned (p. 133). It is indeed conceivable that they were made in this way, the roughed-out bone discs being moulded on the chuck of a lathe to which they had been attached in some way. A simpler method might also have been used: a simple forked implement could have been inserted in the twin (or multiple) blind holes which occur on the bases of some of these pieces and used as a handle to spin the roughly-shaped bone disc in a suitably-shaped hollow in a stone. The result would be almost as symmetrical as that obtainable on a lathe. The bone discs closing the ends of certain Roman period handles or the cylindrical gaming pieces from Taplow, Buckinghamshire, may have been lathe-turned or they may have been produced with a profiled centre-bit. The cylindrical walls of the Taplow pieces (p. 134) are more certainly turned.

In Britain pre-Norman lathe-turned bone objects are otherwise limited to a few spindle whorls, but a carefully-made Migration Period box from Pflaumheim, Main-Tauber (R. Koch 1967) can be recognised from its precisely-cut regular outlines as having been turned. Koch has also noted that a comparable cylindrical box was found in a female grave of the seventh century at Gammertingen, Hohenzollern. A turned ivory box found in excavations at Jarrow, Tyne and Wear, may be from the eleventh century (Professor Rosemary Cramp, personal communication).

From the eleventh century onwards the practice seems to have become more common. Among the earliest lathe-turned products of this period are crossbow nuts, examples of which come from Goltho Manor, Lincolnshire in the late eleventh century and from Wareham Castle, Dorset, early in the following century (p. 160). Later in the medieval period, turned nuts of antler (and sometimes ivory) become fairly common. Bone styli or parchment-prickers are frequently made in this way, their machine-made regular appearance distinguishing them from dress pins even when only a fragment survives (pp. 124-5). These also make their appearance around the time of the Norman Conquest and to the same period may be attributed the bobbins of antler ornamented with multiple circumferential grooves (Figure 100) discussed on pp. 183-5. From Hitzacker, Elbe, Wachter (1976) notes evidence for the technique by the thirteenth century at the latest, in the form of a turned needle-case and a rough-out.[2]

No lathes of this period are still in existence although some possible fragments have been found at Hedeby (Dr Kurt Schietzel, personal communication). These would almost certainly have been pole lathes such as were used in the manufacture of wooden bowls (MacGregor 1978a). An illustration of a lathe of this type appears in a thirteenth-century manuscript in the Bibliothèque Nationale, Paris (ms Lat 11560, f. 84(1), reproduced in Salzman 1964) and accounts of them are given by Salzman, Hodges (1964), G.B. Hughes (1953) and Salaman (1975). Smaller bow-driven lathes may also have been used for producing jet and amber beads and rings, and for small items of bone. In the early post-medieval period lathe-turned bone objects, some of them handles, are known from sites such as Basing House, Hampshire (Moorehouse 1971) and Sandal Castle, Yorkshire (MacGregor 1983).

From the late sixteenth century, the development of more efficient lathes, some incorporating steel leaf springs instead of simple poles, led to tremendous advances in turning techniques especially in German ivory-working centres such as Nürnberg. The products of these centres are among the most extravagant examples of baroque taste, featuring hollow-turning of spheres-within-spheres, helical spirals and other astonishing feats of technical virtuosity (Plumier 1749).

Drilling

Traces of the use of drills are commonly found on artefacts of skeletal materials, particularly on articles of composite structure such as combs (p. 73) and caskets (p. 200).[3] Although a considerable number of early drill-bits are known (Peterson 1951; Wilson 1968, 1976) most of them are shell-bits (or spoon-bits) which, although effective on fibrous material like wood, would make little impression on bone, antler or ivory. Gaitzsch (1980), however, illustrates twist drills as well as spoon-bits from the Roman period. The punches which have been postulated as having been used for perforating bone and antler (Hrubý 1957) would seem to be very questionable; for these dense and compactly-structured materials, implements incorporating well-defined pointed cutting ends would have been more appro-

Figure 35: Rosary bead maker using a bow-driven lathe or drill, from the fifteenth-century *Hausbuch der Mendelschen Zwölfbrüderstiftung* (f. 13ʳ) (For an account of the complete manuscript see Treue *et al.* 1965)

Schleswig (Figure 36), each drilled with one or more holes from which such pieces have been cut (Ulbricht 1980a). Of necessity, the material which originally occupied the area within these perforations was not destroyed in the drilling process, so that some form of hollow bit must have been used. Many of these discoid pieces have no deep central indentation as might have been made by a centre-bit. Instead it is necessary to envisage an implement resembling a modern crown saw or a surgeon's trepanning saw, each of which has the form of a hollow cylinder with a toothed cutting edge and can be mounted on a simple handle as an auger (Salaman 1975). Although they are uncommon finds, a few examples of such tools are known from the Roman period, when they are thought to have been exclusively used in surgery: examples come from a physician's grave at Bingen (Como 1925; R. Waterman 1970; see also Figure 37) and from Niederbieber (Gaitzsch 1980), both in the Rheinland-Pfalz. There seems to be no reason why craftsmen working in the very materials for which trepanning saws were developed should not have had equal access to them and, indeed, it is difficult to account for the manufacture of discoid gaming counters without such an implement.

Scribing

Apart from saw- and knife-cut ornament, the most commonly encountered forms of decoration on bone and antler objects are inscribed ring-and-dot motifs. Occasionally, the concentric ring elements display an irregularity which indicates that they were executed freehand (MacGregor 1974), but the vast majority are perfectly symmetrical and must have been produced with an implement of the centre-bit type. This type of decoration is occasionally referred to as 'compass-drawn'[4] but simpler tools with fixed-radius scribing points would seem to be more probable than variable compasses. Equally, symmetrical double-ring-and-dot motifs (Figure 107) show that some of these implements may have had two or more scribing points at differing radii, although two single-toothed implements of differing dimensions could have been used successively to the same effect. The concentric rings sometimes incised on the surfaces of discoid playing pieces

priate, in the form either of angular-section awls for smaller perforations or of centre-bits, in which the cutting element describes an arc around the centre point, for larger holes. While awls are among the most common implements on archaeological sites, none has been found in circumstances specifically associated with bone working. Centre-bits, on the other hand, are unknown from early contexts, although tools employing the principles of the centre-bit were certainly used for the production of ring-and-dot ornament from the period considered here (see below). A fifteenth-century German illustration of a rosary bead maker shows a bow-driven horizontal drill with radiating spikes at the tip, which would be ideal for this purpose (Figure 35).

Implements of a rather different type, with larger dimensions, may also be postulated on the evidence of discoid playing pieces (Figure 72), as well as spindle whorls cut from jaw bones (Figure 101). A large series of jaw bones (bovine mandibles) has been recovered in

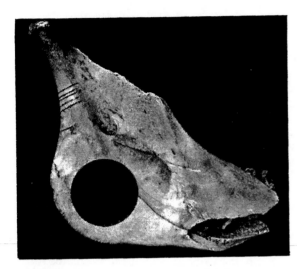

Figure 36: Early medieval bovine mandible from Schleswig with disc excised to form a spindle whorl or gaming piece

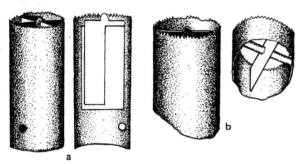

Figure 37: Roman trepanning or crown saws of bronze (scale 2:3) from Bingen (after Como)

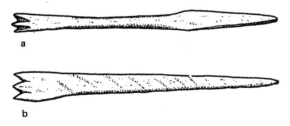

Figure 38: Centre-bits or scribing tools from Slavic settlements at Staré Město (after Hrubý) and Levy Hradec (from Tempel, after Pić) (scale 3:4)

(Figure 72) and spindle whorls (Figure 101) carry similar implications. Few implements capable of producing ornament in this fashion have so far been noted from an archaeological context: Hrubý (1957) has published an iron tool shaped rather like a drill-bit, terminating in a central point flanked on either side by another point (Figure 38a); the lateral points are of unequal length but seem to be equidistant from the centre, so that in use only a single circle would have been described around the centre point. A similar implement comes from Levy Hradec, Bohemia (Figure 38b).

A second type of scribing implement may also be postulated. This produced incised lines at a fixed distance from the edge of the material, so that we may envisage a stop which followed the outline of the piece and one or more teeth which executed the decorative grooves. The principle involved is therefore similar to that of a present-day carpenter's mortice gauge, except that there was unlikely to have been any facility for adjustment. Evidence for the use of these implements comes from casket mounts and combs: in the latter case, the border lines which follow the profile on certain Viking age combs (Figure 50a-b) may be noted and also, more strikingly, the double border line found on some end plates of complex outline from the same period (Figure 50d). Grooves of this type are usually flat-bottomed in section, suggesting that a small chisel-like point was employed. No appropriate implements have yet been found.

Rouletting

A recent find from excavations at Coppergate in York has added a new technique to those recorded for bone decoration. The object (Figure 107c) is a wooden box lid decorated with bone strips cut from split ribs which, in turn, are ornamented with zig-zag and linear patterns of impressed dots, having the appearance of being rouletted.[5] This technique, which is more appropriate for soft materials such as leather or (unfired) pottery, may have been used in conjunction with one of the softening methods discussed below (p. 63): only with prior softening does it seem likely that sufficiently deep impressions could have been made with a rouletting wheel. No extant examples of the latter are known.

Gauging

For certain tasks, notably the production of tooth plates for composite combs, the use of some sort of gauge or template seems to be implied. As noted below (p. 75), the teeth on combs of this type were invariably cut after the blanks had been riveted between the side-plates. In order that the junctions between adjacent tooth-plates always coincided precisely with one of the saw cuts for the teeth, it seems necessary for the blank tooth-plates to have been cut to predetermined sizes corresponding to whole numbers of teeth. This could have been achieved either with a rule or gauge on which the appropriate spacings had been marked, or else with a series of templates of suitable dimensions. One comb from Abingdon (Figure 39) displays scribed lines running from the ends of the saw-cut teeth; they are extremely irregular compared with the teeth themselves, however, and seem more likely to be of secondary origin than to be marking-out lines. The more regular lines to be seen on the end-plate of a comb from Elisenhof,

Schleswig-Holstein, illustrated by Tempel (1969) are more certainly guidelines for the saw.

Clamping

One type of implement has tentatively been identified as having been used to secure small pieces of material while they were being worked. Characteristically, these implements consist of two elements of antler (Figure 91) joined by a stout iron rivet. Each antler piece is D-shaped in section, the flat edges being contiguous; viewed from the side, the opposed faces of the antler grips diverge from one another towards one end. The method of use, as suggested by Jankuhn (1943), is for the material being worked (such as tooth-plates for composite combs) to be inserted between the open jaws at one end. These are then made to clamp around the object by means of a wedge hammered into the opposite (closed) end, the iron rivet marking the fulcrum point. One of the clamps discussed below, from Ytre Elgsnes, Norway, was found along with other tools in what was originally interpreted as a smith's grave (Simonsen 1953); more recently, Tempel (1969) has suggested that the entire tool-kit might be considered equally appropriate for a comb-maker.

Figure 39:   End-plate from a double-sided comb found at Abingdon, Oxfordshire

Riveting

Composite items of skeletal materials were frequently assembled by riveting. The mounts discussed below (p. 197) were attached to their wooden caskets or articles of furniture in this manner and all combs of composite construction (p. 82) were assembled by this technique. Two alternative methods of riveting can be found in each of these groups of objects, one using bone (or antler) and the other metal. The use of bone pegs has the advantage that incised decorative schemes can be continued over their heads; it should be noted, however, that the use of bone rivets on combs is both rare and largely limited to the Celtic world. Iron rivets were most commonly used for all purposes. A few Early and Middle Saxon items, such as the Taplow gaming pieces (p. 134), make use of bronze rivets, but these remain uncommon until the beginning of the medieval period, when the rivets of combs, for example, are more frequently of bronze, and also used in greater numbers (p. 75).

Softening and Moulding

The techniques already mentioned in this section have been applicable equally to all the raw materials under discussion. On the question of softening and moulding, however, the differing physical properties of these materials demand individual consideration; only bone and antler may be considered together for these purposes.

Two objectives may be distinguished in this context: softening may be induced temporarily either with a view to altering the shape of the artefact (or the raw material) before restoring it to its original hardness, or it may be used to facilitate the process of shaping or decorating by making the material easier to cut.

Bone and Antler

As a preliminary to bone-working in the Roman period it has been suggested (Schmid 1968) that softening in water would have been a normal practice. Discussion of whether and by what means bone and antler may have been softened in both earlier and later periods has been most intense among archaeologists in Poland.[6] In particular, K. Żurowski has conducted practical tests over the past thirty years and published his findings in a number of papers (Żurowski 1953, 1973, 1974). Żurowski's interest was first aroused by traces of working (particularly in the form of knife-cuts) on antler artefacts: he deduced that, since antler is a comparatively hard material, these cuts could have been made only after preparatory softening of the raw material. The fact that preliminary softening is a normal practice among antler and horn workers in contemporary Slavic folk cultures had come to the notice of other archaeologists and ethnologists (e.g., Moszyński 1967); inadequate appreciation of the quite different properties of these two materials has, however, led to inconclusive results being obtained when these methods were applied indiscriminately during experimental attempts to induce softening (Żurowski 1974).

In order to bring about temporary softening of bone and antler, the material may be immersed in an acid solution: present-day exponents of Russian folk art use vinegar (acetic acid) in solution for this purpose. Looking for naturally occurring acids which would have been available to bone and antler workers in the past, Żurowski settled on sorrel (*Rumex* sp.), a plant rich in oxalic acid, the remains of which have occasionally been excavated from layers of early medieval date (Żurowski 1974). Having prepared a soured broth of sorrel leaves, he immersed a red deer antler in the solution; every two days attempts were made to cut it with a knife and in this way he was able to demonstrate progressive softening until, after six weeks, the antler could be cut like wood. On being removed from the solution and allowed to dry, it regained its original hardness within four days. Further experiments by the same author employed sauerkraut, sour milk and buttermilk, with which greatly accelerated reactions were obtained, the antler becoming soft within two to three days (Żurowski 1973).

Also according to Żurowski (1974), reversible reactions could be obtained with diluted chloric acid as well as a range of organic acids, including acetic, lactic, propionic and butyric acids, and with various preparations based on cabbage, gherkins and the like. The roots, as well as the leaves, of sorrel, were said to be effective for this purpose (Kluk, quoted in Żurowski 1974). (Non-reversible reactions were said to be induced by solutions of tartaric, oxalic[7] and sulphuric acids.) The chemical mechanism involved in the reversible reactions is given by Żurowski as follows:

Softening
$$2[Ca_3(PO_4)_2] \cdot CaCO_3 \uparrow CO_2 \xrightarrow[\text{acid}]{} CaHPO_4$$

Hardening
$$2H_2O \xrightarrow[\text{from the air}]{CO_2} 2[CA_3(PO_4)_2]\, CaCO_3$$

Żurowski's attractive hypothesis has been adopted by a number of his colleagues. Cnotliwy (1956, 1969) has suggested that the standard method of antler-working in Slavic period and medieval workshops was for the material to be first of all sawn into appropriate lengths and subsequently softened, before further shaping with a knife or draw-knife. Hrubý (1957) states that antler finds from Moravia confirm the practice of softening in sorrel-derived acid, while Schoknecht (1977) concludes that softening pits would have been a normal adjunct of comb-makers' workshops. Żurowski himself interprets pits full of antler fragments found at Błonie near Warsaw as acid softening pits.[8]

Considering the complex and intimate nature of the union between the organic and inorganic elements in bone structure (pp. 2-4) these claims seemed inherently unlikely to be valid, for, having once removed mineral from the bone it would be quite impossible to replace it. A series of tests were therefore carried out by the writer in association with Professor J.D. Currey, in order to clarify the situation. Using the method for establishing the modulus of elasticity outlined on p. 27, a number of standard test specimens were manufactured from a single shed antler of red deer. These were then immersed in bulk quantities of lactic acid (sour milk, pH 4.32), acetic acid (malt vinegar, pH 2.83) and oxalic acid in the form of a solution of sorrel leaves (*Rumex acetosa*, pH 3.57), for periods of six, twelve, twenty-four, forty-eight and ninety-six hours respectively, before being loaded in three-point bending on an Instron table testing machine. Full details of the results will be given in a forthcoming paper, but it can be said here that none of the methods of chemical softening discussed above can truly be said to be reversible. All the acids mentioned act on the bone by removing the mineral fraction, the action progressing from the outer surface of the bone to the interior. Whereas the consequent impairment of the structure might be acceptable in the making of, for example, folk-art carvings of the present day, it seems unlikely that it could have been tolerated in the manufacture of implements or items such as combs, particularly when (as argued on pp. 28-9) advantages of a lower order of magnitude were appreciated and seized on. Two recent accounts of bone and antler working (Ambrosiani 1981; Ulbricht 1978) reject the possibility of chemical softening. In one case (Ulbricht 1978) after practical experiments with sorrel softening the antler was found to have been robbed of its resilience and left dull and lifeless. To these objections may be added another: if, as

suggested on pp. 49-50, comb-workers operated on an itinerant basis all the year round, there would have been no attraction in a working method which demanded several days or even weeks of preliminary softening, particularly if the operation was dependent on the seasonal availability of the softening agent.

A degree of softening sufficient to account for the working traces which prompted Żurowski's investigations is in any case attainable by the simple expedient of soaking the tissue in water. Long shavings were easily detached with a knife from the antler shown in Figure 40a, after forty-eight hours softening in cold water. After soaking for a similar length of time, a second piece of antler was placed in boiling water for fifteen minutes, after which it could be cut with even greater ease (Figure 40b). Boiling for seven to eleven hours, as practised experimentally by Szafrańsky (quoted in Żurowski 1973), is not only unnecessary but is likely to impair the quality of the tissue by leaching out collagen. Boiling in oil, as postulated by Cnotliwy (1956), would be equally unnecessary, not to say costly.

The alternative aim in inducing softening, namely to allow the bone or antler to be bent into a new shape before rehardening, may now be considered. Prompted by discoveries of Neolithic armlets made from split ribs which had been bent into an arc,[9] Żurowski (1974) set about reproducing the softening processes which were clearly involved. He was able to replicate a bone armband of this type by splitting a bovine rib and immersing it in a bath of sour milk: after some days he was able to bend the plate of bone into a ring, which was then bound up and allowed to dry. When the bindings were removed, the plate was found to retain its new shape.

Evidence for some similar practice is more common in the Roman period when narrow armbands or bangles of bone or antler (pp. 112-13) were made by bending a thin strip into a ring and securing it in position with a bronze band. Unfortunately, nothing is known of the medium used for softening these bracelets.

From later periods there appears to be no evidence of finished items produced by bending in this way, but on the basis of thirteenth or early fourteenth century finds from Dobra Nowogardzka, Cnotliwy (1969) has suggested that long strips (some of 19cm or more in

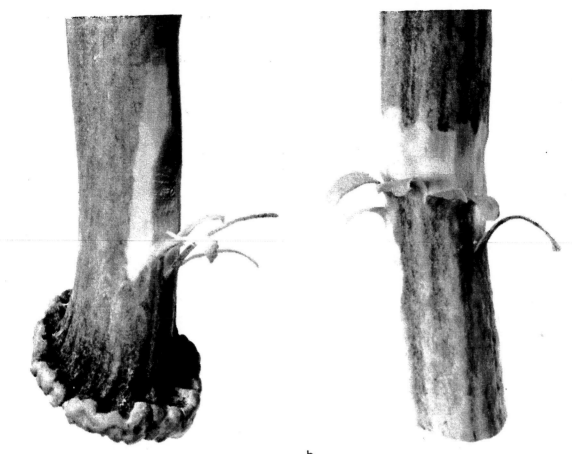

a   b

Figure 40: Slivers cut with a knife from red deer antler softened in water: (a) after 48 hours soaking in cold water
(b) after 48 hours soaking in cold water followed by 15 minutes in boiling water

length) cut from naturally twisted antlers may
have been straightened after preliminary softening and before manufacture into casket
mounts.

Softening for the purposes of bending can
hardly be denied, for the evidence is unequivocal. The method used may have been one of
those mentioned above, but there is no means
of telling. For the ornamental purposes to
which these pieces were put, consequent
impairment of the raw material's mechanical
properties may not have been considered
unacceptable.

Ivory

Elephant ivory has a unique combination of
working properties which are considered

exemplary by artists and craftsmen all over the
world, and it seems unlikely that it would
normally have been subject to preliminary
softening before carving in the normal way.
Digby (1926), however, notes that Siberian
mammoth ivory was softened in very hot water
prior to working by native craftsmen and
Sandys-Wunsch (nd) recommends soaking
mammoth ivory in vinegar for two or three days
prior to carving.

Evidence for softening elephant ivory for
special purposes has also been noted elsewhere
in the past. Panels or tablets of ivory measuring
up to 75cm square were much favoured by
eighteenth-century portrait painters such as
Ross, Thorburn and Newton, who found that
they made excellent vehicles for their art.
These dimensions far exceed those which could

be achieved by cutting cross-sections or longitudinal-sections from tusks, and clearly result from an alternative method of production. Williamson (1938) explains that these panels were cut from around the circumference of the tusk after the ivory had been softened with phosphoric acid; while still soft they were flattened out under pressure, washed and dried, after which they regained their former consistency. H.E. Cox (1946) states that the phosphoric acid should be in solution of specific gravity 1.130 and that ivory, once treated in this way, can be rendered soft again merely by immersing it in warm water. Volbach (1952) mentions that a method of softening and flattening ivory had also been used by craftsmen in the classical world, but gives no details of the method employed.[10] Theophilus, on the other hand, gives a range of techniques for ivory softening as used in the eleventh century, including heating in wine or vinegar or over a fire, annointing with oil and wrapping in leather (Hawthorn and Smith 1963).

Horn

As already stressed, the composition of horn is quite distinct from that of antler and hence the methods employed in working it can be very different. This is particularly true in the case of softening and moulding, which have for centuries been essential processes in the horner's repertoire.

Rendering horn soft and malleable is achieved simply by the application of heat, although delicate control is needed to avoid damaging the material. (No chemical change is therefore involved here, although Żurowski (1974) mentions an alternative method of softening in which horn may be boiled in a solution of wood ash.) Following some weeks of soaking in a tub or pit, the keratinous horn sheaths were separated from the bony cores and set to boil in a cauldron. After one to one-and-a-half hours' boiling, the horn was taken out and held over a fire with a pair of tongs or with a special toothed warming tool (Andés 1925), to evaporate the excess water and further soften it by gentle and even application of heat; it was then ready for 'breaking' or opening. According to the account of a York horner working in the first quarter of the present century (recorded in Wenham 1964), one of two methods of cutting would normally be used, depending on the desired shape of the resulting horn plate: after the solid tip had been removed, the cut could be made either in corkscrew fashion, to produce an elongated rectangle when opened out with the aid of a pair of tongs, or else a straight cut could be made from the tip to the base, giving a squarish plate (Figure 41). Andés stresses that the cut is normally made along the weakest line, namely the inside of the curve. The whole of the above process had to be carried out quickly and efficiently, while maintaining the appropriate temperature: too much heat would scorch the horn and not enough would result in it readopting its former curvature.

After some preliminary trimming and removal of blemishes with the aid of a scraping knife or spokeshave, the plates of horn could then be returned to the cauldron for resoftening, after which they were further pressed

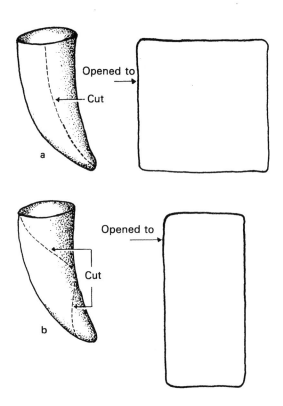

Figure 41: Alternative methods of horn breaking, as practised in early twentieth-century England (after Wenham)

between heated iron plates, the smooth surfaces of which had been smeared with grease.[11] Final smoothing and trimming was then all that was necessary before the plates were ready for manufacture into items such as combs, boxes, etc.

Exceptionally thin and translucent plates, such as were used in the windows of lanterns (hence, probably, the Middle English form *lanthorn*), were produced by selecting suitably light horns, soaking them in water for about a month, and then delaminating or splitting them into two or more leaves before subjecting them to pressure as above. Andés (1925) mentions that translucency could be improved by smearing the horn plates with oil and warming them over a fire, or else by boiling them in three parts water to one part waste fat, before pressing them for half an hour and finally laying them in a dish of cold water. A fine globular lantern incorporating plates of this sort is described by Way (1855) and several smaller lanterns are illustrated by Hardwick (1981). Individual leaves of horn, bearing marks from preparatory grinding and polishing processes, have been recovered from Tudor levels at Baynard's Castle, London (Armitage 1982).

Sheets of horn could be welded together by pressing them between greased plates at temperatures higher than those employed in the processes described above (Wenham 1964). The steel plates were heated over a fire and placed in a press, where tallow was applied to them. When the temperature was judged to be right, the horn plates were introduced and pressure applied. After a few minutes the plates would begin to 'run' and the pressure would be further increased. On cooling off, they would be stuck fast together, provided the appropriate delicate balance of temperature and pressure had been maintained.

Andés (1925) gives a recipe for enhancing the 'elasticity' (toughness) of horn, involving a solution of three parts nitric acid, fifteen parts white wine, two parts vinegar and two parts rain or river water. After treatment in this way, it is said that horn combs could withstand being trodden on without breaking.

The methods described here have been in common use for at least the past three centuries and many of them probably have much earlier origins. Blümner (1879) quotes Pausanius on the softening of horn in the second century

AD, and mentions a striking range of utensils known from classical literary sources. In most surviving early artefacts in which horn was used other than in its complete form, too little survives of the organic material to demonstrate whether it had been worked in this way. The plates on the Benty Grange helmet (pp. 154-5), however, were judged (Bruce-Mitford and Luscombe 1974) to have been softened and bent into shape. A fragment of thin horn with incised decoration, perhaps originally from a box or casket, found in a medieval context at York (Figure 107b) may be an early piece of pressed or delaminated horn. The series of horn combs with riveted side-plates (Figure 52) seems to consist of the entire thickness of the horn, which has simply been flattened and filed.

The full potential of horn as a versatile raw material was perhaps only fully recognised during the last century; several British Patents — e.g., 6402 (1899), 1021 (1908), 163, 219 (1920) — have been filed for processes involving the manufacture of such diverse items as umbrella handles, cigar holders and electrical switch covers from small scraps or powdered horn which, after treatment, was reconstituted and moulded in dies under heat and pressure.

Colouring

Some evidence can be mustered to show that colouring was occasionally used to enhance the appearance of objects made from skeletal materials. Occasionally colour contrast was provided by the employment of sheet-metal backing behind a pierced, openwork design (pp. 91, 199), while at other times colour was applied directly to the material. Green seems to have been a particularly favoured colour: green-stained pins have been recovered from Roman excavations at Rochester, Kent (Harrison 1972) and York (MacGregor 1978a), and again in York, a Viking period buckle, highly polished and deeply coloured to look like bronze, was found in early excavations in the city (D.M. Waterman 1959; colour illustration in Roesdahl *et al.* 1981). A green-stained die from Lincoln (Lincoln Archaeological Trust, unpublished) came from recent excavations in Flaxengate. Traces of red staining have been noted on a Migration Period comb from Holzgerlingen, Württemberg (Veek 1931); on

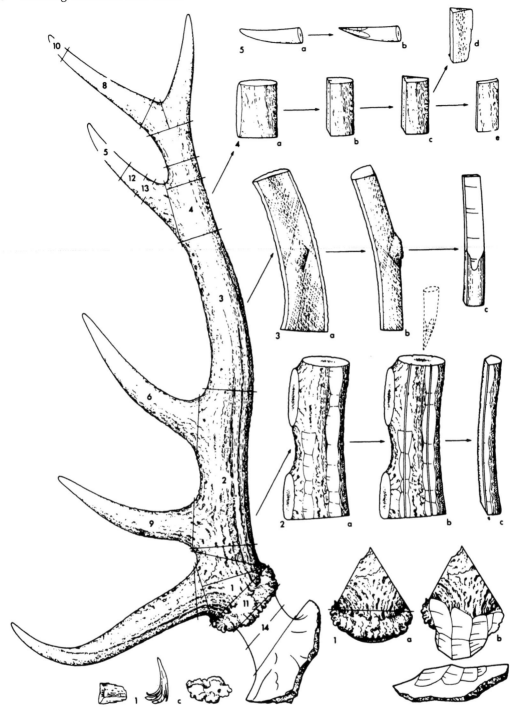

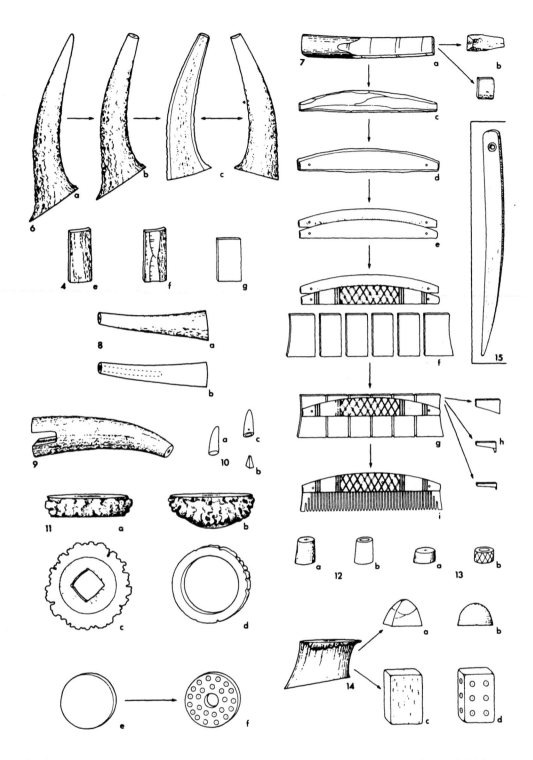

Figure 42: Schematic representation of methods of cutting up and utilising antler at Hedeby (after Ulbricht)

Note: Parts of the antler were used for comb making (1-6); composite combs were produced from a number of these elements in well-defined stages (7); other parts of the antler were used in the production of various small items (8-14); a needle made from an unlocalised piece of antler is shown in 15. The scheme is a generalised one: not all antlers were so exhaustively utilised and neither were all the elements for a single comb necessarily made from the same antler.

the Fife casket (Anderson 1886); on the Lewis chessmen (Madden 1832); and on a number of ivory book covers.

Other instances occur of colour being applied as inlaid pigment, commonly used to highlight incised decoration on Roman age bone carvings from Egypt (Marangou 1976). Schmid (1968) has noted the use of black, seemingly 'ivory black' mixed with beeswax, to emphasise incised ornament on Roman hinges (p. 203) from Augst, and on contemporary bone objects in the Naturhistorisches Museum, Basel. Veek (1931) mentions the use of white 'incrustation' to heighten incised decoration on a Migration Period comb from Oberflach, Württemberg, and traces of blackening have been found on a Viking comb from Birka in Sweden (Kristina Ambrosiani, personal communication). In England there appears to have been a fashion for filling incised details on certain Romanesque ivories with black pigment (Beckwith 1972) and finds of dice and playing pieces from Ludgershall Castle, Wiltshire, with traces of black, white or red pigment show that the technique was extended to quite mundane objects (MacGregor, forthcoming).[12] A number of Roman bone pins are known which have their shanks sheathed in gold leaf, a treatment more commonly given to carved ivory book-covers, playing pieces and the like; it was also applied to the clothing of carved figures and to other details on the bone-mounted caskets of the Embriachi (Dalton 1909).

According to the *Plictho* of Gioanventura Rosetti (written in Venice, 1548), bone could be dyed green in a solution of red vinegar containing copper fillings, Roman vitriol, roche alum and verdigris (Edelstein and Borghetti 1969). An alternative method mentioned by the same author was to place the bones in a copper vessel containing a mixture of goat's milk and verdigris, which was buried for several days in a mound of horse manure to keep it warm. Theophilus, writing in the first half of the twelfth century, recommends the use of madder for staining bone red (Hawthorn and Smith 1963), while Andés (1925) and Forbes (1955) give a wide range of vegetable and other dyes suitable for colouring skeletal materials, some of which would have been available to the medieval craftsman. D.V. Thompson (1935) lists numerous documentary sources giving medieval recipes for dyes and pigments. W.E. Cox (1946) notes a range of organic and inorganic dyes which were available to Chinese ivory carvers, some of which could also have been utilised in the West.

Evidence from Industrial Waste

On the basis of large amounts of waste material and half-finished pieces, Ulbricht (1978) was able to reconstruct in some detail the various methods of utilisation employed by the Hedeby antler workers (Figure 42). Comb-making was the principal activity represented, but other items were also produced, often utilising those parts of the antler which were unsuitable for combs. Although treatment varied according to the particular form of the antler concerned, the usual starting point was the removal of the tines by sawing them flush to the beam. In general, the lower parts of the beam were reserved for side-plates, appropriate strips of compact tissue being produced by cutting off a suitable length of beam and quartering it with a saw, the irregular outer surface and the cancellous material from the core being subsequently smoothed away. An alternative method, often employed when an irregular number of strips was to be produced from a single length of antler, was for the plates to be outlined with longitudinal grooves cut through the compact tissue and subsequently detached with the aid of an antler wedge driven into the cancellous centre (Figure 34). Side-plates might also be produced by selecting a suitably shaped tine and sawing it in half lengthwise.

The upper parts of the beam, which tend to adopt a twist, were usually reserved for sawing into shorter cylindrical lengths, from which tooth-plates were detached either by sawing or splitting off plaques of compact tissue. Other items such as handles or wedges might occasionally be produced from tines. The dense tissue within the burr produced ideal material for spindle-whorls or gaming pieces, while gaming pieces and dice were also cut from the pedicles attached to the antlers of slaughtered deer.

Ulbricht's analysis of the Hedeby material is the most systematic exercise of its kind yet undertaken, but elements of the same techniques have been noted wherever large-scale antler-working has been discovered. Ambrosiani (1981) has produced a break-down of the waste material from Ribe, showing that it conforms to a large extent with the Hedeby finds; she notes some points of particular interest. The special favour with which pedicles were regarded as raw material for gaming pieces and the like was illustrated by the fact that only one intact pedicle was found, compared with twenty-nine burrs from which the pedicles had been sawn. A further disparity among the finds concerned the proportion of unutilised tines to burrs: whereas the average red deer antler might have sported five or six points, Ambrosiani noted that waste material contained only twice as many tines as burrs, indicating that a significant proportion of them had been utilised. The relatively low numbers of cancellous fragments found in all but one area at Ribe were tentatively explained (Ambrosiani 1981) as resulting from the dumping of this material elsewhere or, perhaps, the extensive use of rasps and files in its removal, which would leave only small crumbled particles.

At Lund a somewhat different method of removing the cancellous tissue must have been adopted, as triangular core fragments from quartered beams are common: Christophersen (1980b) notes over four hundred examples and produces an explanation of their formation.

Other accounts of waste material, providing fewer details, but containing at least some elements in common with those already mentioned, cover the Baltic settlements from Schleswig-Holstein to Gdansk (Cnotliwy 1958, 1970; Hucke 1952; Schoknecht 1977; Schuldt 1980), Moravia (Hrubý 1957) and England (MacGregor 1978a, 1982a).

Notes

1. Cnotliwy (1969) noted similar grooving on antlers from Dobra Nowogardzka, Szczecin, but there, in the late thirteenth or early fourteenth centuries, final separation of the strips was by sawing.

2. An unstratified bovine metatarsal (Figure 29c) found at Billingsgate, London (M. Rhodes in D.M. Jones 1980) represents a typical waste product of the turning process; the outer surface has been roughly whittled before being turned on the lathe, the articular ends finally being sawn off and discarded.

3. K.A. Wilde (1953) suggests that the rivet holes on combs from Wolin have been burned rather than drilled, but this seems unlikely. No contemporary evidence for this practice has been found elsewhere.

4. It is also occasionally said to be punched (see, for example, Dryden in *Archaeol. J.* 39, 422; Galloway 1976) but this method would probably not be effective. Schoknecht (1977) suggests that it could have been used after the material had been softened, but there seems to be no evidence for this. According to one report (*Britannia* 2, 299) a Roman bone comb from London bears the maker's name stamped on either side, but the comb is in fact made of wood.

5. I am grateful to Mr D.J. Rackham for pointing out this feature.

6. Hrubý (1957) mentions evidence of softening from Czechoslovakian finds, but does not elaborate on the matter.

7. Oxalic acid is in fact the principal softening agent contained in sorrel, which Żurowski describes elsewhere as the most likely *reversible* acid.

8. There seems to be no reason to interpret these as other than rubbish pits.

9. For these Neolithic armlets made from split ribs see Czerniak *et al.* (1977) and Maciejewski *et al.* (1954).

10. The technique of softening ivory seemingly had an even greater antiquity, however, as is suggested by a further instance dating from the upper Paleolithic period and found at Vladimir, east of Moscow. In this case, the objective was to soften the ivory with a view to eliminating the natural curvature and, since the tusk in question was from mammoth rather than elephant (Żurowski 1973), the curve would have been considerable. A spear made entirely of mammoth ivory was found in association with two skeletons, the spear being so straight that it could only have been made by softening the raw material from which it was made and straightening out the curvature. No evidence has yet been produced to suggest which technique might have been involved in this process, and Mr D.J. Rackham has pointed out (personal communication) the crucial nature of the species identification here, since there existed a straight-tusked contemporary of

the mammoth, namely *Elephas nomadicus*.

11. In the 1740s a box press with a screw pressure control was developed for this purpose (A.B. Hughes 1953), several iron plates and plaques of horn being interleaved within it. An account of its use in nineteenth-century Kenilworth is reproduced in Drew (1965).

12. The need to distinguish opposing sets of otherwise identical playing pieces would have encouraged the use of colour in this particular context.

6. Artefacts of Skeletal Materials: a Typological Review

In the following survey every attempt is made to relate the various categories of artefacts produced in skeletal materials to the considerations already discussed. The primary concern in each case is to highlight the features which recommended these materials to the craftsmen concerned and the conditioning influences exerted on the finished products by them. The objects are located within a general functional context, and aesthetic matters more appropriate to the art historian are not stressed. The range of items considered is not exhaustive but includes the majority of those most commonly found in northern Europe since the Roman period.

Combs (Figures 43-53)

Throughout the period under review combs were articles of everyday use at every level of society, so that from the most modest of late Roman cemeteries to the flourishing urban centres of the medieval period, they form one of the commonest classes of finds. When recovered from burials they are found associated with either sex and all ages: only occasionally can certain types be shown to be associated with particular groups, as at Schretzheim, Bayern, where double-sided combs were found to be particularly common in female burials (U. Koch 1977), and at Birka in Sweden where Ambrosiani (1981) has found certain types to predominate with burials of one sex or the other.

In the Migration Period in particular, combs seem to have had a potent symbolic significance. They were frequently included, often burned or deliberately broken, in cremation burials. Symbolic miniature combs were sometimes made especially for interment, and representations of them are occasionally found stamped on cremation urns (Vierck 1972). A Frankish grave slab from Niederdollendorf, Nordrhein-Westfalen, which shows (apparently) the deceased combing his hair, is thought

to represent an affirmation of life after death (Böhner 1950). During earthly existence too, hair could have a very particular significance: long hair was a sign of nobility and perhaps even of magical power among the Franks (Wallace-Hadrill 1962) and combs no doubt acquired a special significance by association. For evidence of attention paid to the hair by the Rus we have the testimony of Ibn Faḍlän (c. 920-30), who noted among these northern traders the daily custom of washing the hands, face and hair in a basin of water, over which they then arranged their hair with a comb (Togan 1939). The Scandinavians settled in England were equally fastidious about their appearance, leading John of Wallingford to comment in the mid twelfth century on the powerful attraction exerted over English womanhood by these well-groomed Norsemen who combed their hair every day (Vaughan 1958).

In the Pictish realms of Scotland combs again held some powerful meaning, as may be judged from their frequent appearance on symbol stones (Allen and Anderson 1903). Even on later medieval funerary sculpture in Scotland, they remained a favoured symbol in some areas (Steer and Bannerman 1977).

A more prosaic explanation for their widespread use at a time before personal hygiene had acquired any significance in everyday life might be that they performed a useful role in the control of lice (Grohne 1953). Traces of lice or nits might be detectable with the aid of a microscope, but the few recorded instances of microscopic investigation have produced equivocal results.[1]

From a technological standpoint a distinction may be drawn between one-piece combs, made from a single block of material, and composite combs, in which several structural elements are united by rivets.

One-piece combs of bone and antler have the disadvantage of being limited in size by the dimensions of the available raw material. This restriction is rendered particularly acute since, for the reasons given on p. 28, the teeth had always to be aligned 'with the grain'. Larger combs of one-piece construction were produced in cetacean bone and in elephant ivory, in which the dimensional restrictions were less acute.

In manufacturing one-piece combs, as much preliminary shaping as possible was done before the teeth were finally cut. This was particularly important in the area of the teeth themselves, as it was to the comb-maker's advantage to minimise the finishing to be done on individual teeth. Half-finished one-piece combs illustrating this procedure come from Lund (Blomqvist 1942), Schleswig (Ulbricht 1980) and Amsterdam (Amsterdams Historisch Museum 1977).

Combs of wood, mostly boxwood, are common in the Roman period (p. 78); Dark Age examples are scarce, but finds of highly accomplished wooden combs as at Buston Crannog (Munro 1882) and Ledaig Crannog (ibid.), both in Strathclyde, suggest that the tradition survived until the medieval period when box combs once again became more common. A series of Roman Iron Age iron combs is known from north-eastern Europe (Thomas 1960) and a few miniature bronze combs come from Roman contexts (Neville 1855; Todd 1969). One-piece metal combs are uncommon in the Dark Ages; an example in bronze from Whitby, Yorkshire (*Yorkshire Archaeological Journal* 29, p. 350), finds a close parallel from the Frisian terps (Munro 1890) and a metal comb from Altessing, Bayern is mentioned below (p. 87).

Although they were more complicated to manufacture, composite combs accounted for the vast majority of those made in northern Europe from the late Roman Iron Age until the Middle Ages. These combs were entirely a north European 'native' development, although by the late third and fourth centuries they were widely distributed in military and civilian settlements throughout the Romanised regions, reflecting an increasingly large 'barbarian' element in contemporary society.

The evidence provided by manufacturing remains clearly demonstrates the way in which the task of producing a composite comb was tackled, and several practical attempts at reconstructing the methodology have been made (Ambrosiani 1981; Galloway and

Newcomer 1981; Pietzsch 1979). (An explanation of the terminology used is given in Figure 43.)[2] As mentioned elsewhere (p. 28) composite combs of true bone are comparatively uncommon, the most frequently used material being red deer antler. The usual practice, as demonstrated by remains from the centres mentioned above, was first of all for the tines and terminal burr of the antler to be sawn off, leaving the thick main beam intact.[3] The beam was then sawn into appropriate lengths for the long side-plates and shorter tooth-plates, before being cut or split lengthwise into strips. The cancellous tissue in the centre of the beam was cut away and the resulting billets of dense outer tissue were sawn or shaved with a draw-knife and finally filed to the required thickness — about 0.3cm for the tooth-plates and 0.5-1cm for the side-plates. A pair of strips was selected to form the side-plates: these were cut and filed into the desired shape, smoothed and polished, and the decoration (if any) incised on the prepared surfaces. Such decoration was usually saw-cut, but knife-cut ornament is also found. Tempel (1969) notes evidence for marking out decorative schemes before their execution. To facilitate symmetrical shaping and decoration, the side-plates may have been temporarily riveted or pegged together at this stage: at Hedeby, Jankuhn (1943) found a pair of plates temporarily united by wooden pegs, and Ulbricht (1978) has similarly interpreted a number of unmounted side-plates with single rivet holes at either end, found at the same site.[4]

The prepared side-plates were then separated and the blank tooth-plates inserted between them. The sides of the tooth-plates would have been carefully filed so that they lay parallel with one another and they would have been accurately matched in thickness.[5] Tempel (1969) notes various refinements in which the tooth-plates are narrowed towards the back or diminished in thickness towards either end of the comb (see Figure 50a). It is apparent from cut marks frequently found on the side-plates that the teeth were invariably cut after the entire assemblage had been riveted together. Numerous examples are known of assembled combs with uncut tooth-plates, as at Richborough, Kent (Bushe-Fox 1949), Dublin (National Museum of Ireland 1973), Wirdum, Groningen (Tempel 1969), Hedeby (ibid. and

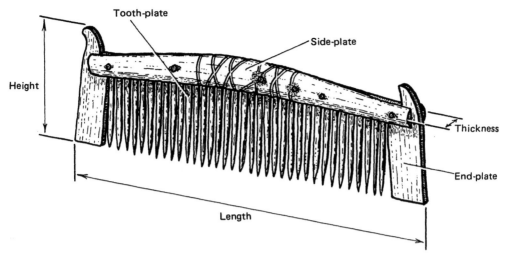

Figure 43: Terminology used in the description of composite combs

Ulbricht 1978) and Lund (Blomqvist 1942). It is noteworthy that there is rarely any unevenness of tooth spacing at the junctions between the plates, so that they must have been cut to widths representing whole numbers of teeth — a task demanding particular care when double-sided combs were being produced. Most probably this would have been achieved by matching the individual tooth-plates against templates or ready-made examples known to be of satisfactory size, and it is unlikely to have involved accurate gauges or finite units of measurement.[6] Theiltoft (1977) postulates an 'adjusting plate' among the tooth plates, whose size could be varied to achieve their desired overall positioning.

When it came to riveting the tooth-plates in position,[7] the most common practice was for one rivet to be inserted at every second join: often it was only the end-plates which were actually pierced, the intervening plates generally being found to have only half a rivet hole notched on one edge. This was not invariably the case, however: Tempel (1969) notes a variety of alternative conventions which may be encountered. Iron rivets were more commonly used than bronze, except on some Viking age and medieval combs of Scandinavian type: Long (1975) dates the adoption of close-set bronze rivets at Trondheim to the early thirteenth century.

After they had been riveted in place, the tooth-plates were trimmed at top and bottom.

In the case of single-sided combs the ends of the tooth-plates projecting beyond the back were sawn off (resulting in characteristic trapezoidal waste pieces)[8] and filed flat to the back; in more elaborate combs decorative crests were fashioned from these projections. In the case of the edge destined to carry the teeth (both edges in double-sided combs) tooth-plates were trimmed to a uniform length ready for sawing.

As mentioned above, sawing the teeth *in situ* at this stage often resulted in cut marks extending on to the edges of the side-plates. In some cases these marks are purely haphazard but in others they have been carefully executed in a more or less decorative manner, as can be seen particularly well on examples from Perth, where cut marks from half the teeth mark one side-plate while those from the other half mark the opposite one (MacGregor, forthcoming). This practice represents a decorative refinement of the normal practice of sawing the teeth at an angle, first one side and then the other, often resulting in an angular base to the cut.[9] It was normal for an area to be left in reserve (i.e., without teeth) at the extremities of the end-plates, and for the last few teeth to be cut progressively shorter, both features adding protection to the delicate teeth. To judge from recent practice among manufacturers of horn combs, the final shaping and polishing of the teeth may have been a more lengthy and elaborate process than can easily be detected: in workshops still operating in early twentieth-century York, no fewer than seven separate stages were involved in the preparation of teeth (Wenham 1964). Tempel (1969) notes some instances of teeth apparently pointed by cutting rather than by abrasion, and suggests that some form of softening would have been a prerequisite for any such treatment (see, however, p. 64).

Just why such a complex method of manufacture should have developed can be explained in terms of the raw materials used. Remembering that its mechanical properties recommended antler rather than bone for comb manufacture (pp. 28-9) and that the disparity in performance between the longitudinal and transverse axes demanded that the teeth should always be cut 'with the grain' (pp. 27-8), one-piece combs were inevitably limited in size by the amount of compact tissue which could be won from a single transverse section of antler.[10] The successive means by which first two and later several plates with the required orientation of the grain were united are described below (pp. 82-95).

An alternative explanation, offered by W.R. Wilde (1863), was that composite construction allowed damaged tooth-plates to be replaced without the necessity of buying an entire new comb. Although such an advantage would hardly justify the additional effort involved in manufacturing a composite comb, individual tooth-plates certainly could be replaced and, if carried out competently, such repairs would be difficult to detect. While observing that broken combs appear normally to have been discarded rather than repaired, Tempel (1969) notes a variety of repairs, including instances of second-hand plates with differently-spaced teeth being used as substitutes. Extra saw cuts on the side-plates of combs from Castell-y-Bere, Gwynedd (Butler 1974) and from Oslo (Wiberg 1977) indicate re-cutting of teeth on replacement tooth-plates. Redundant rivet holes on the Castell-y-Bere comb carry similar implications, as does the mixture of bronze and iron rivets found on three combs from Birka (Ambrosiani 1981). Fragmentary combs found at Sarre (Brent 1865) and Kingston Down (C.R. Smith 1856), both in Kent, have been mended in a different way, both combs having had individual teeth replaced by small bronze pins, while the side-plates on an unprovenanced Anglo-Saxon comb in the Ashmolean Museum,

Oxford (unpublished) have been replaced by a sheet bronze strip.

Combs made from the columnar limb bones of cattle and horses are not so well represented in the period under review but these would have been subject to the same sorts of structural limitations as those made from antler. Evidence from the eighth century for the production of composite combs from the limb bones of horses has been found in Münster, Nordrhein-Westfalen (Winkelmann 1977); the style and method of manufacture of the combs produced there are consistent with those established for antler combs. The use of cattle and horse metapodials in comb-making has been noted at Roskilde (Theiltoft 1977) and cattle long-bones were again exploited at Dorestad, where tooth-plates were also found to have been cut from cattle mandibles (Clason 1980). Some use of bone in comb making has also been detected from eighth-century Ribe (Ambrosiani 1981). Tempel (1969, 1979) notes a considerable proportion of bone combs among marshy coastal settlements such as Aalsum, Emden and Elisenhof: even in these areas which were environmentally unfavourable to red deer, however, antler combs still predominate.

Instances are known of composite combs incorporating elements of both bone and antler, the side-plates being of one material and the tooth-plates of the other. Considering the mechanical superiority of antler (pp. 28-9), one might expect the side-plates (which are less severely stressed in use) to be of bone, and some combs of this type are indeed known. A comb from a *Grubenhaus* at Hayton, Yorkshire, had antler tooth-plates, but the side-plates were judged to be bone, 'possibly from a scapula or skull' (R.T. Jones in S. Johnson 1979). Tempel (1979) notes the occurrence of bone side-plates in eighth-century Frisia, postulating that local shortages of antler may have been partly responsible for this development. The use of split ribs for side-plates has been noted on a comb from York, resulting in an abnormally flat cross-section (MacGregor 1978a),[11] but this type is not well known. In early medieval Lund, on the other hand, there is a distinct trend towards the use of bone for side plates, with an accompanying change in favour of more angular cross-sections (Blomqvist 1942; see also J. Persson in

Mårtensson 1976).[12] This particular combination of materials is not invariably observed, however, and despite the fact that they have less to recommend them from a mechanical point of view, combs are also found which combine antler side-plates with bone tooth-plates. Paulsen (1967) writes of Alamannic combs commonly being made in this way, and instances are also noted from Dorestad by Clason (1980), from Hedeby by Ulbricht (1978), from Schleswig by the same author (Ulbricht 1980a), and from Lund by Persson (in Mårtensson 1976).

In the latest phases of occupation at Hedeby, several composite combs made entirely of bone were found (Ulbricht 1978), foreshadowing a general move towards the use of bone and away from composite construction in the Middle Ages.

The occurrence of residual material in later layers of the urban settlements producing evidence for the use of composite combs in the Middle Ages makes it difficult to identify the moment at which their manufacture finally ceased. No doubt they lost ground progressively to more easily produced one-piece combs, although they co-existed for several centuries before the struggle was decided. Thun (1967) places the end of Scandinavian production in the mid-fourteenth century and Chmielowska (1971) produces similar findings from Poland. Among the latest stratified examples in the British Isles are those from Perth, where there are several double-sided combs from late thirteenth or fourteenth-century contexts.

One-piece Combs: Typology

From the early centuries of our era two distinct traditions of comb-making can be detected, one of them native to northern Europe and the other introduced from the Mediterranean area through northward Roman expansion.

'Germanic' Single-sided Combs (Figure 44a, b)
These are cut from a single block of material, usually antler, and are invariably single-sided. The most commonly encountered form has a round back; the sides may diverge slightly or be more markedly flared. In cross-section the back is thick and heavy and is often concave on its uppermost surface; it tapers towards the teeth, which are sometimes separated from the back by a raised bead on either side. The back often attracted incised decoration, usually of ring-and-dot motifs or intersecting arcs; in the Elbe region in particular, pierced decoration is also common (Thomas 1960). According to Thomas, the type is distributed predominantly in north-eastern Europe and in Scandinavia; the earliest examples appear in the first or second centuries, while on Gotland they have been noted from contexts as late as the fourth century (Nerman 1935).

The type is not well represented in Britain, but a round-backed example with incised decoration of late Iron Age type may be noted

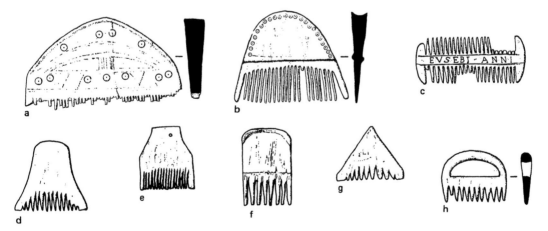

Figure 44: One-piece combs: 'Germanic' single-sided from (a) Stenåsa and (b) Vallstena; Roman double-sided from (c) Rome (Cabrol and Leclerq); Anglo-Saxon miniature from (d) Caistor-by-Norwich (Myres and Green) (e) Bidford-on-Avon (Humphreys *et al.*) (f-g) Lackford (Lethbridge) (h) Bowermadden

from Ghegan Rock, Lothian (Laidlay 1870).

'Germanic' Miniature Combs (Figure 44d-g)
The natural heirs of the Germanic tradition represented by those described above were diminutive one-piece combs which were made specifically as tokens for deposition with the dead. While some of these have been manufactured with a certain amount of care, the majority were only roughly shaped. The coarsest examples are indeed much too crude to have served any practical purpose: one of those from Lackford, Suffolk (Lethbridge 1951) and two from Abingdon, Oxfordshire have short V-shaped teeth of no useful value whatever, while on another of the Abingdon combs only four teeth are actually cut, the remaining five merely being indicated by grooves (Leeds and Harden 1936). It seems, therefore, that these combs are to be counted along with other scaled-down implements such as shears, tweezers and knives, as having a symbolic value only and being made entirely for funerary purposes. Only one example, from West Stow, Suffolk, has been noted from a domestic context (Myres and Green 1973). In addition to those already mentioned, examples may be noted from Spong Hill, Norfolk (Hills and Penn 1981), Cambridge (Hollingworth and O'Reilly 1925), Bidford-on-Avon, Warwickshire (Humphreys *et al.* 1923) and Wallingford, Oxfordshire (Leeds 1938).

It has been noted that these miniature combs, like many of the (apparently) deliberately broken full-sized combs recovered from cremation cemeteries, have rarely been burnt in the funeral pyre (Lethbridge 1951); others have been subjected to the fire, however, and in some areas of the Continent it is unburnt combs which are unusual (Myres and Green 1973). Roes (1963) illustrates one example of a miniature comb from Frisia, but otherwise the type is found predominantly in Anglo-Saxon contexts of about the fifth century.

Other Miniature Combs (Figure 44h)
A number of miniature combs from Roman Iron Age or Dark Age contexts in Scotland and Ireland are distinguished from those discussed above both culturally and functionally. Finds from four broch sites in Orkney and Caithness are listed in the discussion of a fifth comb from the Broch of Burrian, Orkney (MacGregor 1974); the most accomplished of these is a

round-backed example from Bowermadden, Highland Region (Anderson 1883). An unstratified comb from Lagore, Meath (Hencken 1950), is more reminiscent of those from pagan Saxon contexts, but presumably can have no connection with them. Perhaps they were used as beard combs: they certainly appear to have been functional and not merely symbolic.

Roman Double-sided Combs (Figure 44c)
Two rows of teeth are normally present on Roman combs, one set being markedly coarser than the other. Mediterranean examples are known in ivory[13] usually with convex ends (Cabrol and Leclercq 1938). Although this form also occurs in northern Europe it is normally encountered in boxwood; two such combs were found at Portchester, Hampshire (Cunliffe 1975) and one at Winchester (P. Galloway in G. Clarke 1979), while over twenty were recovered at Vindolanda, Northumberland (Birley 1977). Others are known from the Continent (de Boe and Hubert 1977; Roes 1963). Combs with squared ends were also found among those from Vindolanda and are known elsewhere, as at Chew Valley Lake, Avon (Rahtz and Greenfield 1977). Some one-piece combs of bone have been dated to the Roman period: one example has been published by the British Museum (1964) but it has every appearance of being of medieval or later date.[14]

Dark Age and Romanesque 'Liturgical Combs' (Figure 45)
From the late Roman period onwards single-piece combs for domestic use were almost entirely eclipsed by those of composite construction. The few one-piece combs known at this time are of massive construction and are often heavily ornamented. They are distinguished from contemporary composite combs by their adherence to Mediterranean tradition and also by their raw material, usually ivory; others, however, of undoubted north European manufacture, are occasionally found in cetacean bone. These were clearly not items of everyday use and have in the past been designated 'liturgical combs'. Lasko (1956) has pointed out the absence earlier than the thirteenth century of any evidence for the liturgical use of combs, although it may well be that wealthy prelates and other dignitaries of the church of Rome

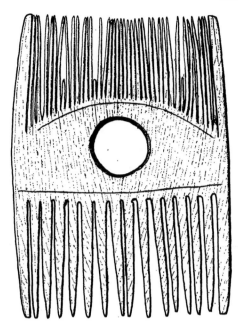

Figure 45: One-piece elephant ivory comb from the tomb of St Cuthbert at Durham (after Lasko) (scale 1:2)

were among the most enthusiastic donors and recipients of such items. Bede records that 'an ivory comb adorned with gold' accompanied a letter from Boniface to Queen Æthelburh of Northumbria about 625, imploring her to strive to 'kindle the spark of the true religion' in her husband, Edwin (Colgrave and Mynors 1969). Alcuin too was the recipient of an elaborately wrought comb and, in a letter of about 794, eulogises its properties to his benefactor, Archbishop Riculf of Mainz (Allott 1974):

I rejoice greatly in your prosperity, and I have rejoiced much in your loving gift. As many thanks as the present has teeth! It's a remarkable animal with its two heads and sixty teeth — and such beautiful ivory, though it's not as big as an elephant! The beast did not frighten me — its appearance is delightful; I had no fear those gnashing teeth might bite me, but their gentle caresses smoothed the hair of my head beautifully. I did not look at the ferocity of the teeth but loved the affection of the sender.

Although devoid of ornament, the ivory comb found with the remains of St Cuthbert at Durham is of this general type. Measuring 16.3 by 11.85cm, St Cuthbert's comb has been cut as a longitudinal section from an elephant tusk;

one side of it displays features which show the original proximity of the pulp cavity, while both ends include traces of the outer 'bark'. It has coarse teeth on one side and fine on the other; the depth to which the fine teeth are cut diminishes towards the centre, giving the central reservation an arched outline. Incised lines delimit the toothed area at the top and bottom of the reservation and there is a large central perforation.[15] The proportions of the comb and its constituent features are carefully planned on a mathematical module (Lasko 1956). The teeth show signs of having been sawn obliquely from either side, the base of the cut subsequently being filed flat. By comparing the comb with other known examples of this type, Lasko has been able to demonstrate its contemporaneity with Cuthbert's burial and subsequent translation at the end of the seventh century, although it remains unclear whether it was manufactured in Northumberland following east Mediterranean models or whether it is itself of Coptic origin. There was certainly no Northumbrian tradition of manufacturing combs of this type but the skills implicit in its sophisticated design would have been available in local *scriptoria* and the possibility of a special commission being carried out for the burial of the local saint cannot be ruled out.

D.M. Wilson (1961) has published a one-piece comb of walrus ivory in the British Museum, dated by its carved ornament to the late tenth or early eleventh century. Like those previously mentioned, this comb has coarse teeth on one side and fine on the other. The central reserve is carved on one side with a pair of Romanesque felines and on the other with an interlaced snake in Ringerike style (Figure 46).

A further comb of this type was recovered during recent excavations at York Minster (York Minster Archaeology Office, unpublished); the surviving fragment shows that it was cut from a single plate of cetacean bone and its carved ornament, featuring collared beasts with back-turned heads and lip-lappets, suggests a date in the eleventh century.

The most accomplished example of this type is now in the British Museum. This large walrus ivory comb, 22cm in length, combines pierced anthropomorphic and vegetable ornament with lion masks, geometric motifs and an inscription in relief, the style of the whole suggesting a date

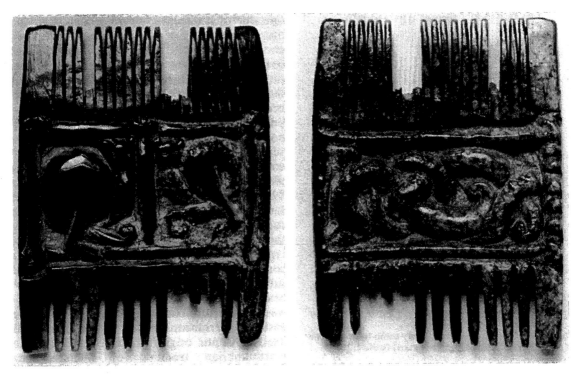

Figure 46:   One-piece comb of walrus ivory, now in the British Museum

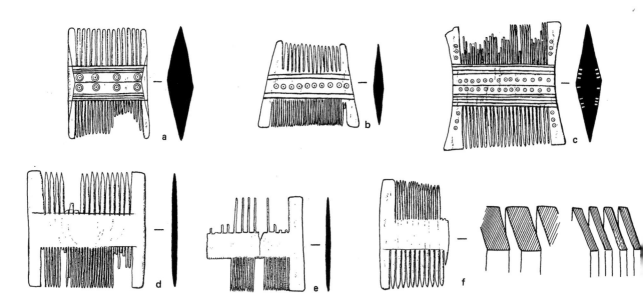

Figure 47:   One-piece combs from (a) Uppsala (Broberg and Hasselmo) (b) Örebro (Broberg and Hasselmo) (c) Schleswig (d) London (e) Southwark (Kenyon) (f) Buckingham (Hall) (scale 1:2)

in the late eleventh or twelfth centuries. The comb itself was found in Wales and, while a German origin has been considered in the past (Dalton 1909), it is now accepted as of English workmanship (Beckwith 1972).

Early Medieval One-piece Combs (Figure 47a-c)
From the eleventh century, one-piece combs for everyday use began to gain favour once more over those of composite construction. Although antler continued to be used for some of them (e.g., Andersen 1968; Schuldt 1980; Thun 1967), a marked preference for skeletal bone can be detected at this time (p. 32). Whereas metapodials, principally those of horses, had been most intensively exploited up to this point (p. 30), they were of insufficient size to provide the large, flat plaques of bone required in the manufacture of this new style of comb, and we must envisage that other skeletal elements, notably tibias, were utilised. No manufacturing waste from this industry has yet been noted.

The characteristic form of these combs is almost square in outline, often with concave ends and invariably with a set of coarse and a set of fine teeth. Some are more elongated in either the vertical or the horizontal plane (e.g., J. Persson in Mårtensson 1976) and others are longer on one side than the other, resulting in a trapezoid outline, but the chronological implications (if any) of these variations have not been fully examined. They all have a lentoid section which results in teeth which are very wide from front to back, however slender they may be in profile. Incised lines often mark the boundaries of the central reserve, providing a guide for the depth to which the teeth were to be sawn. Teeth were normally cut with the saw held at an angle, first from one side of the comb and then from the other, leaving characteristic criss-cross cutting marks on their edges and a rhomboid centre section. Ulbricht (1978) points out the greater security given by this arrangement to the teeth. Blomqvist (1942), however, illustrates a straight-cut comb from Lund, showing that this advantage was not invariably seized upon. Among the earliest stratified examples are combs from Lund (Blomqvist and Mårtensson 1963), Oslo (Molaug 1975; Wiberg 1977), Ribe (Andersen 1968), Hedeby (Ulbricht 1978), Wolin (K.A. Wilde 1953) and Szczecin (Leciejewicz *et al.* 1972), all of them of

the eleventh or twelfth centuries. A diminutive comb from Wallingford, Oxfordshire, is likely to be of similar date: it was found at the same time as the ivory seal described on p. 127, but any stratigraphic relationship between them is unestablished (*Proceedings of the Society of Antiquaries of London* ser. 2, 8, 469). Thun (1967) suggests that the type fell from fashion in the latter part of the fourteenth century.

Although one comb from Wallingford has been mentioned, British examples of this type are hard to find: it may be that the majority of early medieval combs were produced in horn (pp. 95-6) or in wood rather than bone. Boxwood combs similar in style to those just described are known from Perth (unpublished), York (York Archæological Trust, unpublished), and Southampton (Platt and Coleman-Smith 1975), the latter dated to the thirteenth century. Dunlevy (1972) lists several others and includes combs of this type in ivory and bone as well as wood in her class H, a type which survives until the seventeenth or early eighteenth centuries.

Late Medieval and Later Combs (Figure 47d-f)
Four bone combs from Southampton illustrated by Platt and Coleman-Smith (1975) have significantly flatter and more slender cross-sections than those described above. The earliest of these, from Cuckoo Lane, comes from a context dated 1375-1425; the remaining three, distinguished only by more slender central reservations, date between the early sixteenth and first half of the seventeenth centuries. Three similar combs from Basing House, Hampshire are dated by Moorhouse (1971) to the late medieval period, and contemporary examples are illustrated from Southwark by Dennis (1978) and from Northampton by G. Oakley (in J.H. Williams 1979). Of three slender-section combs excavated from sixteenth or seventeenth-century contexts at Plymouth, two had rounded ends and the other was rectangular (Fairclough 1979).

Two ivory combs of similar type from Amsterdam are dated between about 1580 and 1634 (Amsterdams Historisch Museum 1977). A seventeenth-century comb from the same source is of interest in that the teeth have been cut on one side only; the intact side, however, has been carefully prepared so that they would require only minimal shaping after they were cut.

On a sixteenth-century double-sided comb from Southwark, Kenyon (1959) noted that the teeth were cut obliquely rather than at right angles to the principal axis, one set being more acutely angled than the other. The material of the Southwark comb is described in the excavation report as bone, but an explanation for the occurrence of obliquely-cut teeth has been offered which suggests that they developed in response to structural limitations imposed by the use of elephant ivory. In discussing an ivory double-sided comb from a mid seventeenth-century context at Buckingham, D.J. Rackham (in Hall 1975) notes that the obliquely-cut teeth were cut in opposition to each other, a practice which, he deduces, would minimise the potential loss of strength and rigidity posed by the laminar structure of the ivory when cut in the form of teeth (Figure 47f). Dunlevy (1972) notes that carved decoration is scarcely found on these slender combs and that their thinness would indeed have discouraged it. She also mentions, however, a richly-painted comb of (perhaps) the sixteenth-century: it is conceivable that some of the combs recovered from archaeological contexts may also have been painted in this way, but that the pigment has failed to survive.

Alongside these rather modest combs for everyday use, a taste developed from the fourteenth to the sixteenth centuries for impractically large but decorative double-sided combs. Although boxwood is more frequently encountered among combs of this type (Pinto 1952), ivory was valued more highly, and a number of production centres specialising in them developed in northern Italy, France and England (Koechlin 1924; Longhurst 1929; Maskell 1905). They display an elongated H-profile and a lentoid section thick enough to permit decorative panels to be carved on the ends. The central reserve is also frequently carved and in some instances is expanded at the expense of the teeth to provide more space for tender scenes and legends which show that these costly combs frequently served as gifts between lovers.

A feature of some of these later double-sided combs is that the teeth on one side may be separated from one another by a space of half a centimetre or more. An example of this type from Bergen is illustrated by Herteig (1969); others have been published from Southwark by Kenyon (1959), from Hull by P. Armstrong (1977), from Basing House, Hampshire, by Moorhouse (1971) and from Somerset by Rahtz and Greenfield (1977), who note (quoting I. Noel Hume) that this type was common from at least the sixteenth until the eighteenth centuries, with more refined forms incorporating curved ends continuing until the nineteenth.

A single-sided comb from Southampton, with widely-spaced teeth and gently curving back, is dated stratigraphically to the early eighteenth century (Platt and Coleman-Smith 1975). Dunlevy (1972) reproduces a still-life painted by E. Colyer (died 1702) which shows a comb of this type, seemingly of tortoise-shell, along with a double-sided ivory comb. Dunlevy postulates an origin for the type as early as the medieval period and mentions the possibility that some later examples may have had applied plaques or gems on the back.

Composite Combs: Typology

For over a millennium composite combs were produced in a wide variety of forms, with too many variations in size, shape and decoration to be exhaustively catalogued here. Various surveys of the products of particular periods or geographical areas have already been produced and the reader is referred to these for treatment in greater detail. The present survey of the most commonly encountered types makes no claim to be comprehensive.

Single-sided Composite Combs

At the opening of our era bone and antler combs were characteristically of one-piece construction with a semi-circular back (see Chmielowska 1971; Thomas 1960). Their length (as defined in Figure 43) was limited by the fact that the teeth had to be cut 'with the grain' of the raw material in order to gain the maximum mechanical advantage (pp. 27-8). As a first step in overcoming this problem, techniques were evolved in the late first or second centuries of uniting two antler plates side-by-side: these involved either passing rivets lengthwise through both plates (Figure 48a) or riveting a bone or antler plate along the side (Figure 48b). Thomas (1960) lists sixty-three examples of this type, largely concentrated in an area between the Elbe and the Vistula, but with some examples from Jutland and southern Sweden. One example is in the Museum of London (Figure 48a). Once the principle of composite construction was established it was quickly developed to allow larger numbers of tooth-plates to be combined, and towards the end of the second century a new type appeared, the first of the so-called 'triplex' combs (German *Dreilagenkämme*). These are so named because of their method of construction, in which the tooth-plates are sandwiched between a pair of connecting plates or side-plates; the term is an unsatisfactory one, however, as it obscures the fact that the central layer consists of not one, but several, elements.

Round-backed Combs (Figure 48c-e)
In these early composite combs the tooth-plates (up to about six in number) were riveted between a pair of side plates whose rounded back echoed the shape of one-piece combs. In early examples a massive cross-section, expanding towards the back, also recalls one-piece prototypes. The tooth-plates in this type frequently terminate in a line some distance below the apex of the back, the space above them being packed out by a separate filling strip which was also riveted in position. In the course of the following two centuries this filler disappeared and the tooth-plates regularly ran through to the back of the comb. Although there is an easterly bias among the Continental examples catalogued by Thomas (1960), they occur at least as far west as Frisia (Roes 1963). In England they appear at Richborough (Bushe-Fox 1949), in fifth-century contexts at Sancton, Yorkshire (Myres and Southern 1973) and Caistor-by-Norwich, Norfolk (Myres and Green 1973), in a sixth-century burial at Lackford, Suffolk (Lethbridge 1951), in a Saxon hut at Lower Warbank, Kent (Philp 1973), and at West Stow, Suffolk (West 1969). The end-plates on some combs, such as that from Lackford, terminate vertically, while on others, including those from Caistor-by-Norwich and Lower Warbank, they are outswept. The chronological implications of these and other variations have yet to be finally explored.

Triangular-backed Combs (Figure 48f-h)
Within a short time of making their first appearance at the end of the third century or early in the fourth century, triangular-backed combs quickly challenged those with round backs as the most favoured type, particularly in the area west of the Elbe. Thomas (1960) distinguishes between those in which the height is comparable to the length, and others of more elongated form; in a third variant the tooth-plates extend beyond the back to form either carved projections, often zoomorphic, or a continuous decorative crest with pierced ornament. The latter type is widely distributed, both on the Continent — for example, from Lauriacum in Austria (Deringer 1967b), Cologne (Fremersdorf 1928), Issendorf, Niedersachsen (Janssen 1972), Cortrat, Loiret (Böhme 1974) and Furfooz in Belgium (Nenquin 1953) — and on English sites including Richborough, Kent (Bushe-Fox 1928, 1949), Winchester, Hampshire (Biddle 1970), Colchester, Essex (Hull 1958), Lackford, Suffolk (Lethbridge 1951), Caistor-by-Norwich, Norfolk (Myres and Green 1973) and Sancton, Yorkshire (Myres and Southern 1973).

The large expanse of the triangular side-plates attracted decoration which often took the form of multiple ring-and-dot motifs bounded by incised border lines (Figure 48g-h). Other motifs encountered less frequently include incised zig-zags, such as appear on an elongated triangular comb from the Late Roman cemetery at Neuburg, Bayern (E. Keller 1979) and on an example from Richborough in which the design is formed of offset triangles (Bushe-Fox 1928).

Combs featuring equilateral backs (with or without outswept end-plates) remained in use well into the fifth century, for example at Lackford (Lethbridge 1951) and Caistor-by-Norwich (Myres and Green 1973). More elongated forms survive for another two or three centuries, as at West Stow (West 1969) and at Wiesloch, Baden-Württemberg (Stein 1967), the latter dating from the eighth century.

Rectangular-backed 'Handled' Combs (Figure 48i-j)
The third and final *Dreilagenkamm* in Thomas's typology for the Roman period combines side-plates of more or less rectangular outline with a central extension forming a handle. Amongst those of the fourth and fifth centuries, distributed mostly eastwards of the Rhein, the 'handle' is most commonly a simple lobed or bell-shaped projection (Thomas 1960). On later

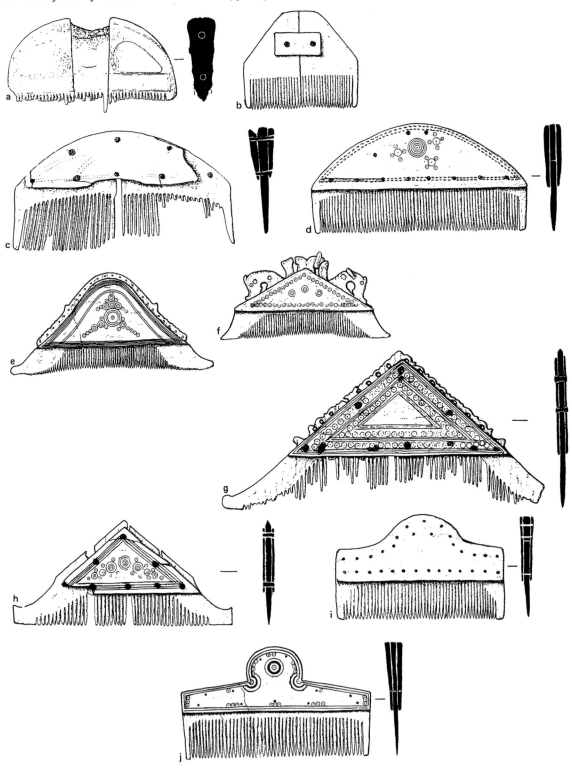

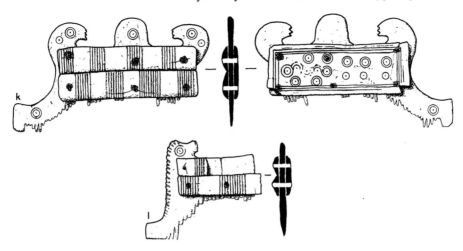

Figure 48: Composite combs (scale 1:2): (a) unprovenanced (b) Baltic area (Pietzsch) (c) Vallstena (d) Zauschwitz (Pietzsch) (e) Utrecht (Vollgraff and van Hoorn) (f) unprovenanced (Salin) (g) Winchester (Biddle) (h) Newark-on-Trent (i) Trebur (Behn) (j) Broa, Gotland (Nerman) (k-l) York

combs, such as sixth-century examples from Schretzheim, Bayern (U. Koch 1977), the lavish proportions of the side-plates contrasts with the minimal size of the projections, but on Scandinavian versions of this type, found mostly on Gotland from the fifth to the eighth centuries, the 'handles' have well-developed T-shaped or mushroom heads (Nerman 1935).

Whatever its profile, the 'handle' is in some instances cut as an integral part of the side-plates, as on examples from Heilbronn, Württemberg (Veek 1931), Trebur, Rheinland-Pfalz (Behn 1938), Wiesbaden, Hessen (Schoppa 1974), and Dittenheim, Bayern (Dannheimer 1962a). Excavations at Ózd in Hungary produced not only a finished example of this type but also a roughed-out side-plate: this was in the form of a plate of compact tissue from an antler beam cut at the base of one of the tines, the junction providing a natural extension needing only minimal shaping to render it immediately usable (Párducz and Korek 1959). On other combs the 'handle' is cut as an integral part of the central tooth-plates, to either side of which a separate set of plates is riveted: a comb of this type from Elsterebnitz, Sachsen, was replicated by A. Pietzsch (1979) and another from Lorch in Austria is illustrated by Deringer (1967b). On yet other examples, the 'handle' exists merely as an extension of the tooth-plates, without any side-plates (U. Koch 1977; Roes 1963).

Barred Zoomorphic Combs (Figure 48k-l)

A preponderance of early discoveries in Holland (Boeles 1951; Roes 1963) led to the epithet 'Frisian' being applied to these combs (MacGregor 1975a), but recently Hills (1981) has argued for the adoption of a more neutral descriptive title. Several elements which occur in the various combs already described are combined in this type. They are basically rectangular in shape, usually with a central extension or 'handle', and have outswept end-plates with zoomorphic terminals. The side-plates form a diagnostic feature of this type, a single deep, flat side-plate on one side being matched by a pair of bars of plano-convex section on the other side. Decoration on the single side-plate commonly features ring-and-dot ornament within border lines, while the bars most frequently display bands of incised lines.[16] To the English examples already published (MacGregor 1975a) a handsome addition has come from Peterborough, Cambridgeshire (Mackreth 1978) and over thirty examples have been recovered during excavations at Spong Hill, Norfolk (Hills 1981; Hills and Penn 1981).

The late fourth or fifth-century dates suggested by earlier finds from York (MacGregor 1975), Caistor-by-Norwich, Norfolk (Myres and Green 1973) and Lackford, Suffolk (Lethbridge 1951) are confirmed by the larger number of securely-stratified combs from Spong Hill (Hills 1981).

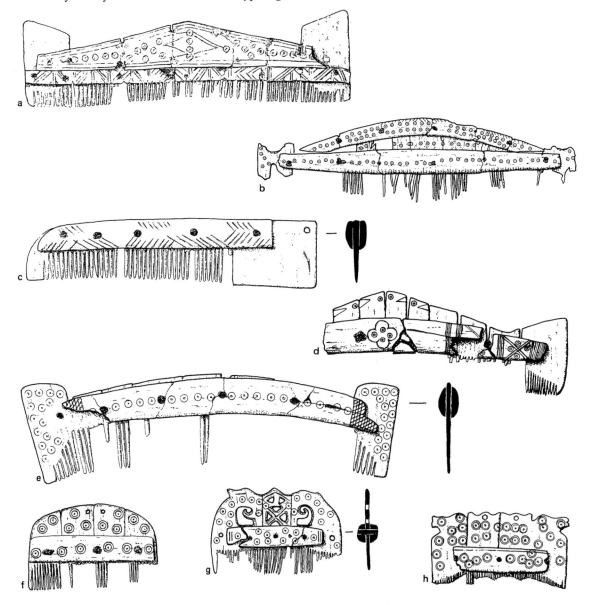

Figure 49: Composite combs from (a) Hayton (Johnson) (b) New Wintles Farm (c) Hedeby (Tempel) (d) Southampton (Addyman and Hill) (e) Sutton Courtenay (f) Buckquoy (Ritchie) (g) Dun Cuier (h) Lagore (Hencken) (scale 1:2)

Other Barred Combs (Figure 49a, b)

A disparate variety of early post-Roman combs are united by a common feature in the form of a secondary set of side-plates. A recent find of this type comes from a *Grubenhaus* at Hayton, Yorkshire (S. Johnson 1978); the dimensions of the principal side-plates are perfectly adequate for their normal functions but an additional set of plano-convex plates has been added under-

neath (Figure 49a). The depth to which the teeth are cut and the multiple saw-cuts marking the lower edge of the extra bars show that the latter were an original feature and were not applied secondarily for strengthening or repair. On other English combs with extra side-plates one set follows the curving outline of the back while the other is straight, leaving an area between them in which the upper parts of the tooth-plates are visible, as on a comb from New Wintles Farm, Oxfordshire (Figure 49b). On one example from Cambridge (Ashmolean Museum, unpublished) and one from a well-appointed double inhumation grave at Dunstable, Bedfordshire, dated about 600 (C.L. Matthews 1962), this intervening area is decorated with incised vertical lines. A third comb in this group comes from Garton Slack, Yorkshire (Mortimer 1905), and an end-plate from another has been found in York (MacGregor 1982a). The latter piece is so close in style to another detached end-plate found at Dorestad (Roes 1965) as to suggest a Frisian derivation for the York comb.

Continental finds of this type are indeed concentrated in the Frisian area; examples of combs with varying profiles but with extra side-plates are common among finds from the terps (Roes 1963). They appear to be unknown in Scandinavia, although a comb from Grave 854 at Birka has a pair of grooved side-plates which imitate this form (Arbman 1943). Scattered examples are known from Germany, as at Pfullingen, Baden-Württemberg (Cabrol and Leclercq 1938), Thaining, Oberbayern (Dannheimer 1962b), Donautal-Regensburg (U. Koch 1968), Schretzheim, Bayern (1977), and Weimar, Thüringen (Götze 1912). A date range from the fifth or sixth centuries to the eighth is suggested by these finds.

Asymmetrical Combs (Figure 49c)
The choice of raw material among early examples may have played an important part in determining the form of these combs. Several of them are found with the side-plates formed from two halves of an entire tine, and it is the irregular curving form of the antler which gives them their diagnostic shape. Others, perhaps the majority, are straight-backed, and may belong later in the series (Roes 1963), while some, including examples from Hedeby and Birka (Tempel 1969), are made of bone in which no controlling factors of this sort could have been present. Nor can the raw material have played any part in the development of another feature commonly found on these combs, namely the presence at the butt end of one tooth-plate with no teeth cut in it. Presumably this formed a useful finger-hold, while at the same time providing a convenient (though not invariably exploited) field for

incised decoration. Most of the Continental examples have been recovered from the Frisian area (Hübener 1953; Roes 1963), but more southerly examples are known from Bourges, Berry (Cabrol and Leclercq 1938), Lauterhofen, Bayern (Dannheimer 1968) and Donautal-Regensburg (U. Koch 1968). One comb of this type from Domburg, Walcheren (Roes 1963) incorporates both coarse and fine teeth, and another from Altessing, Bayern is unusual in being made of bronze with iron side-plates (Stein 1967).

Hogbacked Combs (Figure 49d, e)
A distinct group of combs may be recognised in the long hogbacked (i.e., concavo-convex) variety, often provided with large 'winged' end-plates. Of three combs of this type recovered at Burwell, Cambridgeshire (Lethbridge 1931), one was found at the chest of a (probably middle-aged female) skeleton, where it had been suspended by a cord with a red and a green bead at either end. A similar comb comes from a burial at Kingston Down, Kent (C.R. Smith 1856), while others from non-funerary contexts are known at West Stow, Suffolk (West 1969) and Southampton (Addyman and Hill 1969).

Some hogbacked combs lack the characteristic flaring end-plates of those described above. Since many of these lack ends of any kind, however, the distinction may often be more apparent than real. One complete example of a small comb of this type with rather deep side-plates was found with the skeleton of a young girl at Cambridge (Walker 1912).　•

The Netherlands, and particularly the Frisian coastal area, again provides most Continental examples (Hübener 1953; Roes 1963).

A date in the seventh and eighth centuries may be suggested for most combs of this type, although some Viking age combs exhibit a similar profile.

High-backed 'Celtic' Combs (Figure 49f-h)
A group of short combs with high backs which extend well above the side-plates has a distribution within the late Celtic rather than the Germanic realms. Comparisons have been made (e.g., Dunlevy 1969; Laing 1975) between the zoomorphic treatment of the backs of some of these combs with that on late Roman metalwork, but the comb type is never

found in Anglo-Saxon contexts. Zoomorphic ornament of this type occurs on Irish combs from Carraig Aille, Limerick (S.P. Ó Ríordáin 1949), and Lagore, Meath (Hencken 1950), and on one Hebridean example from Dun Cuier, Barra (A. Young 1956).

On other combs in this series which lack these zoomorphic motifs, the projecting crest may take the form of an open arcade, as on certain Irish examples (e.g., Hencken 1950) while others have backs in the form of a simple or sinuous curve. The side-plates are frequently short and flat, often bowed outwards along their long edges; in some instances they terminate well short of the margins of the end-plates while on others they extend for the entire length of the comb. Typical examples come from Lagore (Hencken 1950) and from three settlements in the Orkneys — Burrian (MacGregor 1974), Buckquoy (A. Ritchie 1977) and Burwick (Anderson 1883).

The type appears to have survived until about the eighth century. A derivation in the fifth century would be necessary to account for correspondences with late Roman zoomorphic ornament if, indeed, any such correspondence were accepted as valid.

Combs with Deep, Thin Side-plates (Figure 50a-c)
These correspond with the 'Group A' combs identified by Kristina Ambrosiani (née Danielsson) at Birka (Danielsson 1973). They are characterised by elongated side-plates with a straight lower edge and a gently curved upper edge; in section the side-plates have a low plano-convex profile, the ratio of depth to thickness being greater than about 3.5:1. In the course of further research the same author (Ambrosiani 1981) has distinguished three sub-types on the basis of ornamental motifs contained within the incised border lines which characteristically mark the side-plates of these combs: A1 may have no decoration within the border lines or it may have bands of vertically-oriented incisions; A2 has ring-and-dot motifs; A3 has interlace ornament, often in the form of a central band flanked by elongated fields echoing the shape of the side-plate. The group as a whole dates from the beginning of the ninth to the mid-tenth centuries, with A3 combs belonging to the latter half of this period. Ambrosiani's Group A incorporates elements of various typologies established at settlements other than Birka, including combs of type 5 established at Wolin by K.A. Wilde (1953); types 1-2 identified at Hedeby by Jankuhn (1943) and types 1-3 from the same site in Tempel's (1969) classification; Group 1 as identified at Dorestad by Hübener (1953); and types 1 a-d and 2 a-d in Davidan's (1962) typology for Staraja Ladoga. In addition to these and to contemporary north European sites where they are widely distributed — for example at Århus (Andersen *et al.* 1971), Menzlin (Schoknecht 1977), Elisenhof (Tempel 1979) and the Frisian area (Roes 1963) — combs of this type are well known in the British Isles. Typical examples come from Caistor,

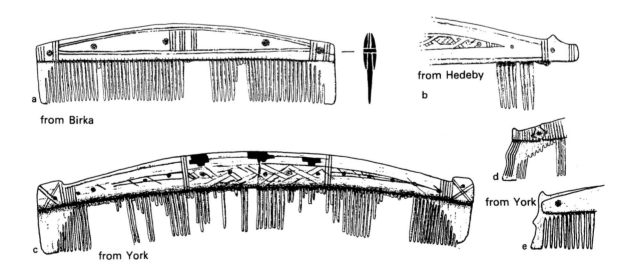

a from Birka

b from Hedeby

c from York

d from York

e

Figure 50: Composite combs from (a,f) Birka (b) Hedeby (c,e,g,i,j) York (h,o) London (k) Lund (Blomqvist) (l) Freswick (m) Oslo (Wiberg) (n) North Elmham (Wade-Martins) (o) River Thames (scale 1:2)

Lincolnshire (F.H. Thompson 1954), Dublin (Dunlevy 1969), South Uist (Grieg 1940; MacLaren 1974) and Jarlshof, Shetland (A.O. Curle 1935; Hamilton 1956).

Ambrosiani (1981) suggests an origin for the type in Scandinavia. Many combs of this type noted at Birka incorporated side-plates made from elk antlers whose palmate forms may have had an initial conditioning effect on their stylistic development which later came to be carried beyond the area in which elk antler was readily available.

Within this broad grouping are found stylistic variations too numerous to mention here, including many of the twenty-four varieties of terminals catalogued by Tempel (1969).

Combs with Shallow, Thick Side-plates (Figure 50d-h)
This series corresponds with the 'Group B' combs identified at Birka by Danielsson (1973). They are characterised by side-plates which are both shallower and thicker than those just described, with a ratio of depth to thickness less than about 3.5:1. Sub-groups identified on the basis of ornamental features include B1, with single or multiple lozenges, which dates from about 900 to the later tenth century, and B2-4, featuring, respectively, vertical lines, ring-and-dot ornament, and no ornament whatever, which survive into the eleventh century (Ambrosiani 1981). Ambrosiani's Group B combs incorporate types 1 and 2 as established at Wolin (K.A. Wilde 1953); type 3 in Jankuhn's (1943) classification for Hedeby, and types 4-6 in Tempel's (1969) typology for the same site; also type 2 as isolated by Davidan (1962) at Staraja Ladoga.

Combs of this type are widely distributed in the Viking period, both on the Continent, as at Århus (Andersen *et al.* 1971) and Elisenhof (Tempel 1979), and in the British Isles at York (MacGregor 1978a and 1982a; Richardson 1959; D.M. Waterman 1959; Wenham 1970), Dublin (Dunlevy 1969) and Jarlshof (Hamilton 1956).

Ambrosiani suggests an origin for the type in the southern Baltic region, contrasting the result of using locally available red deer antler (producing more rounded plates of compact tissue) with the flatter plates of elk antler which conditioned the development of type A combs in their Scandinavian homeland.

Combs with Trapezoidal Side-plates (Figure 50i)
By contrast with the curving cross-sections characteristic of those discussed above, the side-plates on combs of this type are angular and faceted. One sub-group features two major planes which meet in a low-pitched angle along the median, while a second type has an additional medial facet. Although they first appear in Holland and northern Germany in the eighth century they become more widespread in the tenth and eleventh centuries, reaching Scandinavia (Tempel 1969), northern Poland (Cnotliwy 1958; K.A. Wilde 1953) and the British Isles, as at Dublin (Dunlevy 1969), York (D.M. Waterman 1959) and Aberdeen (Way 1847).

The most favoured form of decoration among those with two major facets is a pair of incised longitudinal lines marking the median, with ornamental motifs (often secondary groups of lines) arranged symmetrically on either side. Those combs with an additional facet along the centre of the side-plate commonly have bands of incised lines arranged alternately on the lateral and medial facets to form a chequer pattern (Figure 50i).

Tempel (1969) notes that at least some of the Frisian combs are made of bone rather than antler. Conceivably this factor could have had some determining influence in the evolution of the angular side plates which characterise combs of this type.

Combs with Rectangular-section Side-plates (Figure 50j-k)
In cross-section the side-plates on combs of this type are basically rectangular, although the edges are normally rounded and the principal face is often decoratively profiled with longitudinal grooves. The back is almost invariably straight and may be from about 10cm to some 30cm or more in length. The end-plates may be cut square or in a curve, or may project decoratively above the back. Bronze rivets become increasingly common on later examples. The type is widely distributed in early medieval Scandinavian settlements such as Lund (Blomqvist 1942; J. Persson in Mårtensson 1976), Trondheim (Long 1975), Bergen (Herteig 1969) and Oslo (Wiberg 1977), in Denmark at Ribe (Andersen 1968) and at Århus (Andersen *et al.* 1971), and as far south as Hamburg (Tempel 1969). In the British Isles

they occur from the Shetland Islands (*Proceedings of the Society of Antiquaries of Scotland* 71, 22; Hamilton 1956), Freswick, Highland Region (A.O. Curle 1939) and from Dublin (Dunlevy 1969). The date range indicated by these finds is from the tenth to the thirteenth centuries.

Bone rather than antler is the most commonly used raw material for this type, a fact which no doubt played an important part in determining its form (Ambrosiani 1981).

False-ribbed Combs with Arched Backs (Figure 50l-m)

A group of small single-sided combs falls outside the range hitherto discussed. Two of these from England are related to one another by their high arched backs; by their deep and flat side-plates incorporating a false rib along the bottom; by T-shaped openings which pierce the flat areas; and by their use of close-set bronze rivets. One of these, from London, is said to be made from only three plates of material, all the teeth and associated zoomorphic terminals being cut on a single element; the T-shaped openings are stained green 'as though originally filled with bronze' (R.A. Smith 1909). The other comb, from Northampton, is said to have been 'associated with an urn burial' (Smith 1902), but the association can hardly have been a meaningful one. A third comb (Figure 50l), from Freswick Sands, Highland Region, belongs to this same group although it lacks the pierced motifs of the others.

Although Baldwin Brown (1915) suggests an Anglo-Saxon date for this type, there can be no doubt that it is of later Scandinavian origin. Arched profile combs of this form are assigned to the thirteenth century at Trondheim, where they occur with zoomorphic terminals similar to those found on the London comb (Long 1975). An example dated to the latter half of the twelfth century from Oslo is illustrated by Molaug (1975). Combs with T-shaped perforations backed by sheet bronze date from the early twelfth to the thirteenth centuries at Bergen and Oslo (Grieg 1933; Wiberg 1977) while at Lund a similar date is suggested for a series with high perforated side-plates with false ribs, but without zoomorphic terminals (Blomqvist 1942; J. Persson in Mårtensson 1976). Floderus (1934) illustrates a rather

longer comb from Västergarn, Gotland, with the same cross-sectional profile, in which the side-plates are pierced with cruciform perforations backed with sheet metal. In England only one other instance of this type of decoration has been noted on a comb — from Clifford Street, York (Figure 50c) — but the same technique of backing pierced ornament with metal sheeting occurs on casket mounts and gaming pieces of about the twelfth century (pp. 199, 207).

Handled Combs (Figure 50n-o)

Combs with a side handle (or 'whip handle') enjoyed a certain popularity from about the seventh century until the early medieval period, but securely-stratified examples are few. The problem of fitting a comb with a suitably robust handle was overcome in either one of two ways: the most common solution was to take an antler tine and cut a longitudinal slot in it, starting from the tip and occupying about half the length, into which tooth-plates were riveted in the usual manner; alternatively, two elongated plaques of antler were cut so that, when placed together, there was a space into which the tooth-plates could fit at one end while at the other the plaques were riveted directly together, so forming a rigid composite handle. In every case noted, iron rivets were used. The majority of those with one-piece handles have been made from fairly straight tines, but one or two display an attractive curve; whenever this is the case, the teeth are invariably on the inside of the curve. In some instances the tines are faceted to give them a hexagonal cross-section; an interesting example of this type, found in the Thames, while having all the morphological characteristics of an antler comb, is said to have been made of wood (Winter 1906).

On the Continent the type is found infrequently in Alamannic contexts (Christlein 1966) and one example of (perhaps) Frankish date may be noted from Belgium (de Loë 1939). Three such combs found at Dorestad may be dated tentatively within the period 700-850 (Roes 1963). A handled comb of the Viking period was found at Birka (Arbman 1943) while early medieval examples are known from Bergen (Grieg 1933) and Lund (Blomqvist 1942).

The initial impetus behind their widespread distribution has been attributed to the activities of Frisian merchant seamen from emporia such as Dorestad (D.M. Waterman 1959), an assertion which may find some support in the fact that decoration is often confined to one side of the handle only, a feature noted on other Frisian combs by Tempel (1972). The distribution of handled combs in England, where they are limited to the east and south of the country, is also in accord with this suggestion. Examples come from York (MacGregor 1978a; D.M. Waterman 1979), Whitby (Peers and Radford 1943), North Elmham, Norfolk (Wade Martins 1970), Bedford (*Proceedings of the Society of Antiquaries of London* ser. 2, 12, 115), London (Wheeler 1935; Marsden 1970), Rochester, Kent (Harrison and Flight 1969) and Southampton (Addyman and Hill 1969). The Southampton comb is unique among English handled combs in having two rows of teeth, but finds parallels in Scandinavia (Grieg 1933; Herteig 1969) and in the Netherlands (Trimpe-Burger 1966).

Double-sided Composite Combs

From about the third to the thirteenth centuries double-sided combs were manufactured alongside those with teeth on one side only. Those of Roman age are normally provided with coarse teeth on one side and fine on the other, the element of choice so offered to the user presumably representing the principal reason for the development of this method of construction. During the Migration Period, however, the distinction in spacing between one row of teeth and the other was not always observed, but in Viking age and early medieval combs the convention was followed almost universally, perhaps encouraged by the increasing popularity of one-piece double-sided combs which invariably have differentiated teeth. It has been suggested (Roes 1963) that these combs were a Roman invention, but they seem rather to represent a 'barbarian' interpretation of the true Roman single-piece combs described above (p. 78).

Roman Period Combs (Figure 51a-c)
Compared with most later types, composite combs of the Roman period are relatively short in comparison to their depth. Many are provided with a single pair of side-plates which are usually rather flat in cross-section with the edges bevelled or decoratively profiled with longitudinal grooves. Typical examples are found both on the Continent, as at Vermand and Abbeville in north-east France (Haupt 1970), Furfooz, Belgium (Nenquin 1953), Breisach, Baden-Württemberg (Nierhaus 1938), Lauriacum (Deringer 1967b) and elsewhere in Austria (Deringer 1967a), as well as in England, at Langton, Yorkshire (Corder and Kirk 1932), Thorplands, Northamptonshire (G. Oakley in Hunter and Mynard 1977), Colchester, Essex (P. Crummy 1981) and Lankhills, Hampshire (P. Galloway in G. Clarke 1979).

Combs incorporating a second pair of side-plates are also encountered. The two sets of side-plates are usually widely spaced and the intervening area is often pierced with decorative holes. Keyhole shaped cut-outs, as occur on combs from Askrig (Manby 1966) and Beadlam (Stead 1971), both in Yorkshire, are also to be found on contemporary Continental combs, for example from Steinfort, Luxemburg and Jakobwüllesheim, Nordrhein-Westfalen (Haupt 1970). One such comb, from Altenstadt, Südbayern, with cruciform cut-outs between its double bars, dates from the latter half of the fourth century (E. Keller 1971).

Decorative profiling of the end-plates is common on both types of comb, particularly, it would seem, from the second half of the fourth century (E. Keller 1971). Various curved, dentilated and other forms of carved ornament are exhibited on the series of thirteen combs from Lankhills (P. Galloway in G. Clarke 1979), twelve of which are positively dated later than about 365, and by others from Keill Cave, Strathclyde (J.N.G. Ritchie 1967), Spong Hill, Norfolk (Hills and Penn 1981) and Alchester, Oxfordshire (Iliffe 1932). Zoomorphic ornament is common on double-barred combs such as those from Langton, Yorkshire (Corder and Kirk 1932) and on the Steinfort and Jakobwüllesheim combs mentioned above (Haupt 1970).

Dark Age Combs (Figure 51d-h)
Double-sided combs of post-Roman date adopt an elongated outline and mostly display plain, rectangular end-plates. There is little to distinguish Anglo-Saxon combs with simple plano-convex side-plates — such as those from Bantham, Devon (A. Fox 1955), Southampton (Addyman and Hill 1969), Sutton Courtenay,

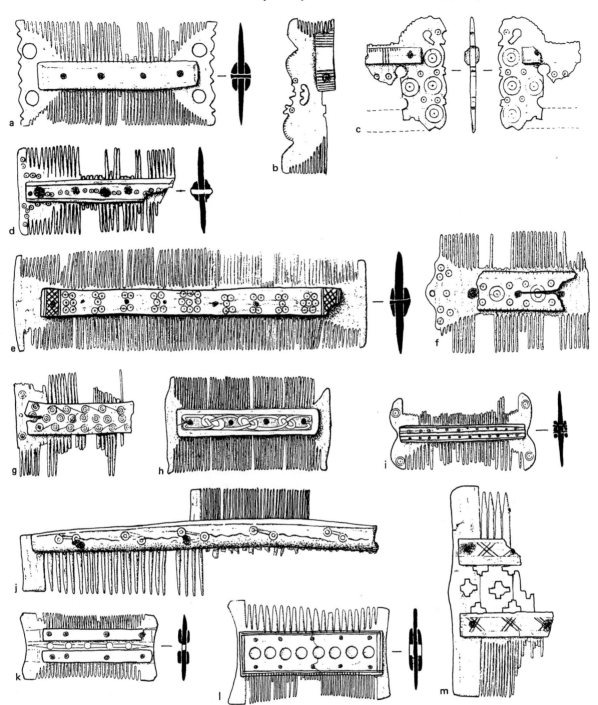

Figure 51: Composite combs from (a) Lankhills (Clarke) (b) Langton (c) Beadlam (Stead) (d) Bantham (Fox) (e) Ford (Musty) (f) Settle (Swanton) (g) Dun Cuier (h) Ardglass (Rynne) (i) Freswick (j) York (k) Oslo (Wiberg) (l) London (m) Schleswig (scale 1:2)

Oxfordshire (Leeds 1923), West Stow, Suffolk (West 1969) and from Whitby (Peers and Radford 1943) and Driffield (Mortimer 1905) in Yorkshire — from those of later (early medieval) date. On the Continent these simple combs are found in Merovingian contexts, as at Hollogne-aux-Pierres, near Liège (Alenus-Lecerf and Dradon 1967), amongst Alamannic burials at Hailfingen, Baden-Württemberg (Stoll 1939) and Nordendorf, Bayern (Franken 1944), and from the Frankish cemeteries at Köln-Müngersdorf (Fremersdorf 1955) and Köln-Junkersdorf (La Baume 1967). Others displaying deeper side-plates with flatter cross-sections, often decorated with incised lines on the upper and lower margins, are found in some numbers at Weimar, Thüringen (Götze 1912) but are less common in England. Other forms of ornament found at this time are limited to incised lines and ring-and-dot motifs.

Widely-spaced side-plates continue to be favoured: an example from Merdingen, Südbaden, has circular holes drilled between bars ornamented with incised chevrons (Fingerlin 1971). An unprovenanced tooth-plate from a comb of ths type is in the museum at Alnwick Castle, Northumberland (Bruce 1880). Contiguous bars are also found at this time: an example from Saintes, Charente-Maritime (Barrière-Flavy 1901) finds a parallel from the Köln-Müngersdorf cemetery (Fremersdorf 1955).

Roes (1963) illustrates a series of Carolingian combs which are made to standard single-sided (notably hog-backed) patterns except that they have short row of teeth projecting for a limited distance along the back, a type which she names 'semi-double' combs. Another example, from an eighth-century grave at Pfullingen, Baden-Württemberg is illustrated by Stein (1967).

Among combs of this type are some which, it has been suggested (e.g., Meaney and Hawkes 1970; Musty 1969), have all the teeth cut on a single plaque of bone. None of these claims stands up to examination.

One group of combs from within the British Isles with a single pair of side-plates as described above is distinguished from Anglo-Saxon combs both in form and in geographical distribution. In proportion, these combs are closer to the Roman originals, being rather short in comparison with their height. The side-plate cross-section is usually deep and flat and the area left in reserve at the extremities of the tooth-plates is rather narrow. Several combs of this type display sinuous outlines to the end-plates, some of them incorporating a perforated central convexity; one of these, from Lough Corcreevy, Tyrone, is threaded with a bronze ring for suspension (Dunlevy 1969). The majority come from Ireland, where they range in date from about the third to the ninth centuries. Outside Ireland they are most numerous around the Atlantic coast of Scotland, from Buston Crannog, Strathclyde (Munro 1882) in the south, through Dun Cuier, Barra (A. Young 1956) to Buckquoy (A. Ritchie 1977) and Burrian (MacGregor 1974) in the Orkneys. A comb from Dinas Powys (Alcock 1963) in South Glamorgan displays the ogival outline commonly encountered on these combs, and an easily recognisable outlier comes from Victoria Cave in north-west Yorkshire (Swanton 1969).

Viking and Early Medieval Combs (Figure 51i-m)

Long double-sided combs with plano-convex bars survive into the Viking period (e.g., Roesdahl *et al.* 1981; D.M. Waterman 1959) including 'semi-double' combs as discussed above (J. Persson in Mårtensson 1976). From this time onwards, however, there is a tendency for combs to become shorter, perhaps under the influence of small one-piece combs which appeared around the twelfth century. A short comb of this type, dated to the eleventh or twelfth centuries, has been noted from Thetford, Norfolk (Knocker 1969) and a number of them (executed in bone) come from Århus (Andersen *et al.* 1971).

Side-plates on early medieval combs are often heavily profiled and set with numerous small rivets, commonly in a double row. Perforated side-plates backed with sheet bronze occur on double-sided as on contemporary single-sided combs (p. 91); an example from Tommarp in Sweden has T-shaped perforations (Thun 1967), another from Ribe in Denmark features cruciform cut-outs (Andersen 1968) while a further example from London has circular holes (London Museum 1940). Double side-plates also remain popular, occurring on a number of Irish sites (Dunlevy 1969) and from thirteenth or fourteenth-century levels at Jarlshof, Shetland (Hamilton 1956).

Scandinavian combs of this type are common in medieval urban settlements such as Lund (Blomqvist 1942; J. Persson in Mårtensson 1976), Oslo (Wiberg 1977), Bergen (Herteig 1969) and Ribe (Andersen 1968). Decorative cut-outs between the bars are common.

While some combs continue to be produced with plain, rectangular end-plates (Andersen *et al.* 1971), decorative profiles become increasingly popular, including concave, convex and double convex forms (Figure 51i); combinations of any two of these may occur on the same comb and a range of more complex forms may also be encountered (Ambrosiani 1981; Andersen 1968; Blomqvist 1942; Grieg 1933; J. Persson in Mårtensson 1976; Wiberg 1976). In some combs the two rows of teeth may be offset, so that one row finishes short of the end, as on an example from Freswick, Highland Region (A.O. Curle 1939).

Horn Combs (Figures 52-3)

Although it is suggested elsewhere (p. 51) that the rise of the horn industry in the medieval period may have contributed to the eclipse of bone and antler working, horn combs, which would almost certainly have been the major products of this industry, are scarce indeed. This apparent dearth may be partly explained by the relatively poor capacity of horn to survive prolonged burial, although excellent preservation may be encountered under suitable environmental conditions.

The capacity of horn to be moulded into large, flat sheets allowed single-piece combs of dimensions large enough to suit almost any purpose to be produced without difficulty. Three double-sided horn combs from England incorporate a feature which is therefore difficult to explain, each having a pair of riveted bone side-plates (seemingly made from ribs) of the type which serve to connect the individual tooth-plates on bone and antler composite combs. The first of these (Yorkshire Museum, unpublished) is said to have formed part of a Roman grave group found in York in the nineteenth century; the second (Figure 52) is an undated find from Queen Victoria Street, London, whose side-plates are marked with tell-tale saw cuts showing that, as with composite combs, they were assembled before the teeth were cut; the third comb was recovered from a ninth or tenth-century pit at Milk Street, London (Museum of London, unpublished). Comparison of the generally trapezoidal outline of these combs (having one row of teeth shorter than the other) with those of early medieval one-piece bone combs, certainly favours the date suggested by the Milk Street comb rather than that from York, but further finds must be awaited before the chronological span of this type can be identified with certainty.

Horn combs of Dark Age or Viking date are

Figure 52: Horn comb with riveted bone side-plates, from Queen Victoria Street, London

Figure 53:   Horn comb from London Wall, London

practically unknown on the Continent (Tempel 1969), but Ambrosiani (1981) notes some evidence for their production at both Ribe in Denmark and at Dorestad in the Netherlands.

Six horn combs from Dublin (Dunlevy 1969, 1972) have in common a rather massive form, with a deep central reserve and comparatively short teeth. Their respective ratios of height to length range from about 1:1 to 1:2 and there is also some variation in outline. They range in date from the twelfth to the fourteenth centuries. A comb from London Wall (Figure 53), dated to the sixteenth or seventeenth century, displays similar features. Continental examples are also rare: Dunlevy (1972) mentions one fourteenth-century horn comb from the Frisian terps.

The more recent history of horn combs can be charted from surviving examples (Hardwick 1981) and from the reminiscences of those who worked in the horn industry in its last days. Among the latter the recollections of J.W. Rougier (quoted in Wenham 1964), who joined his family's horning business in York in the last decade of the nineteenth century, provide a valuable record of the craft practices current at that time. The historical evidence for horn comb-making in Kenilworth, Warwickshire, has been reviewed by J.H. Drew (1965).

Comb Cases (Figure 54)

Composite combs were frequently provided with protective cases to minimise the possibility of damage to the teeth. These were often of bone or antler, but not invariably so: a hog-backed comb from an Anglo-Saxon burial at Lowbury Hill, Berkshire, was found with the remains of a case made of wood and leather (Atkinson 1916), while a Viking age comb from Birka was enclosed in a leather pouch (Arbman 1943). Among other graves at Birka comb cases were associated particularly with male burials (Ambrosiani 1981); perhaps the remaining combs there and at least some of those found elsewhere may originally have had some form of organic case.

Cases of skeletal material often display constructional and decorative features which reflect those of the corresponding comb. Antler is the most commonly used material although bone is also encountered. A group of fragments from Viking age comb cases found at York are made from split ribs; it has been suggested (MacGregor 1982a) that this mechanically inferior material, which was used only rarely for combs themselves, may have been thought acceptable for this purpose since cases were rarely subjected to the stresses which had to be borne by combs.

Roman comb cases for single-sided combs normally consist of a single pair of rectangular side-plates, deep enough to enclose the whole length of the teeth, separated by a pair of vertically-oriented spacer-plates at the ends. The whole structure is fastened with iron (or, occasionally, bronze) rivets. It has been noted (Nenquin 1953) that some combs, notably those with outswept end-plates, are too wide to slide directly into their cases: the need to fit in first one end and then the other provided a measure of security for the comb, since in order to get it out again the process had to be reversed. Sometimes an additional slip of antler was inserted to close the gap between the bottoms of the bars. When accompanying a comb with a projecting crest, the projecting edge of the closing strip on the case might be carved and pierced in a similar manner: a triangular-backed comb from Thivars, Eure-et-Loire, has a matching case with this feature (Barrière-Flavy 1938). In other instances, carved zoo-morphic projections on the back of the comb are matched by corresponding treatment of the spacer-plates: fourth and fifth-century instances are found at Lorch in Austria (Deringer 1967),

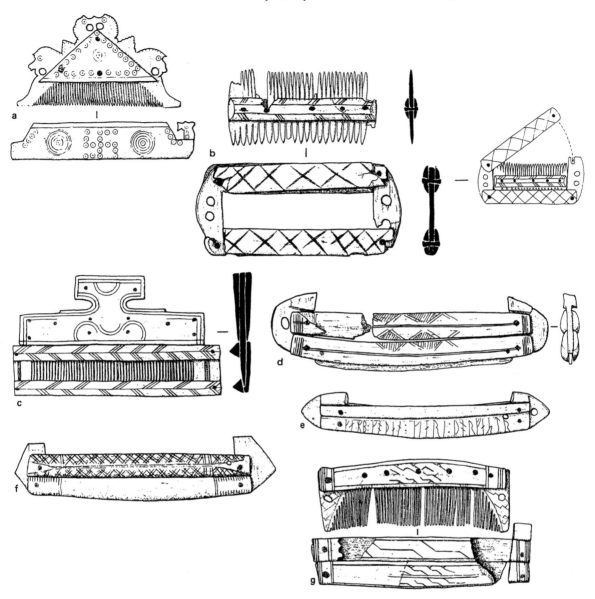

Figure 54: Comb cases (scale 1:2) from (a) Lauriacum (Deringer) (b) Kremsdorf (Deringer) (c) Gotland (Nerman) (d) Northampton (Williams) (e) Lincoln (British Museum) (f) York (g) Skaill

Furfooz, Belgium (Nenquin 1953) and in Frisia (Roes 1963). There appear to be no records of any finds of Romano-British comb cases.

In the fifth century cases appear which match the method of construction of barred zoomorphic combs (p. 85), having a single, deep side-plate on one side and two plano-convex or triangular-section bars on the other.

Continental examples may be noted from Issendorf, Niedersachsen (Janssen 1972), Dittenheim, Bayern (Dannheimer 1962), Wildau, Brandenburg (von Müller 1962) and from Frisia (Boeles 1951; Roes 1963), while in England they occur at Spong Hill, Norfolk (Hills 1981; Hills and Penn 1981), Lackford, Suffolk (Lethbridge 1951) and Girton College,

Cambridge (MacGregor 1975a). The form of the case cannot, however, be taken in isolation as an infallible indicator of the type of comb with which it was used: triangular-backed combs have been found in association with such cases at Spong Hill (Hills 1981) and at Obermollern, Thüringen (B. Schmidt 1961), while on Gotland examples of rectangular backed combs with central 'handles' occur with cases of this general type but featuring widely-spaced instead of the usual contiguous bars (Nerman 1935).

Elsewhere on the Continent, cases featuring a single pair of deep side-plates survive well into the Migration Period (e.g., Roes 1963). In some of these there is a marked convexity of the lower edge (e.g., Pietzsch 1979). On others the side-plates are fairly straight but the closing strip between them projects with a convex or angular outline and is sometimes perforated with a central slot, as on examples from Schretzheim (U. Koch 1977) and Marktoktoberdorf (Christlein 1966) in Bayern, Tocâne-Saint-Apre, Dordogne (Barrière-Flavy 1901) and in Frisia (Roes 1963). Since suspending the case by this slot would simply result in the comb falling out, we may assume that it was in fact threaded with a tie to hold the comb in position.[17]

At this time, however, it is double-sided comb cases which predominate. In the usual method of construction (Figure 54b) the two pairs of side-plates are located at opposite extremities of the spacer-plates, the gap between being filled by the side-plates of the comb. Access for the comb is normally arranged by pivoting one pair of side-plates at one end; the spacer-plate at the other end pivots at the bottom, its free end being notched to engage with a rivet joining the side-plates, so holding the case shut. One of the spacer-plates is commonly slotted for suspension. The type is uncommon in Anglo-Saxon England, but an example from Driffield, Yorkshire (Mortimer 1905) is linked by its form and decorative scheme of double arcades enclosing ring-and-dot motifs to a large series on the Continent. These are common in Frankish cemeteries such as Köln-Mungersdorf (Fremersdorf 1955) and Köln-Junkersdorf (La Baum 1967), and, more particularly, amongst Alamannic burials in Württemberg (Stoll 1939; Veek 1931) and Südbaden (Fingerlin 1971; Garscha 1970), Bayern (Franken 1944; U. Koch 1968, 1977)

and in upper Austria (Deringer 1967 a, b).

Two cases of splendid appearance but of unusual type come from Migration Period contexts at Weilbach, Hessen (Schoppa 1959) and at Schretzheim, Bayern (U. Koch 1977); these are 'double-sided' comb cases in the sense that each houses a pair of single-sided combs, inserted in opposing directions.

Viking age and early medieval comb-cases featuring a single pair of side-plates are also well known, but at this time it becomes common for the case to have two pairs of contiguous side-plates, the back of the comb forming a third matching element when it is in position.[18] All three bars may be identical in appearance, but instances are also found in which the upper bars of the case have an angular section while the lower bars and the side-plates of the comb are plano-convex, as in several instances at Birka (Arbman 1943). Whether the case has one pair of side-plates or two, small lengths of antler of appropriate size and section are occasionally riveted to the tops of the spacer plates so that, when the comb is inserted, the line of its back is extended to match those of the side-plates of the case (e.g., Blomqvist 1942; J. Persson in Mårtensson 1976; Wiberg 1977). The spacer-plates themselves are often made unnecessarily long so that they project from the ends of the case, forming decorative rectangular, trapezoidal or trefoil terminals (Blomqvist 1942; Chmielowska 1971; J. Persson in Mårtensson 1976; Schuldt 1980; K.A. Wilde 1953). In the British Isles rather short combs seem to be most frequently provided with cases and examples come from Skaill, Orkney (Grieg 1940), York (Hall 1977; MacGregor 1978a), Northampton (G. Oakley in Williams 1979) and London (R.A. Smith 1909). A case of this type from Lincoln bears a Runic inscription identifying its maker by the name Thorfast (British Museum 1923). Longer examples are also known, as from Dublin (National Museum of Ireland 1973) and Freswick, Highland Region (A.O. Curle 1939). In some instances a hole is drilled through the side-plates of the case, matching a corresponding hole in one of the end-plates of the comb. A peg or tie passing through these holes would have held the comb in the case.

Comb cases are normally adjuncts of composite combs and largely disappeared with them in the fourteenth century.

Mirror and Other Cases (Figure 55)

From the late thirteenth century until about the middle of the fifteenth, richly ornamented ivory mirror-cases were among the most popular products of French ivory carving schools (see, for example, Koechlin 1924; Longhurst 1929). These cases, designed to hold small circular mirrors, mostly of metal, were made in two elements with an internal recess for the mirror. The suitably tender scenes (lovers in a garden, the storming of the Castle of Love, and so on) carved on the outer faces are frequently contained within a circular frame, often with four angular supporters which impose an over-all square format (Figure 55). Related pairs of valves have occasionally been recognised but the method by which they were attached to one another is not always clear.

A series of what may be cheaper versions of mirror-cases provide one of the rare instances of composite construction in bone during the medieval period. To meet the need for material which is both appropriately large in area and of sufficient thickness to allow relief carving on the outside and a recess on the inside, three strips of bone (presumably from cattle or horse long-bones) were riveted together by means of cross-bars at the top and bottom. A well-preserved example from Warburg, Niedersachsen, is illustrated by Schultz (1965), and two representatives of this type, one of them complete (Figure 56), are in the Museum of London. Drilled holes on the cross-bars of the London pieces may indicate the former presence of pivoting doors. All three display castellated architectural forms, a feature also found on smaller one-piece cases from Esneux, Belgium,[19] and from Hitzacker, Elbe (Wachter 1976). The latter piece has both elements intact and retains two glass discs within its ovoid internal recess. The latter were so diminutive, however, as to be useless as mirrors. Wachter's identification of the piece as an amulet may well be correct: one might imagine a lock of hair or some similar relic enclosed between the glass discs. The architectural allusions of certain lead-alloy pilgrim badges (Hansmann and Kriss-Rettenbeck 1966) may lend further support to this suggestion.

Toilet Sets (Figure 57)

From about the sixteenth century toilet sets of bone began to achieve widespread popularity. The British Museum collections include a variety of decoratively carved implements such as ear scoops, some of them with an integral tooth-pick (Figure 57a,b). Others formerly in the Guildhall Museum (1908) are now in the Museum of London, including examples combining an ear scoop with a pair of tweezers (Figure 57c, d).

More complex sets in which several implements are united by a single bronze pivot are also encountered. Four elements with flattened shanks and perforated terminals deriving from such a set have been found in a sixteenth-century context at St Michael's House, Southampton (Platt 1976), and excavations at Aldwark, York, have produced an almost complete set in which the same range of implements is riveted to a decorative base plate (Figure 57f).

Buttons and Beads (Figure 58)

Prior to the medieval period buttons are unknown, while beads, although common in glass, amber and other media, are infrequently

Figure 55: Ivory mirror case, unprovenanced, Ashmolean Museum

Figure 56:   Bone mirror case from London (obverse and reverse)

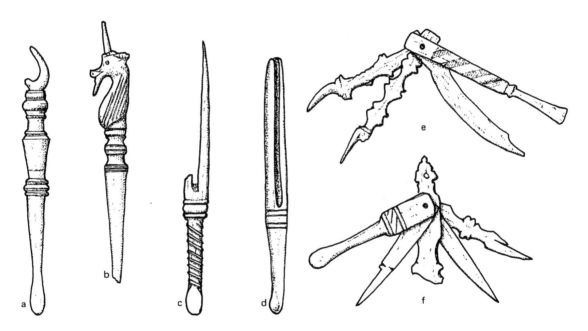

Figure 57:   Toilet implements (scale 3:4): ear scoops (a-b) from London; scoops combined with tweezers (c-d) from London; composite toilet sets from (e) Southampton and (f) York

found in skeletal materials. Exceptions are known from England at Lankhills, Hampshire (G. Clarke 1979) and at Spong Hill, Norfolk (Hills 1981) and are sparsely represented at Krefeld-Gelep, Nordrhein-Westfalen (Pirling 1966). A single bead, said to be of ivory, comes from a Viking age male burial at Skeabost in Skye (Lethbridge 1920). Individual finds of this latter sort may have been worn as much for amuletic as for decorative purposes.

From the medieval period come numerous waste fragments from long bones drilled repeatedly with holes, ranging from about 0.5cm to 1.5cm in diameter (Figure 58a-e). Whether these represent waste from bead-making or button-making (or indeed both) seems impossible to decide. It is clear that one or the other is involved, however, since it was evidently the material removed by drilling which was being sought. The profile of the holes shows that they were drilled first from one side of the bone and then the other; the discovery of some fragments with the resulting discs of material not yet removed confirms this fact. The implement used was evidently a centre-bit with a curving profile and with an extended central point which, when it had penetrated the bone from one side, allowed the drill to be aligned on the same spot from the other. A collection of ten drilled fragments came from a series of fourteenth or fifteenth-century pits at King Street, Coventry (Gooder *et al.* 1964) and others have been found at York (MacGregor 1982a), King's Lynn (Clarke and Carter 1977), Northampton (Oakley in Williams 1979), London (M. Henig in Tatton-Brown 1974) and at St Mary's Hospital at Ospringe, Kent (G.H. Smith 1979); examples with beads (or buttons) still in place come from Hull (Armstrong 1977) and Lincoln (Colyer 1975). All of these appear to date from the late medieval period, but, surprisingly, others are said to come from pre-Conquest levels at Flaxengate, Lincoln (C. Colyer, quoted in Clarke and Carter 1977).

Detached beads found in Hull correspond to

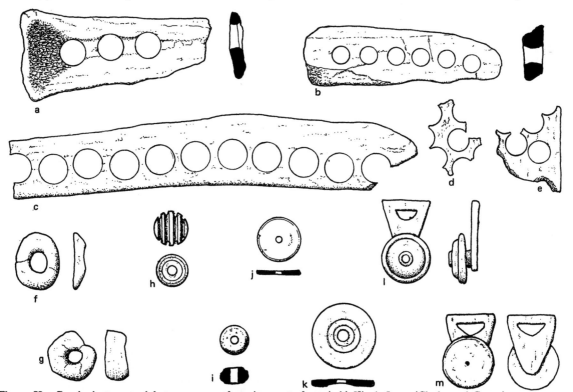

Figure 58: Beads, buttons and fasteners: manufacturing waste from (a-b) King's Lynn (Clarke and Carter) (c-e) London; beads from (f-g) Spong Hill (Hills) and (h-i) Northampton (Williams); buttons from (j) Northampton (Williams) and (k) London (Tatton-Brown); button-and-loop fasteners (l) unprovenanced (Wilde) and (m) Musée de Dijon (scale 2:3)

the broadly spherical shapes which might be expected from these waste pieces; one example found there still had an unsmoothed flange of tissue around its circumference marking the area where it was detached from the parent bone. Others have been noted from Hangleton, Sussex (Holden 1963) and from Ludgershall Castle, Wiltshire (MacGregor, forthcoming). Two beads from the latter site were found together with a bone swivel, the function of which was unclear although it was evidently not from a necklace. Large numbers of beads, including seventeen matching examples, were found in a mid sixteenth-century context at Coventry, West Midlands (Woodfield 1981).

Finds which correspond more closely to the dimensions of modern buttons are thin, flat discs of bone, usually with a central perforation (Figure 58j-k): excavations at St Aldates, Oxford (M. Henig in Durham 1977), Worcester (Carver 1980), and at Faccombe Netherton (MacGregor, forthcoming), Southampton (Platt and Coleman-Smith 1975) and Winchester (Collis 1978), all in Hampshire, have produced examples of these, while a disc from Ospringe, Kent, having four perforations, is even more akin to the buttons of the present day. These discs are both larger in diameter (average 4cm) than the perforations in the bones discussed above, and much thinner than the products of these bones would be; they correspond rather to the thickness of scapula blades, but the only perforated scapulae so far noted, from Silchester, Hampshire (Boon 1974), are of Roman date.

An unusually rich find from excavations in Saint-Denis has produced a vast amount of evidence for the manufacture of bone beads, so far published only provisionally (Meyer 1979). From a rubbish pit dated to the late fifteenth or early sixteenth centuries came over 1,200 discarded articular ends of cattle metapodials, and about 1,000 rough-outs for beads of various shapes which were being made from the corresponding shafts, evidently for use in rosaries. From the evidence of these rough-outs and from written accounts of the *corporation de patenotriers* of Paris, Meyer has reconstructed the working methods of the bead-makers as follows: after sawing the ends from the metapodials, the shafts were split into rods, which were in turn cut into appropriate lengths for beads; these blanks were then drilled longi-

tudinally and finally mounted on a lathe for shaping. Centrally-perforated discoid buttons were also found among the waste, together with bone plaques from which they had been cut. Could it be that these so-called buttons are themselves paternoster beads, perhaps for marking out the decades of rosaries?

In more recent years, horn buttons came to be widely used. D.P. White (1977) has described the method by which blanks were cut from sheets of horn which had been flattened under heat and pressure, lathe-turned to produce a rim, and scoured by prolonged rotation in a barrel; holes were then drilled in the blanks before they were given a final polish in a barrel with jeweller's rouge. From the nineteenth century, an alternative production method appears, using die-stamped reconstituted horn.

Button-and-loop Fasteners (Figure 58l-m)

Among the Roman button-and-loop fasteners reviewed by J.P. Wilde (1970) are a number made of bone. Two principal types can be recognised: those of Wilde's Class Xa are of solid construction, with the head cut as a circular boss on a triangular shank, while those of Class Xb are composite, having a separate discoid head riveted to the shank. Of eleven examples catalogued by Wilde, none of which is later than the first century in date, three (from Pompeii and Vindonissa) are of the solid variety, while the remainder (from Vindonissa, Hofheim and Wiesbaden) are riveted. To these may be added a more recent find from the Flavian fort at Hayton, Yorkshire (Johnson 1978), and one from Dijon (Musée Archéologique de Dijon (nd)).

Toggles (Figure 59)

Another group of objects found commonly, but difficult to interpet, are so-called toggles, made from long-bones such as the carpals and metapodials of pigs and sheep. They are modified by a single perforation cut through the centre of the shaft. They have been interpreted as fasteners, possibly for personal dress (e.g. Curle *et al.* 1954) or, more plausibly, as bobbins for winding wool (e.g. Bantelmann 1955; Wild 1970). An alternative suggestion by Hrubý

(1957) is that they may have been mere playthings, to be mounted on a twisted string and spun first one way and then the other (Figure 59c). They occur in Iron Age contexts, as at Glastonbury, Somerset (Bulleid and Gray 1917), and remain common until the medieval period (G. Oakley in Williams 1979). Wild (1970) lists several Roman period examples from Britain but notes that they are not found on Continental sites at this time.

Buckles (Figure 60a-j)

The main stylistic developments in buckle design seem always to have taken place in metal and, although buckles are known in bone and occasionally in ivory from the early Roman to the late medieval period, the majority are copies of metal types. While bone tissue undoubtedly performs better under compression than in tension, its mechanical properties were evidently quite adequate for this task. Predictably, breaks are most common on the hinge pivots, which endured most of the stress.

Metal prototypes have clearly influenced the scrolling outlines featured on buckles of first or early second-century type found at Colchester, Essex (P. Crummy 1977), Richborough, Kent (Cunliffe 1968) and Saalburg, Bayern (Oldenstein 1976). In each of these (Figure 60a-c) the loop terminates in a well-defined flange from which projects a pair of hinges; the tongue (which survives only on the Colchester buckle) terminates in a similar hinge and pivots on a

metal pin which passes through all three sockets. The absence of corresponding belt-plates of Roman age suggests that the buckle may have been attached directly to the looped end of the leather belt; later buckles of the sixth and seventh centuries incorporating similar hinges are, however, fitted with bone or ivory belt plates riveted to the end of the strap and incorporating hinge elements (Moosbrugger-Leu 1967). Equivalent fittings of the Roman period may yet be found.

A simpler Roman type featured a plain crescentic loop with expanded terminals, drilled to carry a metal pin on which the tongue pivoted. Examples come from Risstissen (Ulbert 1970) and from Rheingönheim (Ulbert 1969) on the *Limes* and from Ozengel, Kent, the latter formerly published as Saxon (G.B. Brown 1915). Oldenstein (1976) illustrates a late second and third-century type of ring buckle, among which examples in bone are occasionally found. One of these, from Niederbieber, Rheinland-Pfalz (Figure 60d), has its iron tongue still intact.

Among bone finds supposedly (but not certainly) of Roman date from London, C.R. Smith (1859) illustrates two buckles. One has an oval loop grooved for the tongue and a projecting plate, cleft to receive the end of the belt and drilled for two rivets; in the other buckle the loop is carved within a rectangular plate perforated by two rivet holes and incorporating the pivot for the tongue, the whole buckle decorated with incised ornament and relief mouldings.

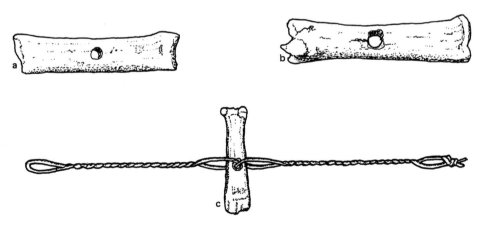

Figure 59: Toggles (scale 3:4) from (a) Freswick (Curle) and (b) Northampton (Williams); (c) suggested method of use as a toy (Hrubý)

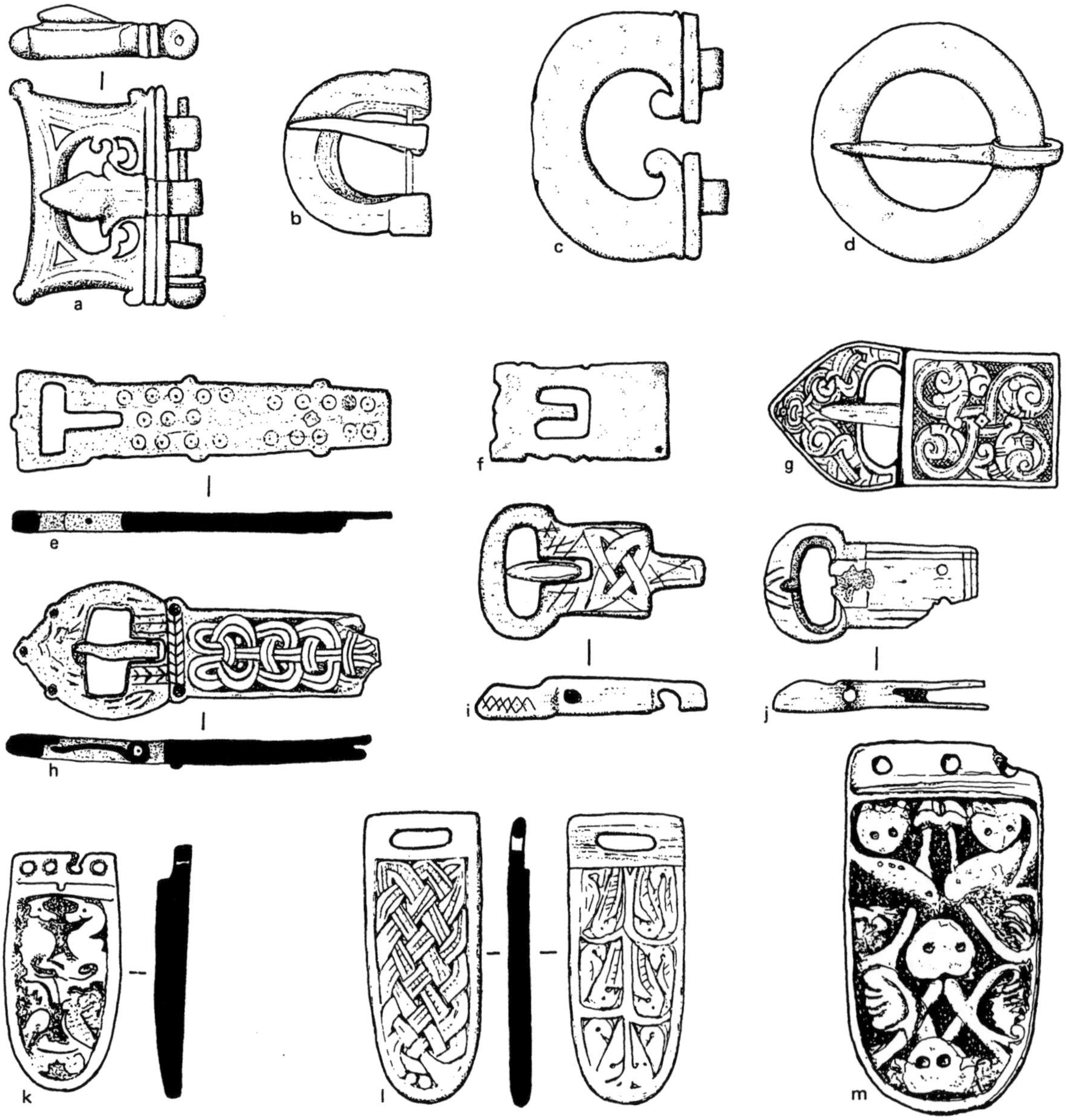

Figure 60: Buckles and strap-ends (scale 2:3): from (a) Colchester (Crummy) (b) Ozengel (Baldwin Brown) (c) Richborough (Cunliffe) (d) Niederbieber (Oldenstein) (e) unprovenanced, Alnwick Castle (f) Austmannadal (Roussell) (g) Lewis (Dalton) (h) Goodmanham (i) York (j) Goltho (Beresford) (k) London (l) York (m) Leicester (Brønsted)

Among the earliest post-Roman buckles in skeletal materials are the elaborate bone or ivory 'reliquary buckles' of the sixth and seventh centuries discussed by Moosbrugger-Leu (1967) and Werner (1977). This type, which is limited in distribution to south-west Germany, Swizterland and south-eastern France, features a large buckle plate joining the loop in a hinge and is often hollowed out to receive a relic. Their specifically Christian significance is emphasised by the iconographical content of the carved ornament on some examples and by incised scriptural passages on others.

Finds from the Frisian terp mounds illustrate the more commonly worn types of Carolingian and later buckles. Roes (1963) illustrates a variety of types, including some abandoned in the course of manufacture. The simplest of these has a fixed tongue projecting inwards from the loop; the belt would have been held in place merely by tension. Although this example, from a terp at Ferwerd in the Netherlands, may indeed be early, the presence of a more decorative buckle (Figure 60f) of the same type (but with a slotted base to take the captive end of the strap) in a medieval farm at Austmannadal, Greenland (Roussell 1941) shows that it was not exclusively an early type. The other Frisian finds range from a simple elongated type, with two fixing holes and an integral bar to carry the tongue, to more developed forms with well-defined loops in which the tongue formerly pivoted on a metal axis. Two unprovenanced buckles in the Alnwick Castle Museum, Northumberland (Bruce 1880), are probably contemporary with these Dutch finds.

A tenth-century origin can be proposed for a bone buckle from Goodmanham, Yorkshire, on the basis of the incised Borre style interlace ornament on the plate (Figure 60). The plate is slotted at the base for a strap, originally held in place by four (or five) bronze rivets. The tongue is also of bronze, its base wrapped round an integral bar cut in the solid bone. Two further buckles from the city of York may also date from the tenth or eleventh centuries (D.M. Waterman 1959), and one of these, stained a uniform dark green, has a conventionally slotted base with two rivet holes while the other (Figure 60i), carved with an interlace knot, terminates in a curious notched projection.

Like the chessmen with which it was found (p. 139) a buckle from the Isle of Lewis in the Outer Hebrides (Figure 60g) is of walrus ivory. It comprises a deep, pointed loop and a rectangular plate, the latter slotted at the base for a strap which was held in position by four rivets inserted from the back. The tongue pivots on a bronze pin. The front surface is covered with interlace decoration within a reserved border; an origin in the twelfth century may be proposed on the basis of both this and the accompanying chessmen.

The use of bone for the manufacture of buckles continued throughout the medieval period: the deserted medieval village at Goltho, Lincolnshire (Beresford 1975) produced two examples (one of which is illustrated in Figure 60j) and that at Wharram, Yorkshire, produced another (D. Andrews in Hurst 1979); Hrubý (1957) illustrates a twelfth or thirteenth-century example found in Moravia with elaborate incised and pierced decoration, while Tauber (1977) reproduces simpler versions from Frohburg, Switzerland. Roussell (1941) has published a cetacean bone buckle with a zoomorphic loop from medieval Kangersuneq in Greenland.

Strap-ends (Figure 60k-m)

Strap-ends of bone would have formed a natural complement to the buckles described above and a few examples of these can be cited, although none is earlier than the ninth century in date. Brønsted (1924) describes one such example from Leicester, with incised ornament in the form of opposed beasts and masks in acanthus foliage (Figure 60m). A further example from London (Figure 60k), probably contemporary with the Leicester piece and seemingly made of morse ivory, also displays opposed animals (and, perhaps, birds) but without accompanying foliage, and has four holes for fixing-rivets at the base (R.A. Smith 1909). An unfinished strap-end of similar form and with only rudimentary incised ornament is in the British Museum (unpublished). From Lund in Sweden comes one example with low relief decoration in Borre style (Blomqvist and Mårtensson 1963), a near contemporary of the Goodmanham buckle described above. A recent find from York (Figure 60l), slotted from front to back and decorated with incised plant and interlace ornament, is also from the tenth century (Roesdahl *et al.* 1981).

Amulets (Figure 61)

Whether to guard against the malevolent influence of the 'evil eye', a concept which survived until recent times (Elworthy 1958), or against any number of physical ailments or calamities, amulets played an important part in the lives of North European peoples through-

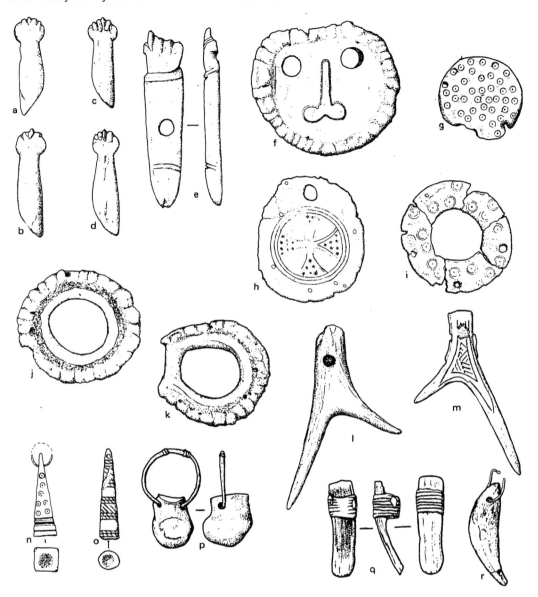

Figure 61: Amulets (scale 1:2) from (a-d) Verulamium (Wheeler) (e) Southwark (Kenyon) (f) Malton (g) Barrington (Foster) (h) Rittersdorf (Böhner) (i) Polhill (Philp) (j) unprovenanced, British Museum (k) unprovenanced, Museum of London (l) London (m) York (n) Aargau (Werner) (o) Bern (Werner) (p) Kingston Down (q) Ducklington (Chambers) (r) Sleaford (Thomas)

out the period under review. Their talismanic significance has been reviewed elsewhere (e.g., Budge 1930; Deonna 1956; Hansmann and Kriss-Rettenbeck 1966; Meaney 1981); here they are discussed according to raw material and type.

One of the principal types to make its appearance in the Roman period is in the form of a 'fig hand' carved in the round and sometimes associated with a phallus. The 'fig hand', in which the fingers are clenched and the tip of the thumb protrudes between the index and second fingers, has maintained its popularity in the Mediterranean world as a protective against the evil eye to the present day. Protection could be gained by making the gesture with the hand or by wearing an amulet carved in the same form (Elworthy 1958). Phalli are among the most widespread of Roman symbols for good fortune. The use of certain raw materials such as coral and jet in the manufacture of these amulets endowed them with additional protective powers but there is no indication that bone or antler were considered especially efficacious in this context (Hansmann and Kriss-Rettenbeck 1966).[20] Budge (1930) illustrates a number of examples in a variety of materials from the Roman world. In England four realistically carved fig-hand amulets from Verulamium each terminate in stylised phalli and are pierced laterally through the wrist (Wheeler and Wheeler 1936), while an alternative type, perforated centrally from front to back, occurs at Wroxeter, Shropshire (Bushe-Fox 1913), Southwark, Surrey (Kenyon 1959) and Fishbourne, Sussex (Cunliffe 1971). On the Continent an amulet of the latter type may be noted from Risstissen on the Danubian *Limes* (Ulbert 1970) while a rather different variety, sharply curved and longitudinally grooved, is recorded from Oberstimm, Bayern (Schönberger 1978) and from Baden in northern Switzerland (Lunz 1974). A single British example of this latter type comes from Silchester, Hampshire (Stephen Greep, personal communication).

Evidence that antler did have some special talismanic significance is provided by representatives of the second major group of Roman amulets, which are invariably cut from the bases of shed antlers. The denticulated edge common to this type, which has drawn comment from various authors, is no more than the natural coronet of the burr, chanelled and perforated by the presence of blood vessels in the velvet during growth (p. 12). One or more holes may be drilled in the disc to permit suspension, possibly from a belt or harness. Some appear to have been worn without further elaboration, as in examples from Pfünz (Winkelmann 1901), Rheingönheim, and Marköbel (Ulbert 1969) on the German *Limes*, from the region of Langres in central France (Lebel 1956) and Neris in Bourbonnais (Vertet 1958), and from La Chapelle-du-Mont-de-France, Saône-et-Loire (Lebel 1956). More commonly, a device is found carved on one face. Most widely favoured was the phallus; instances may be noted in the British Isles from Newstead, Borders Region (J. Curle 1911), Corstopitum (Corbridge), Northumberland (M. Green 1978), Malton, Yorkshire (Corder 1948) and Caerleon, Gwent (M. Green 1978), and on the Continent from Vechten in Holland (Hatt *et al.* 1955), Froitzheim (Barfield 1968) and Rheingönheim (Ulbert 1969) in Germany and from Vindonissa in Switzerland (Hatt *et al.* 1955). Other devices are occasionally found carved on amulets of this type: Roes (1956) illustrates one example from Nijmegen Museum which combines phalli with a bull's head and Vertet (1958) reproduces a medallion from Vichy featuring a dog lying with its head on its paws. Lebel (1956) illustrates three examples from the region of Langres and from Saint-Reverien, Nièvre, each of which has been profiled with a lathe or centre bit to reproduce a regular circular surface, and a similar roundel from Sens, Yonne, is reproduced by Hatt *et al.* (1955).

The popularity of these discoid amulets seems to span the whole of the Roman period[21] and related types survived until perhaps the seventh or eighth centuries. None of these carry phalli or other representational devices in relief, however, but instead feature incised ornament, usually in the form of ring-and-dot motifs. The cemeteries at Barrington (Foster 1884) and Burwell (Lethbridge 1931), both in Cambridgeshire, have each produced examples of this type (Figure 61g). Similar discs come from the Migration Period cemeteries at Ciply, Hainaut (Faider-Feytmans 1956) and Maastricht, Holland (Hatt *et al.* 1955), as well as from Dorestad (ibid.; Roes 1963) and elsewhere in the Netherlands (Roes 1956, 1963). Ten examples were found at Schretzheim, Bayern, all with female burials of the second half of the sixth century (U. Koch 1977). In the case of the Dorestad disc and on one unprovenanced example illustrated by Roes (1963) the ring-and-dot motifs are in a cruciform arrangement, which also appears more formally as scribed or compass-drawn crosses on amulets from Maastricht (Hatt *et al.* 1955) and from Rittersdorf, Rheinland-Pfalz (Böhner 1958). Compass-drawn petal or star motifs also occur (Hatt *et al.* 1955; Faider-Feytmans 1956; U. Koch 1977).

All these latter discs are distinguished from

those of the Roman period by their decorative treatment, by their thinness, and by the fact that the irregular burr, if it survives at all, is no more than a ragged edge to the disc, being abraded flat and contrasting with the relief border which it forms naturally around the Roman amulets. Some have a single suspension hole and others have smaller, irregular holes around the border; in certain cases the latter are natural features of the coronet, as mentioned above, but others may have been used in mounting the disc, as exemplified by a related group of annular amulets (Figure 61i).

These annular pieces are made in the same way as the discs described above except that the centre is cut away and the small holes around the periphery seem more definitely functional. Two such pieces, each covered with ring-and-dot ornament, were found at Burwell, Cambridgeshire (Lethbridge 1931), both of them associated with the remains of chatelaines. The Burwell amulet is mounted with a bronze suspension loop and has several peripheral holes showing signs of wear, one of them being fitted with a wire ring; the excavator is surely correct in his assertion that it hung from the girdle with various small appendages dangling from it, and we may add that it almost certainly was endowed with talismanic powers. Other examples come from Spong Hill, Norfolk (Hills and Penn 1981), Yelford, Oxfordshire (Ashmolean Museum, unpublished) and from Polhill (Philp 1973) and Eccles (Detsicas and Hawkes 1973), both in Kent, the latter examples dated to the seventh century. A similar piece from Londesborough, Yorkshire is thought (Swanton 1966) to have been used along with a loose iron pin as a form of annular brooch.

Amuletic powers may perhaps be ascribed to a further group in which only the peripheral coronet is retained (Figure 61j-k). The fact that some at least of these also served a practical function as girdle rings or buckles need not deter us from this conclusion in view of the special significance which, on the evidence given above, was certainly attributed to the burr. (The occurrence of specialised reliquary buckles in the sixth century (Werner 1977) provides an interesting parallel development.) English examples of the simple annular form come from fifth or sixth-century cremations at Lackford, Suffolk (Lethbridge 1951), Spong

Hill, Norfolk (Hills and Penn 1981) and Newark-on-Trent, Nottinghamshire (Newark-on-Trent Museum, unpublished), while Vertet (1958) illustrates a find from Vichy, Bourbonnais. Roes (1963) has suggested that they may have been worn as pendants and has also noted that some examples from Frisia are large enough to have been used as bracelets by children or even adults; as a further alternative, she speculates that some may have been tied round the necks of animals to protect them from harm. Meaney (1981) suggests that identical finds from Finglesham, Kent, and Long Wittenham, Oxfordshire, were used as bag rings of the type more commonly found in ivory and discussed below on pp. 110-12. The polish which marks the inner face of these rings would be consistent with any of these functions or with their being used as girdle fasteners. This latter suggestion finds support in the form of one find from Whitby Monastery, Yorkshire in which one side is cut as though to take a strap (Peers and Radford 1943); another, although described as a pendant (Guildhall Museum 1908), is seemingly a simpler version of this type, and an angular variant comes from Lagore Crannog, Meath (Hencken 1950).

A rather later group of antler pendants based on tines (Figures 61l-m) may also be interpreted as amulets. With the exception of one example from London (Figure 61l) all those found so far come from York: they include four finds from early excavations in the city (D.M. Waterman 1959) and one from more recent investigations (MacGregor 1982a). This new find is cut from the palmate tip of a fallow deer antler,[22] while the others are of red deer. All appear to date from about the tenth or eleventh centuries. Auden (1909) suggested that the early finds from York may have been worn to promote success in hunting, but this view may be too narrow an interpretation in view of the esteem in which antler was generally held: Pliny is an early advocate of the beneficial powers of the stag, vested in antler and other parts of its body (quoted in Meaney 1981). As late as the seventeenth century, many benefits were held to derive from potions made from various parts of its anatomy (particulary the antlers) and the stag was described as 'a world of remedies, of commodities and advantages for men' (D. Murray 1904).

One of the most geographically widespread

types of talisman among the Germanic peoples of the late Roman and early post-Roman period is that which Werner (1964) has shown to derive from Roman 'Hercules club' amulets. They are distributed over some eighty find-spots from the Ukraine to England and date from the fourth to tenth centuries. Some are circular in section and ornamented with bands of incised lines; examples include those from Perdöhl, Schwerin (Werner 1964) and Lackford, Suffolk (Lethbridge 1951); others are rectangular in section and are more commonly ornamented with ring-and-dot motifs, as on those from Nassington, Northamptonshire (Leeds and Atkinson 1944) and Wallingford (Leeds 1938) as well as Souldern, Oxfordshire (Kennett 1975). Others have incised lines, as at Spong Hill, Norfolk (Hills and Penn 1981). The Wallingford amulets are certainly made from antler tines, whose natural shape is so appropriate that it would be surprising if the major part of this series did not prove to be made from the same source, particularly in view of the favour in which antler was held for the manufacture of the other amulets described above.

Bones from other parts of mammal skeletons occasionally also occur as amulets, although no general preferences can be detected. Examples include a phalanx from an unidentified carnivore, found at Petersfinger, Wiltshire (Leeds and Short 1953), a bone tentatively identified as the pisiform of an ox, from Nassington, Northamptonshire (Leeds and Atkinson 1944), and what is possibly an innominate bone of a sheep from Kingston Down, Kent (G.B. Brown 1915). All of these are grave finds and all are more or less complete bones provided with bronze wire rings for suspension. Meaney (1981) mentions further finds of unidentified bones possibly used as amulets, and adduces modern ethnographic parallels to shed light on their use.

Some instances of fish bone amulets may also be mentioned: finds of various fish bones from Saxon graves at Dunstable, Bedfordshire (C.L. Matthews 1962) and Wallingford, Oxfordshire (Leeds 1938) find an interesting analogue from the Viking settlement at Hedeby, Schleswig-Holstein, where a perforated vertebral centrum was identified (Lepiksaar and Heinrich 1977) as halibut, a species which became the fish to be eaten during fasting (*Heilbutt* — holy fish) and

may have had some special pre-Christian significance. A number of perforated fish vertebrae have been noted from hitherto unpublished excavations in York and East Anglia (Andrew Jones, personal communication), so that the type promises to become better known in the future. Many may have gone unrecognised and different interpretations have been placed on others; hence one possible example from a late Saxon context at Marefair, Northampton has been published as a roller or guide (Oakley and Jones in Williams 1979) and another from medieval Southampton is identified as a gaming piece (Platt and Coleman-Smith 1975).

Finally, amulets made from the teeth of various species may be considered. The simplest of these are unmodified, probably being carried around in a small bag. Examples include a collection of human teeth found in a grave of about the fifth or sixth century at Dunstable, Bedfordshire (C.L. Matthews 1962) and isolated horse and cattle teeth from a number of Anglo-Saxon inhumations (Meaney 1981). The use as amulets of pigs' teeth, particularly in the form of boars' tusks, can be traced back to the late Roman period; they were particularly favoured by Germanic mercenaries and were worn mounted in pairs in bronze or silver sheaths. Boon (1975) discusses examples from Kent, Segontium, Gwent, Silchester, Hampshire and North Wraxall, Wiltshire (see also Hawkes and Dunning 1961), while Continental finds, notably from Monceau-le-Neuf, Aisne, are described by Böhme (1974) and Werner (1949). Some continuation of this tradition is detected by Meaney (1981) in a find from a sixth-century warrior's grave from Stowting, Kent, but most pig's teeth amulets of the Dark Ages are associated with women (perhaps, in Meaney's opinion, evoking fertility rather than ferocity, as in the male equivalent). English examples come from Waterbeach, Cambridgeshire (Meaney 1981), and from Cassington (Leeds and Riley 1942) and Wheatley (Leeds 1917) in Oxfordshire, all perforated for suspension, while one from Londesborough, Yorkshire, is set in a bronze sheath (Swanton 1966). Others, including representatives from Germany, France and Belgium, are discussed by Meaney (1981).

Perforated bears' teeth, as commonly found

in Alamannic and Frankish graves (Garscha 1970; Martin 1976; Sage 1973; other references in Meaney 1981), are not so far recorded in Britain, but Anglo-Saxon beaver teeth are well-known. Evidently it was an animal held in some esteem:[23] the beaver teeth from Ducklington, Oxfordshire (Chambers 1975) and Wigberlow, Derbyshire (Ozane 1963) are mounted in gold, while that from Dunstable, Bedfordshire, was found on a necklace strung with amethysts (C.L. Matthews 1962) and another from Castle Bytham, Lincolnshire, came from a grave containing a jewelled brooch (*Archaeological Journal* 10, 81-2). A further example, from Bidford-on-Avon, Warwickshire, is mounted in bronze and fitted with a suspension ring (Humphreys *et al.* 1923). They are less frequently found on the Continent, but are known from Schretzheim, Baden-Württemberg and Villey-Saint-Étienne, Meuse (Salin 1959).

The teeth of dog, fox and wolf have proved difficult to distinguish from one another, but all have been identified with greater or lesser degrees of certainty from Roman and Anglo-Saxon graves. Two canines of dog or wolf, both perforated for suspension, were found with a sixth-century inhumation at Wheatley, Oxfordshire (Leeds 1917) and another came from Abingdon, Oxfordshire (Leeds and Harden 1936). Other finds are mentioned by Meaney (1981), including two metal-mounted fangs from a *c.* sixth-century woman's grave at Milton-next-Sittingbourne, Kent. G. Clarke (1979) describes two perforated canine teeth of unidentified species found at Lankhills, Hampshire.

Keratinous claws of birds or animals may have been more common as amulets than the surviving tentative indications might suggest. These include a terminal phalanx of a white-tailed eagle (which may have been buried with the claw intact) from Alfriston, Sussex (Griffith 1914) and a sixth-century perforated animal claw from Glen Parva, Lincolnshire (R.A. Smith 1907). Meaney (1981) suggests that the carnivore phalanx from Petersfinger mentioned above (p. 109) may have been worn with the claw still attached and finds several literary references to the use of claw amulets ranging from the time of Pliny to the present century.

Ivory 'Bag Rings' (Figure 62)

Large-diameter ivory rings occur in numerous early post-Roman graves, and over forty find spots have been noted in England alone by Myres and Green (1973). They pose problems on two fronts: the first is concerned with function, the second and more important with the origin of the raw material.

In general, these rings are of comparatively large size, reaching some 15cm or more in diameter; they are usually sub-rectangular or D-shaped in section, having a maximum width in the region of 2.5cm. A surface examination of the structural features of the ivory shows that each ring represents a single transverse section, cut near the root where the tusk is developed to its maximum diameter and where the pulp-cavity forms a natural internal void (p. 17). Since ivory has a tendency to delaminate with time and an adverse environment, the majority of these rings survive only in fragmentary form. On occasion, as in the case of a discovery at Mitcham, Surrey, delamination has been so complete as to lead the excavators to believe that the ring had originally been built up from a number of individual sections (Bidder and Morris 1959), but this is certainly erroneous. Evidence of contemporary repairs suggests that in some instances this process of disintegration may already have begun before burial: one example from Beckford, Worcestershire (Figure 62b), incorporates two pairs of thin bronze plates each joined by radially-set rivets; quite possibly they were intended to clamp together the constituent lamellae already showing a tendency to split apart, although they could equally well have been designed to repair accidental breaks. Similar repairs have been carried out on rings from Hundsbach (R. Koch 1967) and Marktoberdorf (Christlein 1966), both in Bayern.

The widely-held opinion that these rings were used as bangles seems no longer tenable. One example, found with a skeleton in a grave at Mitcham, Surrey, was said at one point to have been discovered 'on the left fore arm' (Bidder and Morris 1959), but elsewhere is stated as having been found 'where the left arm should have been' (ibid.); another, from Driffield, Yorkshire, occurred 'near the right wrist' of the skeleton of a young woman (Mortimer 1905). In both instances the impli-

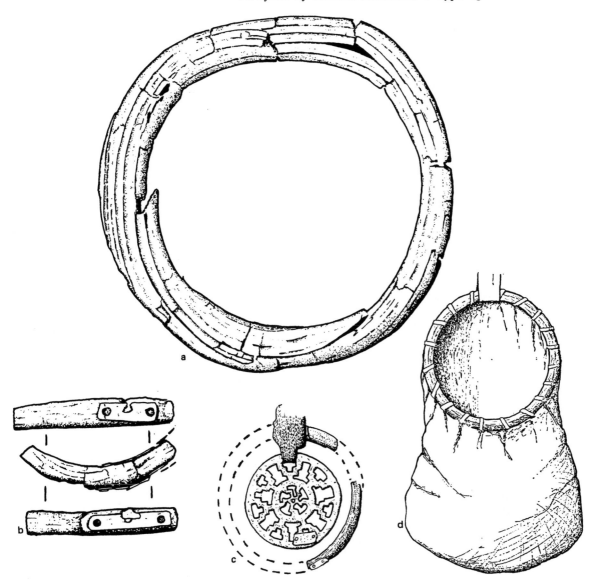

Figure 62:   Ivory bag rings from (a, b) Beckford and (c) Marktoktoberdorf (Christlein); (d) reconstruction after Myres and Green (scale (a-b) 2:3)

cation is that the rings were found alongside the hips and this accords with the position most frequently noted elsewhere, and with the contention that they were worn suspended from the waist, either as part of a châtelaine or in association with a bag.[24] A convincing reconstruction, reproduced in Figure 62d, is offered by Myres and Green (1973), who note that these objects are almost invariably found with the remains of women. On the Continent a number of rings have been found in Alamannic graves associated with pierced bronze discs (Christlein 1966; R. Koch 1967; U. Koch 1977; Vogt 1960). The possibility that the discs served as closing flaps for pouches similar to those described above is attractive, but several instances have been noted in which the disc and the ring are joined by a rigid bronze band (Christlein 1966; Vogt 1960). Vogt offers an alternative method of reconstructing such a bag which, on the evidence of Alamannic finds, was normally of leather: in this hypothesis, the ivory ring and the bronze disc together provided the means of closure (Figure 62c).

With regard to the source of the ivory, the possibilities have already been discussed elsewhere (p. 40). It may simply be reiterated here that utilisation of locally-obtained fossil ivory should not be ruled out at this stage. Furthermore, David Brown has pointed out (personal communication) that although exotic imports from the Mediterranean can be found in a considerable number of Anglo-Saxon graves, they tend to be associated with burials of later date than those of the fifth to sixth centuries, which produce these rings. Myres and Green (1973) may be correct in their assertion that ivory rings were imported from this area, perhaps through the agency of Byzantium (in a finished condition, to judge from the absence of other contemporary artefacts in this material), but they must have arrived by some quite different commercial mechanism from that which introduced the other Mediterranean material.

Bracelets (Figure 63)

All the bracelets considered here are of late Roman origin and of a single basic type. All are made from slender strips of bone, antler or ivory, averaging 5mm in width and 2mm in thickness, and being ovoid or rectangular in section; the strips are bent into a circle of c. 7cm diameter and the ends are fastened together by one of a variety of techniques, the latter providing the only means of distinguishing different groups.

A series of forty-two bracelets recovered from the Lankhills cemetery at Winchester, Hampshire, has provided a useful basis for typological classification, from which three basic groups have emerged (G. Clarke 1979). In the first of these (Figure 63a), the two ends of the bone strip are transversely ribbed and are frequently pierced as well; the ends are enclosed in a sheath of sheet bronze (or, occasionally, silver), held in place by being pressed into the depressions on the bone. No rivets were found at Lankhills with bracelets of this type, even those with drilled ends; conceivably the holes could have been used to pull the ends together while the bracelet was being shaped. The second type (Figure 63b) has plain terminals, joined within a plain cylindrical sheath, each end being fixed in place by a single iron rivet; bronze sleeves are most common, but others of iron are also recorded. In Clarke's third type (Figure 63c) there is no sleeve, the ends of the bracelet simply being tapered, overlapped, and riveted in place. All these types were current in the fourth century, the first-mentioned group perhaps predominating in the latter part of the century.

All but two of the Lankhills bracelets are undecorated and plain bracelets with various terminals predominate elsewhere, for example at Catterick (Hildyard 1958) and York (RCHM 1962) in Yorkshire, at Lydney Park (Bathurst 1879) and Gloucester (Hassal and Rhodes 1974) in Gloucestershire, Chew Valley Lake, Avon (Rahtz and Greenfield 1977) and Chichester, Sussex (Down 1979). Decorated examples are also known, however. In addition to one example from Lankhills, flanked on either side of the sleeve by three transverse grooves and multiple oblique ones,

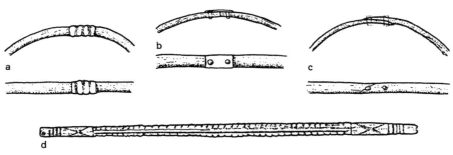

Figure 63: Bracelets (scale 3:4): junctions with (a) ribbed sleeves (b) plain sleeves and rivets (c) overlap and rivets (after Clarke); (d) expanded bracelet with carved ornament from Richborough (Bushe-Fox)

decorated bracelets come from Portchester, Hampshire (Cunliffe 1975) and Richborough, Kent (Bushe-Fox 1926). E. Keller (1971) illustrates plain and ornamental bracelets from Südbayern, including two from Valley, each ornamented with a single row of incised ring-and-dot motifs, and a broad version from München-Harlaching with occasional large motifs separated by two rows of smaller ring-and-dot ornament.

Ivory bracelets are less common in the Roman period, but G. Clarke (1979) lists eighteen from Lankhills. Of these, two formed unbroken circles and were judged to be transverse sections of tusk. The remainder incorporated sleeves of bronze or silver which were judged perhaps to have joined two semi-circles which, on the evidence of two bracelets, were thought to have been cut transversely from the tusk. An alternative suggestion put forward by Clarke was that the ivory had been cut as long strips and bent into shape. The problem could be easily resolved by microscopic examination of the ivory structure, which is quite distinctly different in the longitudinal and transverse axes.

The means by which the strips of bone or antler (and, conceivably, ivory) were softened and bent into shape is unknown, but techniques of softening in general are discussed on pp. 63-6.

Additional items identified elsewhere as bracelets are discussed here under amulets (p. 108) and bag rings (pp. 110-12).

Pins (Figure 64)

Until the general adoption of buttons in the medieval period, pins formed one of the principal forms of fastening clothing; others included brooches, straps and ties. Each of these groups is more or less appropriate to a particular kind of garment; the pins discussed here, for example, would not be well suited for use with tight-fitting clothing but are more likely to have been associated with loose cloaks and tunics, presumably made in fairly open-weave material. It is clear, however, that quite radical differences in clothing styles may fail to register any changes in the pins themselves. Some attempts to infer variations in clothing styles in this way have nonetheless been made; Schwarz-Mackensen (1976) has noted that, with

one exception, the women buried at Hedeby in Scandinavian-style dress (represented by a pair of brooches at the shoulders) never have accompanying pins; she has further suggested that the occurrence of bronze or bone pins in certain Viking-period graves on Gotland and their absence from contemporary graves at Birka suggests a different (or additional) element in the dress worn on Gotland at this time. In analyses of this kind, however, the possibility that different burial practices rather than different modes of dress may be represented must be borne in mind: the dearth of pins from graves at Birka, for example, is not matched by a corresponding scarcity from the settlement area where, on the contrary, bone pins are very numerous (Kristina Ambrosiani, personal communication).

The fact that some bone pins would have been used as hair pins must also be borne in mind. The remains of a young Roman woman discovered at York included a bun of hair at the back of the head held in place by a number of polygonal-headed pins of jet (RCHM 1962). The same function has been noted for metal pins of the Roman and Merovingian periods on the Continent (Schwarz-Mackensen 1976), and in Anglo-Saxon England the position in which certain pins have been found in inhumation burials also suggests some use as hair pins (G.R. Owen 1976). Evidence for this practice is harder to find in the Viking period (Schwarz-Mackensen 1976) but it certainly occurs in western Scandinavia (Kristina Ambrosiani, personal communication).

It is interesting to note that the Roman hair pins mentioned above, along with many jet pins of the Roman period, are identical in form with contemporary examples in bone. The same is true of certain metal (mostly bronze) pins, but in this case the relationship may have been technological rather than purely stylistic. The likelihood that bone originals were used for preparing moulds for casting bronze pins has been borne out by the discovery of clay moulds with impressions made by associated bone pins at a number of Scottish sites, including Dunadd, Strathclyde, the Mote of Mark, Dumfries and Galloway, and the Brough of Birsay, Orkney (Stevenson 1955a; C.L. Curle 1982).

Whereas antler was favoured above bone in the production of many categories of artefact, it seems that limb bones were generally more

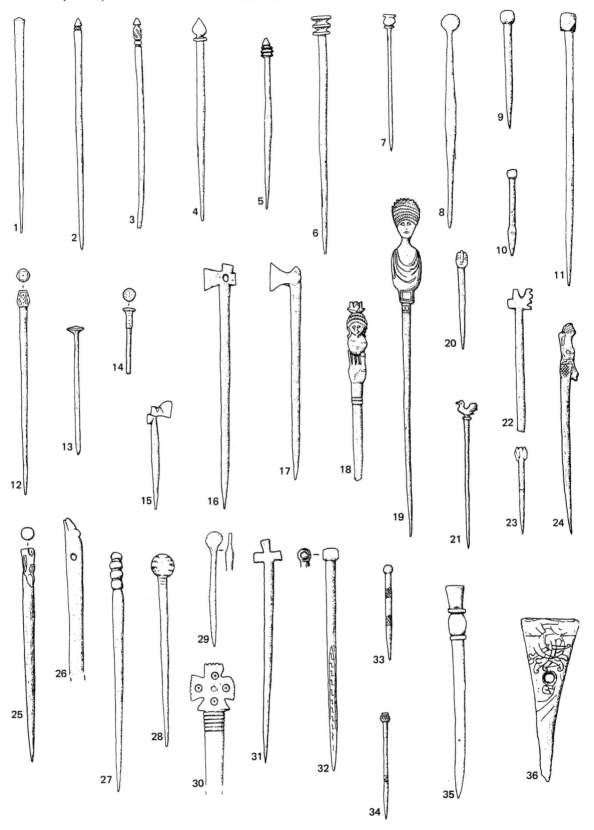

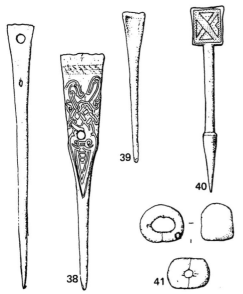

Figure 64: Pins (scale 1:2): headless from (1) York (2) Gadebridge (Neal (3) Scole (Rogerson) (4) Portchester (Cunliffe) (5) Colchester (Crummy); bead and reel from (6) Portchester (Cunliffe) (7) Chalk (Johnston); spherical from (8) Chalk (Johnston) (9-10) Burrian; polygonal from (11) Portchester (Cunliffe) (12) York; nail from (13) Chalk (Johnston) (14) Jarlshof; axe from (15) Scole (Rogerson) (16-17) Jarlshof; anthropomorphic from (18, 19) London (20) Denny Abbey (Christie and Coad); zoomorphic from (21) Lydney (Bathurst) (22) Portchester (Cunliffe) (23) Burrian (24) Jarlshof (25) York (26) unprovenanced, Ashmolean Museum; segmented from (27) Driffield (Mortimer); disc from (28) Lincoln; small disc from (29) Burrian; cruciform from (30) Bury (31) Jarlshof; loose ring from (32) York; thistle from (33) Buston (34) Buckqouy (35) Jarlshof; expanded from (36) London (37) York (38) London; pig fibula from (39) Burrian; late hipped pin from (40) Birka; pin head from (41) Burrian

popular for making pins. With the exception of the pig fibula pins discussed below, in which one end of the whole bone is used without a great deal of alteration, most pins are cut from the sides of limb bones of large ungulates, mostly horses and cattle. Since all identifying characteristics are usually lost in this process, little can yet be said with greater precision about patterns of utilisation. Occasional traces of cancellous tissue or the occurrence of other features identifying the raw materials as limb bones are all that we have to guide us; the small perforation in a pin from York Minster (Figure 64 no. 37) for example, is the natural nutrient foramen of such a bone, connecting the periosteum with the medullary cavity (pp. 8-9). The discovery of antler rough-outs and finished pins in a context dated about 300 at Chalk, Kent (D.E. Johnston 1972) has, however, been taken to indicate that antler also played some part in this industry.

In view of the ready availability of raw materials and the comparatively simple preparative processes necessary for some of the plainer pins, many of these would have been manufactured by the individual as required. It seems likely that many of the pig fibula pins, for example, would fall into this category. At the other end of the scale, some highly competent pins, such as those with zoomorphic heads, carved to very high standards (pp. 118-19), seem to speak of professional production. Manufacturing sites are occasionally identified: one Roman production site has been mentioned above and another is reported from Cambridge (*Britannia* 7, 341). Unfinished Viking age pins were found at Jarlshof, Shetland (Hamilton 1956) and other suggestions of on-the-spot manufacture have been found at Hedeby, (Schwarz-Mackensen 1976). Elsewhere only stray examples of unfinished pins can be found to suggest localised preparation: examples of roughly-whittled blanks for pins have been found at Gadebridge Park, Hertfordshire (Neal 1974), Winteringham, Lincolnshire (Stead 1976), and Buston Crannog, Strathclyde (Munro 1882). All show traces of working with knives only. Few pins have been found to be lathe-turned, although some Roman examples apparently were (e.g., Gracie and Price 1979). In the medieval period lathe-turning seems to provide an almost infallible indicator that the object in question is a parchment-pricker (pp. 124-5) rather than a pin.

Two principal components may be considered in a typological classification of pins, namely the shank and the head. Some pins lack a head of any kind, the upper end of the shank simply terminating in a straight cut or a rounded or pointed end. In the case of these headless pins the shank is either straight (parallel) sided and tapered only at the tip, or else it tapers smoothly along its entire length. On the other hand, while some pins with distinct heads have shanks which fall into one or other of these categories, many of them also taper from the centre towards the head, resulting in a marked swelling in the middle of the shank. This swelling would have had the effect of holding the pin more securely in position when it had been thrust through the weave of the material (or, indeed, through the hair). Some pins, notably those of about the seventh or eighth centuries, have bands of incised lines or cross-hatching around the shank (Figure 64, nos. 33-4) which, in addition to any decorative value, would have had the virtue of impeding any tendency for the pin to slip out of position. Another more effective measure to keep the pin in place was the development on the shank of distinct hips (Figure 64, no. 10), formed by a sharp expansion about two-thirds of the way towards the tip. Stevenson (1955a) has suggested a late Roman or fifth-century origin for these hipped pins, but so far none has been found in a context demonstrably earlier than the sixth century. Early examples come from Little Wilbraham, Cambridgeshire (Lethbridge 1951), Burwell, Cambridgeshire (Fox 1923) and Shakenoak, Oxfordshire (Brodribb *et al.* 1972). Those few that are known on the Continent appear to be no earlier than the British examples and indeed are thought to be derived from them (Roes 1963). Bronze hipped pins dating from about the eighth to the tenth centuries come from York (D.M. Waterman 1959), Whitby (Peers and Radford 1943) and Southampton (Addyman and Hill 1969), while Huggins (1975) illustrates a contemporary example from Waltham Abbey, Essex. The final appearance of hips is on a series of short pins of the eleventh or twelfth centuries, discussed on p. 121.

While some distinctions can, therefore, be made on the basis of the shank, the top of the pin, with or without a distinct head, usually provides more diagnostic features. A selection of some of the more commonly-encountered types follows.

Headless Pins (Figure 64, nos. 1-3)

Although lacking a head, pins of this type are made with equal care to that of their more ornamental counterparts. The top of the pin may be flat or slightly conical. The shaft invariably tapers smoothly from its widest point at the head to the tip, and never has a central swelling. N. Crummy (1979) has suggested that this type belongs to the earlier part of the Roman period, finally losing its popularity during the first half of the third century. Support for this assertion comes from finds at York (MacGregor 1976b), Leicester (Kenyon 1948), Gadebridge Park, Hertfordshire (Neal 1974) and Dover, Kent (Philp 1981). Others have been recovered from later deposits, but are susceptible of being residual.

One group of these pins features a rather narrow top to the shank, around which one or more grooves are cut circumferentially; occasionally an area is left in reserve between two of the grooves, to be decorated with oblique incisions or other ornamental features. The occurrence of a pin of this type in a Claudian context at Chichester, Sussex (Down 1978), demonstrates an early start to its currency which, to judge from data collected by N. Crummy (1979), terminated contemporaneously with undecorated pins of the same form. Recent finds from Dover (Philp 1981) tend to confirm Crummy's conclusions, which were based on a survey of ten British sites.

Conical-headed Pins with Flanged Shanks (Figure 64, nos. 4-5)

On this type of pin an enlarged head terminating in a conical tip may have, immediately below it, from one to five flanges, projecting from the top of the shank. On evidence from Portchester (Cunliffe 1975) and Clausentum (Cotton and Gathercole 1958) in Hampshire, from Gadebridge Park, Hertfordshire (Neal 1974) and Colchester, Essex, N. Crummy (1979) postulates a life-span for the type from the mid-second century to the late fourth or early fifth centuries. Corroboration for this claim is given by finds from Frocester Court, Gloucestershire (Gracie and Price 1979), Chew Valley Lake, Avon (Rahtz and Greenfield 1977), Chichester, Sussex (Down 1977) and Springhead, Kent (Penn 1968), all dating to the third or fourth centuries. The type did not survive the Roman period.

Bead-and-reel Headed Pins (Figure 64, nos. 6-7)

N. Crummy (1979) dates this type from about 200 until the late fourth or early fifth centuries, the earliest example coming from Chichester and being dated tentatively to the second century or later (Down 1974). The type was among those apparently being made at Chalk, Kent (D.E. Johnston 1972).

Spherical-headed Pins (Figure 64, nos. 8-10)

N. Crummy (1979) suggests that this type does not make an appearance until about 200. Support for this claim comes from Scole, Norfolk (Rogerson 1977), Icklingham, Suffolk (West and Plouviez 1976), Latimer, Buckinghamshire (Branigan 1971), Billingsgate, London (D.M. Jones 1980) and Dover (Philp 1981). Stephen Greep (personal communication), however, has established that the type is represented by the mid-second century at Walbrook, London, and elsewhere.

Although they decline in numbers from the fifth century, some continuity up to the Norman period can be demonstrated. Examples from Little Wilbraham, Cambridgeshire (Lethbridge 1931), Swindon, Wiltshire (unpublished) and Sarre, Kent (Payne 1892), combining spherical heads with short hipped shanks, date from the sixth or seventh centuries, and from about this time the type takes on a vigorous new lease of life in the north. Since a review of these Scottish pins was published by Stevenson (1955a), new finds have come from Dark Age sites at À Cheardach Mhor, South Uist (Young and Richardson 1960), Dun Cuier, Barra (Young 1956) and Dùn an Fheurain, Strathclyde (J.N.G. Ritchie 1971), while others have come from Viking age levels at Jarlshof, Shetland (Hamilton 1956) and at Buckquoy, Orkney (A. Ritchie 1977). In England spherical headed bone pins found at York (Waterman 1959) and at Cuerdale, Lancashire (where they were thought to have secured a bag containing a silver hoard of about 903) (T.D. Kendrick 1941),[25] may owe their presence to Norse influence, although discoveries of similar pins of bronze, probably of *c.* eighth to tenth-century date at Whitby, Yorkshire (Peers and Radford 1943), York (D.M. Waterman 1959)

and Southampton (Addyman and Hill 1959), may point to a parallel survival in the south. Spherical-headed bone pins make a final appearance in the eleventh and twelfth centuries with the series of short hipped pins discussed on p. 121.

Polygonal-headed Pins (Figure 64, nos. 11-12)

The term describes pins with heads in the form of a cube with chamfered corners. On evidence from Colchester and elsewhere, N. Crummy (1979) postulates an introduction for this type from the mid third century. Two examples were found amongst possible pin-making debris dated *c.* 300 at Chalk, Kent (D.E. Johnston 1972), and jet pins of the same form were found in the preserved hair of an adolescent female burial at York (RCHM 1962).

Although they occur in bronze in the Anglo-Saxon cemeteries at Shudy Camps, Cambridgeshire (Lethbridge 1936) and at Lackford, Suffolk (Lethbridge 1951) and in later Saxon contexts at Whitby (Peers and Radford 1943), York (D.M. Waterman 1959) and Southampton (Addyman and Hill 1969), there appear to be no firmly-dated post-Roman examples in bone before the Viking period, when they occur at York (D.M. Waterman 1959). The heads of these later pins are proportionally smaller than those of the Roman period and the facets are decorated with incised ornament. Others were found in post-Roman contexts under York Minster, but the presence of residual Roman material in the same layers has made it impossible to decide on their true date (MacGregor, forthcoming). Jankuhn (1943) illustrates an example in wood from the Viking age settlement of Hedeby, but the type is not represented among the bone pins from that site (Schwarz-Mackensen 1976), nor among those from the other major Scandinavian settlements.

Nail-headed Pins (Figure 64, nos. 13-14)

A Roman origin for this type is demonstrated by finds from York (MacGregor 1978b), Gadebridge Park, Hertfordshire (Neal 1974), Leicester (Kenyon 1948), Shakenoak, Oxfordshire (Brodribb *et al.* 1968, 1971), Frocester Court, Gloucestershire (Gracie and Price 1979) and Portchester, Hampshire (Cunliffe 1975), ranging in date from the third to the fourth centuries. From well beyond the northerly Roman frontier comes an example from broch-period levels at Clickhimin, Shetland (Hamilton 1968). Others probably of the seventh to ninth century come from the Broch of Burrian, Orkney (MacGregor 1974), Dunadd (Stevenson 1955a) and Buston Crannog (Munro 1882), both in Strathclyde, and the Mote of Mark, Dumfries and Galloway (Stevenson 1955a), as well as from Cahercommaun, Clare (Hencken 1938). Burrian and Buston both produced bronze pins of the same pattern. Hamilton (1956) illustrates two Viking age bone pins of this type from Jarlshof, Shetland, both with plain collars extending for about 1cm below the head.

Axe-headed Pins (Figure 64, nos. 15-17)

Pins of widely differing forms were carved with axe-shaped heads in the late Roman period; they vary from small but realistically-proportioned types like those from Scole, Norfolk (Rogerson 1977), Lincoln (Figure 64, no. 15) and Richborough, Kent (Bushe-Fox 1949) to a large but ineffectual-looking example from Leicester (Kenyon 1948).

In the centuries immediately following the Roman period the type falls from favour, although some examples of distinct style from the Frisian terps illustrated by Roes (1963) may be of Merovingian date. Others are more probably of Viking origin and it is to this period that three examples from Jarlshof, Shetland, belong (Hamilton 1956). References to parallels in metal are given in Schwarz-Mackensen (1976).

Anthropomorphic Pins (Figure 64, nos. 18-20)

Roman pins of this type include one group showing an outstretched hand and another carved with a human head. A series of pins showing a hand, many of them holding a bead between the thumb and forefinger, is illustrated by von Gonzenbach (1951), all of them apparently of the first or second centuries. Other examples come from Richborough, Kent (Bushe-Fox 1932, 1949). Down (1978) tentatively identifies a small socketed bronze hand of this type as the head of a bone pin.

Pins showing human heads vary from clumsily-executed types such as those from Icklingham, Suffolk (West and Plouviez 1976) to artistically-made versions showing a female bust with an elaborate coiffure or head-dress, such as those illustrated by J. Curle (1911) from Newstead, by Bushe-Fox (1949) from Richborough and by the British Museum *Guide* (1964). A pin in the Museum of London (Wheeler 1930) shows such a bust held in an outstretched hand, a type represented in Continental excavations of the first and early second centuries (von Gozenbach 1951).

Both of these Roman types can be identified with some certainty as hair pins rather than dress pins, and examples are known in bronze and in precious metal as well as in bone (von Gonzenbach 1951). The symbolic significance of this series has been discussed by Henig (1977), while hands holding eggs or pomegranates are treated by Arthur (1977).

Post-Roman finds of pins with human features are rare; excavations at Denny Abbey, Cambridgeshire (Christie and Coad 1980) produced one example (Figure 64, no. 20) from a twelfth-century context, but the presence of quantities of residual Roman material on the site means that an earlier origin for the pin cannot be ruled out. Hencken (1950) illustrates two pins with human heads from Lagore Crannog, Meath, but otherwise they do not appear to have been favoured after the end of the Roman period.

Zoomorphic Pins (Figure 64, nos. 21-6)

Although they are not common in the Roman period, pins with zoomorphic heads occur occasionally at this time. The most common type, found at Gadebridge Park, Hertfordshire (Neal 1974), Lydney Park, Gloucestershire (Bathurst 1879) and Chichester, Sussex (Down 1978) takes the form of a cockerel, perhaps alluding to Mercury. This scarcity continues in the succeeding centuries: a single example, found at the Broch of Burrian, Orkney, and featuring two horses' heads, dates from about the seventh or eighth century (MacGregor 1974). The closest analogies for this piece include a bronze pin in the National Museum of Ireland (E.C.R. Armstrong 1922), and an example in bone carved with two opposed birds from a Frisian terp illusrated by

Roes 1963. The National Museum of Antiquities in Edinburgh has in its collection a stray find from North Uist, in the form of a pin with a bird-like head arranged at a right-angle to a swelling shank. All of these pins are probably broadly contemporary with that from Burrian, while two zoomorphic pins from Lagore, Meath (Hencken 1950) may be a little later in date.

Four zoomorphic pins from Jarlshof, Shetland, are all closely related stylistically and are probably the products of a single craftsman. The discovery of two unfinished pins of this type at Jarlshof indicates that they were being made on site. The heads of these pins are aligned with the shank (Figure 64, no. 24), a fact which Hamilton (1956) has contrasted with the normal practice with 'native' pins on which the heads tend to be arranged at right angles to the shank (see above). All are carved to a high standard, a characteristic particularly noted on other Viking age zoomorphic types in Schwarz-Mackensen's (1976) survey of pins from Hedeby, Schleswig-Holstein. Here pins closely comparable with those from Jarlshof are shown from Traelnes in Norway and Sigtuna, Sweden, together with related types in which the ornament is purely incised, as from York (Figure 64, no. 25). Several of them have a perforation through the head or between the jaws, a feature found on a further group of more robust pins whose heads terminate in stylised jaws or beaks. Schwarz-Mackensen illustrates examples from Hedeby and from Birka in Sweden; the example shown here (Figure 64, no. 26) from an unknown source, is in the Ashmolean Museum, Oxford.

The taste for zoomorphic treatment survived to the ultimate phase of bone pin production, for among the small-hipped pins of *c.* twelfth-century date discussed below are some carved in the form of a cockerel and bearing a disconcerting resemblance to the Roman pins which began the series.

Segmented-head Pins (Figure 64, no. 27)

Few representatives of this type have so far been noted, yet despite their apparent rarity they clearly form a well-developed type of which more representatives may yet be expected. Bone pins of this type have been found at Driffield (Mortimer 1905) and at Whitby (Peers and Radford 1943), both in

Yorkshire. Comparable examples in bronze have been noted from Culbin Sands, Grampian Region, and Birsay, Orkney, by Laing (1973). Their form recalls the segmented glass beads occasionally found in Anglo-Saxon graves.[26]

Disc-headed Pins (Figure 64, no. 28)

Laing (1973) and Stevenson (1955a) claim a Roman origin for this type, though they do not appear to be common at this time. It seems equally possible that the scarce bone pins in this series evolved from the better-known disc-headed bronze pins of late Saxon date, in which the heads were formed by hammering out the end of the shank into a large flat field or by fitting a separately-wrought disc head. Examples of the former type, stamped with ring-and-dot motifs, are known from York (D.M. Waterman 1959), Whitby (Peers and Radford 1943) and Southampton (Addyman and Hill 1969). A more ambitious example with a composite head ornamented with a cruciform design (originally one of a suite of three linked pins) was found at Birdoswald, Cumbria (Cramp 1964) while a similar pin, bearing a representation of two confronted winged beasts comes from York (Cramp 1967). Scottish metal pins with disc heads include a group in silver found with the late ninth-century hoard from Talnotrie, Strathclyde and a more modest but carefully-executed pin from the Broch of Burray, Orkney (Stevenson 1955a). The eighth or ninth-century date suggested by these metal pins agrees with that postulated for the few bone pins of this type from the Continent, all of them from the Frisian terps (Roes 1963). The few stratified examples of this type from England, include one of probable Middle Saxon date from Northampton (Oakley in Williams 1979) and one from an eleventh-century context at Lincoln. An unprovenanced example now in the British Museum is illustrated by Jessup (1950).

Small Disc-headed Pins (Figure 64, no. 29)

A group of short pins with flattened heads, sometimes forming a complete disc and sometimes cut away on the underside to form a fan shape, seems at present to have a predominantly Scottish distribution and to be absent in the Roman period. A few examples are now known in the south, however, including one from York (York Archaeological Trust, unpublished) and a group from Swindon, Wiltshire;[27] one example in bronze was found at Whitby (Peers and Radford 1943). Several bone pins of this type are also known from the Frisian area (Roes 1963).

Cruciform-headed Pins (Figure 64, nos. 30-1)

Jarlshof in Shetland has produced two of the cruciform-headed pins so far noted, one (Curle *et al.* 1954) an early find and the other (Hamilton 1956) from more recent excavations at the site. A more elaborate example now in the Ashmolean Museum, Oxford, comes from Bury, Suffolk, while an unpublished cruciform pin from Roscommon, now in the British Museum, has a markedly expanded upper arm and smaller cross bars, strongly reminiscent of a styliform pin from Whitby Monastery (Peers and Radford 1943). Some at least may have some Christian significance: a tenth or eleventh-century date seems most likely for all of them.

Loose Ring-headed Pins (Figure 64, no. 32)

Although this type is undoubtedly best suited to production in metal and bone, representatives are unlikely to be numerous, though some finds have already been made. One example from York is illustrated in Figure 64, no. 32, and another is in Norwich Castle Museum (D.M. Waterman 1959), the latter still fitted with its bronze ring. Other examples of this type, also with the remains of rings *in situ*, come from Hedeby and Birka (Schwarz-Mackensen 1976); the same author illustrates further types of perforated pins, some of which may have had metal or leather rings.

Thistle-headed Pins (Figure 64, nos. 33-5)

Two groups may immediately be distinguished within this class, all of which come from Scotland: on the one hand there are short pre-Norse pins (Figure 64, nos. 33-4) including those from the Broch of Burrian and Buckquoy in Orkney (MacGregor 1974; A. Ritchie 1977) and Buston Crannog in Strathclyde (Munro

1882), and on the other more robust pins (Figure 64, no. 35) such as those found in Shetland at Jarlshof (Hamilton 1956). The Buston pin (Figure 64, no. 32) has a shank ornamented with bands of cross-hatching (see p. 116), while there are three circumferential grooves on the Burrian pin. Those from Jarlshof are all uniform in style, although one of them is from pre-Norse levels and the others are of Viking date.

Expanded-head Pins (Figure 64, nos. 36-8)

Although their shape seems to have been inspired by the natural form of the pig fibula pins discussed below, the expanded heads of these larger pins are not conditioned in the same way by the bones from which they were made. Instead they have been cut from the shafts of limb bones, as can be seen from occasional surviving features (p. 9). The flat expansion at the top (extending in some instances to half the total length of the pin) presents a broad field, which invited decoration, and this opportunity was grasped on a number of examples, most notably in the case of a large paddle-shaped pin from London, decorated with Ringerike-style ornament (Figure 64, no. 38). The type is at present known in England only from the Viking period as at York (D.M. Waterman 1959) and good parallels are to be found in tenth and eleventh-century Scandinavia and northern Germany (Grieg 1933; Schwarz-Mackensen 1976). The similarity of certain late Saxon bronze styli from Whitby, Yorkshire (Peers and Radford 1943) suggests, however, that earlier examples may yet be forthcoming.

Pig Fibula Pins (Figure 64, no. 39)

Pins of this group present an interesting illustration of the way in which specific bones were chosen for specific functions. The fibulae of pig present a shape which immediately recommends itself as a pin: the diaphysis or shaft is neither so thin as to be over-fragile, nor so thick as to need thinning down. At the proximal end it expands to form a natural head while around the middle of the shaft a second area of expansion can either be trimmed off at a stroke while pointing the tip or, by slicing it slightly lower, can be incorporated in the shank of the pin so that it impedes any tendency to slip out of place (see p. 116). The head may be perforated or left intact but, so far as we can tell, there need be no difference in function between the two types. Those with perforated heads have sometimes (Hamilton 1956; Brodribb *et al.* 1972) been claimed as needles, but in most cases this seems unlikely to have been the case, for the perforations rarely show any sign of wear and they often occur on untrimmed heads which would be inconveniently wide for most sewing purposes. On the other hand, some wear has been noted in the perforations on pins from Feltrim Hill, Dublin (Hartnett and Eogan 1964) and Ambrosiani (1981) has suggested that such pins might have been useful for mesh knitting. In most cases, however, the perforations may simply have had a retaining cord passed through them, the pins being used to secure an article of dress in one of two ways. They could have been paired, one at each shoulder, as in some inhumation burials of the Migration Period on the Continent (Nerman 1935) and joined by a cord in the manner of certain Anglo-Saxon union pins (Leeds 1936); alternatively, they could have been used as a primitive form of safety pin, with a cord passed through the perforation and tied around the tip.

Pig fibula pins were mundane, everyday objects and frequently display no great degree of elaboration beyond occasional trimming of the head. This ornamentation is usually limited to cutting down the natural expansion of the articular end to form a distinct head, either squarish in outline or with jagged indentations. These latter pins, which appear to be limited to the Viking period, are the last efflorescence of the type, whose origins can be traced back to the pre-Roman Iron Age. They seem to have been particularly common in Ireland during the Early Christian period — there are 131 from Lagore, Meath (Hencken 1950) and 82 from Cahercommaun, Clare (Hencken 1938), and they occur on broadly contemporary settlements in Scotland (MacGregor 1974; A. Ritchie 1977) and England (Brodribb *et al.* 1972; Leeds 1923). They remain common in the Viking period, as at York (MacGregor 1982a) and at Hedeby (Schwarz-Mackensen 1976), and survive in some numbers from early medieval Scandinavian settlements such as Lund (M. Lindström in Mårtensson 1976), Oslo (Wibert

1977) and Århus (Andersen *et al.* 1971).

Post-Conquest Hipped Pins (Figure 64, no. 40)

In a last burst of popularity before the use of bone pins finally diminished, a new series of hipped pins makes an appearance at, or soon after, the time of the Norman Conquest. They are characterised by rather stubby shanks with well-marked hips, and by prominent heads in a variety of forms. Most common are spherical heads, which may have a perforated loop at the top: one example comes from Pleshey Castle, Essex (F. Williams 1977) and numerous others have recently been published from Castle Acre, Norfolk (S. Margeson in Coad and Streeter 1982). A second variety, with a rectangular head notched round the edges and perforated in the centre, is again represented at Castle Acre and at Pleshey Castle. Winchester, Castle Acre and York have produced a third type featuring a head shaped as a cockerel. Their small size and frequent provision for attachment to a thread or cord suggests some special function for pins of this type, such as the attachment of a particular style of head-dress. The only parallel noted from outside southern England is a single example from Birka in Sweden (Figure 64, no. 40).[28]

Globular Pin-heads (Figure 64, no. 41)

In addition to pins made entirely of bone, as described above, an interesting group of pin heads made of ivory or bone may be noted here, most of them from Scotland and Ireland. Three principal types may be distinguished: a solid variety, usually of antler, known from three Orkney and two mainland Scottish brochs (MacGregor 1974; Stevenson 1955a) and from Buston Crannog, Strathclyde (Munro 1882); a hollow type cut from the shaft of a long-bone, usually sheep, distributed in the north and west of Scotland and in Ireland where there are numerous examples from Ballinderry, Offaly, with one outlier from Corbridge, Northumberland (Hencken 1942; MacGregor 1974; Stevenson 1955a); and a series made from animal teeth, all at present from Orkney (MacGregor 1974; Stevenson 1955a). Stevenson has suggested an origin in Roman pins with large heads of jet. A 'spherical bone handle to an iron tool' of the Roman period from Lydney Park, Gloucestershire (Bathurst 1879), seems to be an example of the solid type of pin-head mentioned above, mounted on an iron pin.

Spectacle Frames (Figure 65)

A recent find from the Trig Lane exacavations in the City of London has added a new category to the list of everyday items made of bone. From a securely-dated mid fifteenth-century context, a pair of bone spectacle frames was recovered, providing at once the earliest dated spectacles yet found in Europe and the only examples in bone. The following description is summarised from accounts of these spectacles published by Michael Rhodes (1980, 1982).

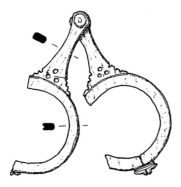

Figure 65:   Spectacle frames from London (after Rhodes) (scale 2:3)

The frames consist of two symmetrical elements of bone,[29] united by, and pivoting about, an iron rivet. Each element comprises a circular rim, seemingly cut with a centre-bit, the inner face being grooved to receive a lens of about 3cm in diameter. The arms by which the rims are joined each feature a wide base, notched with three small holes. Opposite either arm a three-lobed projection is carved on the outer edge of the rim; both rims have been deliberately split through the centre of the projections, which have then been bound tight with copper wire.

The functions of the various features described above have been explained by Rhodes. The triple notches on the arms are designed to improve the grip of the spectacles when clamped to the nose;[30] the fact that they occur on either side presumably indicates that the lenses were identical and were interchangeable between left and right eyes. Rhodes suggests that the lenses were used primarily for close-focusing, being worn low on the nose and allowing the wearer to look over the rims for normal viewing. The pin-holes drilled in the expanded base would have helped relieve the 'blind-spots' created by the arms of the frames projecting in front of the eyes and would themselves have acted as an aid to focusing. Finally, the split projections[31] are explained as a means of allowing the rims to be temporarily expanded to allow the lenses to be fitted, after which the gap was closed by binding with copper wire.

Further references for the early history of spectacles, the importance of the Netherlands in their early production and the development of manufacturing in London from the mid-fifteenth century, are given by Rhodes (1982).

Writing Materials (Figures 66-7)

In the classical world the stylus and waxed tablet were used for a variety of purposes from school exercises and accounting to literary compositions. Two or more tablets were sometimes bound together by rings or thongs to form a *codex* which, as well as for jotting down everyday ephemera, could be used as a legal document whose privacy was ensured by threads or tapes sealed by witnesses. The normally encountered materials are iron and bronze for the styli and wood for the tablet, although ivory tablets are also found (E.M. Thompson 1912). A number of literary references to the use by monks of styli and waxed tablets in Anglo-Saxon England are recorded by Thompson and by Peers and Radford (1943). Waxed tablets dating from the later medieval period are known from Italy and Germany (E.M. Thompson 1912; Warncke 1912), while one example in wood with characters in Irish and Latin still inscribed in the wax is in the National Museum of Ireland (Coffey 1909). An old find from Springmount, Antrim, of an entire 'book' of waxed wooden leaves (Armstrong and Macalister 1920) has taken on a new interest by more recently being dated to the seventh century (Hillgarth 1962). Only one other example of a Dark Age writing tablet is

Figure 66:   Cetacean bone writing tablet (obverse and reverse) from Blythburgh

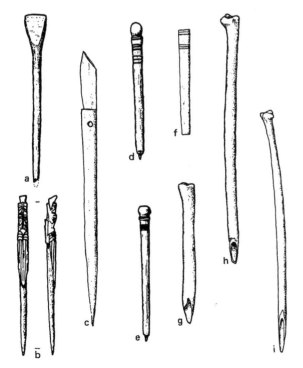

Figure 67:   Writing implements (scale 1:2): styli from (a) Whitby (b) York (c) Lund (Mårtensson); 'prickers' from (d) Whitby (e-f) Jarrow; 'pens' from (g) Norwich (Hurst) (h) Coventry (Hurst) (i) Cambridge

known from the British Isles: this, made of cetacean bone and found at Blythburgh, Suffolk (Figure 66), has a characteristic recessed area in which the wax was spread, and two perforations by which it could have been bound to a second tablet in the manner described above. A seventh or eighth-century date for this piece is indicated by a panel of low-relief interlace carved on its unrecessed face which, to judge from surviving bronze rivets, was originally overlaid with an equal-armed cross (British Museum 1923). Secular writing tablets of later medieval date occur in elephant ivory, often richly carved on their covers with romantic subjects. The main production centres were in France: Koechlin (1924) discusses several examples of fourteenth-century origin, including one in which six leaves coated with wax within raised borders are contained within a pair of ornamented covers, the whole being provided with a protective leather case.

Roman styli of bone seem to be rare in Northern Europe: the large number of objects identified as such from London (Wheeler 1930), for example, are all more likely to be medieval prickers (see below). Iron appears to have been the most favoured material at this time, contrasting with a post-Roman preference for bronze. Of those published examples in bone, one from Whitby, Yorkshire (Peers and Radford 1943) compares broadly in outline with those in metal from the same site, although it lacks the usual circumferential bands on the shank. D.M. Waterman (1959) mentions that some objects with spatulate heads normally identified as pins could have served as styli: one particularly likely example from York (Figure 67b) is carved in dragonesque form, with a projecting spatulate tongue which could have served as an eraser, an essential element on any stylus (D.M. Waterman 1959; see also Ward Perkins 1949).[32] In a forthcoming consideration of writing materials from Winchester, Hampshire, David Brown expresses doubt that styli could ever have been made from bone since, he suggests, it would have been necessary to heat the spatulate end in order to melt the wax and to facilitate erasure. There seems to be no supporting evidence for this theory, however, and indeed the mention of a *corneum graphium* among the personal relics of St Desiderius, who was murdered in the mid-seventh century (quoted in Peers and Radford

1943), may indicate the contrary.[33] Among the items which *could* have served as styli may be included a crutch-headed bone object found at York (York Archaeological Trust, unpublished), which corresponds in shape to certain styli made of metal and to others illustrated in Romanesque manuscript illuminations (reproduced in Mårtensson 1961). The same author illustrates what may have been an alternative form, featuring a blade-like terminal (Figure 67c).

A more common type of bone implement seems to belong to the medieval period. It is characterised by being lathe-turned, with an ovoid or spherical head and a short, tapering or parallel-sided shank; the shank is usually ornamented with one or more bands of multiple incised lines and is invariably tipped with an inset metal point, usually of iron but sometimes of bronze, or even silver. Unstratified examples from London have been published as of Roman origin (Wheeler 1930), and others from Whitby have been associated with the Saxon material from that site (Peers and Radford 1943), but all are likely to have come from medieval levels.[34] Others of equally equivocal stratigraphic origin come from Jarrow, Tyne and Wear, where one example, lacking a ball head and terminating instead in a flat top (Figure 67f), may be of pre-Conquest date (Professor Rosemary Cramp, personal communication). A group of five such implements come from a thirteenth-century well at York Minster (MacGregor, forthcoming), while two further examples from Southampton (both lacking their tips but almost certainly styli rather than pins, as published) are from the thirteenth and early fourteenth centuries respectively (Platt and Coleman-Smith 1975). Examples of similar date come from Norwich (Clarke and Carter 1977), Oxford (Henig, in Durham 1977), London (Tatton-Brown 1974) and Eynsford Castle, Kent (Rigold 1971), while others have been noted from a late fourteenth or fifteenth century context at Bordesley Abbey, Worcestershire (Rahtz and Hirst 1976) and from sixteenth-century rubble at Ospringe, Kent (G.H. Smith 1979).

While the medieval date of these objects may, therefore, be taken as certain, their function has not hitherto been convincingly explained. Their identification by several of the above authors as styli is difficult to support, since all these objects lack the essential spatulate eraser at the head, while the metal tips featured by all the complete examples show that they are certainly not pins. In his forthcoming report on writing materials from the Winchester excavations, David Brown makes the convincing suggestion that these implements are in fact parchment prickers. It was the custom of medieval scribes to lay out the pages of their manuscripts with great care (see Ivy 1958). Vertical margins were drawn at the edges of each column and horizontal lines guided the hand of the scribe in his task. The spacing of these horizontal lines was controlled by a series of small pricked holes on either side of the page: variations in the positioning of these holes — whether within the text area, on the inner and outer margins, at the extreme edges of the page, executed before or after the page was folded — all have been shown to be of significance in assigning manuscripts to particular *scriptoria*, or to a particular period of time (see, for example, Lowe 1935; Ker 1960). The character and alignment of the prickings can be equally illuminating to the expert eye (L.W. Jones 1946). The advantage of pricking manuscripts in this manner lay in the way that several pages could be laid out at any one time by superimposing two or more bifolia and pricking through several leaves at once. Coveney (1958) states that the normal Late Saxon insular practice was for an entire quire of four double leaves to be folded and pricked at once. Subsequent ruling could also be carried out on more than one sheet at a time since, at least until the mid-twelfth century, ruling was executed with a dry point, which made a furrow on the upper side of each sheet of parchment (often the hair side) and a corresponding ridge on the reverse. The lead point or plummet progressively replaced the dry point from around the twelfth century and was in turn superseded by ink in the fifteenth (Diringer 1953; L.W. Jones 1946).

Since some of the implements described here seem to be from after the twelfth century, it seems unlikely that they can correspond to the dry point used for ruling (*ligniculum*), as this practice had lapsed by that time. It remains a distinct possibility, however, that they could be prickers, since pricking outlasted dry point ruling. Early sources mention two categories of pricker: the *circinus*, denoting compasses or dividers with sharp points, and the awl, *subula* or *punctorium*. L.W. Jones (1946) discusses various forms of perforation which could have resulted from each of these implements (as well as a putative pricking wheel provided with multiple spikes); among these are circular holes similar to those which might be made by the items being considered here. In addition, Brown comments on the useful 'shoulder' formed by the bottom of the shank, which would prevent the iron tip from penetrating too deeply and forming an undesirably large hole. The overall size of the implement is well suited to this use while the ball head, so inappropriate for a stylus, *may* have served as a burnisher to treat small blemishes in the parchment, since many of them show signs of wear or polishing on some part of the head.[35]

Further categories of writing equipment may be noted here. A number of goose radii with obliquely cut and pointed ends have been tentatively identified as medieval pens. Hurst (1965) describes one from a thirteenth or early fourteenth-century pit at Barn Road, Norwich, and three more from Coventry, West Midlands. Other examples come from broadly contemporary contexts at St Aldates, Oxford (Henig, in Durham 1977), Boston, Lincolnshire (Moorhouse 1972), Leicester (Mellor and Pearce 1981) and London (Tatton-Brown 1974). Hitherto unpublished examples are in the Museum of London collection and in the Ashmolean Museum, Oxford (Figure 67l), the latter found in Cambridge; another has been found more recently in the excavation of the College of the Vicars Choral at York (York Archaeological Trust, unpublished). In a discussion of this type of objects, Biek (in Hurst 1965) notes that they lack the split ends which give added flexibility and, perhaps, capillarity, to quill pens, but concludes that they could have been used as lining pens if loaded with viscous ink and held with the open side upwards, almost horizontally. The similarity in form of a Roman bronze pen from London (Wheeler 1930) is of interest here, although the 'nib' on this Roman implement is cleft. Residues of ink on those from Coventry were deemed to be of doubtful antiquity, but the pieces from York and Boston certainly have contemporary ink stains on them. An alternative function suggested by Biek was for scooping out or measuring quantities of softened oak galls for preparation with boiling water as ink, while other suggestions made elsewhere (in Moorhouse 1972) include pipettes for charging quill pens and 'economisers' for broken quills, the end of the quill being inserted into the hollow bone.

Brief reference may be made to parts of two pen cases of eleventh or early twelfth-century English workmanship, one (of maple wood) found in Lund, Sweden (Blomqvist and Mårtensson 1963) and the other of walrus ivory from London (Beckwith 1972). The sliding lid of the London case is made from a single piece of material, but the sides are jointed and riveted together in the middle; the joints may formerly have been covered by metal plates.

From later in the medieval period come two horn ink-wells now in the Museum of London (London Museum 1940) both making use of the natural hollow cylindrical shape of the raw material.

Also of interest in this context is the interpretation placed on a bone plate inscribed with a runic legend on one side and acquired (though not necessarily found) in Derby. Bately and Evison (1961) have suggested that it might have been used as a ruler or spatulate implement for turning pages of manuscripts, or as a reading aid, adding that the two holes at one end could have served for the attachment of a ribbon or strap, the whole forming a decorative book mark.

Seal Matrices (Figures 68-9)

Although the use of wax seals in conjunction with writing tablets is known from the Roman period (p. 122), it was not until the late Saxon period that matrices for use in sealing letters made their appearance, the earliest known example being the bronze matrix of Bishop Ethilwald of Dunwich, now in the British Museum (British Museum 1923). This example dates most probably from the 860s, from which time there also survives a series of orders issued

Figure 68:   Seal matrix of walrus ivory (obverse and reverse) from Wallingford

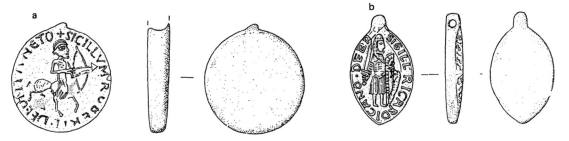

Figure 69: Seal matrices of (a) walrus ivory from Witney and (b) bone from Old Sarum (scale 2:3)

by Pope Nicholas I stressing the necessity of sealing correspondence (Heslop 1980). In the succeeding centuries the use of seals became increasingly widespread, particularly from the time of Edward the Confessor, and, although they never challenged the popularity of those made of bronze, matrices made from skeletal materials became reasonably common. The need for a medium with good working properties, capable of being carved to a reasonable depth and with no marked surface texture, ensured that morse and (later) elephant ivory were most widely used. The earliest and most accomplished example is that found in 1879 at Wallingford, Oxfordshire (Figure 68). On one side this walrus ivory matrix is carved with the bust of a man holding an upright sword, surrounded by the legend *SIGILLUM GODWINI MINISTRI*, 'The seal of Godwin the Minister'; a lobate handle projects from the top, carved in relief with a prostrate Satan surmounted by God the Father and God the Son. On the reverse is a second matrix, showing a seated female figure surrounded by the inscription *SIGILLUM GODGYÐE MONACHE D[E]ODATE*, 'The seal of Godgyða, a nun given to God'; the reverse of the handle is undecorated. The precise dating of the two sides and their relationship to one another has provoked much discussion, recently summarised by Heslop (1980): Godwin's matrix seems most likely to date from about 1040 or a little before; the Godgyða inscription is probably a little later, although Dolley (quoted in Okasha 1971) gives it primacy over Godwin's. The simlarity in design between this and other matrices on the one hand and contemporary coinage on the other (as commented on by Heslop) may indicate that matrices were sometimes produced by craftsmen whose principal employment was as die cutters. A near-contemporary matrix, now lost, was discovered near Amiens in the nineteenth century, and it too was carved on both sides, one face carrying the device of an archdeacon called Fulk and the reverse a bishop of the same name. Both presumably belonged to the same person and were cut at different stages in his career (Heslop 1980).

A date in the mid eleventh century or a little later has been suggested for a second morse ivory matrix in the British Museum, cut with a seated sword-bearing figure and the inscription *SIGILLUM WULFRICI*; a suspension lug above carries indistinct zoomorphic ornament (Hastings 1977; Heslop 1980). Two further matrices in the same material are to be dated to the following century: one of these (Figure 69a), carved with the figure of Sagittarius surrounded by the legend *SIGILLUM ROBERTI DE FONTANETO*, was found at Witney, Oxfordshire; the other, identified as *SIG SNARRI THEOLENARII* — 'The Seal of Snarr, The Toll Gatherer' — is from York. The latter piece shows a figure (perhaps Snarr himself) in a wide-sleeved gown girdled at the waist, carrying a bag which presumably holds the fruits of his toll collecting. It has a perforated suspension lug at the top, a feature formerly present but now broken on the Witney matrix. An unfinished matrix of the same type, found near the Guildhall in London, is in the Museum of London.

Three somewhat similar twelfth-century matrices are published by Goldschmidt (1926). The first is of French workmanship and is identified by its inscription as belonging to St Stephen's Cathedral, Sens; the second bears within an architectural setting a bust identified as that of a twelfth-century pope, Lucius, and an inscription around the edge relates it to Holy Trinity Cathedral, Roskilde; the third matrix displays a figure identified as William, Abbott of St Martin's, but, although it is of French origin, the abbey in question has not been located. The Roskilde and St Martin's pieces, although twice the size of those from York and Witney, are close to them in form, having similar suspension lugs, and are also of walrus ivory.

The common alternative form of seal, a pointed oval or vesica shape, is represented in bone by a matrix from Old Sarum, Wiltshire (Figure 69b). This is an early example of a personal seal in this form: Cherry (1972) notes only one other example earlier than the thirteenth century. On it a mail-clad knight defends himself with sword and shield against attack from a determined, though puny, beast; the surrounding inscription reads *SIGILL RICARDI CANO. DEBR*, the final element probably alluding to the place of origin of its owner, Richard Cano. The face of the matrix is slightly convex and there is a loop handle at the rear. A date in the mid twelfth century seems most likely for this piece (Cherry 1972).

The same shape occurs on a walrus ivory matrix in the British Museum collection, attributed to St Alban's Abbey, Hertfordshire, and dated to the twelfth century (Tonnochy 1952), and on a sixteenth-century elephant ivory matrix of the Archbishopric of Merioneth, now in the Ashmolean Museum, Oxford. The latter example has an integral lathe-turned handle.

Perhaps the most elaborate example in ivory of the die cutter's craft is the double-ended matrix of Sir George Carey, dated *c.* 1586: it is charged on one face with nine armorial quarterings and on the other with a three-masted man-of-war (Tonnochy 1952).

No ivory seals of later date have been noted, but later bronze matrices were commonly fitted with ivory handles.

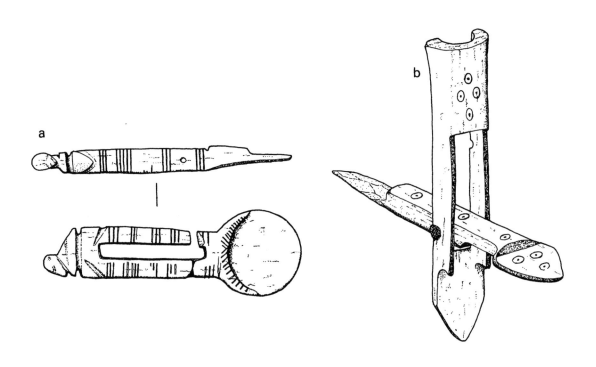

Figure 70:   Coin balances of bone: balance arm (a) from Castle Acre (Coad and Streeter) and complete balance (b) from Smyrna (scale 1:1)

Coin Balances (Figure 70)

Excavations at Castle Acre, Norfolk, have produced the only known English example of a coin balance of the trebuchet or tumbrel type in bone (S. Margeson in Coad and Streeter 1982).[36] Only the horizontal balance arm survives (Figure 70a): it incorporates a flat circular platform with a well-defined segmental lip along the innermost edge of its upper surface, and a longitudinally slotted shank with a transverse pivot hole; the shank has a carved anthropomorphic terminal and is ornamented with groups of incised lines. The vertical member on which the surviving arm originally pivoted is now missing. Among contemporary bronze balances the vertical element is usually the more complex, incorporating a slot through which the balance arm passes, a finial at the top and a point at the bottom; the latter allows the balance to be set up in an instant by being stuck into any convenient surface (see, for example, Galster 1961). In the case of the Castle Acre balance a simple pin with a pivot at its upper end would suffice which, when not in use, could be folded up into the slot on the arm, where there is a recessed housing for it on the underside.[37]

The use (and abuse) of coin balances of this type has been discussed by Galster (1961) and Mayhew (1975), although in each case references are to bronze instruments. Their function was to distinguish coins whose weights (and hence whose bullion value) had been diminished through wear and tear or by deliberate clipping; the balance is made for use with one denomination only, and is so adjusted that coins of good weight tip the balance arm and fall off, while underweight coins fail to do so. (The well-defined lip on the Castle Acre balance permits precise location of the coin, obviating the possibility of cheating which Mayhew discovered while experimenting with a bronze balance of this type.) The same author (1975) notes another dubious practice associated with this instrument, in which coins at the upper end of the weight range acceptable to medieval mint masters could be identified and relieved of their excess silver. For this reason unauthorised possession of a trebuchet came to be regarded as sinful and, in some countries, it was illegal for private citizens to own one.

Although no other European balances of

bone have been noted, two examples in the Ashmolean Museum, Oxford, are of interest. One of these (Figure 70b) is from Smyrna: it comprises a slotted vertical member cut from a long-bone, probably of sheep or goat, and a solid horizontal arm which pivots on an iron pin (now broken). Of the second balance, which is unprovenanced, only the broken vertical member, of the same design as that from Smyrna, now survives.

Dice (Figure 71a-e)

The earliest known British dice are from Iron Age contexts and are parallelepiped rather than cubical (Figure 71a). At least ten pre-Roman sites have produced dice of this type (see D.V. Clarke 1970, for references), while the latest example in the south, from Coygan Camp, Dyfed, may be dated to the second century AD (Wainwright 1967). Clarke suggests that the later absence of parallelepiped dice from the highly Romanised south may be explained by the wholesale adoption there of the Roman six-sided cubical dice, along with other facets of Roman material culture. In those regions lying beyond the limits of intense imperial influence, however, the type lingered on for several centuries and, indeed, may not have even gained currency in the first instance until around the second century AD, by which time it was already disappearing from the south.

In Scotland parallelepiped dice occur on a number of broch and wheelhouse sites with lengthy post-Roman occupation, although any association with the later rather than the earlier phases is in every instance probable rather than demonstrable. In Ireland, on the other hand, several examples from Ballinderry, Offaly (Hencken 1942) and Lagore, Meath (Hencken 1950) clearly do belong to the post-Roman period, some of them dating from perhaps as late as the ninth century.

The choice of raw materials used in the manufacture of parallelepiped bone dice varies to some extent from that noted below for the cubical variety: the majority are made from the shafts of small long bones, comparable with the metapodials of sheep, and indeed their characteristically elongated shape may be seen as resulting from this repeated selection. A corollary of this choice is that the ends are usually

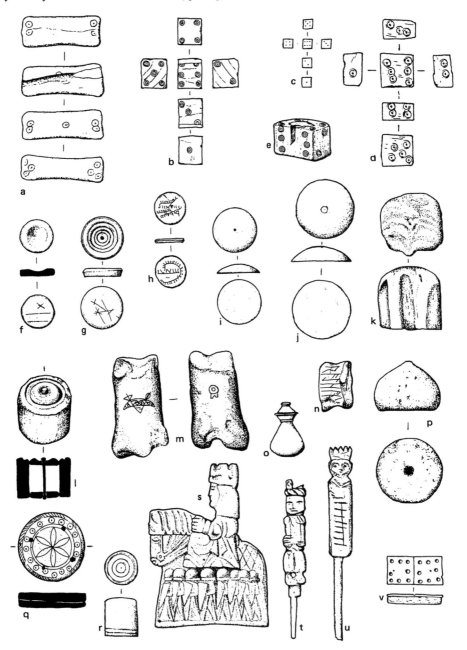

Figure 71:   Dice and gaming pieces (scale 1:2) Dice: parallelepiped from (a) Burrian; cubical from (b) Frocester Court (Gracie and Price) (c) Gilton Town (d) Norwich; plugged from (e) Richborough (Bushe-Fox). Gaming pieces: from (f) Dover (Philp) (g) Ewell (Hassall and Tomlin) (h) Southwark (Sheldon) (i) York (j) Kingston Down (k) Faversham (l) Taplow (m) Burrian (n) Caistor-by-Norwich (Myres and Green) (o) Jarlshof (p) Goltho (q) Trim Castle (Sweetman) (r) Ludgershall (s) Salisbury (t) Southwark (Turner and Orton) (u) London (v) Plymouth (Fairclough)

open and hence the values are normally restricted to the four elongated sides, the numbers 1 and 2 usually being omitted. Antler is also used on occasion, however, as well as entire small bones, but the solid ends of even these dice do not normally carry values.

The dice in use throughout most of northern Europe in the period under review were of the Roman cubical type. Bone and antler are the materials most commonly used in their production. The comparatively large areas of dense tissue offered by antler would seem to have made it a more attractive substance than bone for producing large cubical shapes of uniform appearance; in particular, the base of the antler near the burr, together with the pedicle which supports it, are excellent sources of dense tissue, at least during certain seasons (p. 12). The larger Roman dice, recorded, for example, from York (Wenham 1968) and Dover, Kent (Philp 1981) are most probably derived from this source, while the dimensional limitations of the available raw material would ensure that most bone dice would be of smaller size (*c.* 1cm square or less). Such dice are known from London (e.g., Guildhall Museum 1908), where recent excavations in Southwark produced evidence of manufacture as well as finished products (Turner and Orton 1979). An alternative method of production allowed larger dice to be produced. This involved cutting a section from the shaft of a long-bone and stopping up the medullary cavity with a bone plug, so producing a more or less regular, solid cube. Dice of this type have been noted from Richborough (Bushe-Fox 1949) and London (Guildhall Museum 1908); several unprovenanced examples are in the Ashmolean Museum, Oxford.

The most readily available ivory, in the form of ungulate teeth, is neither as uniform in structure nor as easily worked as bone or antler. Early ivory dice are rare, but one example from Frocester Court Roman villa, Gloucestershire (Figure 71b) has been identified as ivory, seemingly from hippopotamus, (Gracie and Price 1979). A possible dice box of bone is recorded from London (Guildhall Museum 1908).

Dice from Migration Period contexts, as, for example, those from the Gilton Town cemetery in Kent (C.R. Smith 1856), conform closely to the Roman model. In later times,

however, total symmetry was apparently thought less important (or perhaps at times, even undesirable), so that dice are not infrequently found with one axis distinctly and presumably deliberately longer than the others. Scandinavian dice are frequently of this type (Petersen 1914; du Chaillu 1889; Müller-Wille 1978), and it may be that the type is exclusively Scandinavian in origin. One example, however, comes from Dorestad (Clason 1980). A die from Lincoln with this characteristically elongated shape appears to be made of walrus ivory, further suggesting a Viking origin. Other dice show the opposite bias, with one axis markedly shorter than the others. One example from York Minster (MacGregor, forthcoming) is shaped in this way; the trait is carried to such an extreme on a twelfth or thirteenth-century die from Botolph Street, Norwich (Norwich Survey, unpublished) that throwing any values other than those on the flat sides must have been extremely difficult. In every case the values are marked with dots or with ring-and-dot motifs.

On irregularly-shaped dice of these types, certain patterns may be detected in the method of numbering: an elongated die from a Viking period ship burial in Brittany has the values 1 and 2 on the two small ends, which would have been most difficult to throw (du Chatellier and le Pontois 1909), a feature echoed on certain dice from Scandinavia (Petersen 1914). The Dorestad die mentioned above has the value 1 on either end, with 3, 4, 5 and 6 on the other faces (Clason 1980), as have others from Nes, Norway (Graham-Campbell 1980). The Norwich die previously described is marked so that 1 and 2, on the smallest sides, would be most difficult to throw, followed by 3 and 4 on the intermediate sides and 5 and 6 on the largest and most-readily thrown faces. It seems possible therefore, that variations in shape may prove to be useful indicators of date.

On cubical dice the convention most commonly observed since the Roman period is for the values to be arranged so that opposite faces always total seven: thus 6 is opposite 1, 5 is opposite 2 and 4 is opposite 3. Deviations from this pattern do occur, but mostly, it would seem, within the medieval period from the thirteenth century onwards. During this period an alternative method of numbering was commonly used, in which 1 appears opposite 2,

3 opposite 4 and 5 opposite 6. Four examples of this numbering system have been noted on Norman dice from Castle Acre, Norfolk (S. Margeson in Coad and Streeter 1982); nine from Winchester on dice dating from the thirteenth to the fifteenth centuries (D. Brown, forthcoming); thirteen from Dublin (National Museum of Ireland 1963) — though the dates of these are not given — one from Southampton (Platt and Coleman-Smith 1975) dated 1200-1250; one from a late medieval or sixteenth-century context at St Mary's Hospital, Ospringe (G.H. Smith 1979); one sixteenth-century example from Streatley, Bedfordshire (Dyer 1974); one unstratified die from Water Newton, Huntingdonshire (C. Green 1964), and individual unpublished dice from Lincoln and York. Scandinavian examples are known in bone (Ambrosiani 1981) and an example in wood comes from the French medieval settlement at Colletière, Isère (Colardelle and Colardelle 1980).

It is established that certain board games current in the Roman period depended on dice for determination of the movements of the pieces on the board, the best known being *duodecim scripta* and a variant known as *tabula* (Austin 1935; Bell 1960). Then as now, not all board games involved the use of dice, however, and neither did all dice games involve playing men, but the games of *ludus latrunculorum* and *terni lapilli* are of this type, according to Bell. Cubical dice of the Anglo-Saxon period are so scarce and our knowledge of contemporary board games so scanty, that only minimal conclusions about their use can be drawn. The dice from the Gilton Town grave (see above) were unaccompanied by playing pieces and are so nearly identical in size that they could easily have formed a pair for the casting of lots, without any involvement in board games. Some Anglo-Saxon associations of dice and playing men have nonetheless been noted, and a 'decayed bone object resembling a die' was found with 56 plano-convex playing pieces in a grave at Shudy Camps, Cambridgeshire (Lethbridge 1936); 2 dice in Grave 198 at Sarre, Kent, were accompanied by 40 plano-convex counters (Brent 1868); a pair of dice along with 46 bone playing pieces was recovered from a grave at Keythorpe Hall, Leicestershire (R.A. Smith 1907). Near-contemporary finds with similar associations on the continent include those from Hemmoor-Warstade, Niedersachsen, where one grave produced 3 dice and 9 playing pieces (Waller 1959) and Gudendorf, Niedersachsen, where Waller found 2 dice with 3 counters. A number of associations of sets of playing pieces accompanied by dice may also be noted from the Viking period; of several sets of playing pieces found in the Birka graves, one was accompanied by 3 dice (Arbman 1943), while the 2 dice from the Île de Groix ship burial in Brittany were found with 19 playing pieces (du Chatellier and le Pontois 1909). It seems fairly certain, therefore, that the moves in at least some of the board games played during these periods were determined with dice.

The casting of lots with dice is recorded in the Norse sagas: in *St Olaf's Saga*, for example, ownership of a tract of land is decided on the throw of a pair of dice (du Chaillu 1889).

Dice games have long attracted the displeasure of moralising authors, an indication perhaps of their widespread popularity: Strutt (1876) records that ten different dice games of the twelfth century are known by name and that even the bishops and clergy were not immune to their appeal.

Gaming Pieces (Figures 71-4)

Just as certain games achieved periods of widespread popularity before being superseded by others, so periodic changes of fashion in the design of gaming pieces can be recognised. Correlation of particular pieces with particular games is not always easy, however; some types of counter probably being used in more than one game and, conversely, several varieties of playing pieces being used in a single game. The latter suggestion has been made in connection with a large cache of counters recently discovered in a Roman fort in Cumbria. R. Turner (in Potter 1979) has suggested that 119 bone counters of various types found together with 7 glass counters in the late second or early third century destruction levels of a barrack block at Ravenglass may all have been used in games in which some differentiation of the pieces is a necessary feature. (References to Roman games are given above.)

Typical Roman counters are discs of bone averaging some 1.5 to 2.25cm in diameter and

3mm in thickness (Figure 71f-i). Long-bones of cattle or horse provided the raw material: the rectilinear bevelled edges sometimes found on the bases of these counters, interpreted by one writer as the result of wear from use in a game 'in the nature of tiddly-winks' (Kenyon 1948), have been shown elsewhere (MacGregor 1976b) to be the naturally-curved edges of the bone. In order to minimise the visual intrusion of these features, the internal surface of the (whole) bone was normally used for the obverse of the counters.

While some Roman counters are hand-cut, the majority are produced on a lathe or with a centre-bit. Among the most common types are those with countersunk (dished) obverse surfaces, those with multiple concentric rings turned on the obverse, and those with flat surfaces. No chronological distinction can be drawn between these various types, all of which occur at, for example, Ravenglass (Potter 1979), York (MacGregor 1976b), Leicester (Kenyon 1948) and Dover (Philp 1981).

Graffiti in the form of symbols or letters are commonly found scratched on the bases of counters, but only occasionally do they form recognisable words (Wright 1946). These basal graffiti are often extremely faint, so it seems unlikely that they played any part in the game itself. *X*, *V* and *X* are most commonly encountered. In discussing a find of 9 bone counters from Ewell, Surrey, Hassall and Tomlin (1977) note that the latter symbol, represented on 4 counters, stands for *denarii*: this fact, together with the occurrence on some counters of the words *REMI[TTAM] L[I]B[ENTER]* (*I shall pay back willingly*), leads them to suggest that the counters had been used as gambling tokens.

Ten counters from a group of 12 found at Southwark bear on either face (or on both) personal names in association with what have been interpreted as stylised garlands (I. Schwab in Sheldon 1974). Sometimes the edges as well as the faces bear numbers. Such edge numbers are usually more deliberately carved but would still have been difficult to read during play (especially as many are inverted), and must have had some secondary significance.

A few Roman counters display a plano-convex section (e.g. MacGregor 1978b) but this type is found much more commonly in the succeeding centuries. Although some groups may have adopted this pattern after settlement in England, the occurrence of counters of this type in certain continental cemeteries such as at Klietzen, Halle (Laser 1965), Hemmoor-Warstade, Niedersachsen and Gudendorf, Niedersachsen (Waller 1959) demonstrates a currency there at least as early as in England.

While many of these plano-convex counters are quite plain, others are ornamented with incised dots or with ring-and-dot decoration, the number of dots varying between one (for example on a counter from Kingston Down (Figure 71j)) and ten, in the case of some of the 28 counters from a cremation barrow at New Inns, Derbyshire (Bateman 1861). As Bateman observed, the number of motifs on the most prolifically-decorated pieces is too great for them to have been counted easily, so that the number present is unlikely to have had any significance in the game.

Several of the sites on which these counters have been found (see Ozanne 1963 for a list) have produced large groups of them. Leeds (1924) records 10 or more from Asthall Barrow, Oxfordshire; 14 came from a single cinerary urn at Sancton, Yorkshire (Myres and Southern 1973); a cremation urn at Loveden Hill, Lincolnshire, produced 45 (Lincoln Museum, unpublished), while among the 50 or 60 counters accompanying a burial at Sarre, Kent were many of plano-convex outline (Brent 1865). These large numbers imply that whole sets of counters were being interred, a suggestion supported by the fact that 22 counters of white bone in one urn at Caistor-by-Norwich, Norfolk were accompanied by 11 of a black material, probably shale (Myres and Green 1973). About half the bone counters from an urn at Lackford, Suffolk (Lethbridge 1951) appear to have been deliberately blackened (Myres and Green 1973).

As mentioned above, many counters of this plano-convex shape come from cinerary urns, including examples from the fifth century, as at Lackford (Lethbridge 1951), Caistor-by-Norwich (Myres and Green 1973) and Spong Hill, Norfolk (Hills 1974; Hills and Penn 1981). Others, including the examples from Sarre (Brent 1865) come from inhumation graves from as late as the seventh century.

A second type of playing piece found in Anglo-Saxon contexts is that made by modifying a horse molar tooth, so that the grinding surface becomes the base and the root is rounded off to form a high dome or conical shape. Their contemporaneity with plano-convex counters is demonstrated at Sarre, where both types occurred in a single grave (Brent 1865). A large series of these pieces in the British Museum (Figure 71k) is thought to have come from Faversham, Kent (British Museum 1923); the slightly ambivalent wording of the British Museum *Guide*'s description has led several writers (e.g., Wheeler 1935) to conclude that similar teeth were found in Taplow Barrow, Buckinghamshire, while H.J.R. Murray (1952) has further conflated finds from the two sites in his statement that Taplow, Faversham and Basingstoke have all produced playing men in the form of short hollow cylinders made from horses' teeth with the opposite ends closed by discs united by a silver pin; the playing men from Taplow (see below), however, have nothing in common with those from Faversham. An unstratified example of a horse's tooth playing man, from Cheapside, is in the collection of the Museum of London (Wheeler 1935) and another (unpublished) was found in recent excavations in York, but is again unstratified. Continental parallels may be noted from the Frisian terps (Roes 1963) and from Scandinavia (Wheeler 1935).

By contrast with the above, the cylindrical pieces from Sutton Hoo were, to judge from the (preliminary) published description of their laminar structure (Bruce-Mitford 1975), of elephant ivory.

The Taplow playing men mentioned above are, as yet, unique. Found with a rich burial of the seventh century (J. Stevens 1884) were thirty cylinders turned from the hollow shafts of horse metapodials, each about 20mm high and 30mm in diameter; the ends of these cylinders were closed by discs of the same material, linked by a central bronze pin (Figure 71l). To judge from additional finds of loose bronze pins from the barrow, ninety or more pieces may originally have been buried (Bruce-Mitford 1975). No other pieces of similar construction are known.

According to H.J.R. Murray (1952) *tafl* (and its later variant, *hnefatafl*) is the only board game known to have been played by the Saxons. All these men (and all the contemporary gaming boards) may have been used in

one version or another of this game.

An instance of the natural shapes of certain animal bones recommending themselves for utilisation as playing men is that of astragali or 'knuckle bones'. One astragalus was found with a plano-convex counter in one urn at Caistor-by-Norwich while a second urn from the same site, mentioned above as containing 33 plano-convex pieces, also produced 35 astragali, 15 or more of them from sheep and at least 2 from roe deer (Myres and Green 1973). One roe deer astragalus (Figure 71n) was distinguished from the others by its large size and dark brown colouring, and also by having an inscription in runes on one face (Wrenn 1962). Later (medieval) astragali used as playing pieces have been recovered from Amsterdam (Amsterdams Historisch Museum 1977).

Phalangeal bones formed an alternative to astragali, their natural shape allowing them to be stood on end with ease. A single phalanx from Saxon Southampton inscribed with Frisian runes and published as a trial piece (Addyman and Hill 1969) may conceivably have been a playing man, and the same interpretation has been proposed for two phalanges from the Broch of Burrian, North Ronaldsay, one of them (Figure 71m) bearing an undoubted Pictish symbol and probably dating to the seventh or eighth centuries (MacGregor 1974). Several examples have been recovered from the Frisian terps (Roes 1963) and from excavations in Amsterdam (Amsterdams Historisch Museum 1977) while twentieth-century village communities in Friesland are said to have amassed large numbers of them. These were used in games in which the bones were placed in long rows on the ground (or on frozen river surfaces), the object being to strike the furthermost phalanx with a throwing stick or long-bone (Roes 1963).[38] It has been suggested (MacGregor 1974) that the presence of large numbers of bovine phalanges in the absence of other parts of the skeleton on the Dark Age site of À Cheardach Mhor, South Uist, may reflect similar practice, though the possibility cannot be overlooked that this apparent selection is merely the result of some quite different practice, such as a particular method of skinning (p. 30).

The use of knuckle bones for a variety of children's games survived until the last century. Micklethwaite (1892) mentions that pottery playing pieces were being manufactured in the shape of bone originals in his day. Metal versions also became popular from the sixteenth century onwards (Amsterdams Historisch Museum 1977), but the practice of casting metal pieces from bone originals has a considerable antiquity: a recent Roman find from London is of a bronze playing piece, the model for which was certainly an actual astragalus (Ferretti and Graham in Bird *et al.* 1978).

The influx of new cultural traits which accompanied the arrival of large numbers of Norse settlers in the ninth and tenth centuries brought a new form of playing piece, onion-shaped or hemispherical with a flat bottom, often provided with a basal peg-hole. Although some of these domed pieces have shapes reminiscent of the horses' teeth playing pieces mentioned above (pp. 133-4), they are often of considerably larger size, a factor linked to a new source of raw material, namely large cetaceans. These provided dense and heavy bone in quantity, without the inherent limitations of ungulate bone which, for all its potential size, tends to be arranged either in hollow tubes or as a layer of dense cortical tissue over a spongy internal mass (pp. 8-9) Red deer antler bases provided a satisfactory alternative, but there does seem to be a strong correlation between the appearance of this new type of playing piece and the cetacean bone, to which Scandinavian (particularly Norwegian) communities had greater ease of access.

Four playing pieces of this type in the National Museum of Ireland may have originated in the Viking cemetery at Kilmainham (Bøe 1940); a further example, with the classic onion shape mentioned above, was found at Jarlshof, Shetland (Curle *et al.* 1954), and another was recovered from a long-house at Drimore, South Uist (MacLaren 1974). A more recent discovery, from Goltho Manor, Lincolnshire, is illustrated in Figure 71p. Sets of such playing pieces are known in cetacean bone or antler from Dorestad (Clason 1980) and from Birka (Arbman 1943).

Another specifically Viking age playing piece is a piriform variety, in which a bulbous bottom is surmounted by a knop; the base is again often drilled to take a pin. A single example (Figure 71o) from Jarlshof (Hamilton 1956) may be compared with a series of fourteen found at Boge, Gotland (*Proceedings of the Society of Antiquaries of London* 15, 273). Examples of this type, executed in walrus ivory and including some unfinished pieces, have come from recent excavations in Dublin (Dornan 1975).

Hnefatafl was the game most favoured in the Viking period. Several appropriate boards are known (H.J.R. Murray 1952) and an illustration of the disposition of the pieces survives from the reign of Athelstan (J.A. Robinson 1923). The rules of the game are given by Bell (1960).

Within a few decades of the Norman conquest a new class of gaming counter made its appearance — flat, discoid, averaging 4-5cm in diameter and about 1cm in thickness (Figure 72).[39] Three groups may be isolated in terms of raw material, the respective qualities of which impose quite marked stylistic differences in the treatment accorded to each. Antler discs are among the most numerous, usually transversely cut from the thick beam, although instances are also found of their having been cut longitudinally, as demonstrated by the direction of the spongy tissue: in transversely-cut pieces the cancellous tissue, which consists of a limited area of closely-set pores, usually runs axially from the centre of the upper surface to the centre of the lower one while in longitudinally-cut discs it may sometimes be distinguished running diametrically from one side of the disc to the other. Discs cut in either axis of the antler (Clason 1980) from near the base or from its supporting pedicle (Ambrosiani 1981) may show little evidence of any spongy tissue (p. 12) and in any case the bulk of any antler disc consists of solid tissue. Examples are known from York (Benson 1906) and Goltho, Lincolnshire (MacGregor, forthcoming). Continental pieces come from Scandinavia (Mårtensson 1976) and from Rubercy in Calvados (Lorren 1977).

Bone discs are also fairly plentiful, usually cut from the conveniently thick mandibles of cattle (Figure 72b); others (Figure 72c) are known in cetacean bone and yet others are of composite form (Figure 71q), built up from several discs of antler or bone,[40] some of them being fairly ornate.[41] Those cut from mandibles are usually from the angle of the jaw; in addition to the characteristic sandwich effect of the cancellous tissue seen in section, they are

Figure 72: Discoid gaming counters of (a) antler (b) jaw bone (c) cetacean bone (d) walrus ivory. Included in (b) is a side view of a jaw bone counter, showing characteristic sandwich structure; the mandibular foramen has been cut through on this example and appears as a groove on the right hand side. The disc shown in (d) is cut as a longitudinal section through the centre of the walrus tusk

often perforated by a large hole, the mandibular foramen (Figure 72b), which is sometimes mistaken for an artificially drilled hole, the discs then being taken for pendants. In the early medieval town of Schleswig, numerous jaw bones have been found with circles neatly excised from them for the production of discs of this type (Figure 36). Other bone counters are thought to derive from cattle ribs (Margeson in Coad and Streeter 1982).

In most instances, decoration on bone counters of this type is limited to ring-and-dot motifs or compass-drawn petal designs incised lightly on the surface (Figure 72a). Many such discs are known with large central perforations, this feature frequently leading to identification of these items as spindle whorls (p. 187), but in Scandinavia they are accepted by some authors as playing pieces (see, for example, Ambrosiani, 1981; J. Persson in Mårtensson 1976). Antler counters often follow suit, but this material, like cetacean bone, permits a more deeply-cut treatment, as on cetacean counters from London (Figure 72c) and from Iona Abbey (*Proceedings of the Society of Antiquaries of Scotland* 87, 203) and on an antler counter from Rubercy, Calvados (Lorren 1977).

Discs of elephant or morse ivory are much less numerous. They would have been more expensive in the first instance and thereafter often had deeply-cut decoration lavished on them, as was permitted by their uniform structure and excellent working properties. Few of the beautifully carved ivory counters in the national collections (e.g., Beckwith 1972; Dalton 1909; V.B. Mann 1977) have any provenance, and many are known to have been imported from the Continent by collectors. A few early medieval examples have been found in the British Isles, however, among which may be noted one example in walrus ivory from Melrose Abbey (*Archaeological Journal* 9, 297), one found in a garden in Leicestershire and showing, perhaps, Jeremiah being cast into the pit (*Proceedings of the Society of Antiquaries of London* 11, 316-7), and a third from London carved with a masculine figure, perhaps Bacchus (Dunning 1932). A series of carefully prepared but uncarved discs in the British Museum displays the typical structure of morse ivory (Figure 72d); they may represent blanks of raw material as traded to carvers.

The only similarly-shaped pieces in other materials which can be compared with those mentioned above are a few examples in bronze, showing some signs of having been enhanced with enamel; all of them come from Ireland, where the best provenanced of them was 'found by Mr Patrick Donohue while preparing his garden for planting potatoes . . . near Durrow, Co. Laoighis' (Roe 1945).

Although they are frequently referred to as draughtsmen (e.g., Beckwith 1972; Dalton 1909; Longhurst 1927; Westwood 1876) these large discoid counters are more properly to be identified with the game of tables. H.J.R. Murray (1941, 1952) describes tables as a series of games rather than one, played with either two or three dice. Its currency can be demonstrated as early as the eleventh century. The playing men (and hence the boards on which they were used) are invariably larger than those used in draughts, which did not become popular until after 1500.

At some point, as yet imprecisely defined but probably in the eleventh century,[42] a whole new series of playing pieces makes an appearance in England. These are generally agreed to have been used together in a single game, namely chess. The formal evolution of these pieces from the Islamic realms and ultimately from India, is traced by H.J.R. Murray (1913) and Wichmann and Wichmann (1964). Simplest among them are cylindrical 'pawns', represented by early medieval examples from Ludgershall Castle, Wiltshire (Figure 71r), by two others in the British Museum (Dalton 1909), and by one from Steigerwald, Bayern (Wichmann and Wichmann 1964). These are parallelled in jet at the Mote Hill, Warrington (J. Kendrick 1853) and in wood at Colletière, Isère (Colardelle and Colardelle 1980). Whereas the British Museum pieces are naturally solid, being made of antler, the Ludgershall Castle piece has been manufactured from an antler tine, plugged at the end with a second piece of antler to disguise the cancellous core. A further interesting feature of this piece is that the concentric circles which have been incised on the plugged upper end contain traces of red colouring matter, no doubt to distinguish the men of one set from those of the opposing side. Of two cetacean bone pawns found with more elaborate playing pieces at Witchampton, Dorset, one pawn (like several other pieces) was said to have been 'purposely blackened by the action of fire in order to distinguish them from the uncoloured men' (Dalton 1927).[43] The use of jet as a common alternative to bone in the manufacture of pieces of this type presumably also reflects the need to distinguish opposing men.

Found with the cylindrical piece at Warrington was a representative (again in jet) of a second group of these playing men, identified as knights. These may be circular or sub-rectangular in section and are usually

a   b   c   d

Figure 73:   Early chess pieces: knight (a) of antler from Helpstone and castle (b) of bone from London, each plugged in the centre; bishop (c) of cetacean bone from Witchampton; king (d) of antler from London

provided on the upper edge with a single projection, often fashioned into a stylised zoomorphic head. An example in antler from Helpstone, Northamptonshire (Figure 73a) has had the cancellous tissue removed from its centre and replaced by a plug of solid material in the manner already described. Two knights were among the collection of pieces found at Witchampton (Dalton 1927). Examples from Steigerwald, Tübingen, and Châtenois, Vosges are illustrated by Wichmann and Wichmann (1964) while examples in wood come from Colletière (Colardelle and Colardelle 1980) and from Amsterdam (Amsterdams Historisch Museum 1977).

Closely related to this latter group is a series of pieces distinguished by two projections or heads instead of one and normally described as bishops. An example of this type is in the collection of the Museum of London (Pommeranz-Liedtke 1964) and two more are in the British Museum (*Archaeological Journal* 39, 422), all of them from London. Others come from Northampton Castle (ibid.), and also from Beverley (H.J.R. Murray 1913) and Witchampton (Figure 73c) in England and from Steigerwald (Wichmann and Wichmann 1964) in Germany.

The castles in this series are again represented in jet (Dunning 1965; *Interim* 8 no. 1, 19; D.M. Waterman 1959) as well as bone. Two examples made from plugged sections of

long-bones are in the Museum of London (Figure 73b), one of them found in Tokenhouse Yard, London. Another from Woodperry, Oxfordshire is illustrated in *Archaeological Journal*, (1896, 122). Wichmann and Wichmann (1964) illustrate one from Châtenois, Vosges. All are characterised by a wide V-notch cut in the uppermost surface.

Finally, among these earliest chessmen the king and queen pieces are basically cylindrical in shape with a slightly projecting lower half or a rebated upper half (Figure 73d), being distinguished from one another only by size. An example of this type in the British Museum is mentioned by H.J.R. Murray (1913) and another from Rievaulx Abbey, Yorkshire is illustrated by Dunning (1965). A representative of this series in wood comes from Colletière, Isère (Colardelle and Colardelle 1980). Scapula (1956) illustrates a piece of this type from the Butte d'Isle-Aumont, Aube, a settlement which was apparently devastated and abandoned in the tenth century, and Wichmann and Wichmann (1964) illustrate two from Châtenois, Vosges. More elaborate versions have a separate head projecting from the top of the cylindrical body, as in one example in the British Museum (Figure 73d), and others from Old Sarum, Wiltshire (F. Stevens 1933a) and South Witham, Lincolnshire. This last piece has lost most of its head, but part of it survives in its socket, held in place by a transverse antler pin (MacGregor, forthcoming). A twelfth-century date has been suggested for the Old Sarum king (F. Stevens 1933a), while that from South Witham was found in a thirteenth-century layer. Apart from this latter example, however, none of the English pieces comes from a context which can be dated with any degree of precision, although dates for them between the eleventh and the thirteenth centuries are most widely favoured.

Among early chessmen of this type decoration is usually limited to incised, circumferential lines, ring-and-dot 'eyes' on those pieces with face-like projections, and other ring-and-dot motifs. An interesting feature of the latter is that they are frequently joined together in groups by incised lines, a device rarely encountered on any other type of artefact. It may be that this too reflects the Islamic background of these early chessmen. Pinder-Wilson and Brooke (1973) have commented on groups of ring-and-dot motifs arranged in the form of a stylised tree which occur on an ivory casket now in York Minster and on other caskets of 'Siculo-Arabic' types; they note similar devices on one ivory chessman of this early type, to which other examples from excavations at St Albans, Hertfordshire (Chris Saunders, personal communication), and in various museum collections (Wichmann and Wichmann 1964), may be added. It seems plausible to suggest that the tradition of grouping motifs in this way may have been taken over from the Islamic world, along with the stylised forms of the pieces themselves. As the impact of European taste made itself felt on them, elaborate representational carving in false relief came to cover every surface, as on various pieces from French and German collections illustrated by Goldschmidt (1926) and Wichmann and Wichmann (1964), as well as on a king piece from Kirkstall Abbey, Yorkshire (Way 1849).

Although these simple types survived in use until at least the late twelfth century, wholly realistic pieces were also in production by this time. Perhaps the best known early chessmen from the British Isles are those found in 1831 on the Isle of Lewis. In contrast with the schematised pieces described above, the Lewis men are wholly naturalistic and remarkably accomplished in their execution. Of the seventy-eight pieces found (belonging to several sets), the identity of each is immediately apparent to any present-day chess player, except perhaps for that of the castles, represented here by helmeted warders carrying a sword and shield. All are carved in a simple but powerful style; the outlines are uncomplicated, with facial features and details of dress represented either in low relief or with incised lines and dots. The material is identifiable as walrus ivory from the marbled dentine structure visible on the bases and, in some instances, in the longitudinal axis (Figure 74). The carver has capitalised on the irregularities of structure, the 'graining' being used, for example, to enhance the flanks of the knights' horses or to heighten the effect of folds in the vestments of some of the bishops (Figure 74). When first reported (Madden 1832), some of the pieces retained traces of dark red stain.

Although the Lewis find is of outstanding importance, individual pieces now in Florence, Paris and Stockholm (Goldschmidt 1926) bear sufficient resemblance to show that it was not an isolated phenomenon. As on the Lewis pieces, it is common to find the principal figures in other early medieval sets sitting enthroned or mounted on horseback. The latter pieces sometimes incorporate a number of footmen disposed around the horse, which may serve not only to emphasise the importance of the rider but also to broaden the base. An example from Salisbury, Wiltshire, is shown in Figure 71s, and others are illustrated by Goldschmidt (1926), Lindahl (1980) and Wichmann and Wichmann (1964). Progressive refinement led to the production of virtuoso carvings such as a distinctive series of thirteenth-century pieces in which knights do battle with one another or with dragons amid foliate scrolls. A French origin has been claimed in the past for some of these (Goldschmidt 1926) but recent opinion identifies them as English (D.A. Porter 1974). Chess pieces continue to the present day to provide the turner and carver with an outlet for stylistic improvisation, but the basic forms of the pieces have been established since the Middle Ages.

Excavations in Southwark have uncovered an early sixteenth-century pit containing refuse from the manufacture of dice (p. 131) together with a number of anthropomorphic pieces terminating in elongated pegs at the base (Turner and Orton 1979). The type seemingly survived until the nineteenth century, to judge

Figure 74:   Chess pieces of walrus ivory from Lewis: (a-b) bishop, (c-d) knight

by examples illustrated by Bell (1981), who identifies them as outdoor chess pieces, the pointed bases being simply stuck in the ground. Examples from Southwark and from the British Museum are shown in Figure 27t-u.

Under the heading of gaming pieces, dominoes may also be mentioned. Fairclough (1979) illustrates three examples from post-medieval contexts at Plymouth, Devon. One of these (Figure 71v) is of composite construction, a thin bone plaque bearing the values being riveted to a wooden base. Curiously, both ends of this piece bear the value 8, while one of the others is numbered 9 and 1. A more conventional domino from Southampton is given a probable eighteenth-century date (Platt and Coleman-Smith 1975), but the earliest dated piece comes from a context judged to be not later than the sixteenth or early seventeenth centuries at Oxford (M. Henig in Lambrick and Woods 1976). A similar example from the same site was unstratified.

Skates (Figures 75-6)

The skates described below represent one of the most widespread categories of bone artefact, although their identification as such is still challenged from time to time. The conclusion by Tergast (1879) that they were used to smooth textiles also found favour with Kjellberg (1940), who dismissed them as skates after a trial run on the ice. An alternative claim, that they were used in working some soft material such as leather, was postulated by Semenov (1964) on account of microscopic wear marks found on the base (cf. Figure 75), which he was unable to reconcile with marks on modern skates. Subsequently it was shown

Figure 75: Photomicrograph of characteristic wear marks on a bone skate from York. Despite inevitable random scratches, the dominance of the fine striae in the main axis of the skate is clear

(MacGregor 1975b) that Semenov's conclusions were based on a misapprehension of the manner in which these skates were used, and that wear marks comparable with those on ancient skates could indeed be built up on modern replicas used in the appropriate fashion. Some writers (e.g., Barthel 1969) who recognise most skates for what they are, nonetheless find some evidence to suggest that similar implements were used in leather-working. No such objects have been noted in this survey.

The majority of skates are made from metapodials or, less frequently, radii of horses and cattle (tabulated in MacGregor 1976a); a few utilised leg bones of deer occur (e.g., G. Done in Poulton 1980) and skates made from donkey metapodia have also been identified (Clason 1980). Although certain written sources in Latin refer to the use of *tibias* as skates, the term seems to have been used to imply 'shin bones' rather than tibias in the current ana-tomical sense; no tibia skates have been found. Other skeletal elements were also used: skating on cattle ribs is recorded from Germany (Balfour 1898a), Holland (Wichers 1888) and England (MacGregor 1976a), while skates made from horse mandibles with a wooden platform fixed over the teeth are known to have been used in the nineteenth century (Balfour 1898b).

In the case of the leg-bones considered here it is usually the anterior side of the bone which has formed the contact surface with the ice, although a few instances have been noted where the plane of wear is on the posterior side (Barthel 1969; Clason 1980; Süss 1978). Wear is sometimes so advanced that the medullary cavity is exposed, but preliminary grinding of the surface, attested both by wear marks and by recorded practice in the nineteenth century, may have accounted for some of this attrition. On some skates from Scandinavia and Finland the medullary cavity is exposed (sometimes for its entire length) on the upper surface of the skate, as a result of flattening to improve the foothold (Berg 1943; Hyltén-Cavallius 1868; Vilppula 1940). Some lesser trimming is common elsewhere, sometimes accompanied by rough transverse cuts to improve the foothold (MacGregor 1976a).

Pointed and/or upswept toes are common features, presumably intended to improve per-formance on irregular ice or in light snow (Figure 76). Strap holes are also common, about one in three skates having either a vertical or horizontal toe hole and about two in every three having an axial or transverse heel hole (tabulated in MacGregor 1976a). Vertical holes at the front and rear indicate sledge runners (p. 144) rather than skates: the sugges-tion (Schuldt 1960) that some vertically-perforated runners served as skates with a wooden platform pegged to the top is unsupported by any evidence. In the case of axial heel holes the straps were wedged in position by a wooden peg driven into the hole, several such pegs having been found in position, sometimes in association with leather thongs (e.g., M. Cinthio in Mårtensson 1976). Iron loops or nails occasionally take the place of holes and pegs. Many have no holes whatever, for it was not essential that skates of this type should be tied to the feet: the skater moved along by pushing between his feet with an iron-shod pole, while keeping his skates flat on the ice and directed forwards (Figure 76e).

Various accounts of the use of bone skates are reproduced in MacGregor (1976a), the earl-iest being from an Arabic source of about 1120 (Minorsky 1942). A vivid description of skating on Moorfields, then on the northern fringes of London, was recorded by William FitzStephen about half a century later (Douglas and Greenaway 1953).

Others, more skilled at winter sports, put on their feet the shin-bones of animals, binding them firmly round their ankles, and, holding poles shod with iron in their hands, which they strike from time to time against the ice, they are propelled swift as a bird in flight or a bolt shot from an engine of war. Sometimes, by mutual consent, two of them run against each other in this way from a great distance, and, lifting their poles, each tilts against the other. Either one or both fall, not without some bodily injury, for, as they fall, they are carried along a great way beyond each other by the impetus of their run, and wherever the ice comes in contact with their heads, it scrapes off the skin utterly. Often a leg or an arm is broken, if the victim falls with it underneath him; but theirs is an age greedy for glory, youth yearns for victory and exercises itself in mock combats in order to carry itself more bravely in real battles.

A prehistoric ancestry stretching at least to the Bronze Age now seems fairly well-established for bone skates. Scattered examples

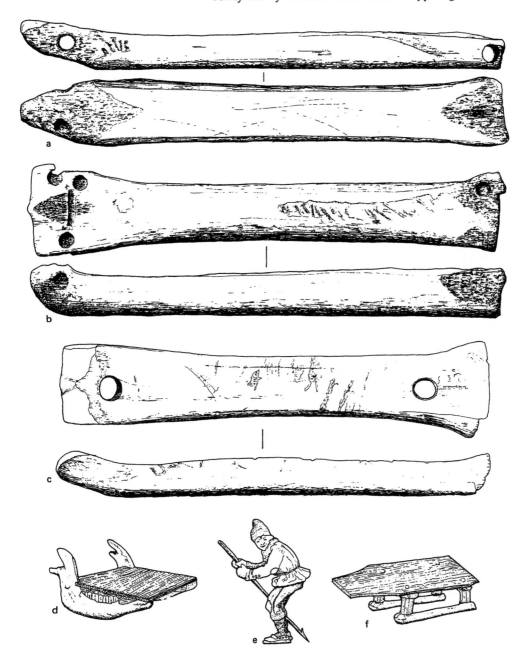

Figure 76: Skates and sledge-runners (scale (a-c) 1:2) skates (a) unprovenanced, Museum of London (b) from London; sledge-runner (c) unprovenanced, Pitt Rivers Museum (d) reconstructed jawbone sledge (Balfour) (e) the method of skating on bones (Herman) (f) sledge with bone runners from Bosnia (Balfour)

of Roman Iron Age date are known, for example from a second to fourth-century settlement near Frankfurt, Oder (Marschalleck 1940) and several contemporary sites in Thüringen (Barthel 1969). They become more common in the succeeding centuries, as in the late eighth and early ninth centuries at Bad Nauheim, Hessen (Süss 1978) and in the Slavic settlements of *c.* 600-900 in Niedersachsen (Jacob 1911; Jacob-Friesen 1974), Schleswig-Holstein (Hucke 1952), at Menzlin (Schoknecht 1977) and Gross Graden (Schuldt 1978) in Schwerin, and in Poland at Gniezno (Kostrzewski 1949), Kołobrzeg (Rulewicz 1958), Szczecin (Leciejewicz *et al.* 1972) and Wolin (Filipowiak 1956). In Russia they survive until at least the twelfth century (Semenov 1964).

In the Netherlands they are common finds from the Carolingian period onwards among the Frisian terps (Roes 1963) and at Dorestad (Clason 1978); later Dutch examples are recorded by Glazema (1950), van de Heide (1956) and Trimpe-Burger (1957). From Belgium one skate is known from a terp in western Flanders for which a Frankish date has ben claimed (de Loë 1939) and three more of twelfth-century origin have been recorded from Grimbergen, Brabant (MacGregor 1976a).

Scandinavian finds begin modestly in the Roman Iron Age (Hagberg 1976) and in the Migration Period (Klindt-Jensen 1951; Stenberger 1955), becoming more numerous in the Viking age as on the military site at Trelleborg (Nørlund 1948) and at the trading settlement of Birka (Arbman 1943; Danielsson 1973). Large numbers have been recovered from medieval urban excavations at Trondheim (Long 1975), Bergen and Oslo (Grieg 1933), Lund (Blomqvist and Mårtensson 1963; M. Cinthio in Mårtensson 1976), Århus (Andersen *et al.* 1971) and Ribe (Ambrosiani 1981).

Finds from the British Isles, ranging in date from the eighth to the thirteenth centuries, are listed in MacGregor (1976). Since that report was published others of about the eighth century have been noted from Bedford (Jane Hassal, personal communication) and of the ninth century from Oxford (M. Henig in Durham 1977); seven separate finds from the City of London have been gathered together by Barbara West (1982). A Saxo-Norman origin is suggested for a utilised red deer metatarsal from Reigate, Surrey (G. Done in

Poulton 1980). A horse metapodial upswept at both ends has been recovered from Aberdeen (MacGregor 1982b) and an undated skate has come from Abingdon, Oxfordshire (Parrington 1979). In the same review will be found accounts of the survival of skates in various parts of Europe up to the present century; further instances have been recorded by Clason (1980) and Hagberg (1976). Together these records show that skates were used for long-distance travel and for fishing over ice, as well as for pleasure.

Sledge Runners (Figure 76c, d, f)

Two distinct types of sledge runner may immediately be distinguished on the basis of raw material; the first and most numerous consists of runners made from long bones, principally the metapodials and radii of horses and cattle, while the second is derived from horse mandibles.

Of these two groups, long-bone runners are the best known and most widely distributed. In appearance they resemble the bone skates already discussed, except that they invariably have fixing holes aligned from top to bottom (i.e. in anatomical terms, in the dorso-palmar plane). These holes were used in fastening the runners to the sledge. Although no more than the runners of such sledges have ever been found in archaeological contexts, the survival of the type into the nineteenth century in various parts of central and northern Europe provides illustrations of the kind of superstructures with which they would have been associated. The simplest form consists of a plank base, pointed or rounded at the front, to the bottom of which the runners were nailed or pegged. A development of this type involved the addition of a three-legged stool on which the user could sit with his feet on a baseboard. This practice was not as precarious as it might seem, for sledges of this type were not (necessarily) used for downhill tobogganing: normally their use was limited to the frozen surfaces of lakes, the motive power being provided by two iron-tipped poles wielded by the sledger in much the same way as those used by bone skaters (p. 142).[44] Sledges of this type are illustrated by Balfour (1898b), Clason (1978), Goldstern (1921) and Herman (1902), while a verbal description of their use in the mid-nineteenth century in Gotland is given by Berg (1971). A refinement of this type took the form of a four-legged stool with the legs fitted directly to a pair of bone runners (Figure 76f). In sledges of this type the feet usually fitted into a perforation cut in the upper surface of the bone only (Balfour 1898b), as distinct from the holes on sledges of the base-board type which had perforations running right through them, sometimes countersunk on the underside to accommodate the head of the nail or peg. In addition to the simplest types illustrated by Čurčić (1912) and Moszyński (1967) there are more elaborate examples with cross-braced legs (Balfour 1898b) or with ornately carved seats (Goldstern 1921).

None of these sledges could be considered as more than children's playthings, but the possibility that some runners from archaeological contexts could have fulfilled a more serious role is underlined by observations made on the Fens towards the end of the last century. Goodman and Goodman (1882) describe sledges mounted with bone runners used by wildfowlers to get within range of their prey over frozen water, the gunner lying prone on the sledge which had mounted in front of it a framework camouflaged with reeds, through which the duck gun protruded. The wildfowler approached the birds by manoeuvering the sledge with a pair of spiked sticks. Balfour (1898b) saw such a sledge on the Fens in 1882, and an illustration of one in use is given by E. Porter (1969). Such an arrangement could also have been useful with a crossbow, although it would have been less satisfactory for conventional archery.

A few bone sledge runners are known from England, although none can be securely dated. One was recovered at Stixwold Ferry, Lincolnshire, during construction work on the Great Northern Railway (*Proceedings of the Archaeological Institute* 1848, xxii); another was found at a depth of 2m in peat at Ramsey, Huntingdonshire (Munro 1897), and a third at a depth of 2.5m on Mildenhall Fen, Suffolk (*The Field* 1893, 990). An unpublished nineteenth-century find from Billiter Street, London is in the Pitt Rivers Museum, Oxford, and another example of Continental origin from the same collection is shown in Figure 76c. Continental finds serve to indicate the chronological limits within which these finds may fall. A few claims have been

made there for a prehistoric introduction, Herman (1902) placing a number of Hungarian runners in the late Neolithic or early Bronze Age, though the secure stratification of these early finds cannot be guaranteed. Čurčić (1912) presents evidence for late Hallstatt sledges of this type in Bosnia. Kostrezewski (1949) finds indications of their use in (perhaps) Slavic levels in Gniezno, Poland; Hucke (1952) notes an example of similar date from Olsborg, Schleswig-Holstein; and a single pair was found in a grave of the Viking period at Helvi, Gotland (Stenberger 1961), along with a pair of bone skates. Sledge runners of the eleventh or twelfth centuries come from Köpenick, Brandenburg (Herrmann 1962) and from Potzlow (Herman 1902) and Teterow (Schuldt 1960; Unverzagt and Schuldt 1963) in Mecklenburg. Others of medieval date come from Wolin and Szczecin in Poland (Rulewicz 1958), from Oslo and Bergen in Norway (Grieg 1933) and the former island of Schokland on the Zuiderzee (van de Heide 1956). On this evidence, it would not be unreasonable to propose an introduction into the British Isles of this type of sledge from as early as the Middle or Late Saxon period, with a proven survival until the early days of the present century, corresponding closely with the chronological distribution of the related bone skates (p. 144).

In the second group of sledges considered here, the mandibles of horses and cattle formed the raw material for the runners. Once again, much of the evidence relating to them comes from ethnographical sources, but a currency at least as early as the medieval period can be demonstrated. In their simplest form they consist of an entire lower jaw with a plank seat fitted over the teeth (Figure 76d). Some illustrations show the user facing in the same direction as the jawbone, as in a well-known engraving after Pieter Bruegel the Elder (reproduced in Ijzereef 1974). Another, after Hendrick Avercamp, shows the jawbone reversed (also in Ijzereef); in either case the sledge is propelled with two spiked sticks, although eye-witness accounts also survive of their use in downhill tobogganing (Berg 1971). One variation on this method of construction involved splitting the jawbone at the front and mounting the two halves parallel to one another on a wooden base (Balfour 1898b), while another apparently employed two jawbones mounted side by side in catamaran fashion (Ijzereef 1974). Evidence for the existence of the latter type of sledge rests entirely on a study of the wear marks on one half of a jawbone from Dordrecht, Holland. From the angle at which the marks crossed the sliding surface of the Dordrecht mandible, Ijzereef calculated that it was probably mounted in this way, while the fact that the vertical ramus had been removed concurred with his suggestion that the innermost ramus of each jawbone would have been cut off for this type of sledge.

Apart from the Dordrecht sledge runner, which is perhaps of the fourteenth or fifteenth century, only one other example has been noted from an archaeological context; from excavations at the Ebor Brewery site in York, a fragment of a similar runner has been recovered from a medieval context (York Archaeological Trust, unpublished).

Contemporary illustrations provide useful proof of their currency and method of use. The earliest of these appears as an incidental illustration in the margin of a Flemish manuscript of the first quarter of the fourteenth century, held in the Bodleian Library, Oxford (MS Douce 5, f. 1a, reproduced in Randall 1966); two more sledges appear in paintings by Pieter Bruegel the Elder, one entitled *The St George Gate at Antwerp*, dated 1555, and the other an *Adoration of the Magi* of two years later (reproduced in Ijzereef 1974). A print after van der Borcht of *c.* 1560 also shows three examples of jawbone sledges (Wichers 1888), while an illustration by Avercamp of *c.* 1620 provides the only evidence for their being used in reverse (reproduced in Ijzereef 1974).

Their survival into the nineteenth century is testified from Brandenburg (Herman 1902) and Pomerania (Balfour 1898), but the period of their initial development has not yet been traced beyond the Middle Ages.

Stringed Instruments (Figure 77)

The remains of any stringed instruments dated earlier than about the ninth or tenth centuries are most likely to derive from lyres. The reconstructed Sutton Hoo lyre (Bruce-Mitford and Bruce-Mitford 1974) gives a good impression of the appearance of the Anglo-Saxon instrument: the hollow sound box and partially-hollowed arms are covered by a thin sound board, and are connected to the symmetrical yoke by mortice and tenon joints; the six strings are anchored to a tail piece at the base of the instrument, pass over the bridge which rests on the sound board and fan out to the pegs set in the yoke. (It should be noted, however, that no tail piece and no bridge were actually found at Sutton Hoo, while the pegs in this instance were made of wood, probably willow or poplar.) Lawson (1978b) numbers excavated examples of such lyres at ten.

By contrast with the lyre, in which the strings pass over the sound board (to which the vibrations are transmitted by the bridge), the true harp has strings rising directly from the sound board, to which they are anchored. Furthermore, while lyres are invariably symmetrically shaped, harps are generally asymmetrical, either rectangular or triangular in outline. The earliest evidence for the introduction of true harps dates to the ninth century (Bruce-Mitford and Bruce-Mitford 1974; Fry 1976); representations on stone monuments of this period in Scotland show them as tall as the player, while a smaller variety, played on the knee, is illustrated in the Bodleian Library Caedmon MS *Junius* XI, possibly produced in Northumbria and dating from the late tenth century. No material remains of harps such as these have yet been positively identified, although it is possible that some of the pegs mentioned below may have come from instruments of this type.

Bone tuning pegs, around which the instrument strings were coiled and by which their tension was adjusted, are among the most commonly found elements in bone. An important group of Roman pegs with squared heads and swelling shanks comes from the Hungarian fortress of Intercisa on the Danube (Alföldi 1957) and a few others have been published (but not recognised) by the Musée de Dijon (nd). Although increasing numbers of pegs have been discovered in recent years, earlier claims for an Anglo-Saxon currency, largely based on unstratified finds from Whitby monastery in Yorkshire (Peers and Radford 1943; Fry 1976) have not been substantiated. Evidence from stratified finds can now be brought to bear and in no instance can an origin earlier than the medieval period be demon-

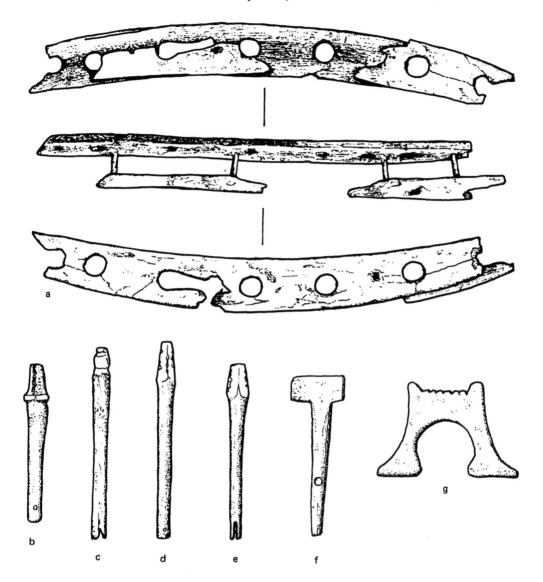

Figure 77: Elements from musical instruments (scale 3:4): wrest plank (a) from Abingdon (Leeds and Harden); tuning pegs from (b-e) Whitby (Fry) (f) Lincoln; bridge (g) from Birka (Salmen)

strated. The earliest securely dated piece is that from Wallingstones, Herefordshire, assigned to the late twelfth century (Lawrence 1978b). An unpublished example from Jarrow, Tyne and Wear, may be contemporary with that from Wallingstones (Professor Rosemary Cramp, personal communication), while a peg from Ludgershall Castle, Wiltshire, comes from a context dated to the end of the thirteenth century (MacGregor, forthcoming). Lawson (1978b) quotes further examples of the fourteenth century from Winchester, Hampshire, and the fifteenth century from Gloucester, while others of the fourteenth or fifteenth centuries have been recovered in Oxford (M. Henig in Durham 1977).

All those found have in common a small transverse perforation (or, in some instances, a slot — see Figure 77e) close to one end, through which the string was passed. The proximity of these holes to the tip of the peg in many examples indicates that they were inserted in the wrest plank from the rear, and not in the manner of the Sutton Hoo instrument.[45] Occasionally, as on the peg from Castle Bellingham, Louth (Lefroy 1870), the friction of the string has resulted in some lateral grooving on either side of the hole. Fry (1976) has taken the general absence of metallic staining in the region of the perforations as an indication that strings of organic material such as gut or horsehair were used. Lawson (1978b), on the other hand, while conceding that organic strings would have been more appropriate for Anglo-Saxon instruments fitted with soft wooden pegs, notes a correlation between the first appearance of metal strings and the introduction of bone pegs about 1100.[46]

At the opposite end of the peg, the circular-section shank may expand to form a spatulate grip (expanded into a T-shape in the case of a sixteenth-century example from Lincoln (Figure 77f) and another possible peg from York (both unpublished), which would allow the tuning to be adjusted by hand; alternatively, it may taper to a square-section terminal, implying the use of a key or tuning wrench. Several of the Whitby pegs display some wear on the heads from the use of such a wrench (Fry 1976), as does one of those from Oxford (M. Henig in Durham 1977). A number of manuscript illuminations exist showing tuning wrenches in use (Fry 1976), although none has yet been recognised from archaeological sources.

Considering the comparatively late currency of bone tuning pegs as outlined above, it is possible that they were used on a much wider range of instruments than the harps and lyres with which they have hitherto been associated: fiddles and lutes, for example would be possible candidates.

Smaller pegs, perforated near the head rather than the base, were represented by unfinished as well as completed examples at St Aldates, Oxford, where eight such pegs were found along with three others of the type already discussed and some eighty fragments indicating on-the-spot manufacture (M. Henig in Durham 1977). The fragmentary pieces derived from horse metapodials had been cut into strips of about 7mm square in section, apparently by hammering the bone on to a sharp blade, prior to finishing with a knife. Although the profes-

sional status of the manufacturer could not be ascertained with certainty, Henig finds some support for the suggestion that he was an instrument maker who made the pegs as required. The instruments concerned were thought most likely to be of the psaltery type and the deposit was dated to the late fourteenth or fifteenth centuries.

Fittings other than pegs are scarce indeed. An important find (Figure 77a) comes from a fifth-century grave at Abingdon, Oxfordshire, which produced two curving strips of antler (one fragmentary), originally perforated by five regularly-spaced circular holes and united by long iron rivets (Leeds and Harden 1936).[47] Although their significance was not recognised at the time of excavation, these fragments are now accepted as being a set of mounts from the wrest plank or yolk of a lyre (Bruce-Mitford and Bruce-Mitford 1974). Pegs protruding through the perforations would have engaged the ends of the strings, but since no such pegs were found in the grave we may presume that they were of organic material, no doubt wood. The Abingdon find does not stand entirely alone: a near-contemporary antler plaque from Dùn an Fheurain, Strathclyde, has been tentatively identified as a wrest plank mount (J.N.G. Ritchie 1971) while Megaw (1968) has postulated a similar function for a curved antler plate with nine perforations from an Iron Age context at Dinorben, Clwyd.

Another stringed instrument element recorded in bone (or, perhaps, antler) is a bridge found in the 'Black Earth' at Birka (Figure 77g). It dates from about the ninth century and is notched for seven strings. Other examples of bridges are known in metal and, more numerously, in amber (Bruce-Mitford and Bruce-Mitford 1974; Crane 1972; Roes 1965; Salmen 1970), mostly notched for six or seven strings.

Whistles and Flutes (Figure 78)

During their entire development over several millennia, until their decline in the medieval period, bone flutes never developed beyond a rudimentary form. While many examples can be found from as late as the thirteenth century, from which time the history of woodwind instruments is fairly well documented, they

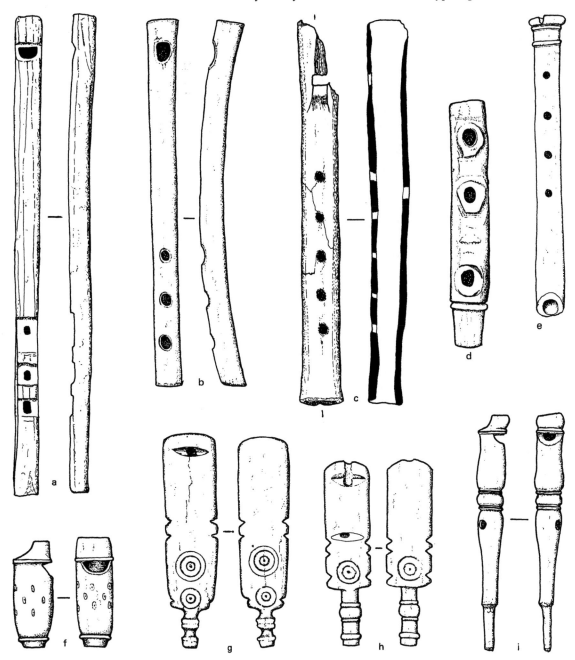

Figure 78:   Whistles and flutes (scale 2:3) from (a) Canterbury (Megaw) (b) Southampton (Platt and Coleman-Smith) (c) Keynsham Abbey (Barrett) (d) London (e) unprovenanced, British Museum (f) Hadleigh Castle (Drewett) (g) Bury St Edmunds (h) Pflaumheim (Koch) (i) Lincoln (Chapman *et al.*)

contributed little or nothing to the musical developments of this period, which were taking place on a variety of more versatile and sophisticated instruments.

All those considered here are end-blown instruments, in which the player's breath was ducted by a block or fipple inserted at the upper end of the pipe and directed against a narrow ledge or voicing-lip cut in the blow-hole, so setting up the essential vibrations in the column of air within the pipe. No such fipples have been found in Britain but a number of examples, all of wood but used originally with bone instruments, have been noted from Holland, Norway and Sweden by Crane (1972). The same author suggests that many flutes may originally have been fitted with fipples of beeswax, while Megaw (1961) postulates clay as an alternative. No evidence for cross-blown bone flutes has been found.

The Latin word for a flute, *tibia*, has a clear anatomical allusion, but Roman instruments of bone have not been noted here. Stephen Greep (personal communication) points out that securely stratified Roman flutes have been found, however, and that they are generally lathe-turned and of composite construction. Long-bones of various mammals, particularly sheep (Brade 1975; Crane 1972; Megaw 1968) but also cattle, pig and dog (Brade 1975), were used in the manufacture of Continental flutes and whistles of the post-Roman period. In England, sheep tibia flutes are known from medieval sites at Lyveden, Northamptonshire (Bryant and Steane 1971), Castle Acre, Norfolk (Lawson in Coad and Streeter 1982) and Ludgershall Castle, Wiltshire (MacGregor, forthcoming); and from a post-medieval context at Wharram, Yorkshire (D. Andrews in Hurst 1979), while utilised deer metapodials have come from twelfth or thirteenth-century levels at White Castle, Gwent (Megaw 1961).

The pneumatic limb bones (particularly ulnae and tibiae) of large birds were also favoured, their long, thin-walled hollow shafts suiting them admirably for this purpose. Particular concentrations of bird-bone flutes have been noted among coastal-dwelling communities on the Continent (Brade 1975), presumably corresponding with a special importance in the diet of these communities of such birds. Bird-bone flutes are by no means limited to these Continental coastal settlements, however, and

examples from England include some of Saxon date from Thetford, Norfolk (Megaw 1960) and Southampton, Hampshire (Holdsworth 1976), along with two from York likely to date from the Viking or early Norman period (D.M. Waterman 1959). Others of medieval date (the twelfth or thirteenth centuries) are known from Canterbury, Kent (Megaw 1969), Ludgershall Castle (MacGregor, forthcoming), Lydney Castle, Gloucestershire (Casey 1931) and Southampton (J.V.S. Megaw in Platt and Coleman-Smith 1975), while an undated bird-bone pipe from Lincoln is mentioned by J. Clarke (1855). The bones in question, where identifiable, are all tibiae or ulnae from crane or geese.

Considerable variation in the quality of workmanship is displayed by these flutes, the best made seeming to be those from Canterbury (Megaw 1969) and from White Castle, Gwent (Megaw 1961). Particular care has been taken with the voicing lip of the latter instrument; it is a finely-cut ledge only 0.5mm thick, set within a rectangular aperture measuring 8 x 5mm. A lathe-turned ivory pipe in the London Museum (Figure 78e) may be of more recent origin than those described above; the upper part is missing and it is impossible to know whether it was originally a simple flute or part of a composite instrument such as a bagpipe. Alternatively, it could be one of the Roman instruments described above.

In an examination of all known flutes from the northern European mainland, Brade (1975) notes examples with up to seven finger holes. The most commonly encountered number is three, which Megaw (1960) observes is the greatest number that can be controlled with one hand.[48] A range of up to an octave and a half was achieved with the Keynsham Abbey pipe, which has five finger holes and a thumb hole at the rear (Barrett 1969). One particular refinement on the Canterbury flute is that the three finger holes are each recessed, a feature paralleled in Britain only on a wooden instrument, thought perhaps to be a reed pipe, from tenth or eleventh-century levels at Hungate, York (Richardson 1959). Although not uncommon on the Continent, thumb holes appear only rarely on English instruments. The flute from White Castle has two, however, a refinement which has important implications for its tonal range (Megaw 1961); similar flutes with two thumb holes are noted from the Continent by Brade (1975).

Megaw (1968) has experimented by playing on these instruments and determining their tonal range, but little evidence for the use of consistent scales could be found: some flutes are evidently pentatonic in scale while others correspond more closely with the diatonic; yet others are non-modal. Megaw concluded that the musical scale familiar to us may have evolved as the result of generations of such instruments being fashioned to similar patterns on standard raw materials, which naturally resulted in the repeated production of a certain range of notes. Brade (1978), on the other hand, reminds us that the playing technique employed with these instruments may have been quite different from that of the present day, using, for example, different methods of fingering.

In addition to the flutes discussed above, a variety of whistles with little or no means of modulation may be noted. Some years ago R. Koch (1967) published a bone whistle from the Migration Period cemetery at Pflaumheim, Baden-Württemberg (Figure 78h) for which no parallel could then be found. More recently a very similar whistle from Bury St Edmunds, Suffolk (Figure 78g) was sent to me for identification;[49] although it lacks an archaeological context there can be no doubt that it is a close contemporary of the Pflaumheim instrument. Both whistles appear to have been cut from the solid wall of a large mammal long bone; the front and back faces are both convex and the flattened sides are each notched twice near the centre and once towards the end. Both terminate in solid, moulded projections. An axial hole drilled in the opposite end is exposed in both whistles by a transverse slot near the lip and in the Pflaumheim instrument by a second hole at the centre; this central hole is missing from the Bury St Edmunds piece which, since it produces no sound, is presumably unfinished.

A second type of whistle, so far found only in Frisia, is also cut from solid bone rather than making use of a natural cavity. From a rounded or squared mouthpiece housing the blowhole these expand to a wide spatulate end. A curious feature common to the complete examples is a central hole drilled from side to side, flanked above and below by other holes drilled from front to back of the instrument; none of these

intercepts the air passage and their significance is unknown. Several examples are illustrated by Roes (1963) and others are listed by Crane (1972).

Stratified whistles of later date are not numerous. Hamilton (1956) interprets a perforated long bone from Viking age levels at Jarlshof, Shetland, as possibly an otter whistle. Chapman *et al.* (1975) illustrate a lathe-turned bone whistle lacking its fipple from an early eighteenth-century context at the Bishops Palace, Lincoln (Figure 78i). Post-medieval horn whistles for various purposes are discussed by Hardwick (1982), who also illustrates examples of combination pieces, including snuff-horns with whistles and a spoon with a whistle on the handle.

Blast Horns and Drinking Horns (Figure 79)

A number of horns have been recognised from Dark Age and later sites, notably in the British Isles. In most cases only the decorative metal mounts have survived, but actual horn fragments were recovered from Anglo-Saxon burials at Taplow, Buckinghamshire (J. Stevens 1884), Broomfield, Essex (G.B. Brown 1915) and Sutton Hoo, Suffolk (Bruce-Mitford 1979). The former presence of others is attested by metal rim-mounts at Sarre, Kent (Brent 1865) and Alton, Hampshire (Evison 1963). Graham-Campbell (1973) has published other mounts from Burghead, Grampian Region. G.B. Brown (1915) mentions that similar rim-mounts were occasionally applied to wooden drinking cups, however, and this possibility should be borne in mind when speculating on the significance of remains like these in the absence of associated organic material. There seems to be no way at present of distinguishing blast horns from drinking horns on the appearance of the rim. Graham-Campbell (1973) suggests that the presence of a suspension loop on the Burghead mount might indicate that it was not a drinking horn, though he does cite other drinking horns which do have loops. To those he mentions may be added an important find from a rich Frankish burial at Cologne (Doppelfeld 1964); the surviving suspension ring on the Cologne horn (Figure 79a) was originally matched by another close to the silver-mounted rim; the

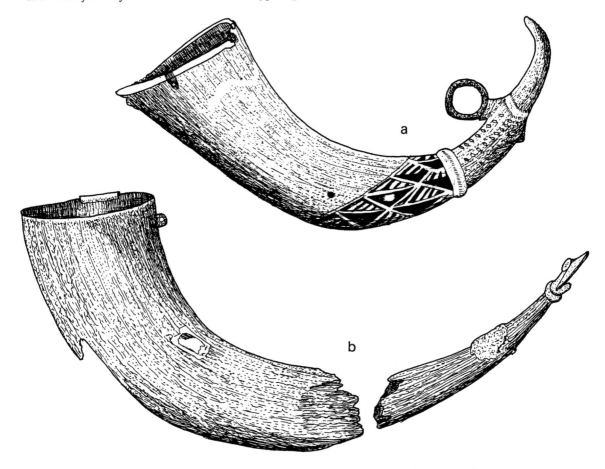

Figure 79: Drinking horns from (a) Cologne (Doppelfeld) and (b) Voll (Ellmers) (not to scale)

remains of a fringed leather band and a leather carrying strap were found, and the horn itself was ornamented near the base with rows of incisions and an area of lozenges.

The occurrence of decorative metal terminals from the other (narrow) end of the horn, must, of course, be indicative of closed drinking horns. Seventeen Viking age drinking horn terminals found in Norway, many of them zoomorphic in form and thought to have been imported from England, are listed by Petersen (1940) and a substantially preserved horn of the same date from Voll, Nordtrondelag (Figure 79b) is discussed by Ellmers (1965).

It is clear from the numbers of mounts found that both classes of horn were much more commonly used than the few surviving cattle horn fragments would otherwise indicate. Little can be said of the beasts from which the horns were derived, except that most were probably domestic cattle. The Sutton Hoo horns, however, were from aurochs (*Bos primigenius*) (Bruce-Mitford 1979), and that found at Cologne is from a goat (Doppelfeld 1964). Elmers (1965) reckons the capacity of the average drinking horn at rather less than half a litre, although some of those mentioned above, notably the Sutton Hoo horns, are very significantly larger.

Later drinking horns of the fourteenth to sixteenth centuries, all fitted with feet or rests and with elaborate silver-gilt mounts, are illustrated by Oman (1944); by this time, he suggests, their use was generally reserved for special celebrations, particularly those of ancient custom.

From seventeenth and eighteenth-century Scotland come several examples of a distinct type of smaller drinking horn, lacking the natural curve of those mentioned above. Hardwick (1981) illustrates several examples and mentions that the manufacturing process involved straightening the warmed horn on a former before applying characteristic incised or lathe-turned ornament; not infrequently, an integral whistle was cut into the base (in anatomical terms, the solid tip) of the horn.

Blast horns also survived throughout the medieval period and formed a practical means of communication, especially in forested areas. Some acquired symbolic importance as tokens of land tenure, and others came to be associated with the maintenance of public peace, such as the horns of Ripon and Bainbridge in Yorkshire which are still sounded regularly today (for an account of such horns see Bridge 1904).

Both drinking horns and blast horns were produced in other materials in addition to that which gave them their name, notably in ivory. Within the context of this survey the most important are those of elephant ivory, sometimes termed oliphants. The configuration of the tusk with its natural pulp cavity is reminiscent of a cattle horn. Poplin (1977b) has noted that the internal surface of the tusk is normally left intact when utilised as an oliphant, the great thickness of the surrounding dentine being carved to produce rich relief decoration. Dalton (1909) notes that whereas the earliest ivory horns were probably used for hunting and other secular purposes, many came to be housed in church treasuries, frequently being used as receptacles for relics. Maskell (1872) describes a sixteenth-century ivory horn of French origin in the Victoria and Albert Museum, carved on one side with hunting cupids and provided with six stops on the other for modulating the note.

Powder Horns

With the invention of gunpowder, the horn industry found an important new outlet for its products. Being both spark-proof and water-proof and naturally funnel-shaped, cattle horn was immediately and widely adopted as the favourite material for the manufacture of priming horns. The open end was usually fitted with a rim and stopper of wood, metal, or some other material, which could be removed in order to fill the horn, while the solid tip was bored out to allow a carefully-controlled flow of powder and was supplied with a bung or cap. Suspension loops might be fitted to either end of the horn; alternatively, the solid tip might be shaved down to a more slender profile except for a moulding left in relief, designed to prevent a suspension cord wrapped round the narrower end from slipping off. Different-sized horns were put to different purposes, from priming and loading small arms to charging cannon. It was common for personal powder horns to be compressed along the line of the curve, a process which, given mature horn and an appropriate temperature, gave the horn permanently flat sides which frequently attracted incised decoration. They remained in common use until the invention of patent cartridges in the nineteenth century. Grancsay (1945) and Hardwick (1981) illustrate various examples from the seventeenth and eighteenth centuries.

Antler provided a popular alternative to horn as a raw material for powder horns, particularly for sporting purposes. The normal practice was for a large red deer antler to be sawn through above the burr and just beyond the junction of the bez tine with the beam, producing a short fork. After the cancellous core had been removed to form a hollow cylinder the two ends of the fork were permanently capped with metal or some other material and a third cap, removable for filling and fitted with a mechanism to allow a charge of powder to be measured out, closed the other end, which became the top of the container. Antler powder horns, which were particularly favoured in Germany in the seventeenth century, frequently have skilfully carved relief decoration, contrasting with the scrimshaw-type work which is more common on those of cattle horn.

In discussing the uses to which the natural cavities of bones and teeth may be turned, Poplin (1977b) illustrates a curious composite powder horn in which the main chamber consists of two symmetrical elements cut from the shafts of horse femurs, tapering towards a nozzle cut from the tibia of a smaller, sheep-sized animal.

Other Horn Containers

Entire horns came to be used for a variety of purposes as containers for various materials. From the late medieval period, they are known to have been used to hold coins. Five examples of such money horns are known from Scottish finds, dated by their contents from the mid-fourteenth to the late sixteenth centuries (Metcalf 1977), and another containing 153 coins of the fifteenth and sixteenth centuries comes from Lübeck, Schleswig-Holstein (Grassmann 1980).

Axle-grease was commonly carried in cattle-horns by carters and coachmen who had to avoid overheating in the wheels of their vehicles, while reapers used them to keep a mixture of grease and sand to aid the whetstone in sharpening their blades (Hardwick 1981). Among other craft practices featuring horns is that of applying slip to pottery, the tip of a horn functioning as a handy reservoir for the slip which was applied through a nozzle of goose quill (Brears 1971).

A more refined purpose to which horns were put in the period from the seventeenth to the nineteenth centuries was the manufacture of snuff mulls. Decorative caps, often of silver, closed the wide end of the horn, and various utensils for preparing the snuff were sometimes attached. They vary in size from entire cattle or rams horns, heavily mounted and designed as table ornaments, to small pocket-sized containers. Among the latter are some of cattle horn which have had the tip heated and twisted into a spiral so that they resemble rams' horns, so making them more easily portable.

Illustrations of these various types of horn are given by Hardwick (1981).

Horn Helmets (Figure 80)

The qualities of lightness and toughness possessed by horn recommended it for use in Dark Age defensive helmets. These were rare and costly articles, however, and would have been worn only by the uppermost echelons of society. M.L. Keller (1909) notes that the word *galea* is glossed *leðerhelm* in some sources, and we may conclude that any battle helmets worn by the rank and file would usually have been of leather. Wilson (1971) observes that on the

Franks casket (Figure 108) only the principal figures wear helmets with nasals and neck guards and there is a corresponding scarcity of these items in contemporary graves. By the eleventh century, however, helmets of one form or another were more generally worn; the *Anglo-Saxon Chronicle* for 1008 records that each eight hides of land had to provide a helmet and a corselet (Plummer and Earle 1892).

Only one helmet bearing evidence of having incorporated horn plates survives in Britain, namely the well-known example found in the middle of the last century at Benty Grange, Derbyshire (Bateman 1861). It came from a grave said to contain no trace of a body save for the hair, but one which produced a silver rim (thought to be from a leather cup), some champlevé enamelwork and fragments of silk, as well as the helmet fragments. The helmet has recently undergone conservation and exhaustive research at the British Museum, from which the following details of its structure have

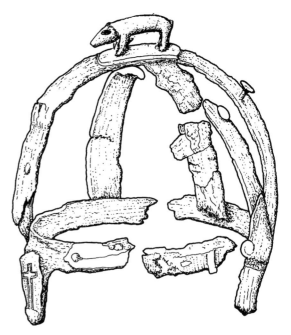

Figure 80:   Helmet from Benty Grange (after Bateman) (not to scale)

Note: Only the iron framework (with various decorative elements) survives, but the layout and structure of the horn plates which it originally incorporated can be seen in the corrosion products.

emerged (Bruce-Mitford and Luscombe 1974). It consists of an iron framework based on a horizontal brow band 25mm wide and 1-2mm thick. From this brow band rises an openwork crown of which the two principal members are arranged at right angles to one another: one of them projects at the back to form a curved neck guard and at the front (where it had an applied silver cross) to form a nasal; the other projects at either side over the ears, the extensions perhaps originally carrying ear-protectors or anchorages for cheek-pieces. The quadrants formed by these major strips were each sub-divided by a narrower tapering iron band, also running from the brow band to the crest. On the inside of this framework would have been a cap of cloth or, more probably, of leather, while on the outside it was covered with strips of horn. Traces of these strips survive as a mineralised pattern on the outer surface of the iron strips, the pattern reproducing the structure of fine parallel lines established above (p. 20) as being typical of horn. The horn has clearly been applied as a series of riveted plates, softened and bent into shape, with the 'grain' of each arranged obliquely to the iron framework and at right angles to that of the adjacent plate, resulting in a chevron pattern visible in the corrosion products. The junctions between the plates, marked by a small ridge of corrosion along the centre of the iron bands, were covered with strips of horn, cut to the same width as the underlying iron bands and fixed to them with silvered rivets. Impressions detected in the corrosion products on the neck guard suggest that further horn plates were fixed between it and the ear pieces to give additional protection. The frame of the helmet was surmounted by a bronze crest in the form of a boar. A date in the latter half of the seventh century would seem to be appropriate.

An excellent parallel for this helmet comes from the grave of a princely youth found under Cologne Cathedral, dating from the sixth century (Doppelfeld 1964). In this instance the helmet was thought to have been constructed as follows. First of all, a stiff leather skull-cap was made, either in one piece or from a series of wedge-shaped panels, probably on a mould. Twelve strips of horn were then cut as sectors of a single circle; for each of these a corres-ponding but slightly oversized leather lining was cut. A brow band of horn was mounted on the skull-cap and the leather-lined horn plates were glued to it, with a strong leather disc applied to the crown. The assembly was then stitched firmly together, using, at least in parts, bronze wires which passed through the leather edgings of the horn plates. Strips of bronze were then applied to the helmet, one passing around the outside of the horn brow band and the others arranged radially to cover the joints between the horn plates, terminating under a finial on top. A mail neck-guard and a pair of cheek-pieces were finally suspended from the rim.

The richness of the Cologne burial serves to emphasise the rarity of these helmets. To describe it as a 'child's version of the *Spangenhelm*' (Lasko 1971), with (presumably) the implication that being constructed of horn rather than sheet metal it should be considered as little more than a toy, seems misleading. Bearing in mind the evidence of the Benty Grange helmet, it is more appropriate to see the Cologne helmet (for all that it was indeed made for a child) as a miniature version of an adult type and not as a useless substitute. The work of fracture for horn has been calculated at an impressively high value,[50] and it would clearly have been quite effective in this role.

Composite Bows (Figures 81-3)

In the Mediterranean world the composite bow found widespread favour from at least the early first millennium BC, although Rausing (1967) estimates that it may have developed some 3,000 years earlier. Many variations in detail are found among the composite bows which came to be dispersed among totally disparate cultures over three continents, but a general-ised description of the type which found its way to northern Europe may be attempted on the basis of Roman period fragments and of more complete extant bows from more recent periods (based on Balfour 1890). The core of the weapon (Figure 81) is a wooden grip, from which flexible arms spring symmetrically on either side. At the extremities of the springy arms are cut rigid 'ears' which, in some instances, continue the line of the curve but, more generally, may diverge markedly from the line of the arms. The nocks, which engage the ends of the bow-string, are frequently rein-forced with bone or antler, let into the ears as

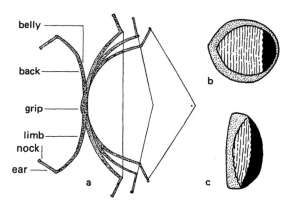

Figure 81:   Composite bows (a) conformation from unstrung to fully extended; sections through (b) grip and (c) limb (after Rausing)

strips, while lateral bridges at the elbows served to control the movement of the string when it was released. Strong strips of cattle horn were fixed with a suitably resilient animal glue to the belly of the bow (that is, the surface of the bow facing the archer when in use); these strips were thickest and strongest towards the grip, gradually thinning out until they terminated at the elbows. The back of the bow (the surface furthest from the user) was covered with sinew, disposed longitudinally along the bow, mixed with glue and moulded in one or more layers onto the wood. This combination of materials resulted in the bow adopting in its unstrung state a 'negative' curve, with its extremities pointing forwards; stringing the bow resulted in the direction of curvature being reversed, producing the classic 'Cupid's bow' shape.

This composite structure produced a number of mechanical advantages, making it inherently unlikely that the type was developed merely in default of suitable timber, as suggested by some authorities (summarised in Rausing 1967). The one-piece long-bow of yew (*Taxus baccata*) which became for a time the English weapon *par excellence*, was particularly suited to the temperate climate of northern Europe, and recent research has shown that the mechanical properties which make yew an excellent reservoir of strain energy are seriously impaired at temperatures above 35°C (Gordon 1978). In composite bows, however, the wooden core played only a minor part in storing the energy induced by the archer stringing and drawing the

bow; instead, this energy was stored partly under tension in the sinew surface moulded to the back of the stave and partly under compression in the horn strips on the belly. Both of these materials function more effectively as energy stores than does yew and lose none of their efficiency up to about 55°C, provided they are kept dry.

A more important advantage enjoyed by the composite bow over the self bow lay in the fact that a greater amount of energy could be stored during the stringing process. Gordon (1978) outlines the principles involved as follows: the energy available to dispatch the arrow is dependent on the distance by which the string is drawn (normally a maximum of 0.6m) and the force applied to it (usually not more than 350 Newtons or 80kg); Figure 82a expresses diagrammatically the means by which the maximum energy available for storage in an unstressed bow[51] can be calculated at about 105 joules, that is, about half the input of the archer. By contrast, composite bows are, as already explained, reflexed when strung, so that a more significant amount of strain energy is already stored in the bow before the archer begins his pull (Figure 82b); in this instance about 170 joules of energy are available at the moment the arrow is fired. In weapons of similar size the composite bow would clearly have a considerable advantage in range over the self bow, but in practice this advantage was used in making composite bows of smaller and more manageable size.

While the horn strips clearly represent the most vital element in the composite bow to be made of the materials under review, premedieval examples seem not to have survived. Only one bow incorporating horn has so far been noted and nothing of certainty can be said about its age; this example, said to have been formed from a single horn,[52] was found in the Fens between Ely and Waterbeach around the middle of the last century; the only details published, apart from the above, are that it was 1.08m long and was broken at one end (*Archaeological Journal* 13, 412; 14, 284; 27, 76).

Bone or antler splints incorporating nocks are better represented, at least in the Roman period (Figure 83).[53] These are characteristically elongated and curving blade-like strips of bone or antler, usually rounded and wider at

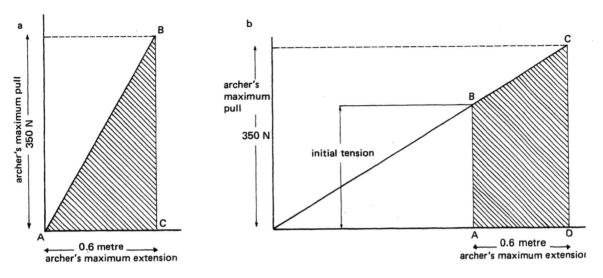

Figure 82: Schematic energy diagrams (after Gordon). Self bow (a) energy stored in bow (ABC) = 0.5 x 0.6 x 350 = 105 Joules. Pretensioned bow (b) energy stored in bow (ABCD) = 170 Joules

Figure 83: Antler splints from composite bows in the Museum of London

one end and irregularly plano-convex in section; the underside is roughened to facilitate glueing to the ear of the bow and the nock for the string is cut into the thinner of the two edges, close to the rounded end. Six of these were found in the fort at Bar Hill on the Antonine Wall in Scotland (MacDonald 1934; Robertson *et al.* 1975), where they are thought to be from the second century and to be associated with the presence of Syrian troops of the Cohors I Hamiorum Sagittariorum. A collection of about fifty splints, thought to be made from rib bones of cattle, came from the destruction levels of a third-century building, evidently an armourer's workshop, in the legionary fortress at Caerleon, Gwent (Nash-Williams 1932; Boon 1972) and a single example of approximately contemporary date was recovered at Silchester, Hampshire (Boon 1974). Birley (1977) illustrates an example from Vindolanda, Northumberland, and a number of antler splints now in the Museum of London are shown in Figure 83. Similar splints, probably of the first century, have been found in the *Schutthügel* at Vindonissa, Switzerland (Eckinger 1933) and they are common finds on the German *Limes* (Rausing 1967; Stade 1933; Walke 1965). Numerous examples found at Carnuntum in Austria came from within an armoury building (Stade 1933). An example from Mainz is illustrated by Klumbach and Moortgat-Correns (1968), who provide further references. Although all the above-mentioned examples were found singly, a complete 'ear' from a Roman-period composite bow, found at Belmesa in Egypt and illustrated by Balfour (1921), shows that in practice they were used in pairs, one fixed to either side of the wooden ear, a conclusion confirmed by Nash-Williams's (1932) observation that some of the Caerleon splints were notched on one side and some on the other.

In the post-Roman era the composite bow enters a period of obscurity in northern Europe. A few physical remains are, however, known from Migration Period contexts, showing some continuation of their popularity or perhaps a new interest stimulated by weapons introduced in folk movements from Eastern Europe: several graves in the Migration Period cemetery at Környe in Hungary produced splints of the type discussed above (Salamon and Erdelyi 1971) and Veek (1931) illustrates exam-

ples of mid fifth century date from Cannstatt, Württemberg. Although composite bows are illustrated in the ninth-century Utrecht Psalter (reproduced in Rausing 1967) no physical remains of Frankish bows have yet been noted. It seems premature to conclude, however, as Werner (quoted in Rausing 1967) has done, that they were not made by the Franks. In Anglo-Saxon England the occurrence of the term *hornbogen* ('horn bow') in *Beowulf* has been taken to equate with bows of this type (*Archaeological Journal* 13, 412; Rausing 1967), and even if the reference was not to the material of which it was made but rather to the shape of the bow, comparison with a pair of cattle horns is perhaps more apposite for the shape of a composite bow than for the simple curve of a self bow. Physical remains are, however, entirely lacking.[54] A number of (apparently unrecognised) splints published from Viking graves in the Ukraine (Arne 1931), while perhaps representing locally-acquired weapons, offer the possibilty of a reintroduction at this time.

For further evidence of the possible currency of composite bows in post-Roman Britain, reference must be made to the question of the use of crossbows (below). While it is possible to construct a crossbow with a one-piece bow, the small size which is desirable in such a weapon would certainly favour a composite structure. Medieval crossbows were invariably made in this way, as were (to judge from the representations discussed below) those of Roman date.

Crossbows (Figure 84)

Two elements in the crossbow are of particular relevance to the present enquiry: one is the bow, constructed in composite fashion in the manner just described, and the other is the nut, which controlled the string release.

The early history of the crossbow has recently been discussed elsewhere (MacGregor 1976c). The earliest archaeological evidence for this weapon comes from two Roman bas-reliefs from Aquitaine (Espérendieu 1908): the first of these, a *cippus* from Salignac-sur-Loire, illustrates a hunting assemblage, including a crossbow with reflexed (i.e., composite) bow; the second, a fragmentary slab found among the

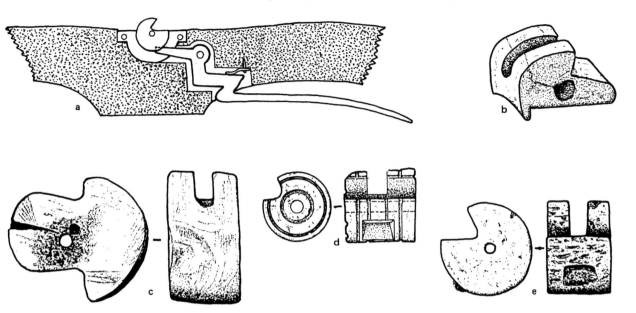

Figure 84: Crossbows (a) cross-sectional view showing positioning of nut in stock and relationship to trigger (after Payne Gallwey); nuts from (b) Burbage (Goddard) (c) Buston Crannog (d) Wareham Castle (Renn) (e) Urquhart Castle (scale (b-e) 3:4)

ruins of a Gallo-Roman villa at Espaly, has a more ambitious composition, showing a hunting scene in which one of the huntsmen carries an unmistakable crossbow and has a quiver at his belt. Whether they were used at this time exclusively as sporting rather than military weapons is unclear.

As already mentioned, most medieval crossbows found in northern Europe would have had bows of the composite structure described above, incorporating horn springs and, perhaps, bone or antler splints forming the nocks. So far, however, only the splints mentioned above have been found, all of them being of Roman date. Documentary reference of 1302 has been noted by de Cosson (1893) to one William Conrad, bowyer to the Tower of London, concerning the supply of 'wiseblase', glue, the sinews of sea-dogs and other necessities for the manufacture of crossbows, and later bills quoted by the same author extend the range of requirements. With the second crossbow element normally executed in skeletal materials — the nut — we are better provided with archaeological remains.

Payne-Gallwey (1903) describes in detail the function of the nut in the crossbow. Cradled in a socket lying across the top of the stock, it was secured by a pin or by strands of gut threaded through an axial perforation; the sear of the trigger engaged in a notch cut in the underside of the nut, which was in some instances protected from undue wear by the insertion of an iron wedge. The bow-string was held under tension in a second notch cut in the upper side, slotted transversely to form twin projections, between which lay the arrow, fitted to the string. Pressure on the lower end of the trigger mechanism disengaged the sear from its notch, leaving the nut free to rotate in its cradle under the tension of the bow-string, until the string was freed and the arrow released.

Both the sculptured representations of Roman crossbows illustrated by Espérandieu (1908) exhibit what could be taken to be nuts of this type. Early excavations at Carnuntum on the Austrian *Limes* produced one example (von Groller 1909), and Roach Smith (1859) reproduces another in his *Illustrations of Roman London*. Both of these items are indistinguishable from medieval nuts and, since neither piece is from a stratified Roman context, their early origins must be doubted.[55] A further nut (Figure 84b), of unusual form, was found in a chalk-cut grave at Burbage, Wiltshire, towards the end of the last century, and was also claimed as being of Roman date (Goddard 1896). This example is quite unlike the normal lathe-turned cylindrical nuts of the medieval period (see below), being flat in section and having a trigger-notch extending across the entire width of the nut. Other items of bone or antler contained in the grave included a pommel, a lathe-turned collar and a strip ornamented with incised border lines and with ring-and-dot motifs. The latter was pierced by a number of iron rivets and is of the same character as the ornamental casket mounts described below (pp. 197-200); Goddard (1896) records the opinion that this example may have decorated the stock of the crossbow, however, and Credland (1980) suggests that the pommel too may have come from this weapon. Precise dating evidence is entirely lacking: a Roman or Saxon date might be acceptable for a formal burial with grave-goods, though the manner in which the body was thrown into the grave (it was found face downwards, with the skeleton apparently twisted and the feet about 1m lower than the head) might suggest clandestine interment. Credland (1980) notes an eleventh-century parallel for an iron hammer head from the same grave, reinforcing the likelihood of a post-Roman date for this as for the other nuts mentioned above.

Another nineteenth-century discovery was made at Buston Crannog, Strathclyde (Munro 1882). The Buston nut (Figure 84c) is made from a sawn section of antler beam, cut near the base to avoid the spongy core. There is an axial perforation, 4mm in diameter; an earlier attempt at perforating the nut, by drilling from either side with a pointed implement, was abandoned at an early stage, presumably when it was realised that the resulting hole would be considerably off-centre. It is clear from the irregular outlines of the piece that it has been shaped entirely by hand and is unused. Like the Burbage nut, the trigger-notch extends across the entire width of the nut from Buston. The seating for the string has an inadequate look, not having been undercut to provide a secure hold in the manner usual in medieval nuts. The eighth-century date generally accepted for the bulk of the material from Buston might also be applied to the nut, although it should be noted that there is a certain amount of residual

Roman material on the site and also that the crannog survived as a small island until the nineteenth century (MacGregor 1976c).

A further important find, whose significance seems not to have been recognised, has been made at the Butte d'Isle Aumont, Aube (Scapula 1956). Among the bone and antler finds from this site is an unmistakable crossbow nut seemingly incorporating a hole for securing an iron wedge. The settlement is said to have been destroyed in the tenth century and, if the nut does indeed belong to the period of occupation of the site, it would be the earliest securely-stratified example to survive.

Whatever its status beforehand, the crossbow enjoyed greatly increased popularity from the time of the Norman Conquest, as can be seen from extant remains as well as literary references. A nut of the typical lathe-turned cylindrical form favoured in the medieval period has been recovered from Goltho Manor, Lincolnshire, where it was found in a late eleventh-century context (MacGregor, forthcoming). Renn (1960) describes a similar example from Wareham Castle, Dorset (Figure 84d), dated to the first half of the twelfth century. Unstratified nuts which may be of early medieval date include examples from Pevensey Castle, Sussex (Credland 1980), and Urquhart Castle, Highland Region (MacGregor 1976c), the latter incorporating the oxidised remains of an iron wedge which had once protected the trigger slot (Figure 84e), a feature also seen on a thirteenth-century nut from Winchester, Hampshire (Credland 1980). Long (1975) mentions three nuts found in recent excavations at Trondheim, Norway, at least one of them from the thirteenth century. Another example from Amsterdam is dated about 1400 (Amsterdams Historisch Museum 1977). From the later medieval period comes a nut from Sandal Castle, Yorkshire, dated 1450-1500 (Credland 1980), and others of uncertain date found in Cambridge and in London are also mentioned by Credland. Complete crossbows incorporating antler nuts and dated as late as the seventeenth century are listed by Mann (1962), including one German example dated 1683 and combining a steel bow with an antler nut.

Two historical references to the collection and use of antler for the manufacture of crossbow nuts appear in the *Close Rolls* of Henry III (*Rotuli Litterarum Clausarum* 2, 50, 63):

Mandatum est Hasculf de Adhelakeston quod omnes perchias de cervo quas penes eo habet de foresta nostra que est in custodia sua habere faciat Philipo Converso balistario ad nuces balistarum faciendas.

It is commanded that Hasculf de Adhelakeston should make over all the antler beams which he has at his disposal from our forest which is in his care to Philip Convers the crossbow-maker for the manufacture of crossbow nuts.

Precipimus tibi quod habere facias Magistro Petro Balistario dimidiam marcam pro nucibus nervis et cornu que emit per preceptum nostrum ad balistas nostras de Corf reperandas.

We order you to make over to Master Peter the crossbow-maker half a mark for the nuts, strings and horn which he bought at our command for the repair of our crossbows at Corfe.

At a later period, in the sixteenth century, Olaus Magnus (1556) mentions that in Scandinavia reindeer antler was much sought after by the makers of bows and crossbows. Together these represent the only historical records of the deliberate gathering of antlers for manufacturing purposes. It is of interest to note that the word *perchia* (also written *perticha*) refers to the beam rather than the whole antler (Turner 1899), and perhaps it was permitted to remove the tines (which were of no use in crossbow-making) before the antlers were rendered up to the Crown.

It is well known that crossbowmen are conspicuous by their absence on the Bayeux Tapestry, a fact which has been taken in the past to imply that these weapons did not enter the Norman armoury until after the Conquest. Morton and Muntz (1972) have observed that the stance and accoutrements of one of the archers shown on the tapestry are more appropriate to a crossbowman, however, and suggest that the weapon itself may have been discreetly omitted from this highly propagandist work, since it was generally considered to be barbarous (its use against Christians later being banned by the Second Lateran Council in 1139). Guy of Amiens, in his *Carmen de Hastingae Proelio*, written within two years of the Conquest, twice (vv. 338 and 411) mentions crossbowmen within the Norman force (Morton and Muntz 1972), while we find that some of the tenants-in-chief recorded in *Domesday* as holding land in Yorkshire, Norfolk and Wiltshire (listed in Ellis 1833) are given the title *arbalistarius*, confirming the existence of these weapons in England within a few years of the Conquest.

Secondary evidence for the use of crossbows in the pre-Norman period is limited to a few passing references in continental written sources (summarised in Morton and Muntz 1972) and to a series of representations on Pictish stones (Allen and Anderson 1903), the significance of which has recently been reviewed by Gilbert (1976). Although the details are unclear, each of the stones concerned illustrates a kneeling hunter pulling the string of his bow with one hand while the other grips the base of what appears to be a stock attached to the bow. Gilbert states that an arrow can be seen outlined on the flat stock of the crossbow illustrated on one stone. He concludes that the weapon represented must be a primitive type without a trigger mechanism, the archer simply pulling back the arrow and releasing it by hand. Far from being, as Gilbert says, 'ideal for stalking . . . since it would require less strength, less space and less movement to fire', such a weapon would be quite impractical, presenting no mechanical advantage to the kneeling archer; furthermore, the manner in which the figure on one stone (the 'Drosten' stone) is gripping the string makes it clear that this is not what is being portrayed. In any case, the identification of the nut from Buston Crannog, if it is indeed contemporary, would render such a hypothesis unnecessary. In each of these sculptured stones the Pictish crossbows are portrayed as hunting weapons. Anderson (1881) may well be correct in his assertion this was the principal role of crossbows among the Picts, while conventional bows were used as weapons of war

Finally, a unique find from the Continent adds one more element to the list of bone crossbow fittings. Tauber (1977) illustrates a fragmentary object with complex facets and perforations which he identifies as a trigger from a crossbow. It comes from Frohburg, Switzerland, where the bulk of the material can be dated between the second half of the eleventh century and the beginning of the thirteenth.

Arrowheads (Figure 85)

Excavations on the site of an eleventh-century Norse farmhouse at Narssaq on Greenland have produced two well-made tanged arrowheads of antler (Figure 85a, b), corresponding closely to contemporary types in iron (Vebæk 1965). Vebæk concludes that the adoption of antler there was prompted by recognition of its fitness and easy availability for this purpose rather than by any sudden difficulty of access to sources of iron. This contention is borne out by the occurrence at Birka, one of the best-supplied of Viking age settlements, of an alternative form of antler arrowhead with a solid, quadrangular section (Figure 85c). Antler and bone had certainly shown their suitability for this purpose in earlier periods, to judge by the numbers of such finds of Roman Iron Age date from Vimose, Denmark (Engelhardt 1869) and others of Iron Age type recovered from the Thames near London (Guildhall Museum 1908). There appears, however, to have been no very widespread production of bone or antler arrowheads during the historic period.

Inspired by material collected by ethnologists among recent hunters in the Yakutsk, Zachrisson (1976) has tentatively identified a second type of arrowhead which had some specialised use in northern Europe. These circular-section antler heads, lathe-turned in some instances, have an axial socket and a profile which expands to a wide, blunt tip (Figure 85d-e). Zachrisson notes one Swedish and two Norwegian finds of medieval date and a fourth example of uncertain date, again from Norway. No such arrowheads have hitherto been identified elsewhere, but it seems possible that certain items which have been differently identified in the past should be reassessed in the light of Zachrisson's paper. From the Groningen Museum collections Roes (1963) illustrates two bone or antler cylinders, each with an expanded lip at one end, one of which has two iron pins passing laterally through it. She also illustrates two similar objects, and another with a pear-shaped and a blind axial hole comes from Carolingian levels at Dorestad. Roes decided that these 'cannot have been anything else but the heads of walking-sticks', but there is a close resemblance between them and the Scandinavian arrowheads identified above. Holdsworth (1976) has compared an antler knob from Saxon Southampton with the Frisian finds mentioned above, and hence this object too might be

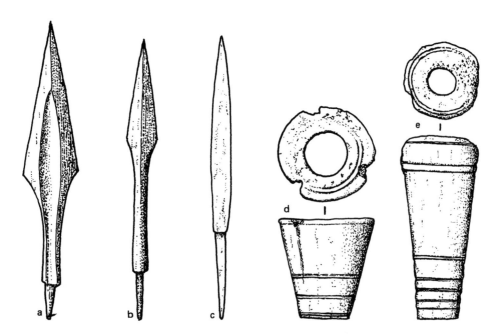

Figure 85:   Antler arrowheads (scale 3:4) from (a-b) Greenland (Vebæk) (c) Birka (d-e) Norway (Zachrisson)

considered as a blunt arrowhead. Like one of the Groningen heads the Southampton piece was fixed in place with lateral pins, one of iron and one of bone. Another item of some interest here comes from a grave at Burbage, Wiltshire, which also produced a crossbow nut (pp. 159-60). This antler knob was originally identified as part of a dagger handle (Goddard 1896) and more recently has been reinterpreted as a pommel from the crossbow already mentioned (Credland 1980), but the possibility that it served as the head of a crossbow bolt cannot be discounted.

Blunt arrowheads of this type could have been used in hunting wildfowl or, as Zachrisson (1976) suggests, small animals such as squirrels.

Scabbard Chapes (Figure 86a-g)

For a comparatively brief period during the late second and third centuries, scabbard chapes of bone were widely issued as part of the auxiliary soldier's equipment. Production of these was no doubt concentrated in some of the major military depots; possible evidence of manufacturing has been noted at Mainz, where a chape was found together with worked and unworked bone fragments (Klumbach and Moortgat-Correns 1968) and in the *Limes* fort at Stockstadt (Drexel 1910), while at Caerleon, Gwent, nine chapes were found in a third-century armoury building where these and other items in bone (p. 158) were being produced (Nash-Williams 1932). The long-bones of cattle (probably tibias) provided the principal source of raw material.

The chapes are generally made in two parts,[56] of which the front element is most commonly rectangular or trapezoidal, the longer (vertical) sides often being slightly concave (Figure 86a-e). The sides curve round to form flanges, widely separated from the front surface at the top and converging towards it at the bottom; the flanges also tend to taper in relation to one another, frequently (but not invariably) towards the top. The rear element is a simple plate which slides within the flanges and displays a corresponding taper. Some examples incorporate rivet holes through which they were fixed to the scabbard, but the majority have no such holes and were presumably glued in place.[57]

In the process of shaping it was common for a central rib (or ribs) and borders on either side to be left in relief and for the chape to be pierced by a pair of opposed pelta-shaped holes near the top; examples are found among those from Caerleon (Nash-Williams 1932), Lydney Park, Gloucestershire (Wheeler and Wheeler 1932) and from Richborough, Kent (Bushe-Fox 1932), while numerous examples from the *Limes* are listed by Oldenstein (1976).

The most common alternative to this decorative scheme features a central elipse in relief, often with an axial rib; some chapes of this type are again pierced by opposed pelta-shaped holes, as on those from Silchester, Hampshire (Boon 1974), Bonn (*Bonner Jahrbücher* 176, 400-1) and Osterburken, Baden-Württemberg (Schumacher 1895), but most feature a pair of incised scrolls near the top of the elipse. One of the Caerleon chapes is of this type (Nash-Williams 1932) and other British examples come from Chester (Newstead 1928) and Richborough, Kent (Cunliffe 1968); several others originating in the *Limes* are illustrated by Oldenstein (1976).

Among chapes of either of the above groups the upper and lower edges may be notched, serrated, or carved into a sinuous outline.

Although less common than the rectangular forms discussed above, circular chapes made on the same principal are also found. Caerleon produced one (Nash-Williams 1932) and Oldenstein (1976) lists several from German military sites. Both of the major decorative devices noted amongst rectangular chapes — midribs combined with pelta-shaped holes and relief elipses with opposed scrolls — are again represented. In one example from Zugmantel, the upper edge is elaborately profiled in the manner of some metal chapes (Oldenstein 1976). A number of circular chapes of bone and ivory of Roman Iron Age date, found in bog deposits at Vimose, Denmark, are described by Engelhardt (1869) (see also Figure 86g).

Scabbard Slides (Figure 86h-m)

From the late Roman period come a few examples of further scabbard fittings identified as slides or suspension loops. These take the form of elongated blocks of bone or ivory, pierced from side to side by a rectangular slot

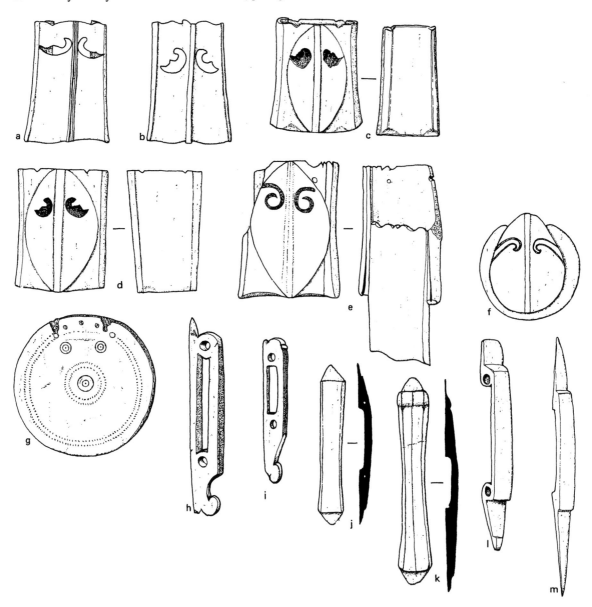

Figure 86:   Scabbard chapes and slides (scale 1:2) (a) Saalburg (Oldenstein) (b) Stockstadt (Oldenstein) (c) Silchester (Boon) (d) Bonn (Münten and Heimberg) (e) Niederbeiber (Oldenstein) (f) Zugmantel (Oldenstein) (g) Vimose (Engelhardt) (h, i) London (Chapman) (j) Worms (Oldenstein) (k) Niederbeiber (Oldenstein) (l, m) Vimose (Engelhardt)

to accommodate the belt or baldric with, above and below the slot, two smaller circular holes by which the slide was bound to the scabbard. For additional stability small tongues project from either extremity. These would have fitted under further bindings on the scabbard. The slides taper gently from top to bottom, with a curving foot or volute projecting from the latter.

To an early (unrecognised) find from Colchester, Essex (Wheeler 1923), Chapman (1976) has recently added to the published list two examples from South Shields, Tyne and Wear, and two from London. From the European mainland come two from Danubian contexts (Trousdale 1975) and four from Vimose in Denmark, well north of the Roman frontier (Engelhardt 1869). As Trousdale has shown, however, the origins of the type as a whole lie further east in Asia, where examples occur from the Near East to China. Their introduction into Europe can no doubt be attributed to the stiffening of late Roman defences with auxilliaries of Near Eastern origin, and as two possibilities, Chapman (1976) suggests Sarmatians or Parthians.

Sword and Dagger Hilts (Figure 87)

Incomplete bone grips from weapons are not always easy to tell apart from those of domestic knives and indeed they may at times have been indistinguishable. Considering the prominence given to the pommel in complete Roman hilts, however, it seems unlikely that grips closed with simple discs could ever have been used for swords, and should be regarded as knife handles. Although grips of bone or antler seem to have maintained only limited popularity beyond the end of the Roman period, finds of pommels and guards are rather more numerous. The practical value of guards made from organic materials (including those of skeletal origin) has been questioned by Ellis Davidson (1962) but the ability of these tough materials to resist even quite savage cutting blows should not be underestimated.

Roman (Figure 87a-e)

The well-known series of Roman sword grips featuring four moulded depressions for the fingers had already made its appearance by the first century, in Britain as well as on the Continent. Most are made from the metapodials of horses or cattle, the former being more regular in section; wood provides the most common alternative (Oldenstein 1976). A simple handle of this type survives on a sword from Newstead, Borders Region (J. Curle 1911). Many bone grips are cut to a rhomboid section and clearly have been shaped entirely by hand, and a good example fixed to the tang of a well-preserved sword is illustrated by Braat (1967).

Unassociated handles of this type come from St Clement's Lane, London (Webster 1958), and from the *Limes* fort of Rheingönheim, Rheinland-Pfalz (Ulbert 1969) (Figure 87c, d). They come also from the Frisian terp mounds (Roes 1963), one of the latter being of ivory and found with a pommel of the same material. Circular-section versions of these handles also exist, sometimes with bands of incised lines on the mouldings to improve the grip, as on an example from Richborough, Kent (Bushe-Fox 1949) and on another (Figure 87b) from Caernarvon, Gwynedd (Boon 1962). Further variants, some of them slightly barrel-shaped and all probably of the second century, are illustrated by Oldenstein (1976); these include an example from Cannstatt, Württemberg (Figure 87a), found together with its pommel. Engelhardt (1869) illustrates several complete hilts from Roman swords, some in bone, some in ivory and some in wood, from Vimose in Denmark.

The most common form of guard to accompany early bone handles is plano-convex in section and ovoid or rounded in plan but that on the Caernarvon sword, which probably dates before 140, is cylindrical (Boon 1962). From the second century others developed with a flatter outline and more angular plan. An alternative type (Figure 87e) of more complex form is less common; Oldenstein (1976) suggests that it owes its shape to metal originals.

The same author notes a parallel development among Roman sword pommels, the spherical or eliptical shapes favoured in the first century, as on the Caernarvon sword (Boon 1962), giving way to flatter and more rounded types. An example from Caistor-by-Norwich, Norfolk, is in Norwich Castle Museum (unpublished). That from Cannstatt illustrated in Figure 87a dates from the mid second century. Smaller pommels found at Zugmantel, Hessen (Jacobi 1909), no doubt served for daggers.

Dark Age and Viking (Figure 87f-k)

Influences from Roman sword hilts can be detected on those of the ensuing centuries, particularly in the form of the grip. Behmer (1939) describes a complete sword hilt from Nydam Mose in southern Jutland which has a grip with finger-mouldings indistinguishable

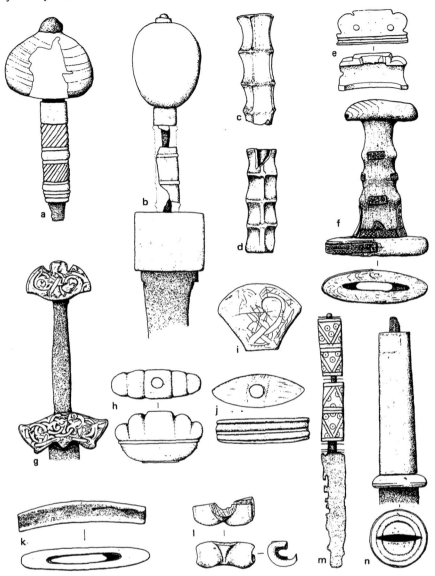

Figure 87:   Sword and dagger hilts (scale 1:3) (a) Cannstatt (Oldenstein) (b) Caernarvon (Boon) (c) London (d) Rheingönheim (Ulbert) (e) Niederbieber (Oldenstein) (f) Cumberland (g) unprovenanced, Nationalmuseet, Copenhagen (Goldschmidt) (h) York (i) London (j) Lakenheath (k) Birka (l) Sandal Castle (m) Bytom (Drescher) (n) Oddington

from those of the Roman period. Something of the same influence can be seen on a complete sword hilt of cattle horn from Cumberland (Figure 87f), although here the grip is ovoid in section and tapers towards the pommel, a feature displayed by an almost intact fifth-century hilt from Evebo, Norway, illustrated by Behmer (1939). The Cumberland hilt is a unique find in terms of its raw material and also in the gold and cloisonné garnet mounts by which it has been dated to the seventh century, although the possibility that the mounts are somewhat later than the horn hilt cannot be discounted. In general, however, grips of skeletal materials appear to have lost favour to those of wood after the end of the Roman period.

The complete hilts from Cumberland and from Nydam Mose both feature guards and pommels which are ovoid in plan and flattened in section, the pommel on the Nydam sword being as large as the guard. A detached pommel and guard of bone or antler from Nydam Mose illustrated by Behmer (1939), have a common eliptical plan, being smaller than the guard and having a small circular perforation for the tip of the tang, while the guard has a rectangular slot for its base.

A feature common to the guard of the Cumberland hilt and to a detached guard of antler from York of late Saxon or Viking origin (D.M. Waterman 1959) is a slot cut on the underside to fit the heel of the blade. A detached guard from the Frisian terps has a similar slot but Roes (1963) takes it to be on the upper (grip) side. Petersen (1919) illustrates many instances of these slots on metal guards and Wilson (1965) mentions it as a common feature on late Saxon swords. More elaborate guards of this period include one example in elk antler, angled towards the blade and decorated with incised Mammen style ornament, from Sigtuna, Sweden (Floderus 1941; Graham-Campbell and Kidd 1980), and one in ivory mounted on the so-called St Stephen's sword, of Scandinavian origin, but now in Prague (Kossina 1929).

Pommels of this period include both simple forms as illustrated by the lentoid example from Lakenheath Fen, Suffolk, illustrated in Figure 87j and the more complex lobed form of catacean bone in Figure 87h, found in a twelfth-century context at York, but likely to be some centuries earlier in origin.

During the ninth and tenth centuries a certain amount of historical evidence can be found to suggest that sword hilts were made by groups of specialist craftsmen rather than by the armourers' workshops in which the blades were made (Ellis Davidson 1962). These craftsmen may also have been employed in the repair of damaged hilts (Jankuhn 1951).

Medieval and Later (Figure 87l-n)

The popularity of skeletal materials in the manufacture of sword hilts was maintained to some extent into the medieval period, particularly in the Scandinavian world. Bergman and Billberg (in Mårtensson 1976) illustrate two bone guards from Lund, Sweden, which they date to the first half of the twelfth century, one with beaked terminals angled towards the blade and the other straight with an incised lozenge pattern. The same authors describe a discoid pommel, also of bone, dated to the twelfth or thirteenth centuries. Goldschmidt (1923) illustrates a sword with an intact guard and pommel of walrus ivory covered with interlacing animal decoration, again dated to these centuries (Figure 87g); the angled guard recalls the shape of the Mammen style grip from Sigtuna mentioned above and is mirrored by the shape of the pommel. Scattered finds from elsewhere demonstrate some continuation of, and variation on, earlier practices.

Drescher (1975) has published a straight-bladed knife from a twelfth or thirteenth-century context at Bytom, Oberschlesien, with a composite handle consisting of two cylindrical elements of bone bounded above and below by plates of copper alloy and lead, between which were originally sandwiched layers of organic material, conceivably horn or leather (Figure 87m).[55] A date in the sixteenth century is suggested for a similar knife in the Guildhall Museum (1908) catalogue.

A single-edged late medieval rondel dagger found at Oddington, Oxfordshire has a cylindrical grip and a discoid guard, both of antler (Figure 87n). An ivory pommel-plate in the form of a scallop shell is among finds from a post-medieval context at Ludgershall Castle, Wiltshire (MacGregor, forthcoming) and excavations at Sandal Castle in West Yorkshire produced what appears to be a unique find in the form of a bone guard from a late medieval ballock knife (Figure 87l) (MacGregor 1983).

Implement Handles (Figure 88)

Under this heading are grouped the handles of tools and utensils (including knives), but not those of weapons, which are considered above.

Roman (Figure 88a-i)

Three basic types may be considered: cylindrical handles into which a pointed tang could

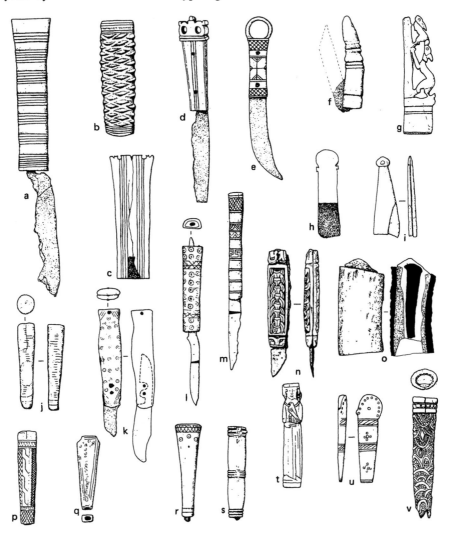

Figure 88:   Implement handles (scale 1:3) from (a) Chew Valley Lake (Rahtz and Greenfield) (b) Icklingham (West and Plouviez) (c) Verulamium (d) Straubing (Walke) (e) London (f) Richborough (Bushe-Fox) (g) Great Chesterford (Tebbutt) (h) Verulamium (i) Shakenoak (j) Weeting (Clarke) (k) Northampton (Williams) (l, m) York (n) Canterbury (Graham-Campbell) (o) Southampton (Platt and Coleman-Smith) (p) Whitby (Peers and Radford) (q-s) Birka (t) Oxford (u) Denny Abbey (Christie and Coad) (v) London (Johnson)

be fitted; paired plates or scales which could be riveted to either side of a strip tang; and handles for folding or clasp knives.

Two raw materials served for the production of cylindrical handles. Antler (often in the form of tines) provided a source of solid tissue into which a longitudinal socket could be drilled and a pointed tang could be wedged. Simple handles of this type come from Carpow, Tayside (Birley 1963), Wakerley, Northampton-

shire (Jackson and Ambrose 1978), and Lydney, Gloucestershire (Wheeler and Wheeler 1932), and on the Continent from the *Limes* (Ulbert 1959). Handles made from the hollow shafts of long-bones, which account for the second major group, would have had to be plugged with wood or some other material in order to give a firm seating for the tang, or in some instances it would have passed through the handle and been secured with a washer at either end. Several knives with terminal washers on the tangs, but with the handles now missing, are among the finds from Straubing, Bayern (Walke 1965). Many handles of this type are lathe-turned and are decorated with raised mouldings or incised decoration, and typical examples come from Richborough, Kent (Cunliffe 1968), Portchester, Hampshire (Cunliffe 1975) and Chew Valley Lake, Avon (Rahtz and Greenfield 1977); a more elaborate hand-carved example with all-over raised lozenges comes from Icklingham, Suffolk (West and Plouviez 1976). Other handles of this type retain the angular cross-section of the original bone; an example made from a bovine metatarsal and ornamented with incised linear decoration is among Roman finds from Borough High Street, Southwark (Ferretti and Graham 1978).

A distinct type of knife handle featuring (and perhaps held in place by) a terminal 'spring-clip' has recently been identified by Greep (1982).

Riveted side-plates are more numerously found on Roman period knives, as probably a satisfactorily firm result could be more easily achieved in this way. They vary in length from about 4cm to a full hand's width of *c.* 10cm. A common type (Figure 88e) features short plates of plano-convex section, waisted in the middle and ornamented with bands of incised lines, often in the form of cross-hatching. Excavated examples come from Caerleon, Gwent (Wheeler and Wheeler 1926), Richborough, Kent (Bushe-Fox 1926), and London (Wheeler 1930) and the German *Limes* (Walke 1965). Others without a medial constriction are also known (H. Chapman in Laws 1976; Guildhall Museum 1908). Intact knives with handles of this sort often have a concave cutting edge and occasionally feature a ring terminal (Figure 88e). A more delicate knife from York preserved in the corrosion products of its iron strip tang the striated impression of what were almost certainly horn plates, although the horn itself had decayed (MacGregor 1978).

Strip-tanged knives were occasionally fitted with more elaborate handles which might have decorative openwork terminals (Walke 1965) or which may be fitted to the blade by means of a slot sawn in the base (Figure 88h); the latter type may be reinforced with notched plates riveted over the junction with the blade.

The simplest clasp-knife handles are those made from antler tines. A ferrule is attached to the basal end of the tine, the pin acting as the pivot of the blade also serving to secure the ferrule, and a slot to receive the folded blade is cut on either the inner or outer curve of the tine. An example of this type from Richborough, Kent (Figure 88f) has previously been published by Bushe-Fox (1928). An alternative form, made of bone and with a wide profile tapering to a finial, has been noted from a second- or third-century context at Fishbourne, Sussex (Cunliffe 1971), and from a late fourth-century layer at Shakenoak, Oxfordshire (Brodribb *et al.* 1973) (Figure 88i). Among the more complex representational handles, one of the most popular was the openwork 'hare and hound' type, also commonly found in bronze. These have been noted in England (Figure 88g) from Great Chesterford, Essex (Tebbutt 1961), and on the Continent from Regensburg, Bayern (Dietz *et al.* 1979), Zugmantel, Hessen (Jacobi 1909) and elsewhere in Germany (von Mercklin 1940), and in France (Lebel 1953; Musée Archaéologique de Dijon nd). Von Mercklin (1940) describes a variety of handles featuring various motifs including animals, dolphins, sword scabbards, gods, human figures and various parts thereof, such as hands, legs and phalli.

Dark Age and Viking (Figure 88j-n, p-s)

A series of simple antler handles of the early post-Roman period carry Ogham inscriptions which, it has been suggested (Macalister 1940), may allude to ownership. Examples come from Aikerness Broch, Orkney (Macalister 1940), Bac Mhic Connain, North Uist (Beveridge 1932) and Weeting, Norfolk (R.R. Clarke 1952), the latter (Figure 88j) retaining the iron tang of what was thought to be a knife. Not all such simple handles need have been for knives: an alternative function for the type is illustrated by a handle found on a two-pronged forked implement from a Saxon grave at Harnham, Wiltshire (Akerman 1855), and a group of bone and antler handles from a tool box of about the eighth to tenth centuries found in Orkney is illustrated by Stevenson (1952). A broadly contemporary date may be suggested for a decoratively incised antler handle (Figure 88p) from Whitby, Yorkshire (Peers and Radford

1943). Among the numerous Viking age and early medieval tanged knives from York illustrated by D.M. Waterman (1959) are two with intact bone handles (Figure 88l-m). From Birka come several smaller examples of varying design (Figure 88q-s). In the north cetacean bone provided an alternative raw material, and a well-made handle cut from solid cetacean tissue came from excavations at Dun Cuier, Isle of Barra (A. Young 1956).

Bone-handled folding knives of the late Saxon and Viking period are becoming increasingly well-known as a result of recent research. I. Goodall (in Williams 1979) illustrates the mechanism of such a knife from Northampton (Figure 88k) and mentions others from Thetford, Norfolk, and Winchester, Hampshire, while Graham-Campbell (1978, 1980) has published another example from Canterbury, with an ornately-carved handle in tenth-century Borre style (Figure 88n).

Medieval (Figure 88o, t-v)

Among the simpler types of tool handle little development may be expected during the medieval period, although closely-dated examples are difficult to find: a number of antler handles from Southampton (Figure 88o) form useful evidence from the period (Platt and Coleman-Smith 1975). It may be conjectured that handles made from the solid tips of cattle horns may have become more popular at this time, although none appears to have survived. Folding knives are indeed rare at this time: Rahtz (1970) illustrates an example from an unsealed twelfth to sixteenth century layer at Glastonbury Tor, Somerset.

More decorative forms appear from the early medieval period onwards. Some rely on incised decoration cut into the surface of the handle, as on a cylindrical bone handle with a plugged butt end (Figure 88v), found at Bush Lane in the City of London and dating probably from the eleventh or twelfth centuries (A.E. Johnson 1974). Others take on anthropomorphic forms, as on examples from thirteenth-century Southampton (Platt 1976), Ludgershall Castle, Wiltshire (MacGregor, forthcoming) and Oxford (Figure 88t). Bencard (1975) has discussed a widespread series of handles dating from about 1250-1350 and carved in the form of a young man carrying a falcon on his arm: to

those listed by Bencard may be added hitherto unpublished examples in the National Museum of Antiquities, Edinburgh, and the Peterborough Museum. Hayward (1957) describes good-quality English knives of the later sixteenth century as often having composite handles of several elements, sometimes of bone or ivory, separated by thin brass washers. On the evidence of the handle from Bytom, Oberschlesien, mentioned on p. 167, origins some three of four centuries earlier seem possible for some examples of this type.

Post-medieval

Riveted pairs of bone or antler scales become common again on knives of the post-medieval period, often with incised cross-hatched ornament (which also improves the grip) and with multiple rivets, frequently of bronze. One example from Hull, North Humberside, has alternating rivets of iron and bronze (P. Armstrong 1977). More delicate handles of bone for small knives and for table cutlery also make their appearance. Those in bone vary from plain cylindrical types with plugged ends as found at St Benedict's Gates, Norwich (Hurst and Colson 1957) to elaborate versions such as an octagonal-section handle with incised leaf and scroll decoration, with rivet-heads covered by bone discs (Goodall and Christie in Christie and Coad 1980). Ivory handles, too, are known in a variety of forms. An attractive sixteenth-century type with a decorative terminal is represented at Ospringe, Kent (G.H. Smith 1979) and a wide range of forms, including skilfully-carved anthropomorphic handles, is illustrated by Ward (1957). T.M. Hughes (1907) illustrates a collection of ivory handles from carving forks and knives from excavations on the site of the Bird Bolt Hotel, Cambridge.

Handles of horn are little known before the eighteenth century, but from that time it became an immensely popular medium for fitting to a variety of domestic utensils, including pen-knives and cut-throat razors (Hardwick 1981). The most common form at this time took the shape of riveted plates of material usually filed into shape and polished to reveal the natural markings; it was sometimes passed through a heated mould to impart impressed decoration with considerable fineness of detail.

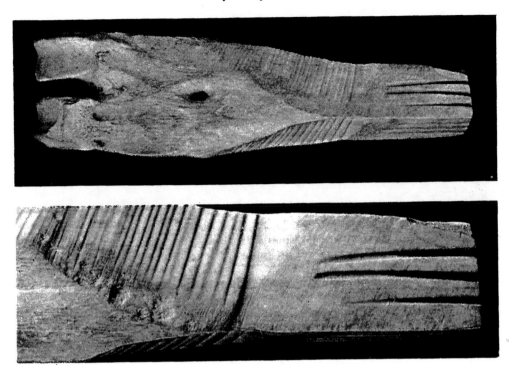

Figure 89:　Pinners' bone from London, with close-up of file marks

Pinners' Bones (Figure 89)

Even before the middle of the sixteenth century, the manufacture of brass wire pins had developed on a large scale. Efficient methods of forming the bulbous heads were quickly discovered but the production of sharp points proved more difficult to streamline so that, until the late eighteenth century by which time the process had become mechanised (Tylecote 1972), it remained customary to file the points individually, using a bone holder in order to improve the grip and avoid bending the pin. Metapodials were normally used, usually those from cattle and horses, as among numerous finds from various localities in London (e.g. Guildhall Museum 1908). These include Baynard's Castle where cattle metapodials appear to have been specially selected for this purpose (Armitage 1977). Sheep bones have also been recorded from Coventry (Chatwin 1934), and from Birmingham (Oswald 1948), both in the West Midlands. Another example from Worcester, although unrecognised as a pinner's bone, came from a pit containing other metal-working debris (Carver 1980). Usually four flat facets were cut into the end of the bone, and two or three grooves made with a saw blade in the long axis; the pins were held in these grooves while the points were being filed, resulting in the bone being marked by diagonal file marks, and frequently also stained green by copper salts from the pins (Figure 89). In addition to those mentioned above, finds of these bones, together with evidence for bronze smithing have been made at Chelmsford, Essex (*Post-Medieval Archaeology* 7, 104) and at King's Lynn, Norfolk, the latter unrecognised in the excavation report (Clarke and Carter 1977).

Hammers (Figure 90)

A number of hammer heads from the Black Earth at Birka have not been published to date. All are cut from solid antler beams and have been carefully shaped and drilled to achieve their final form (Figure 90b).

Five hammers made from shed antler burrs have now been noted from British excavations.

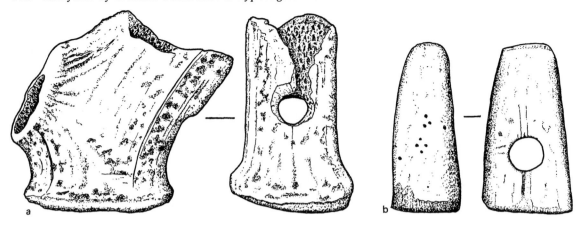

Figure 90:   Hammers of antler (scale 2:3) from (a) Jarrow and (b) Birka

Only one of these (Figure 90a), from Jarrow, Tyne and Wear (Professor R. Cramp, personal communication) is from a stratified context (a thirteenth or fourteenth-century pit), however, so the extent of their currency remains conjectural. Two of these implements were found during excavations at Broad Street, Aberdeen (MacGregor 1982b), where they were unstratified, and another came from a multi-period site at Staines, Middlesex, appearing in an eighteenth-century destruction layer (D. Barker in Crouch 1976). An unprovenanced example, possibly from York, is in the Yorkshire Museum (unpublished). All of these pieces have in common a transverse perforation running through the base of the severed brow tine, into which a narrow handle would have fitted, and all have sustained damage on the face of the burr. They may have been craft tools, used perhaps in sheet metal working. The toughness which is a feature of antler (pp. 27-9) would have suited it admirably for this function, although the coarse appearance of these items contrasts with the hammers from Birka mentioned above.

At least in the last few centuries hammer heads made from the solid tips of cattle horn have been used by silversmiths. Hardwick (1981) illustrates a nineteenth-century example in which the natural curve of the horn is preserved; the wooden haft is fitted through a central transverse shaft hole.

Clamps (Figure 91)

As mentioned above (p. 62), a series of composite implements made of antler or bone identified as clamps is frequently claimed to be associated with comb-making, perhaps being used to hold the tooth-plates during manufacture. While this particular function remains unproven (and indeed their greater suitability for softer materials has been noted in Ulbricht 1978), the identification of these items as clamps is convincing. Each has two elements which, when riveted together, are contiguous at one end and divergent at the other; a piece of raw material placed in the open end would be clamped in place when a wedge was driven into the other, the two elements pivoting about the central rivet.

Clamps of this type are known from Viking age and early medieval contexts at Hedeby (Jankuhn 1943; Ulbricht 1978), at Trelleborg in Denmark (Nørlund 1948) and at Ytre Elgsnes[59] (Simonsen 1953) and Trondheim (Long 1975) in Norway. Others have been noted from Iceland (Eldjárn 1956). Examples of this implement also occur in iron. Some degree of survival in more recent times is implied by examples from ethnographic collections in Norway and Greenland, cited by Ulbricht (1978).

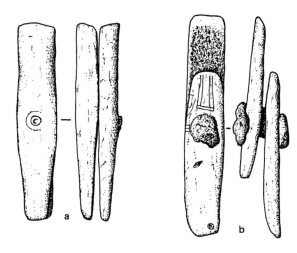

Figure 91: Clamps of antler from Hedeby (scale 1:2)

Planes (Figure 92)

Excavations in 1863 at Sarre, Kent, produced what remains for Anglo-Saxon England a unique find: a small smoothing plane with a stock constructed of antler. The Sarre plane has a sole consisting of a bronze plate with vertical stops at either end and a transverse slot 2.2cm wide to house the blade. The stock measures 13 x 13cm overall and is accurately matched to the sole to which it is attached by three rivets. Although variously referred to as wood and horn (W.L. Goodman 1959), it is in fact made of antler (Dunning 1959; Wilson 1976). It is slotted at an angle to receive the cutting iron, which was probably held in place by a wedge driven under a metal crossbar, although the latter elements are now missing (for a reconstruction, see W.L. Goodman 1959). Towards the rear, the stock is narrowed and transversely perforated by an oval hole to form a finger grip, large enough for two fingers and the thumb.

The small size of the plane marks it as a craftsman's implement rather than a general-purpose tool. Dunning's suggestion that it could have been used in the manufacture of small wooden caskets is quite plausible, while

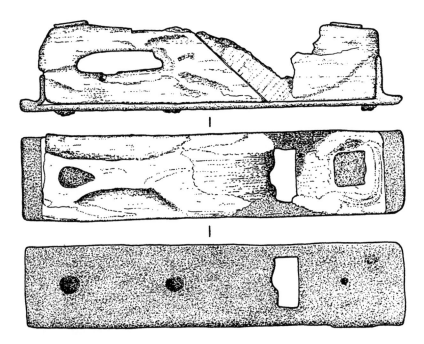

Figure 92: Plane (scale 2:3) with antler stock and bronze sole, from Sarre (after Goodman)

Goodman mentions the manufacture of musical instruments as another possibility.

A number of Roman planes, although of larger size than that from Sarre, provide models on which to base this sole Anglo-Saxon example. A plane from Silchester (reconstructed in W.L. Goodman 1959) shares a number of common features with it, and references to numerous other planes of the Roman period, mostly of the late second or third centuries, are given by Gaitzsch and Matthäus (1980). None of these, however, features antler stocks. Beyond the Roman frontier, a wooden plane dated to the third century was recovered from Vimose in Jutland (Engelhardt 1869), boat-shaped and with the ends turned up in the form of birds' heads. More closely contemporary parallels for the Sarre plane come from the Frisian terps, all of them with antler stocks and distinguished by having carved scroll-like handles which rest against a small upright pillar at the rear, and also a slanting bed for the cutting iron at a slope of about 45 degrees (Roes 1963). Some of these Frisian planes have entire bronze soles while in others an attempt has been made to save on metal by laying it down in thin strips. One example with a wooden stock incorporates on the forepart a panel of incised interlace ornament, on the basis of which Roes dates it and all the Frisian planes to about 700. Wilson (1963) favours a date in the sixth century for this same plane and for that from Sarre.

Recent excavations at Christ Church Place, Dublin, have produced part of a small wooden smoothing plane from a late eleventh-century context (B. Ó Ríordáin 1976). From the published photograph this seems to correspond closely with the Vimose plane mentioned above, being tapered towards its surviving end and terminating in an upturned bird's head.

W.L. Goodman (1959) states that antler continued to be utilised for the manufacture of plane stocks throughout the Middle Ages. This fact, together with the new find from Dublin described here, gives grounds for believing that further finds of antler planes may yet be expected from archaeological contexts.

Points (Figure 93a-f)

Bone and antler points of various types are commonly recovered from excavations, but although they may be resolved into groups on the basis of material and appearance, their respective functions often remain obscure. Two such groups are referred to below under the heading of weaving equipment (pp. 188-9, 192), where they are classified respectively as pin or dagger-beaters, and as thread-twisters. The high degree of smoothness and polish exhibited by many of these implements associated with textile manufacture is not a feature displayed by the other categories of pointed implement.

A series of points manufactured from the metapodials of cattle has been noted from Anglo-Scandinavian levels at Thetford (unpublished), York (MacGregor 1978a, 1982a) and Northampton (G. Oakley in Williams 1979) and on the Continent at Dorestad (Clason 1978). All are made from the proximal ends of the bones, where the flat articular surface is easier to work than the solid projecting condyles at the distal end; the epiphyseal tissue is hollowed out to form an irregular socket connecting with the natural medullary cavity of the bone (Figures 93a, b). The tip is formed by chopping obliquely across the diaphysis; the tips are often smoothed from use and, wherever it can be discerned, the direction of wear is parallel to the axis of the bone, implying that they were used with a thrusting or stabbing action. There is no evidence of any rotary movement. Numerous unstratified examples are held in the collections of the British Museum and the Museum of London, and others have been found in Ipswich, Suffolk (Layard 1908). Layard was of the opinion that points of this type had been used as tips for skating poles (see p. 142), and the same identification is given in the Guildhall Museum *Catalogue* (1908). No supporting evidence has been found for this theory, however, iron tips normally being used for this function. Although the stabbing action suggested by the microscopic wear patterns on the tips is not at variance with such a suggestion, some of the points seem too blunt to have gained any purchase on the ice, while others are so slender that they would almost certainly have broken under any stress of this kind. The question of their having been used as spearheads in the manner suggested for Iron Age points can also be dismissed, as the degree of technological sophistication achieved by urban societies of this period would certainly

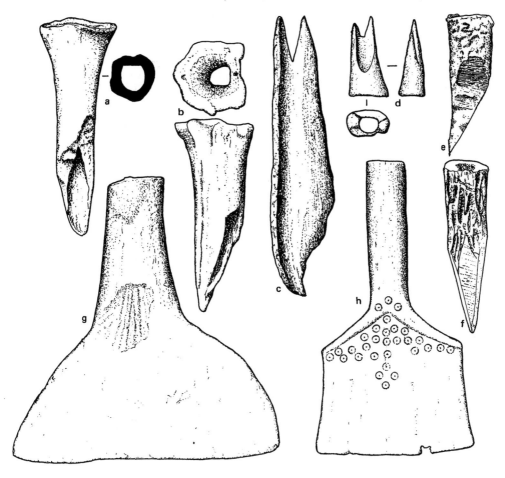

Figure 93: Points (scale 1:2) from (a-c, e-f) York and (d) Waltham Abbey (Huggins); cleavers from (g) Drimore (MacLaren) and (h) Dublin (Ó Ríordáin)

have made such primitive weapons totally unacceptable. The occurrence of six implements of this type in a leather-working shop at York (MacGregor 1982a) suggests rather that they had a craft function. Similar objects, but with more rounded tips, have been identified by Roes (1963) as tallow horns but, while this sort of function might better explain their presence in a workshop (where they could have been used to wax the thread used in sewing), we still lack the evidence to make any firm conclusion.

Another series of points, made from the opposite ends of the metapodials and incorporating the distal articular condyles as the solid butt of a handle, is known from contemporary sites on the Continent. Cnotliwy's

suggestion that some of those from Wolin may have been awls used in leather-working is less persuasive than his alternative explanation, that they were used in basketworking (Cnotliwy 1958). The latter identification was favoured by Roes (1963) for similar Frisian implements.

Mention may also be made of a series of double-pronged points which seem only recently to have been recognised as bona fide tools (MacGregor 1978a, 1982a), although it seems certain that they are more numerous than the paucity of published examples might suggest. The reason for this is that these points are simply the cut or snapped-off ends of bovine nasal bones, which terminate in a natural double prong (Figure 93c). Even their fairly regular length (60-100mm) would not be enough to distinguish them as tools, since this might be a by-product of some butchering technique, but it has been noted among a series of such points from York (MacGregor 1982a) that points of this type exhibit an appreciable amount of smoothing when compared with unutilised skeletal fragments from the same archaeological contexts and that, in particular, the double tips seem disproportionately smooth. The earliest known examples of this type of implement were found in a midden of a late Iron Age fort at Close-ny-Chollagh, Isle of Man, but were only tentatively identified by the excavator as having been utilised (Gelling 1958). One example came from a Roman sewer in York (MacGregor 1976b) and two more were noted from a Merovingian kiln at Huy, Belgium, where they were thought perhaps to have been used in ornamenting pottery (Willems 1973). Two were found during early excavations at Lochlee Crannog, Strathclyde (Munro 1879), and, more recently, six more have come from Viking period levels in York (MacGregor 1982a). Many other examples must lie in museum collections where the fact that they have been utilised has gone unrecognised.

The tentative identification given to the Roman implement from York as a netting tool (MacGregor 1976b) seems less satisfactory now that a larger number has been studied. In particular, it is now clear that the smoothing which has come from handling or utilisation is generally limited to the outer periphery and especially to the points of the implement, the bottom of the terminal U-notch exhibiting little or no wear such as might have been expected had they been used for netting, or as bobbins. The same reservation might be advanced to an identification as thread-twisters, on the basis of comparison with (manufactured) double-pronged implements of the type (Figure 93d) tentatively identified by Blomqvist and Mårtensson (1963), which, along with examples from Portchester Castle, Hampshire (Cunliffe 1976), and Waltham Abbey, Essex (Huggins 1976), form the only comparable parallels (p. 193). Some correspondence may, however, be drawn with a series of double-pronged bones of a different origin which have been noted on the Continent and which have been identified as the fulcral bones of sturgeon. Numerous examples have been found in the Frisian terps and in Dorestad (Holwerda 1930; Roes 1963), in the medieval fishmarket in Hamburg (Roes 1963), and in Eketorp on Öland (Sellsted 1966). Again there is some uncertainty about the extent to which all of these may have been used. Roes' suggestion that they might have been used as forks for eating shellfish, although it cannot be proven, can be reconciled with the slight nature of any wear sustained by these bones and could equally be applied to the nasal bones discussed above. The identification of others from Gniezno in Poland as arrowheads (Kostrzewski 1949) seems less plausible.

Solid antler tines provide an alternative source for pointed implements of various sorts. Tines sharpened to a point with one or more oblique cuts are frequent finds on Viking age sites (Figure 93e, f), though their simplicity of form and lack of direct association permits no precise identification of function. A possible exception is the group of such points marked by transverse grooves, apparently the result of repeated chopping with a blade (Cnotliwy 1970; MacGregor 1978a, 1982a; Schoknecht 1977). It may be conjectured that these cuts are of a secondary nature, received while the tine was being used as a wedge, perhaps in a simple clamping device which held the material being worked. The use of wedges in splitting antlers at Hedeby has already been noted (p. 57) and others would have been used in association with the clamps described on p. 172. As for the remainder, they may have fulfilled a variety of functions as simple pegs. One suggestion (Radley 1971) is that they could have been used to peg out hides in a tannery.

Cleavers (Figure 93g, h)

These implements have long been known in Norway, but with two finds from Drimore, South Uist (MacLaren 1974) and Dublin (B. Ó Ríordáin 1976) respectively, they are only just beginning to be recognised in Britain. In the Norse homeland some fourteen of these implements are known, principally from the north of the country. Two or three of them are said to be made of reindeer antler, while the remainder (like those from the British Isles) are of cetacean bone (Sjøvold 1971). A currency from the Merovingian to the Viking age is postulated for the Norwegian examples, the Drimore and Dublin implements clearly being the products of the latter period. The Drimore cleaver (Figure 93g) is extremely roughly made, its tapering handle merging into a widely flaring blade with little distinction between the two. The Dublin implement, on the other hand, has a well-shaped handle whose outline is carried over the clearly-marked shoulders of a squared spade-like blade, which is decorated with incised ring-and-dot motifs (Figure 93h). Both plain, workmanlike tools and other more decorative examples are known in Norway (Sjøvold 1971), where both flaring and spade-shaped blades are also recorded (Petersen 1951; Graham-Campbell 1980), and some of the Norwegian examples are decorated with more ambitious incised ornament than is found on our Scottish and Irish examples. Their purpose has not yet been established; whereas Sjøvold refers to them as 'cleavers', the fact that Petersen groups them among tanning implements is an indication of the confusion which still surrounds them.

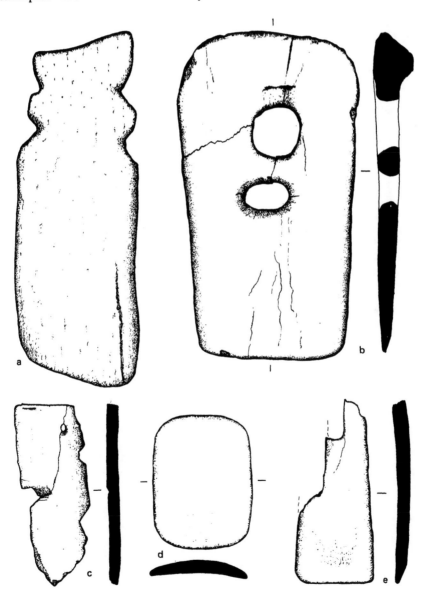

Figure 94:   Cetacean bone implements (scale 1:3) from (a) Foshigarry (Beveridge and Callander) and (b-e) Burrian

Cetacean Bone Implements (Figure 94)

Among the coastal settlements of the Atlantic seaboard there developed a bone industry which was distinct from that discussed elsewhere in these pages, in terms both of its raw material and range of types. The material derives from whales from the surrounding waters, either those caught through pursuit or recovered passively from beached carcasses (see pp. 31-2). In some instances this bone was used to produce items which might have been made further south of ungulate bone or antler (see for example, MacGregor 1974) but there also developed a number of tool types peculiar to the north. Most characteristic are large blade-like implements, notched on either side, as found at Foshigarry, North Uist, and interpreted as blubber mattocks (Beveridge and Callander 1931; Clark 1947); others have been thought to represent shovel blades (MacGregor 1974) and peat spades or oar blades (Crawford 1967). Such wear-marks as are visible on the cutting edges have been thought to favour the blubber mattock interpretation (Rees 1979). Other items are interpreted by Rees (1979) as ploughshares. The range of other tools made from cetacean bone merits a separate study and is too large to attempt here. The references quoted above may serve as an introduction to the topic; for Norwegian material see Sjøvold (1971).

Antler Rakes (Figure 95)

Inherent toughness combined with an appropriate shape led to the selection of red deer antlers[60] for manufacturing implements variously described as rakes, hoes and clod-breakers.

From the point of view of the raw material, two basic types are represented. The most numerous of these comprise implements made from the base of the antler, the beam being cut just above the bez tine; the brow and bez tines thus form a pair of natural tines for the rake, which was then mounted on a haft by means of a socket driven through the centre of the beam section. British examples of this type have been published by Curle (1913a, b) from Newstead; by D.J. Smith (1968b) from Wallsend and South Shields, Tyne and Wear (Figure 95a); by Bagshawe (1949) from Bartlow and Harston in Cambridgeshire and Hadstock in Essex, together with an unprovenanced example in the Museum of Archaeology and Ethnology, Cambridge; by Philp (1973) from Darenth, Kent; and by Rees (1979) from sundry other sites. Dutch implements of the same type, originating in the Frisian terps, are illustrated by Boeles (1951), van der Poel (1961) and Roes (1963).

The alternative form utilises the opposite end of the antler, where two of the upper tines form a natural fork; in this type the beam carrying

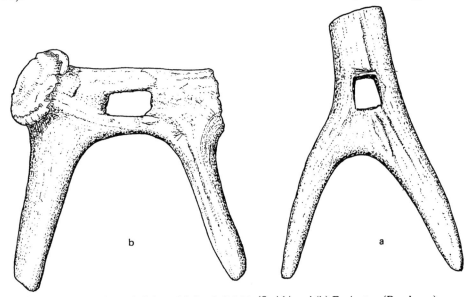

Figure 95:   Antler rakes (scale 3:4) from (a) South Shields (Smith) and (b) Eggington (Bagshawe)

the shaft socket is mounted in the vertical plane, by contrast with the horizontally mounted beam of the other variety. Examples come from Eggington, Bedfordshire (Bagshawe 1949) (see also Figure 95b); Wroxeter, Shropshire (Bushe-Fox 1914); and from Frisia (Boeles 1951; van der Poel 1961; Roes 1963). An unprovenanced implement of this type is also in the Museum of London (Guildhall Museum 1908). The two varieties are complementary to one another, allowing two implements to be produced from a single antler. The shaft-hole in either type may be rounded or square and in some instances there are signs of wear indicating that the handle has been wedged in place (Bagshawe 1949).

Sian Rées (1979) has drawn a distinction between those tools provided with long curving tines and others in which the tines are short and straight. The difference is thought by her to result not from progressive wear but from deliberate choice according to function. The curving shape and comparative fragility of the tines on the first of these types, taken in conjunction with the wear-marks which they sometimes display, suggest to Rees that they served either as a combined rake and pitchfork for gathering straw or, alternatively, as a harrow or seed drill for use on soil which had already been broken up. The former suggestion would square with Stevenson's observations on the wear on the Newstead implement, which seemed to him to have been 'drawn along the ground rather than through it in the manner of a hoe' (Stevenson 1950). This would also account for the gloss built up on an example from Broxbourne, Hertfordshire, thought to have resulted from continual contact with straw (Holmes 1961).[61] The second group of implements, with their short straight prongs sometimes sharpened to chisel-like points, are more likely to have functioned as hoes or rakes for breaking up the soil. Van der Poel (1961) treats these tools as evidence that the terp-dwellers were arable farmers.

All the dated examples of these implements fall within the Roman period, although they represent a distinctly 'native' type of artefact.

Scapula Scoops (Figure 96)

The broad, flat shoulder blades from animals of sheep size and larger form an obvious source of material for the manufacture of scoops, requiring only the trimming of the *spina scapula* to render them instantly usable. Various examples of Roman date and of simple form have been noted from Chester (Newstead 1928), Colchester, Essex (P. Crummy 1977), Newstead, Borders Region (J. Curle 1911), Gloucester (Hassal and Rhodes 1974) and Hayton fort, Yorkshire (S. Johnson 1978), while a more elaborate variety with a well-defined ornamental handle cut from the articular end has been found in York (*Interim* 3, 3, 24). The latter, at least, suggests some domestic function such as handling flour, rather than a heavier industrial use. An example from Billingsgate, London, cut from a bovine scapula, is drilled with a suspension hole and is

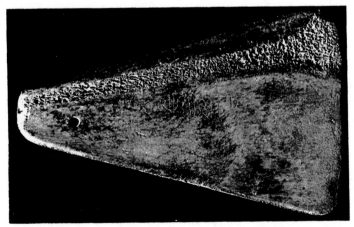

Figure 96: Scapula scoop from London, inscribed *CIIRIIS IIQITIS*. (The site of the *spina scapula* is marked by the band of cancellous tissue)

inscribed *CIIRIIS IIQITIS* (*Ceres Eq[u]itis*) (Figure 96). It has been suggested (H. Chapman in D.M. Jones 1980) that *Eq[u]itis* might be the genitive form of a personal name and that *cera*, wax, is referred to by the other element; if, however, these implements *were* used for handling flour or grain rather than wax, an allusion to the goddess Ceres would not be inappropriate.

Similar scapulae from later contexts include a Viking age find from York, drilled at the neck for suspension (MacGregor 1982a).

Cattle horn scoops of the eighteenth and nineteenth centuries, which were much used by apothecaries, by dealers in dry foodstuffs and in the kitchen, are still to be found in antique shops. Hardwick (1981) illustrates several varieties and notes that the tip of the horn usually served as the handle, either preserved in the round or shaped to form a more elegant grip. These could be made without any need for heat treatment, making use of the natural curvature of the horn. The lack of earlier examples may be due only to the poor ability of horn to survive burial in any but the most favourable conditions.

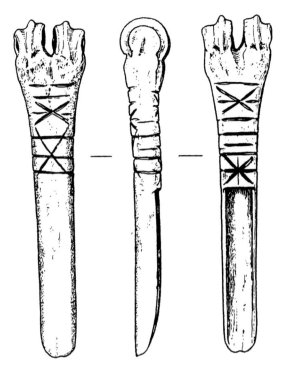

Figure 97:   Apple corer or cheese-scoop (scale 3:4) unprovenanced, Ashmolean Museum

Apple or Cheese-scoops (Figure 97)

These common items are manufactured with ease from the metapodials of sheep. The distal end normally forms the handle, with the articular condyles left intact. The proximal end is cut off and about half the length of the shaft exposed by removing either the anterior or the posterior wall. Shaping the exposed end into a rounded cutting edge renders the scoop ready for use. Decoration in the form of criss-crossed lines and other motifs usually covers much of the handle, often combined with personal initials. All these operations are commonly executed with no more than a knife, conforming with the tradition that scoops of this type were made by young men for their sweethearts.

This notion is nonetheless difficult to reconcile with the general belief that these scoops were used as an aid to eating apples by those who had lost all their teeth. An alternative suggestion, that they were used for coring apples, is more romantically pleasing than a third tradition, that they were used in taking

samples from cheeses to test their ripeness. Since there appears to be a certain amount of evidence to support each of these contentions, it must be assumed that there is some truth in all of them, and that different scoops served different purposes.

Pinto (1969) discusses and illustrates examples in wood, ivory and silver as well as bone, noting that most datable examples are of eighteenth-century origin. Some supporting evidence comes from archaeological excavations as illustrated by one example from Oxford dated to the first half of the eighteenth century by Hunter and Jope (1951), but although there are occasional finds from sites producing earlier material — for instance the unstratified example from Staple Howe in Yorkshire (Brewster 1963) — there seems to be no firm evidence to support Pinto's suggestion that implements of this type were common before the post-medieval period.

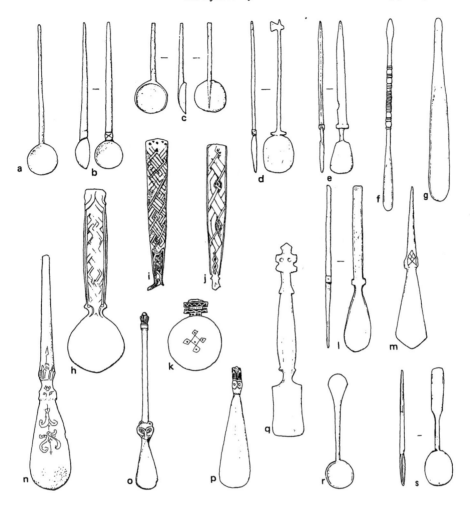

Figure 98: Spoons (scale 1:3) from (a) London (b) Straubing (Walke) (c) Ringstead (Jackson) (d-e) Frocester Court (Gracie and Price) (f) Alésia (Musée de Dijon) (g) unprovenanced, Museum of London (h) Sigtuna (Floderus) (i-k) Birka (l) Lincoln (m) London (n) Winchester (Collis and Kjølby-Biddle) (o-p) London (q) Schleswig (r) London (s) Leafield

Spoons (Figure 98)

Long bones of cattle or horses appear to have provided the bulk of the raw material for manufacturing considerable numbers of bone spoons from the Roman period onwards. The majority of Roman spoons are of tea-spoon size: Wheeler (1930) places those with circular bowls under the early Empire and states that oval or lyre-shaped bowls became prevalent in the third and fourth centuries, but this generalisation is more apposite for metal spoons than for those of bone. In the simplest bone forms, a tapering round or square section handle is combined with a dished, circular bowl, the two joining without any decorative moulding and with scarcely any distinction in level between the two. The type is represented amongst a hoard of seventeen unfinished bone spoons from Woodcuts, Dorset, published (but not acknowledged as spoons) by Pitt Rivers (1887) (Figure 29d, e) and by other unfinished pieces from excavations at Winchester, Hampshire (Crummy 1983). Another example, said to be of ivory, comes from St Paul's Church, Winchester, Hampshire (Collis 1978). Other spoons, from the first to fourth centuries, display a more marked lip at the junction of the handle and bowl (e.g., Cunliffe 1971; Frere 1972; Philp 1981; Townend and Hinton in Bird *et al.* 1978). This develops in some cases to the extent that the handle projects from halfway down the bowl, as on an insecurely dated spoon from Leicester (Kenyon 1948). In some instances the line of the handle is continued as a tapering moulding on the back of the bowl, either finishing at the centre point as, for example, on a spoon from Nun's Walk, Winchester (Collis 1978), or extending almost to the opposite edge, as at Ringstead, Northamptonshire (Jackson 1980). The chronological implications of these variations, if indeed there are any, are not at all clear.

Other forms of elaboration are uncommon, but a late Roman spoon from Straubing, Bayern, has a moulding at the junction of the handle and bowl incised with a saltire (Walke 1965). More ambitious ornamental handles are to be found on a group of late third or fourth-century flat-bowled spoons from Frocester Court villa, Gloucestershire (Gracie and Price 1979), the most complete being shaped in the form of an axe (Figure 98d), a sword (Figure 98e) and a spear, respectively.

A different type of Roman bone spoon has a narrow elongated bowl which tapers smoothly into the handle. Examples may be noted from London (Figure 98g), Lyon (Allmer and Dissard 1888), and from Pfünz on the German *Limes* (Winkelman 1901). They may, perhaps, have been cosmetic spoons.

From the centuries immediately following the Roman period spoons are comparatively rare. A few examples of about the sixth or seventh century are known. A shovel-shaped spoon with well-defined shoulders was found at Jarlshof, Shetland (Hamilton 1956) while others with rather flat, spatulate bowls which expand smoothly from the end of the handle come from Buckquoy, Orkney (A. Ritchie 1977) and from Shakenoak, Oxfordshire (Brodribb *et al.* 1972). To judge from similarly shaped spoons from late Saxon Thetford, Norfolk (unpublished), and those of *c.* eleventh- or twelfth-century date from Goltho Manor, Lincolnshire (MacGregor, forthcoming) and Middle Brook Street, Winchester (Collis and Kjølbye-Biddle 1979), this simple form remained the normal type throughout this period. Broadly contemporary with these latter spoons are two groups which feature decorative mouldings mostly in the

form of animal heads at the junction between the handle and the bowl. The first group, from Winchester, Hampshire, has recently been reviewed by Collis and Kjølbye-Biddle (1979), the bowls being spatulate with rounded ends, tapering towards the handle. They have in several instances incised decoration combining Ringerike and Winchester style ornament; the surviving handles are rounded or ovoid in section and join the bowl with an expanded moulding which, in some instances, represents an animal head. Two of these handles also have broken mouldings at the other end of the handle, suggesting that the spoons may originally have been symmetrically double-ended. A date in the early eleventh century is suggested for these Winchester spoons. A second group of four spoons, all stray finds from London, include three with zoomorphic mouldings and one with a roughly-incised lattice pattern on a simple expanded moulding (London Museum 1940). The bowl shapes on these are quite disparate and of the surviving handles one example, from King William Street, tapers to a point while the other (Figure 98m), from the City, has a cylindrical stem terminating in a trefoil moulding. All of these probably date from the eleventh or twelfth centuries, as does a more accomplished spoon fragment with a dragonesque moulding from Chichester, Sussex (D.M. Waterman 1959).

Scandinavian spoon-makers from the Viking to the medieval period employed antler as well as bone. Their products are characterised by large well-defined bowls and flat strap-like handles, both elements frequently attracting incised interlace and other patterns. Swedish finds include several examples which accompanied burials at Birka (Arbman 1943) and an example in elk antler dated *c.* 1100 from Sigtuna (Floderus 1941). Several Norwegian spoons of medieval date from Bergen and Oslo have been published by Grieg (1933). The type has so far been found in Britain only in wood (D.M. Waterman 1959).

Later bone spoons increasingly reflect the influence of metal prototypes, as shown by examples from Kingsgate Street, Winchester (Collis 1978) dating probably from the seventeenth or eighteenth centuries, and from Leafield, Oxfordshire (Figure 98s), the latter probably of the late eighteenth or nineteenth century. Specialised functions are indicated by the shape of some spoons, such as an unstratified example with elongated bowl and concave handle, from Northampton (F. Williams 1979), which may perhaps be identified as a marrow scoop.

As an alternative to bone, cattle horn and wood were probably widely used, although early spoons in either material are rare. Hardwick (1981) illustrates an eighteenth-century wooden former consisting of two elements with, respectively, a positive and a negative spoon mould. Blanks of horn cut to an appropriate size were softened over the fire and clamped in the mould while they cooled, when the shape was permanently fixed. Similar techniques are used to this day in the manufacture of horn spoons, which are valued for their resistance to staining and to attracting flavour. A number of horn spoons of the sixteenth and seventeenth centuries are listed in the catalogue of the Guildhall Museum (1908).

Knives

A single example of a bone knife has been noted from an English context. It came from a fifth or sixth-century cremation burial at South Elkington, Lincolnshire (Webster 1951). Others displaying a variety of forms and originating in the Frisian terps are illustrated by Roes (1963). The function served by these items is quite unknown: some could have had some practical use, for example in skinning, but the correspondence in form between some of the Frisian pieces and iron-bladed knives suggests that they may have been no more than toy replicas.

Brushes (Figure 99)

Various types of bone brushes have been noted, all of the seventeenth century or later. A detailed typology and chronology has yet to be compiled. All are compound brushes, having multiple tufts. In no instance have surviving tufts been recorded. Those that were of bristle would simply have decayed, but several examples exhibit green staining from copper salts, indicating that the tufts were of fine wire. In either case the technique of fitting the tufts would have been the same. This involved feeding a wire through each of the holes in turn to form a series of loops, into which were inserted half the number of filaments required to fill it. When the wire was pulled tight the filaments were doubled up and drawn into the hole, after which they merely had to be trimmed to a uniform length. One example in the Museum of London is of composite construction, having a separate back-plate which would have covered the heads of the tufts and the wires which secured them. While this latter type may have served as a clothes brush, a number of functions would have been fulfilled by other bone brushes, the smallest of which were toothbrushes.

Few excavated brushes have yet been published. One example from Ospringe, Kent, illustrated by G.H. Smith (1979), exhibits characteristic funnel-shaped perforations linked on the back by grooves to accommodate the wires which anchored the tufts.

The company records of a major manufacturer help to illuminate the later history of the industry. Messrs Kent of London were producing almost 9,000 brushes a week in the 1870s, consuming weekly the long-bones of some 600 head of cattle. Although man-made materials made increasing inroads into the market from this time onwards, it was not until the 1930s that Kent's bone-shaping shop was finally closed (Woodall 1959).

Since the begining of the 19th century, when a British patent was registered, the brush industry has been the major consumer of baleen. After boiling for twelve hours the raw sheets of baleen were cut into strips or filaments whose toughness and flexibility recommended them for use as bristles in brushes varying in size up to large industrial brooms.

Bobbins (Figure 100)

This tentative identification may be proposed for a variety of small, well-made cylindrical objects, the precise functions of which are nonetheless not clearly understood. The most accomplished of these have a narrow axial perforation running their entire length and bands of incised lines cut at the ends; some at least are lathe-turned. Examples have been noted from Ellington, Huntingdonshire (Tebbutt *et al.* 1971), Lyveden, Northamptonshire (Bryant *et al.* 1969), Goltho, Lincolnshire

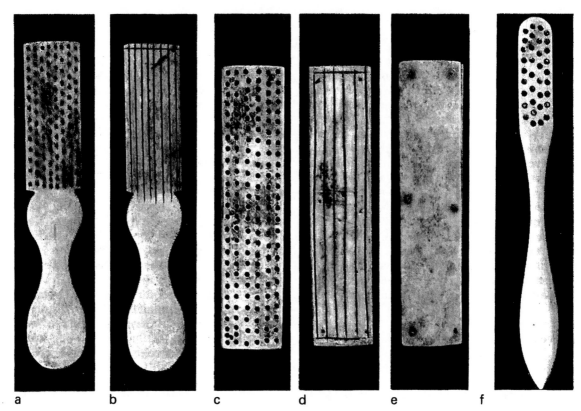

a   b   c   d   e   f

Figure 99: Brushes: (a-b) obverse and reverse, from London (c-e) obverse, reverse and back-plate, from London (f) from London

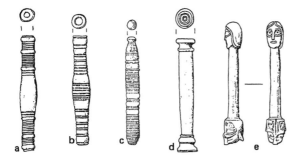

Figure 100: 'Bobbins' (scale 1:2) (a) Goltho (Beresford), (b-d) York, (e) Norwich (Green)

(Figure 100a) (Beresford 1975), York (Figure 100b, c) and Perth (MacGregor, forthcoming), ranging in date from about the twelfth to the fourteenth centuries.

York has also produced a solid circular section rod of antler with expanded ends (Figure 100d) which probably served as a bobbin. An alternative function, however, is suggested by similar balluster-like rods of bone or wood which were until recent years used in Scandinavia, northern Scotland and Ireland to prevent lambs from suckling. Strings tied round the moulded ends were used to fasten the device (known by the Norwegian name of *kjevle*) into the lamb's mouth like a horse bit (Baldwin 1978).[62]

Decorative bobbins are likely to have been favoured by medieval women, however, especially as sewing and embroidery played such a prominent part in their lives. An attractive example of walrus ivory comes from Norwich; at one end it terminates in a female head and at the other in a dragonesque mask (Figure 100e), on the basis of which it is dated to the first half of the twelfth century (B. Green 1973). Another possible bobbin with zoomorphic terminals is in the collections of the British Museum (unpublished).

Textile Equipment (Figures 101-3)

Bone and antler have been utilised consistently in the production of implements for almost every stage of textile production. No doubt it was the excellent physical properties of these materials which recommended them for these purposes, as they are easily shaped in the first instance, are tough and resilient in character, and acquire an ever-increasing smoothness with use, so having progressively less tendency to 'pick up' the fibres being worked. Wood, which was probably the most common alternative for most classes of implement, would have been much inferior in its wearing characteristics; in the case of whorls, where weight rather than toughness was the most important factor, ease of manufacture would have favoured the use of bone rather than the more usual alternatives, pottery and stone.

Combing

Before the process of spinning an even yarn could begin, the raw wool had to be freed from tangles and from foreign matter caught up in the fleece. Two processes may be distinguished. Combing involves the use of a pair of handled combs, each normally set with two or more rows of iron teeth; carding is carried out with a pair of flat, bat-like implements (cards), each set with many rows of short, fine teeth. Today the two processes are complementary. No bone carding combs are known (see Lemon 1972; Patterson 1956; and Wild 1970 for discussions of the process).

Combing was certainly practised in the Roman period and a number of one-piece iron combs of this era demonstrate their currency in northern Europe (Wild 1970). The type of wool comb which survived in use until the nineteenth century, a short-handled T-shaped implement with several rows of long iron teeth, is represented by Anglo-Saxon remains from Wicken Bonhunt, Essex (M.U. Jones, 1975),

Harrold, Bedfordshire (Eagles and Evison 1970) and Shakenoak, Oxfordshire (D. Brown in Brodribb *et al.* 1973).[63] An important example of such an implement is represented by a T-shaped handle of antler (Figure 101 no. 1) from Viking levels at Jarlshof, Shetland (Hamilton 1956). Unfortunately, the Jarlshof handle is now broken through a row of holes drilled to take the teeth; whether there were additional rows or only a single row, as on many Scandinavian combs (Hoffmann 1964), is now unclear.

Spinning

Until the advent of the spinning wheel, spinning was practised with a spindle and whorl, a method with an ancestry stretching back to the Neolithic period (Henshall 1950). The spindle took the form of a rod, measuring some 12-25cm or more in length and usually with a slight swelling on which the whorl was fitted.[64] A wisp of prepared wool was twisted around the spindle, which was then spun and allowed to drop; the momentum of the spinning action was maintained by the whorl, functioning as a flywheel, and in this way the fibres were both extended and twisted into a yarn. When the momentum was exhausted and the yarn spun sufficiently tightly, the newly-formed thread was wound around the spindle, ending with a half-hitch at the top, and the process repeated.

Roman spindles of bone (Figure 101, nos. 2, 3) may be made to high standard, with decorative terminals turned on the lathe (e.g., British Museum 1964) or they may be of simple form with plain ends, either undecorated (Guildhall Museum 1908; Wheeler 1930) or with incised ornament as on examples from Mainz (Behrens and Brenner 1911).

Bone spindles from the succeeding centuries are comparatively few. Perhaps the majority were made then in wood,[65] which has failed to survive except under conditions of exceptional preservation as at Lagore Crannog, Meath (Hencken 1950), Dublin (National Museum of Ireland 1973) and at Colletière, Isère (Colardelle and Colardelle 1980). The numerous double-pointed bone implements sometimes referred to as spindles (e.g., G.B. Brown 1915) are discussed below as pin-beaters. D.M. Waterman (1959) mentions an 'object of uncertain use, possibly a bodkin' from Clifford

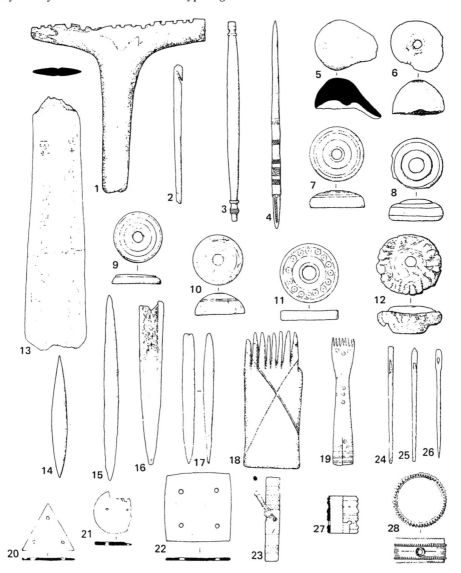

Figure 101:   Textile equipment (scale 1:3): wool comb (1) from Jarlshof; spindles from (2) Southwark (Dennis) (3) London (4) York; unfused epiphysis (5); spindle whorls from (6) York (7) Portchester (Cunliffe) (8) unprovenanced (9) Sibbertswold (10) Shakenoak (Brodribb *et al.*) (11) unprovenanced (12) Lackford (Lethbridge); weaving sword fragment (13) from Wallingford; pin beaters from (14) Sutton Courtenay (15) Southampton (16) York (17) Goltho; weaving combs from (18) Burrian and (19) Birka; weaving tablets from (20) Malton (21) Burrian (22) Birka; needle case (23) from Birka; needles from (24-5) York and (26) Hedeby (Graham-Campbell); thread box (27) from Plymouth (Fairclough); pin-cushion mount (28) from Appleton Roebuck

Street, York, which may be a bone spindle (Figure 101, no. 4).

Weight rather than form would seem to be the critical factor in choosing or manufacturing a whorl, and yet the wide range of weights encountered seems to show no particular clustering. Indeed, the 8g which has been suggested (Ryder 1968a) as an appropriate weight for spinning primitive Soay-type wool is practically never encountered, most whorls being markedly heavier. The weight of the whorl is, in any case, only one of the elements which condition the quality of the yarn, the diameter and length of the fibres being equally critical.[66] It can be said, however, that whorls at either end of the range of weights would not have been interchangeable in their functions. An attempt to assign objective mechanical values to whorls has been made by Oakley and Hall (in J.H. Williams 1979).

One of the most commonly encountered types is that in which the whorl is made from the 'head' or articular condyle of a bovine femur. As mentioned above (p. 2), the epiphyses of certain limb bones become fused to their shafts only in maturity and it seems possible that the widespread practice of utilising these may have developed through the ready availability of unfused heads from immature animals. Unfused epiphyses, however, are small and asymmetrically shaped (Figure 101, no. 5) and the majority of whorls are cut from the fused bones of mature beasts (Figure 101, no. 6). Although cattle femur heads pre-dominate, whorls made from other species are occasionally found, including some derived from human bones (A. Ritchie 1977; Scott 1948). Femur head whorls first appear in the Iron Age or earlier, being represented, for example, among the large collections of bone work from the Glastonbury and Meare lake villages in Somerset (Bulleid and Gray 1917, 1948). They continued in use sporadically from that time until the Viking and Norman periods (e.g., MacGregor 1982a) when they enjoyed a renewed burst of popularity. Of a sample of 23 such whorls found at Lincoln, for example, four are dated to the ninth or tenth centuries, six to the tenth or eleventh centuries and nine to the eleventh or twelfth centuries; the remainder, from contexts dating from the thirteenth to the eighteenth centuries may be residual.[67]

Another instance in which the original form of the raw material has a conditioning effect on the final form of the whorl concerns perforated antler burrs (Figure 101, no. 12) of the type found at Lackford, Suffolk (Lethbridge 1951) and Spong Hill, Norfolk (Hills 1977). There is some doubt whether these objects really are whorls however, similar objects from Sweden having been interpreted as fishing gear (*fiskpuls*) (Kjellmark 1939).

Antler provided the principal source for the other major type of whorl found from the period up to about the twelfth century, in which discoid or sub-spherical shapes were cut or lathe-turned from material cut in cross-section close to the base. The high proportion of solid tissue in this region permitted whorls to be made in which little or no spongy tissue appears, encouraging incised decoration, often in the form of turned rings. Roman whorls in this series include elaborately-turned examples from Portchester, Hampshire (Figure 101, 7), and from Shakenoak, Oxfordshire (Brodribb *et al.* 1971), while others of Anglo-Saxon date were also found at the latter site (ibid., 1972).

Flat, discoid whorls of antler, often with incised ornament (Figure 101, no. 11) make an appearance around the time of the Conquest. The development of this type may have been encouraged by the exploitation at this time of a new source of raw material in the form of mandibles, such bones having conveniently large, flat areas of regular thickness, from which discs of appropriate size could easily be cut. The two sources of raw material are immediately distinguishable from one another, however, those of antler being solid through-out and the jawbone whorls having a band of cancellous tissue sandwiched between two dense outer layers (p. 9). A number of playing pieces of similar date and appearance are noted above, and indeed it is only the central perforation which distinguishes these from the whorls described here (see pp. 135-6). Whereas the solidity of the antler whorls allowed for ornamental carving 2 or 3mm in depth on the upper surface, the structure of the bone whorls necessitated more restrained ornament. Occasionally whorls are found inscribed with a name, perhaps that of the owner (Boeles 1951; K. Jackson in A. Ritchie 1977).

Alternative functions have been attributed in the past to some whorls, including dress-fasteners (A. Young 1956), pendants (Scott 1948), and, in the case of one elaborately decorated example from a male inhumation grave at Dorchester, Oxfordshire, a toggle or sword-knot (Kirk and Leeds 1953). None of these identifications, however, seems very persuasive.

Other media used in the manufacture of whorls include jet, shale, lead, glass and baked clay. The material was obviously not of great importance. Sir Arthur Mitchell (1880) dis-covered an elderly Scottish woman happily using a potato as a whorl, having used nothing else all her life.

Weaving

Until the early medieval period, most textiles were probably woven on the vertical warp-weighted loom (Hoffmann 1964) and the presence of this type is confirmed on many Dark Age and Viking period sites by finds of annular loom weights. An alternative form, the two-beamed vertical loom, is found in pre-Roman Denmark (Hald 1950), however, so that the possibility of some weaving tools being used with this type cannot be ruled out. All the implements so recognised were used to beat the weft into place and they fall into three basic categories: the long sword beater, the shorter dagger beater or pin beater, and the weaving comb.

The sword beater was generally some 25-75cm in length and, being inserted horizontally in the warp shed, could quickly beat up a weft row either in large sections or all at a time, depending on the width of the textile. The origins of these implements seem to lie as early as the Bronze Age (Hoffmann 1964). No Roman weaving swords are known, although they are attested in literary sources (Wild 1970). During the early post-Roman period many may have been made of wood, which has failed to survive.[68] Others of this period, made of iron, have been interpreted as prestige items and are not common finds. The resemblance of some of these latter implements to real swords, except that (in the Anglo-Saxon period, at least) they may have a tang-like extension at the tip, may not be entirely fortuitous, since some examples were apparently manufactured from redundant weapons (Chadwick 1958). While weaving swords of cetacean bone are not uncommon finds in Scandinavia (Lunde 1977; Petersen 1951; Sjøvold 1971) and some are known further south on the continental mainland (Hoffmann 1964), only one example has so far been found in Britain. This fragmentary blade (Figure 101, no. 13), inscribed on either side of a medial groove with two versions of an Old English legend reading *EADBVRH MEC AH . . .* (*Eadburh owns me*), was found in the destruction level of a house dated about 1150 at Wallingford, Oxfordshire (Okasha 1971). Among the more complete Scandinavian swords, the form is in some instances quite schematic, while in others it closely imitates that of real weapons.

Many cetacean bone beaters from Norway have curved blades, a feature which Hoffmann (1964) attributes to the natural shape of the cetacean bones from which they were fashioned. This curvature was of no particular benefit during use, so that the occurrence of wooden weaving swords displaying the same shape, also catalogued by Hoffmann, is a further instance of the morphology of the skeletal raw material conditioning the development of tools in other media.

The shorter dagger or pin beaters (Figure 101, nos. 14-17) were probably used in addition to (rather than instead of) sword beaters, although they survive much more numerously. Perhaps this is a result of their having normally been made of bone (which has a comparatively high survival value) rather than wood, although wooden examples have been noted from Hedeby (Schietzel 1970) and Amsterdam (van Regteren Altena 1970). In addition, they would have been more easily manufactured from more readily available material than the much larger sword beaters, and would also have been more easily lost. Hoffmann (1964) describes the complementary functions of the two types of beater. By contrast with the sword beater, which operated parallel to the weft, the pin beater was inserted between individual warp threads and was used at right angles to the plane of the weft. The transverse grooves which mark some pin beaters were no doubt formed by friction against the warp.

Beaters of the Iron Age 'gouge' type, cut from the long-bones of sheep or goats, as found at Maiden Castle, Dorset (G.M. Crowfoot 1945) survive only rarely into the Roman period: the type is, however, recorded from Langton, Yorkshire (Corder and Kirk, 1932), from various Scottish broch sites (e.g., MacGregor 1974) and from Lagore and Cahercommaun in Ireland (Hencken 1938, 1950), as well as from the Frisian terps (Roes 1963).

Three groups of pin beaters account for the majority of examples from the Roman to the early medieval periods. Most numerous are the so-called 'cigar-shaped' beaters, circular or ovate in section and tapering to a point at either end from an intermediate swelling (Figure 101, nos. 14-15). Very often the maximum girth is not in the centre, with the result that one point is more slender than the other. The choice of point for use on any particular occasion would have depended on the job in hand or the fineness of the cloth being woven. A number of poorly associated cigar-shaped beaters from Roman sites in Britain are listed by Wild (1970) but the same author also cites more securely stratified examples from the Continent, confirming their currency in the Roman period. Numerous examples of Anglo-Saxon date are also known, for example from Wicken Bonhunt, Essex (Bradley and Hooper, 1974), Harston, Leicestershire (Dunning 1952) and from Sutton Courteney and elsewhere in Oxfordshire (Leeds 1923).

An alternative form is provided with a point at one end only, the other being roughly trimmed and frequently displaying a curved section with a certain amount of cancellous tissue on the inside, demonstrating that they were cut from limb bones (Figure 101, no. 16). A number of unpublished examples have been noted from excavations in York, all dating to the later Anglo-Saxon or Viking period. Perhaps these were more general-purpose tools than those described above, or they may have been associated with a particular section of the weaving industry producing one kind of cloth.

A number of pin beaters have been found exhibiting a point at one end and a flat chisel-like butt at the other, suggesting some special usage (Figure 101, no. 17). It seems possible that the chisel end was used across the top of the warp rather than between the individual threads. Several examples come from a structure interpreted as a late Saxon weaving shed at Goltho Manor, Lincolnshire (MacGregor, forthcoming).

Occasional claims are made for other forms of beaters: Moore (1966), for example, has suggested this identification for a pig's tooth found in the Anglo-Saxon settlement at Wykeham, Yorkshire.

Hoffmann (1964) mentions that pin beaters, known by the name of *hraell* in Old Norse literature, survived in use in Iceland along with the warp-weighted loom, until the last century.

In northern Britain it seems that the place of the beater was taken by long-handled bone weaving-combs (Figure 101, no. 18) of the type which made its earliest appearance in Iron Age contexts in the south (Henshall 1950). They also occur on a number of Roman sites listed by Wild (1970), principally in the north, where they may indicate the presence of native weavers producing textiles for the Roman market. They vary in date from the Antonine period at Camelon, Central Region, to the fourth century at Piercebridge, County Durham. In post-Roman Britain they are more difficult to pin-point. One example from the Broch of Aikerness was found with a knife whose bone handle was inscribed with an ogham inscription judged to be of the fifth century or later (Henshall 1950), while at the Broch of Burrian, where occupation of some sort continued until about the eighth century, some at least of the numerous weaving combs were of post-broch (although not necessarily post-Roman) date (MacGregor 1974). Combs from a number of other sites are listed by Bulleid and Gray (1948), Henshall (1950) and Hodder and Hedges (1977). One example was recovered from the Anglo-Saxon cemetery at Kempston, but it has been judged in the past to be residual (Bulleid and Gray 1917). Others, thought to be English imports, have been found in Frisia and, although these are not closely dated, the Anglo-Saxon period might be considered the most likely for their transfer to the Continent (Roes 1963). Two examples have been found in Viking age Birka in Sweden (Arbman 1943; Geijer 1938) (see also Figure 101, no. 19).

As might be expected, antlers and columnar limb bones provided the bulk of the raw material for these implements. The curvature inherent in the latter has led some writers to doubt their suitability for weaving (Cunnington 1923; Hodder and Hedges 1977; Roth 1950), on the grounds that it would result in the displacement of the warp, but G.M. Crowfoot (1945) has maintained that this would not necessarily have been a disadvantage and may even have served a useful function in thrusting the warp threads apart and counteracting the tendency of the web to 'waist' in the middle. Antler was frequently used instead of limb bones and in the Northern Isles cetacean bone was favoured for the manufacture of these implements (MacGregor 1974). The 'fish-tail' terminal displayed by some weaving combs has been compared (Thomas 1961) to the fish symbol in Pictish art, perhaps reinforcing the case for post-Roman survival.

Among the combs from the Broch of Burrian, Orkney, a significant disparity was noted between those with long handles and short teeth and those with comparatively short handles and longer teeth. It was suggested (MacGregor 1974) that this variation might indicate some difference in function, the longer-toothed implements perhaps having been used for combing the wool preparatory to spinning, as has been postulated in the past (Coughtrey 1872). Practical experiments conducted with the more standard form of comb have shown it to function entirely satisfactorily as a weaving comb (Reynolds 1972). There are, however, still a few dissenting opinions. In recent years Alcock (1972) has reiterated the opinion of some earlier writers that they might have been used to disentangle sinews, and a variety of alternative suggestions has been gathered by Hodder and Hedges (1977).

There is a distinct type of long comb which is well-known on the continent (e.g., Herrmann 1962; Schuldt 1960; Trimpe-Burger 1966; Wachter 1972; Ulbricht 1980a), but which seems not to occur in Britain. These combs (Figure 102) have clearly been cut from long-bones, principally the metapodials of cattle, as can be seen from the characteristic foramena and spongy tissue which often survives at the 'handle' end. The teeth are cut long and straight and show secondary shaping only at the tips. There is never any sign of wear further up the teeth suggesting that, despite their length, it was only the extremities of the teeth which came into contact with the material being combed. This fact makes their identification as weaving combs (e.g., Nickel 1964; J. Persson in Mårtensson 1976; Wachter 1976) seem unlikely, when compared with the heavy wear sustained to the very base of the shorter teeth on more certain weaving combs of the type already discussed. It has been suggested (Professor B. Almgren, personal communication), that these implements might have been used in tapestry weaving, but I know of no independent evidence to support this theory. Stratified combs of this type date from about the twelfth to the fourteenth centuries. Nickel (1964) illustrates finished and unfinished combs of this type from Magdeburg, Sachsen-Anhalt, and a production site in Lübeck, Schleswig-Holstein, yielding part-finished combs as well as waste fragments of cattle metapodials from which they were being made, has been dated to the thirteenth century (Stephan 1973). The method of pro-

Figure 102: Long-toothed combs from Schleswig, with close-up of points

duction of these combs has been further elucidated through the manufacture of replicas by Pietzsch (1979).

The majority of the weaving tools of the types discussed here disappeared with the decline of the vertical warp-weighted loom in favour of the horizontal loom.[69]

Notice must be drawn to the remains of a specialist horizontal loom, used purely for band and tape weaving. The only evidence for this type of loom in Britain is in the form of a heddle frame made from centrally perforated bone strips fastened together by a riveted bronze sheath (Bosanquet 1948; Wild 1971). The frame was found on The Lawe at South Shields, Tyne and Wear, and although it lacks any stratigraphic context it has been generally accepted as Roman in origin. Although no other evidence has been found for the currency of this type of loom in Britain, the fact that very similar heddles are known from post-medieval contexts in, for example, Scandinavia (Hald 1946; Hatt 1942; Hoffmann 1964) and Poland (Dobrowolska 1968; Pininska 1974), raises the possibility that the South Shields frame may be some centuries later than has traditionally been accepted. Most tapes and braids of pre-medieval date, however, are usually judged to be tablet woven.

Tablet Weaving (Figure 101, nos. 20-2)

An adjunct (or in some cases, an alternative) to the warp-weighted loom was the method of weaving which employed tablets, small plaques which were often made of bone, although examples in wood, metal, horn and leather are also known. Frequently they were square with a perforation at each corner, but a number of circular tablets with two holes have also been identified (Henshall 1950). During the Roman period in particular, triangular shapes with three holes were also popular (Wild 1970), while hexagonal tablets have also been used at times (Schlabow 1978; Schuette 1956). Sometimes a central hole is also present, and this may be used for an extra warp if especially strong braids are to be produced (Schuette 1956) or, with the insertion of a rod, as an aid to keeping the pack of tablets in order while tying the warps (Dryad, nd). The perforations are frequently marked by smooth radiating grooves worn by friction against the threads. Individual warp threads were passed through each of the holes and the tablets ranged alongside each other in a pack; the weft thread was passed through the shed so formed in the warp, the shed being changed by rotating the tablets before feeding through the next weft thread. Variations in the sequence of rotation produced different patterns; the simplest — quarter turns in unison — gave the effect of a series of parallel cords united by a hidden weft, but by differentially rotating individual or groups of tablets the technique could be used to produce patterned weaves of considerable complexity.

Three methods of keeping the warp under tension may be cited. The simplest (Dryad, nd) is for one end to be secured to a hook and the other to the weaver's belt; alternatively, it may be tied to two pegs at either end of a horizontal frame (Schuette 1956) or suspended from a vertical frame and weighted at the bottom (Schlabow 1978).

Although entire garments such as stoles could be produced by this method (Henshell 1964) it was more commonly used in the manufacture of braids and tapes and in the production of starting and closing borders on textiles woven on the warp-weighted loom. Among the former group may be noted three twelfth-century seal tags woven respectively with 30, 32, and 52 four-hole tablets (Henshall 1964) and the earlier series of braids and bands from the vestments found in St Cuthbert's coffin and thought to have formed part of a gift presented to Cuthbert's shrine by Athelstan in 934 (G.M. Crowfoot 1939). Other examples of tablet-weaving have been found in Anglo-Saxon contexts at Cambridge, Mildenhall and Icklingham (G.M. Crowfoot 1950, 1952) and at Little Eriswell (E. Crowfoot 1966), all in East Anglia; while other discoveries have been made in Irish sites at Lagore, Meath (Hencken 1950), and at Dublin (National Museum of Ireland 1963). The method of tablet weaving integral borders on conventionally-produced textiles is described by Hoffmann (1964), Hald (1950), and Schuette (1956). Even these could be quite complex, as illustrated by a third- or fourth-century textile from Gjeite, Denmark, woven with 137 tablets (G.M. Crowfoot 1939) and a contemporary cloak from Thorsbjerg made with as many as 176 tablets (Schuette 1956).

Actual tablets are, perhaps, more common finds in the Roman period than in the succeeding centuries. In addition to the 27 bone tablets (all of them square or triangular) listed by Wild (1970), examples may be noted from Scole, Norfolk (Rogerson 1977) and from Verulamium (St Albans), Hertfordshire (Frere 1972). Six bone tablets of the eleventh century and one of the twelfth or thirteenth centuries have recently been found in Dublin (National Museum of Ireland 1963): they average about 3.5cm square and have a perforation at each corner, one having an additional small hole in the centre; two have rudimentary decoration in the form of incised lines and one is ornamented on each face with a saltire composed of incised ring-and-dot devices. Raftery (1960) illustrates a further example with four well-worn holes linked by incised lines, found at Rathtinaun Crannog, Sligo. Another Irish find, a triangular plate cut from the naturally flat expanse of an ox scapula and perforated with three unevenly-spaced holes, was discovered at Lagore Crannog (Hencken 1950); it may have been used as a weaving tablet, though the excavators made no such claim for it. A possible tablet of Anglo-Saxon date was recovered from Kingston Down cemetery, Kent; C.R. Smith (1856) describes a 'square flat piece of ivory with a hole at each corner', but unfortunately this object no longer survives, so that it cannot be examined for telltale wear marks. Interestingly, however, the same grave also contained two pin beaters, perhaps adding some weight to the identification of this piece as a weaving implement. Henshall (1950) records two circular tablets from early excavations at Jarlshof and one from the Broch of Burrian; any of these could belong to the period considered here, but none need necessarily do so. A number of square and triangular tablets have been found in Frisia (Roes 1963). In Scandinavia, where there is a long tradition of weaving by this method, the most spectacular find has been that made in the Oseberg ship burial (Grieg 1928), where 52 wooden tablets threaded with an unfinished braid were discovered, along with a loom for tablet weaving, all dated about 850 AD. Two tablets have been recovered from the Black Earth at Birka; one is illustrated by Geijer (1938) and the other is shown in Figure 101, no. 22. More recently a single tablet bearing a runic inscription has been published from Lund (E. Moltke in Mårtensson 1976).

Figure 103: Cetacean bone smoothing board from Birka (with glass linen smoother). Source: Statens Historiska Museum, Stockholm

'Smoothing Boards' (Figure 103)

The series of cetacean bone 'smoothing boards' which is well attested in Norway is represented in Britain by only three examples. The most complete of these from Ely, Cambridgeshire appears to be unfinished (Bjørn and Shetelig, 1940; Roesdahl *et al.* 1981). It incorporates the common motif of confronted animal heads (see Arbman 1943; British Museum 1923; Petersen 1951; Rygh 1885),[70] although these are represented here only in rudimentary form by light incisions. It is also provided with a handle, which is less usual. An incomplete example from the Kilmainham-Islandbridge cemetery is in the National Museum, Dublin; it is of similar form but has had more developed representatives of the zoomorphic heads (Bøe 1940; Graham-Campbell 1980). The third 'board', found in a grave on Arran, Strathclyde, which also contained a styca of Archbishop Wigmund of York (837-54), is even more fragmentary, and displays decoration only of double ring-and-dot devices (Grieg 1940).

The function generally ascribed to these flat plaques is that of smoothing linen (Sjøvold 1971). In Norway they are most frequently found in female graves, the richness of which has been taken to indicate that these plaques, like the weaving swords mentioned above, were items of some prestige. A single example from Sweden, found in a grave at Birka, is illustrated by Arbman (1943) (see also Figure 103).

A number of smaller undecorated cetacean bone plaques found at the Broch of Burrian (MacGregor 1974) may have performed the same function; when first discussed by Anderson (1872), however, they were confidently identified as 'the "rubbing bone" so well known to the Irish hand loom weaver, used for smoothing down the weft as it is woven'.

Miscellaneous

A small number of ancillary objects connected in various ways with textiles may also be discussed here.

Blomqvist and Mårtensson (1963) have published a double-pointed implement cut from the shaft of a long bone which they identify as a thread-twister (see also Graham-Campbell 1980). Although not identical to the find mentioned above, somewhat similar objects have been recovered from late Saxon Thetford, Norfolk (unpublished) and from twelfth-century contexts at Castle Acre, Norfolk (Margeson in Coad and Streeter 1982), Waltham Abbey, Essex (Huggins 1976: see Figure 93d) and Aardenburg in the Netherlands (Trimpe-Burger 1966). Two others are in the British Museum (unpublished). Plaited yarns could have been produced from threads attached to the terminal points and drawn through the tubular shaft of the bone. This function has recently been confirmed by Elisabeth Crowfoot (in Coad and Streeter 1982), who suggests the term 'lucet'.

Bone needles were developed to a high degree of uniformity of style and standard of production in the Roman period. Several varieties may be noted, whose differing forms imply a number of specialised functions, but what these were is unknown (see Kenyon 1948). All are too large to have been used with any but the coarsest materials. The shank of the needle may be parallel-sided or it may expand towards the head. Some parallel-sided needles have a point at the head as well as the base. Various forms of eye are found, including single round holes, intersecting round holes, elongated slots, and various combinations of these. Several examples show signs of having been broken through the eye; the old eye survives as a notch on the head, being superseded by a new perforation cut lower down the shank.

Needles are much scarcer in the succeeding centuries, many of those which have been claimed as such being crudely made from pigs' fibulae, with the articular end perforated but untrimmed. Most of these are held here to be pins rather than needles (pp. 120-1), in view of the lack of wear usually exhibited in the perforations and the comparatively large size of the head. Conversely, however, it might be conceded that some of those with narrowly-trimmed heads may be needles, though they are still rather large. Hald (1950) has sugested that such needles could be used for mesh-knitting items such as stocking or shrouds. Other more certain needles are known from Beckford, Worcestershire (Birmingham Museum, unpublished), Bidford on Avon, Warwickshire (J. Humphreys *et al.* 1932), Lincoln (Lincoln Archaeological Trust, unpublished), Whitby (Peers and Radford 1943), Lagore Crannog, Meath (Hencken 1950) and from Dorestad in the Netherlands (Clason 1980). From the opening of the medieval period metal needles entirely displace all those of bone.

Groves (1973) mentions the former importance of 'pack needles' in securing a wide range of goods for transport in cloth bundles. Sewing on domestic materials would have been carried out with more delicate implements, usually of bronze or iron, for which a number of putative bone cases survive. One such case from the *Limes* fort at Stockstadt, however, contained several fine bone needles (Drexel 1910). Cases manufactured from the shafts of hollow long bones are commonly found in pagan Saxon cemeteries on the Continent (see, for example, Böhme 1974; Jacob-Friesen 1974). A number of Viking period needle-cases found in Scotland have cut from the pneumatic leg-bones of large (goose-sized) birds; sometimes they have a transverse perforation in the centre (Grieg 1940), and one of those from Jarlshof, Shetland (Hamilton 1956) has been plugged with iron at one end. Numerous cases of this type were also found at Birka in Sweden (Figure 101, no. 26). Later medieval needle-cases are characterised by Groves (1973) as being hollow cylinders open at both ends, which carried the needles tucked into a roll of cloth suspended from a string; the tubular case covered this cloth roll when the needles were not in use and was simply slid up the string to allow access to them. A ring passed through the cloth prevented the case from slipping off the end.

From the late eighteenth century an enormous increase took place in the output of sewing accessories in bone and ivory. Groves (1973) illustrates a variety of such items, including needle and thimble-cases, silk-winders, yard measures, lace bobbins, sewing clamps, wax boxes, cotton barrels (Figure 101, no. 27) and pin-cushion holders (Figure 101, no. 28). Many of these are elaborately lathe-turned and intricately carved or pierced. Some are of composite construction, several elements being combined to form sewing sets, the constituent parts of which are linked by integral screw threads. A fragmentary bone cotton barrel of the late eighteenth or nineteenth century has been recovered from excavations in Plymouth, Devon (Fairclough 1979).

Stamps (Figure 104)

Antler tines provide ideal raw material for the manufacture of stamps or dies, the design being cut into the compact tissue at the tip. The majority are identified as potters' tools and are early Saxon in date. A northerly example (Figure 104a) from Dùn an Fheurain, Strathclyde (J.N.G. Ritchie 1971), is probably an import from the East Anglian region, where its pattern can be matched on contemporary pottery and where other known stamps are particularly common. Four of these come from West Stow, (Briscoe 1981; Evison 1979; Myres 1969), one from Illington (Briscoe 1981) and one from Lakenheath (Briscoe 1979), all in East Anglia (Figure 104b, c). Other antler stamps from outside this area include a single example from Shakenoak, Oxfordshire (Brodribb *et al.* 1972 and see also Figure 104d), and two from Southampton, Hampshire (Holdsworth 1980). Later antler stamps whose functions are less clearly defined include one with a wedge-shaped profile, the narrower end of which is carved into six small rectangles, from a wooden tool box of *c.* eighth- to tenth-century date found in Orkney (Stevenson 1952), and a stamp carved with a key pattern (Figure 104e), recovered from a context dated before the middle of the ninth century at Jarrow, Tyne and Wear (Professor Rosemary Cramp, personal communication). Frisian stamps made from antler tines published by Roes (1963) are identified as potters' stamps, but Wahlöö (1972) has suggested that others from early medieval Lund may have been used for ornamenting leatherwork, and the same function was suggested for an implement found at the Broch of Burrian, Orkney (MacGregor 1974).

Small mammal and bird bones also provided suitable material for potters' stamps. Hucke (1952) has noted correspondence in appearance between the cruciform ends of certain unfused phalangeal bones and the impressions found in early Slavic pottery from Schleswig-Holstein, while Briscoe (1981) suggests that the femur head of a hedgehog-sized animal might have been used in the ornamentation of hand-made Anglo-Saxon wares. The hollow shaft of a long bone, found in a *c.* sixth-century urn at Lackford, Suffolk, and ornamented with incised circles along its entire length, has been claimed as a potter's stamp (Lethbridge 1951)[71] and

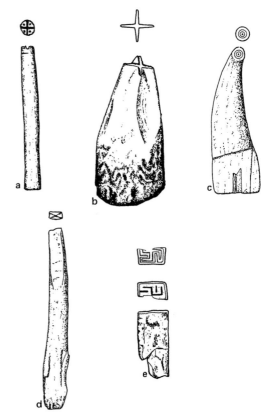

Figure 104: Stamps (scale 1:2) from (a) Dùn an Fheurain (Ritchie) (b) West Stow (Myres) (c) Lakenheath (Briscoe) (d) Shakenoak (Brodribb *et al.*) (e) Jarrow

impressions corresponding in shape to the cross-section of such a bone have been noted (Briscoe 1981). The most elaborate object so far identified as a stamp (now in Moyse's Hall Museum, Bury St Edmunds) consists of a hollow, cylindrical handle with an insert carrying a central dimple at one end. It has been suggested (Briscoe 1979) that the split which now defaces one side of the handle may have been an original feature which could be opened and closed at will with a string binding, allowing inserts with different patterns to be substituted. The idea is an interesting one, but perhaps not entirely convincing. Lethbridge (1951) notes that one urn from Lackford, Suffolk has been stamped around its girth with the molar tooth of a horse, the characteristic form of the grinding surface being reproduced in the clay.

Moulds (Figure 105)

The possible use of so-called motif pieces in the production of decorative metal mounts is discussed below. A contemporary group of Viking age objects may first be mentioned, and these were more certainly used as moulds for the production of cast brooches or other ornaments. All of them are made from antlers, cut close to the burr to avoid the internal cancellous tissue (p. 12). An example from Southampton, Hampshire has recently been commented upon (MacGregor 1980). In this instance a discoid depression has been sunk into the cut surface of the (red deer) antler; this circular area is ornamented with a series of concentric pits and with a sunken border line, so that the resulting ornament would have had concentric rings of small bosses within a raised rim. The expansion marking the site of the sawn-off brow tine has been used to create an ingate, indicating that there would originally have been a second element to form a two-piece closed mould.

Similar moulds of antler have been recovered from only one other site, namely the Viking age settlement at Hedeby in Schleswig-Holstein (Figure 105), and it is on the basis of those finds

Figure 105:   Mould for a cruciform ornament cut on an antler pedicle, from Hedeby (Note opposed holes for registration pins)

that the method of utilisation of these moulds has been elucidated. In discussing an early find from the site, used in the production of quatrefoil ornaments, Jankuhn (1944) suggested that models for *cire perdue* castings had been produced by pressing softened wax into the mould. More recent excavations on the same site have produced further examples, one of them made from reindeer antler and some featuring ingates (Ulbricht 1978). Among those examples which lack ingates, a few nonetheless have holes for registration pins, while some incorporate the remains of such pins in iron. When first published it was assumed (Capelle 1970; Capelle and Vierk 1971) that the newly-found Hedeby moulds, like that from the pre-war excavations, were used to mass-produce models for *cire perdue* casting, the absence of charring or other damage being taken as a sign that molten metal had not been poured directly into the antler matrices. More recently, however, Drescher (1978) has shown by practical experiment that repeated castings of lead and tin ornaments could be made from moulds of this type without incurring more than some slight discoloration. Fifty castings were achieved in one instance, without damage to the mould. The second element in Drescher's reconstructed mould was made of wood and included an ingate, since none was identified on the primary matrix.[72] A discoid antler piece among the Hedeby finds has more recently been tentatively identified as a lid for a mould (Ulbricht 1978). Oldeberg (1966) mentions the more recent use of antler moulds among the Lapps.

The Hedeby finds can be dated to the period between the late eighth or early ninth centuries on the one hand, and the end of the first quarter of the eleventh century on the other. Although the Southampton mould was found in a later context, associated with the demolition of a thirteenth-century wall (Platt and Coleman-Smith 1975), it has been suggested that it dates from the same period as those from Hedeby (MacGregor 1980). No other instances of such moulds have been noted.

Motif Pieces (Figure 106)

These fragments, incised with decorative emblems or with panels of ornament, have in

Figure 106: Motif piece carved on a jawbone fragment, from London

the past been designated 'trial pieces' but, in a recent review of a large body of such pieces in bone and in other materials from Ireland, O'Meadhra (1979) has argued persuasively for the adoption of the more neutral term, 'motif pieces'.

Some of the above do indeed seem to represent no more than first essays or sketches for decorative schemes ultimately realised on other pieces or in other media. This may be especially true of designs incised on flattened bones, such as scapulae, ribs and mandibles, which provide large, flat areas of dense tissue which is, however, of rather limited thickness. Scapulae ornamented in this way may have been found on various Irish sites (O'Meadhra 1979), while decorated mandibles (Figure 106) come from both London (Cottrill 1935) and York (Roesdahl *et al.* 1981), as do rib bones (British Museum 1923; Guildhall Museum

1908; Roesdahl *et al.* 1981; D.M. Waterman 1959).

The comparatively thick walls of columnar limb bones of horses and cattle provide opportunities for cutting in deeper relief and instances of ornamental panels finished to a high standard are found on bones of this category. Examples come from York (Grove 1940) and from a number of Irish sites (catalogued in O'Meadhra 1979).

It is the status of these more accomplished items which has led to questioning of the suitability of the term 'trial pieces', for it is now generally acknowledged that some may have been used as metal-workers' moulds. In order to produce cast plaques from these bones one of the methods of use discussed above under antler moulds (p. 195) could have been used, and this would have involved either making wax models from the bone pattern, for use with the *cire perdue* technique, or casting direct from the carved bone itself. An alternative and more widely canvassed suggestion is that the bone pieces were used as patterns in making thin metal foil panels by the *pressblech* technique. Anglo-Saxon metal dies used in this way have recently been discussed by Hawkes *et al.* (1979). Hawkes suggests two possible methods of producing a repoussé effect with these dies, one involving laying the sheet metal on a yielding surface (such as leather) and hammering the die into it, and the other, which she rightly adopts as the more probable, involving moulding the foil over the pattern with the aid of a burnisher. The latter opinion appears to provide the most attractive explanation of the function of bone motif pieces.

The Irish items catalogued by O'Meadhra (1979) are ascribed dates from the fifth to the twelfth centuries. Few of the English pieces are from stratified contexts, but all appear to belong to the last three centuries of the time-span suggested above, two fragments with Trewhiddle-style ornament from York being stylistically the earliest in the series, dating to the late ninth or early tenth centuries (Roesdahl *et al.* 1981; D.M. Waterman 1959).

Casket and Other Mounts (Figure 107)

Fragmentary bone or antler mounts are common finds on excavations from the Roman to the early medieval periods. Rich finds amounting to hundreds of pieces from composite ornamental schemes have been recovered at Vindonissa in Switzerland, including geometric fragments, lengths of plant-scroll, human figures, animal masks and friezes. Eckinger (1929) has reviewed these, together with others in museum collections in Italy and Germany, coming to the conclusion that they derive from 'parade' or funerary beds. Whether or not these mounts were locally made was unclear to him, but he felt inclined to believe that they might have been imported to Switzerland from Italy. Part of a magnificent Roman couch recently restored in the Fitzwilliam Museum, Cambridge, belongs to a similar class of object, and the mounts from this include many derived from cattle metapodials and some large, flat elements which were probably cut from horse scapulae. The Cambridge couch has been identified as belonging to a group of such objects deriving from north-central Italy in the first centuries BC and AD (Nicholls 1979).

A recent find from Colchester has provided clear evidence for local manufacture of decorative mounts (see p. 45, Figure 29h-j). A series of leaf-shaped and other fragments of late Roman origin were found within the area of a cemetery with an associated *martyrium*; many of these pieces were unfinished and the excavators were led to the tentative conclusion that they might have been intended to decorate coffins (N. Crummy 1981).

Turning to the more ubiquitous casket mounts, a few can be found which feature incised or ajourée inscriptions, as on examples from York, reading, respectively, *DOMINE VICTOR VINCAS FELIX* (*Lord Victor! May you have a lucky win!*) and *S[OR]OR AVE VIVAS IN DEO* (*Hail sister! May you live in God!*) (RCHM 1962). Most of the surviving casket mounts, however, are simple rectangular or mitred strips. Very few plaques with any attempt at representational carving are known and, for the most part, decoration is limited to simple linear or geometrical devices. The origins of the series lie in the late Roman period, and examples of Roman date are known from Lydney Park (Wheeler and Wheeler 1932) and Gloucester (Hassal and Rhodes 1974), Richborough, Kent (Bushe-Fox 1949) and Leicester (Hebditch and Mellor 1973). That from the Anglo-Saxon cemetery at Caistor-by-Norwich, Norfolk, was thought to be perhaps of the late fourth or fifth centuries (Myres and Green 1973). Similar dates may be postulated for other examples from Illington, Norfolk, also noted by Myres and Green, Abingdon, Oxfordshire (Leeds and Harden 1936) and, perhaps, from Dover, Kent (T.D. Kendrick 1937). Rather later in origin are some fragments from a seventh-century cremation in Asthall Barrow, Oxfordshire (Leeds 1924), and a number of decorative bone plaques said to have come from the Irish crannogs of Ballinderry and Strokestown (Munro 1890) may also belong to about this time. Among the later casket mounts found in England are several from a tenth-century refuse pit at Worcester, which also contained a bronze lock-plate (Carver 1980). Another group from South Cadbury Castle, Somerset, represented

Figure 107:   Casket mounts (scale 1:2) from (a-c) York and (d) South Cadbury (Green)

by a number of strips with incised ring-and-dot decoration and a plaque incised with a crude interlace design (Figure 107d), is datable to about the early eleventh century (K.T. Greene, in Alcock 1970). Further casket mounts of the eleventh or twelfth centuries include one group from Ludgershall Castle, Wiltshire, in which the wood had decayed but the strips which decorated the lid were found in their original relationships (*Medieval Archaeology* 10, pl. XV), and others from Castle Acre, Norfolk (Margeson in Coad and Streeter 1982). Two important finds come from Coppergate in York. The first of these (Figure 107a) was found during rebuilding of the corner block of Castlegate and Coppergate at the beginning of the present century (Benson 1906) and the second in 1978 at 16-22 Coppergate (Figure 107c). A third example from York was found in a Saxo-Norman context under York Minster (MacGregor, forthcoming). The latest stratified examples are a series of mounts found in various contexts dating from the early to mid-twelfth century at Perth (MacGregor, forthcoming). On the Continent, several mounts of this general type are known from late fourth or fifth-century contexts, including one from a *Laetengrab* of *c.* 400 at Fécamp, Seine-Maritime (Werner 1962; Böhme 1974); others of Frankish date come from Marœuil, Pas de Calais (de Loë 1939) and Weilbach, Main-Taunus (Schoppa 1953, 1959). One example with undoubted Christian connotations, comes from Heilbronn, Baden-Württemberg (Goessler 1932), and there were several fragments of decorative strip among the contents of a seventh-century grave in the cemetery at Junkersdorf, Cologne (la Baume 1967). Another, virtually intact and thought to be of the eighth to tenth centuries, was found at

Stebbach, Nordbaden (Lutz 1970). Goldschmidt (1918) illustrates a number of other caskets dated on stylistic grounds to about this period (the most impressive being those from Werden, and St Gereon, Cologne), while some fragmentary pieces from Hitzacker may be as late as the twelfth or thirteenth centuries (Wachter 1976). Other fragments from the Frisian terps, although lacking precise dates, will fall within the limits established above (Roes 1963).

In some cases, as in the majority of the fragments from York Minster and in a single piece from Goltho Manor (MacGregor, forthcoming), the raw material used in the manufacture of these strips is antler. Rib bones were also used, however: the Frankish casket from Marœuil was said to be ornamented with strips of split bovine ribs (de Loë 1939). The lids from Ludgershall Castle and Coppergate and a variety of strips from various sites in Lincoln (Lincoln Archaeological Trust, unpublished) are of the same origin, as betrayed by the structure of the cancellous tissue on the back of the strips. Evidence for the utilisation of ribs comes also from the harbour area at Schleswig (Ulbricht 1980a). Among the mounts from York and Perth, those pieces for which bone rather than antler has been used are large flat plaques, the dimensions of which are such that only one bone from the normally available mammalian skeleton could have been used — the broad and flat expanse of the scapula. This source is confirmed by the presence of a band of exposed cancellous tissue on the back of one of the Perth plates, marking the site of the projecting *spina*. The mounts from Lydney Park (Wheeler and Wheeler 1932), and those from Asthall Barrow (Leeds 1924) have both been published as being of ivory, but confusion between ivory and bone has been frequent in the past and it is likely that a fresh examination would prove that in most instances (as here) the materials used were bone and antler. Decorative strips of ivory were commonly used on caskets of Byzantine origin, however, particularly in the ninth and tenth centuries (Talbot-Rice 1968), so that the possibility of this medium being imported into the British Isles cannot be ruled out. A Roman casket mount from Greenwich Park, London, is indeed made of ivory (Stephen Greep, personal communication).

Several of the above strips carry traces of iron corrosion from the rivets which held them in place. On others, bone or antler pegs were used in place of iron rivets. The latter were not only less unsightly than their iron counterparts but also allowed decorative schemes to develop without interruption (the incised ornament being carried over the heads of the flush-fitting pegs after they were inserted). It should be noted that the strips were secured to the flat surface of the wood by the pegs and were not, it seems, inlaid, as some writers have suggested.

A rather limited repertoire of decorative schemes is found on these mounts, being confined for the most part to linear and compass-drawn motifs of the simplest kind. The designs were evidently executed on the strips before assembly, the individual lengths then being cut to fit the space available without regard to the incised patterns. This may be seen clearly on the caskets from Ludgershall Castle and from Coppergate, York. These examples also incorporate what seems to be an otherwise uncommon form of decoration, in which the strips are pierced with large-diameter holes, which were backed with sheet metal in a more or less decorative manner. The gilded sheet copper on the Coppergate casket (Waterman 1959) must have looked quite attractive, but in the case of the Ludgershall box the backing of lead can have added little to its appearance. A richer example from Emden, Ostfriesland, with gold leaf backing to its bone plates, is dated by P. Schmidt (1969) to about the eleventh century. Waterman compares this backed openwork treatment to that found on a number of Irish shrines, particularly of the eleventh and twelfth centuries, and it is also found on a number of composite combs of similar date (p. 91). Large-diameter holes are also to be found on the strips decorating the caskets from Stebbach (Lutz 1970) and the church of St Gereon, Cologne (Goldschmidt 1918), but no mention is made in the published accounts of metal backing.

Most of the examples cited above have been recovered from what are clearly secular — in some instances even pagan — contexts, although one or two of the Continental examples have survived in church treasuries, and several have elements of Christian symbolism in their decorative schemes. The Perth mounts, together with two of the caskets illustrated by Goldschmidt (1918) include plaques with incised equal-armed crosses, as do the gold-backed Emden mounts (P. Schmidt 1969), while the Weilbach casket carries a composite cross on the lid (Schoppa 1953). The Heilbronn casket displays an alternative Christian symbol in the form of a *chi-rho* monogram (Goessler 1932). There seems to be no reason why the type as a whole should be invested with any particular ecclesiastical significance, however, and there can be little doubt that the majority were used for storing small items of personal value rather than as reliquaries. The remains of small wooden boxes without bone decorations are common finds in Anglo-Saxon graves, where they frequently contain trinkets and jewellery, combs and shells (see, for instance, Lethbridge 1931, 1936; C.R. Smith 1856). No doubt most of the decorated examples performed a similar sort of role.[73] Their more elegant counterparts in the Byzantine world, in which panels of figure sculpture are often surrounded by strips ornamented with repeating rosettes (all executed in ivory or bone) (Dalton 1909) fall into the two broad groups. Talbot-Rice (1968) has suggested that those members of this 'rosette group' which carry secular ornament were probably marriage gifts, while those with religious scenes may have contained relics or church treasures.

These applied casket mounts reach their most elaborate forms in the late Viking age caskets formerly associated with the cathedrals of Cammin in Pommern, and Bamberg. The Cammin casket, which was destroyed during the Second World War, was shaped in the form of a house and measured 63cm by 33cm. The basic structure was of wood, covered with twenty-two plaques of elk antler clasped by gilt-bronze mounts. The antler plaques were incised with zoomorphic, anthropomorphic and foliate motifs, filled with overall Mammen-style pelleting (Goldschmidt 1918; Graham-Campbell 1980). The Bamberg casket (now in the Bayerisches Nationalmuseum in Munich) is thought perhaps to have come from the same workshop as that from Cammin. The oak box is, in this instance, covered with thin sheets of walrus ivory held in place by gilt-bronze bands (Wilson and Klindt-Jensen 1966).

Caskets (Figures 108-9)

As well as the decorative bone and antler casket mounts mentioned above, which were used merely to ornament boxes otherwise constructed of wood, a number of caskets made more substantially of cetacean bone panels must be considered.

Some of these, such as the Fife casket (Anderson 1886), rely to an extent on metal fittings to hold them together. Four riveted bronze bands encircle the Fife casket, incorporating the hinge and lock mechanisms; the end panels are dovetailed into the sides, but in addition the vertical corners are covered with decorative metal strips, and each is clamped by a pair of right-angled riveted clasps, with an additional vertical strip in the centre of the panel. The five fields so formed on the long sides and the lid are filled with carved interlace ornament which also embellishes the end panels. All these except the base (judged to be a later addition) display some traces of red staining. Stevenson (1955b) draws attention to certain stylistic parallels which can be detected between the Fife casket and Anglo-Scandinavian stone sculpture. The free rings occurring in the interlace and the hatched pellet-like pattern which fills some of the interstices in the ornament would certainly be consistent with a date in the Viking period.

Pinder-Wilson and Brooke (1973) discuss a large group of 'Siculo-Arabic' caskets of ivory, among which occur rectangular, house-shaped and cylindrical forms. Metal clasps and ivory pins are used in their construction and painted decoration is common to all of them. There seems to have been little or no direct influence from these items on the 'native' north European products of the Norman and early medieval periods.

The most consummate north European piece is undoubtedly the casket found at Auzon, Haute Loire, now in the British Museum and known as the Franks Casket (Figure 108). It stands as the supreme example of its type not only because of its early eighth-century date, but more particularly because it is manufactured without the use of functional metal bindings of the kind mentioned above. The constructional details of the Franks Casket (Figure 109) presumably reflect contemporary carpentry techniques. The intricate method of

Figure 108:   The Franks Casket: views of (top) lid and (below) front panel

jointing is so masterful that it clearly could not have been developed in response to this particular need, and, in the absence of comparably constructed bone caskets, we may assume that the technique was evolved in the production of wooden boxes. The casket, which measures some 23 by 19 by 10.5cm, is made of bone, seemingly derived from the jawbone of a whale. The key to its construction lies in the complex upright members found at the four corners. These are slotted vertically on two adjacent sides to receive the rebated ends of the side plates; in addition, within each of these slots is a pair of rectangular sockets, cut to receive corresponding tenons projecting from the ends of the side plates. (These are best seen

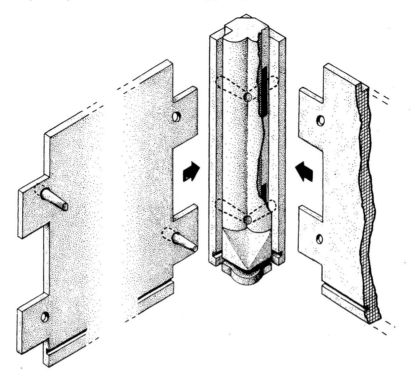

Figure 109:   The Franks Casket: constructional details. Drawing: N.A. Griffiths

on a panel now in Florence, illustrated in Ross 1970). The uprights and the side plates are also channelled horizontally to receive the edges of the bone base plates. Once the four sides and the base had been assembled, the mortice and tenon joints at the corners were secured by rivets or pegs, originally no doubt of bone, driven through drilled holes which intercept each other in pairs at common points on the insides of the uprights; in this way, only two holes (instead of four) are visible on the inside of each upright. Undecorated areas have been left in reserve on the outer edges of the side panels where these pegs emerge; formerly they were covered with decorative silver mountings, now lost (G.B. Brown 1930). To judge from residual metal staining, mounts which were lozenge-shaped rather than rectangular had been fitted to the casket, but doubt has been expressed as to whether these were original.[74] Traces of small feet have been noted under the four corners.

The lid of the Franks Casket (Figure 108), now fragmentary, originally sat on a rebate running around the top edge of the box, secured with a lock on one side. The lock itself was evidently renewed on at least one occasion, to judge from the many fixing holes which survive, although it is possible that some of these were connected with the mounting of a conjectural metal lock plate (G.B. Brown 1930). The fact that the lock was an original feature of the box is shown by the way the carved ornament respects the square field around the keyhole. Curiously, no similar provision was made for the hinges on the opposite side of the casket, so that inevitably they must have concealed part of the carved decoration. This has led to doubts as to whether the hinges (represented now only by rivet holes) could have been original; if they were not, however, and there were no hinges on the casket, then it is difficult to see how the lock could have been effective.

The surviving central panel of the flat lid is rebated along the upper edges of its long sides and would have been overlapped by the flanking panels. An undecorated strip to one side of it (doubtless a late repair) is correspondingly rebated on its underside and is morticed at the ends to engage with the (now missing) edge plates, perhaps reflecting an original feature. Mrs Leslie Webster has suggested (personal communication) that the missing lid panels might have been made of wood covered with decorative plates of precious metal, and this could account for their disappearance, as the casket is said to have been stripped of its metal mounts in the late eighteenth or nineteenth centuries (G.B. Brown 1930). An undecorated field in the centre of the lid was presumably covered by another metal plate, possibly incorporating a handle. From a constructional point of view, Mrs Webster finds the closest parallels in the so-called Brescia casket.

The knife-cut ornament on the Franks Casket is of the highest calibre. It incorporates an Old English runic inscription relating the circumstances in which the whale from whose bones the casket was supposed to have been made was stranded (Page 1973):

fisc flodu ahof on fergenberig warþ gasric grorn þær he on greut giswom/hronæs ban

'The fish beat up the sea[s] on to the mountainous cliff. The king of ?terror became sad when he swam on to the shingle. [This is] whale's bone'

Hinges (Figure 110)

Fremersdorf (1940) was the first to identify as elements from hinges the bone cylinders with lateral perforations which are recorded from a number of Roman period excavations. These individual elements were combined in continuous series, rather like modern piano hinges, to provide pivots for cupboard doors or the lids of chests. Fremersdorf illustrates a plaster-cast of a double-doored cupboard from Pompeii, in which each door has thirty-six such elements running its entire length. Smaller numbers of similar hinges of wood were used on Greco-Egyptian caskets and boxes (Fremersdorf 1940; H. Waugh and R. Goodburn in Frere 1972).

Bone hinges are normally turned from the shafts of hollow long-bones (Figure 110a, b). Fremersdorf (1940) and Schmid (1968) identify cattle metatarsals as the most favoured source

of raw material. The individual elements were articulated by wooden plugs driven into the medullary cavity and wedged in place; 'male' elements, in which projecting cylindrical spigots were cut on the ends of the wooden plugs, mated alternately with 'female' elements incorporating corresponding axial sockets. Fremersdorf and Schmid illustrate examples from waterlogged levels in the *Schutthügel* at Vindonissa in Switzerland, in which the boxwood plugs have been preserved intact; traces of lubricating wax survive on the plugs and on the contact surfaces of the bone cylinders. Two reports on French hinges (Musée Archéologique de Dijon, nd; Pelletier 1971) note traces of drilling or polishing on the internal walls of the medullary cavity, a feature which Pelletier takes as an indication that an iron rod acting as a common axis was passed through several elements in turn. There appears to be no supporting evidence for this assertion in the form of surviving rods or even traces of corrosion. Possibly, some bones had to be drilled out to permit the insertion of an axially-aligned wooden plug of appropriate dimensions.

The hinges were attached alternately to the door and to the framework of the box or cupboard by dowels projecting at right angles from holes drilled in the wall of the cylinder. Schmid (1968) notes that these holes are normally set in a natural longitudinal groove on the external surfaces.[75] By siting the holes in this position, the groove (which was too deep to be removed by turning) would have been hidden from view when the hinge was fitted. According to length, one, two or three dowels might be used. Simple elements, as found at Risstissen (Ulbert 1959), Mainz and Trier (Fremersdorf 1940), Vindonissa (Fremersdorf 1940; Schmid 1968), London (British Museum 1964) and Verulamium (H. Waugh and R. Goodburn in Frere 1972), have a single hole with one wooden dowel; other examples from the same sites have two or more holes in line. French examples come from Alésia and Malain, Côte d'Or, and Besançon, Doubs; excavations at Malain have produced over fifty elements, some unfinished, indicating that systematic production was taking place on site (Musée Archéologique de Dijon, nd). Traces of corrosion products on a hinge from Augst suggest that iron fixing pins may also have been used (Schmid 1968).

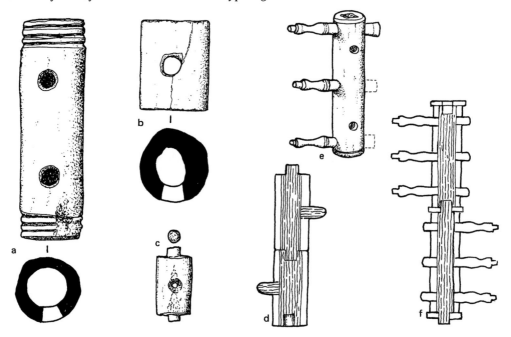

Figure 110:   Hinges: simple (a-c) from Verulamium, with (d) diagrammatic cross-section showing the use of wooden inserts (after Waugh and Goodburn); offset (e) from Maastricht, with (f) diagrammatic cross-section (after Fremersdorf) (scale (a-c) 3:4)

More complex examples (Figure 110e, f), some with three sets of holes passing through both walls of the cylinder in one axis and with two additional sets of holes arranged at right angles to them, are known from museum collections in Brussels, Maastricht, Cologne and Frankfurt-am-Main (Fremersdorf 1940). The dowels associated with hinges of this type are decoratively turned bone pegs, rebated at either end for insertion into the wall of the hinge and the door structure respectively. Unlike the simple wooden pegs described above, whose entire projecting length was buried in the structural timber, these pegs were clearly meant to be seen. Fremersdorf's reconstruction shows the hinge offset from the door and frame by the length of the pegs. Those holes not occupied by pegs are filled by decorative conical plugs of bone which serve no practical function. In addition to the finds mentioned above, a bone dowel of this type may be noted from Alésia (Musée Archéologique de Dijon, nd).

Some cylindrical elements have no lateral holes whatever. These would have been fitted with axial wooden plugs as described above, and would have served as spacers between those which were pegged to the timbers. Several examples from Trier and Mainz are illustrated by Fremersdorf (1940).

Other components are associated with some hinge mechanisms. Fremersdorf identifies small perforated bone discs with lateral extensions as washers which separated the cylindrical elements; the extensions, he suggests, could independently have anchored the column of hinges to an external corner. Decorative finials closed the ends of some hinges; a grave in Cologne produced one example, in which a disc of truncated conical section was secured by a bulbous peg with ornamental flanges (Fremersdorf 1940). A number of turned 'balusters', and 'handles' in the Nuits-Saint-Georges and Dijon Museums (Musée Archéologique de Dijon, nd) may be similarly interpreted.

Decoration on the cylindrical elements themselves is usually confined to incised circumferential lines, either singly or in groups. These have been found on occasion to have been enhanced with inlaid black pigment (p. 70).

An alternative method of producing hinges was to cut them from solid bone tissue. One example of this type (Figure 110c) has been noted from Verulamium by H. Waugh and R. Goodburn (in Frere 1972), who compare it with Egyptian hinges from the Fayûm.

Notes

1. Microscopic examination of a wooden comb of Roman date from Vindolanda, Northumberland, revealed traces of coarse animal hair, probably derived from cattle (Birley 1977). Nits found on a Viking age comb from York were again of a type not found on humans: they compare most closely with a large genus, *Damalinia*, found variously on deer, horses, cattle, sheep and goats (Harry Kenward, personal communication). It is nonetheless difficult to imagine that the primary use of the combs from both sources was other than for personal grooming.

2. The terminology adopted here varies to some extent from, but is not in serious conflict with, that proposed by Galloway (1976). In preference to her 'tooth segment' I have adopted the more self-explanatory 'tooth-plate'; my preference for 'side-plate' over Galloway's 'connecting plate', although less positively descriptive in the majority of cases, acknowledges the fact that some such plates, notably on certain horn combs (p. 95), perform no connecting function.

3. Some tines, however, were used for side-plates. Ambrosiani (1981) notes the under-representation of tines compared with burrs among waste material from Ribe, and deduces that they had been systematically utilised.

4. The possibility that such strips might come from comb cases (pp. 96-8) should also be borne in mind.

5. In a recent replication exercise, Galloway and Newcomer (1981) achieved a standard thickness by placing the roughly-shaped tooth-plates in a wooden jig and filing them all together.

6. Preliminary marking-out of the plates with the positions of the saw-cuts may have been common, but the evidence would normally have been destroyed in the process of sawing the teeth. Tempel (1969) notes one comb from Elisenhof, Schleswig-Holstein, in which incised lines marking the tooth spacing have survived on the end-plate where the teeth have not been cut to their full depth, but more evidence of this nature might have been expected if the practice had been widespread.

7. In their reconstruction of a composite comb, Galloway and Newcomer (1981) found some difficulty in keeping the side-plates and tooth-plates in their respective positions while drilling the rivet holes, and speculate that some combs may have been temporarily assembled with glue before drilling and riveting.

8. These trapezoidal waste pieces have been used by Ulbricht (1978) to estimate the scale of comb production at Hedeby.

9. Galloway and Newcomer (1981) lay some stress on the additional strength imparted to the teeth by an angular base.

10. Such a section would inevitably have to be cut from the peripheral tissue of the antler, the centre being permeated by spongy tissue (p. 12).

11. Similar split rib fragments from Leadmill Lane, York, are interpreted as coming from comb cases (MacGregor 1982).

12. Conversely, Ambrosiani (1981) has noted a strong corelation between, on the one hand, her 'A' type combs (p. 88) with their deep thin cross-sections, which she sees as a Scandinavian development occurring within the area of maximum use of palmate elk antlers, and, on the other hand, her 'B' combs in which the adoption of more rounded cross-sections on the side-plates is matched by a shift towards the use of red deer antler.

13. For a single-sided ivory comb of the fourth or fifth centuries from Wels, Austria, see Deringer 1967a. An example from London, as yet unpublished, has also been identified as elephant ivory (Dr P. Armitage, personal communication).

14. A Roman comb found in London and bearing (apparently) the maker's name, *DIGNUS*, has been published more than once as bone (e.g., *Britannia* 2, p. 299) but is in fact made of wood.

15. Lasko (1956) notes that certain Coptic combs display corresponding circular patterns or inlays in bone or glass, the latter seemingly intended to serve as mirrors.

16. The same features can be found on the corresponding cases for these combs (see p. 97).

17. B. Schmidt (1970) illustrates a comb and case from Stössen, Sachsen-Anhalt which each have a projecting loop in the centre, perhaps reinforcing this suggestion.

18. K.A. Wilde (1953) has suggested that the side-plates were sometimes deliberately curved inward to clamp the teeth of the comb in position. It seems more probable, however, that such curvature as can be seen in some cases results from the bars being compressed while buried in the ground.

19. I am grateful to John Clark of the Museum of London for drawing my attention to the Esneux case.

20. On the talismanic significance of antlers and other parts of deer, however, see Meaney (1981).

21. The tradition stems from at least as early as the La Tène period. What appears to be an amulet of this type, dated no later than *c*. AD 300, is illustrated by Cocks (1931).

22. For this identification I am indebted to James Rackham.

23. In this context it is interesting to note that the Sutton Hoo lyre was stored in a beaver-skin bag (Bruce-Mitford and Bruce-Mitford 1974).

24. In a grave at Cassington, Oxfordshire, an iron ring of comparable size to those discussed here was found. Its cross-section is too sharp for it to have functioned satisfactorily as a bangle and its position, together with the distribution of associated objects, gives support to the identification of both this item and its ivory homologues as bag rings (D. Brown 1977; Leeds and Riley 1942).

25. There seems no reason to surmise (*pace* Edwards 1978) that these pins are of Roman origin.

26. Laing (1973) actually refers to these as 'bead-headed pins'.

27. Details of these pins, found in association with a number of *Grubenhaüser* on Swindon Hill in 1975, were kindly sent to me by Miss Caroline Washbourn.

28. An illustration of what appears to be a similar pin is given by Noss (1976): it is not a dress pin, however, but is being used to open up the pattern in a piece of lace.

29. In an appendix to Rhodes (1982), Dr P. Armitage provides a discussion of the source of the raw material of the spectacles and an analysis of contemporary bone waste from the site of Baynard's Castle, London. Microscopic examination of the structure and the minimum dimensions of the bone from which the Trig Lane spectacles were made lead to the conclusion that a bull metacarpal was used.

30. Rhodes (1982) also discusses the possibility that the spectacles may originally have been fitted with wire supports, as shown in contemporary illustrations. A painting of Virgil by Ludger tom Ring the Elder (1496-1547), now in the Westfälisches Landesmuseum, Münster (No. 1175LM) shows the subject holding a pair of spectacles of this type in place with thumb and forefinger.

31. An incised line marking (and determining) the site of the split is noted on one rim.

32. A somewhat similar dragonesque object from Lund is also identified as a stylus (Mårtensson 1961) though its open jaws appear to have held a ring terminal.

33. Unfortunately, there seems to be no way of establishing whether a *corneum graphium* really was a horn stylus or whether it was some sort of pen.

34. Mårtensson (1961), however, illustrates what appear to be related implements of classical Roman date from Rome itself.

35. Some Scandinavian implements of this category illustrated by Mårtensson (1961) have chisel-shaped rather than ball heads, but this variation has not been noted elsewhere.

36. Dr Margeson kindly discussed this item with me in advance of the published report.

37. An unpublished bronze balance from Smyrna, now in the Ashmolean Museum, Oxford, is made in this way. It has also the added refinement of an adjustable counter-weight.

38. Knuckle bones filled with lead were also used for this purpose (see Amsterdams Historisch Museum 1977).

39. The contemporary introduction of spindle whorls in similar forms and materials is discussed on p. 187. It is possible that some at least of these centrally-perforated discs may yet be gaming pieces rather than whorls.

40. A riveted discoid counter of this type was found at Trim Castle, Meath, where it was identified as being made of antler and having been mended in antiquity after splitting (Sweetman 1978). The structural organisation of antler makes it unlikely that it could have split in such a way, however, and it is probable that this is another example of original com-

posite construction. A further example, found in Cologne, is in the British Museum (Dalton 1909).

41. An interesting example of this type from an eleventh- or twelfth-century context at Schloss Broich, Rühr, has a sheet of bronze interposed between its two riveted discs (Binding 1968). This sheet was exposed through decorative perforations cut in the upper disc in the manner also encountered on contemporary combs and casket mounts. The British Museum counter referred to in note 40 has been similarly treated: Dalton (1909) noted the angular perforations in the upper disc but mistakenly assumed them to have held inlays.

42. On the Continent, evidence for this type may be traced to the ninth or tenth centuries (Binding 1968; Wichmann and Wichmann 1964).

43. Wilson (1970), however, describes them as dyed.

44. Clason (1980) suggests that sledges with bone runners could have been used on the slippery clay of unpaved streets. Any such use would, however, produce uneven wear which would contrast markedly with the polished plane surfaces built up by friction on frozen sheets of water which are a feature of these runners.

45. The perforations on the Sutton Hoo pegs (which are of wood) are at the shoulder, rather than the tip as on most of the bone pegs discussed here, so that the pegs must have been fitted in the reverse of the usual manner. The same is true of a number of fifteenth-century pegs from St Aldates, Oxford (M. Henig in Durham 1977).

46. The tuning pegs too were sometimes made of bronze, and several unpublished examples from Ireland are now in the British Museum.

47. Two Iron Age objects identified as possible wrest planks should also be noted: one comes from Dinorben, Clwyd (Gardner and Savory 1964) and the other from Dùn an Fheurain, Strathclyde (J.N.G. Ritchie 1971).

48. The other hand would then have been free to play a drum.

49. I am grateful to Miss Elizabeth Owles for allowing me to examine this whistle and to mention it here.

50. Unpublished information from Professor J.D. Currey.

51. A self bow, being almost straight in its unstrung form, is invested by stringing with only a comparatively small amount of strain energy.

52. It seems unlikely that this could have been the case, since such a bow would have been hopelessly weak (cf. Balfour 1921). Indian bows made from a single buffalo horn are known, however, and it is conceivable that the Waterbeach bow could have been a recent introduction from the Far East.

53. A tombstone, probably of Hadrianic date, from Housesteads, Northumberland, shows the deceased clasping a composite bow which, according to the scale of the figure, would have been about 1m in length (D.J. Smith 1968a).

54. The only bow to have survived from the Anglo-Saxon period was found at Chessel on the Isle of Wight. It is a self bow some 1.50m in length (Clark 1963). A Viking age self bow was recovered from Ballinderry Crannog 1 (Hencken 1937).

55. Goddard (1896) mentions 'two or three similar catches of Roman date, which have been found in London, existing in the collections of the British Museum', but nothing is known of the origins of these pieces nor of their present whereabouts.

56. Oldenstein (1976) mentions one example from Niederbieber, Rheinland-Pfalz, made from a single piece of bone.

57. Oldenstein (1976) acknowledges the slight possibility that some chapes with pierced decoration could have been riveted through the ornamental openings.

58. A knife handle from Oslo constructed in a similar way from elements of stone and brass is illustrated by Molaug (1975).

59. Tempel (1969) raises the possibility that the burial at Ytre Elgsnes (which produced a variety of tools) may have been that of a comb-maker.

60. Van der Poel (1961) mentions the occurrence of such implements from the terps made of elk antler, but gives no further details.

61. Holmes (1961) thought the evidence pointed to these implements being used in thatching or reed-gathering, rather than in agriculture.

62. Christopher Morris kindly drew my attention to this fact. A bone strip, perforated at either end and found in Viking age levels at

Jarlshof, Shetland, has been similarly interpreted (Hamilton 1956).

63. David Brown mentions the possibility that this implement may have been used in working flax rather than wool. An inventory of spinning and weaving tools contained in the Anglo-Saxon *Gerefa* (late eleventh century) mentions both weaving comb (*pihten*, glossed *pecten*) and wool comb (*wulcamb*) (Liebermann 1903).

64. European communities have generally used the whorl towards the bottom of the spindle, but this is not a universal practice.

65. Wild (1970) notes that even during the Roman period appropriate conditions of waterlogging (as encountered at Vindonissa) result in wooden spindles outnumbering those of bone by about ten to one.

66. Some societies spin without any whorl whatever, while in others a simple expansion at the lower end of the spindle acts as a sufficient energy reservoir. Yet others spin with the spindle resting on the ground, so that its weight has a less direct bearing on the characteristics of the yarn.

67. I am grateful to Jenny Mann of Lincoln Archaeological Trust for providing this information.

68. A wooden weaving sword from Dublin, dated to the Viking period, is illustrated by Ó Ríordáin (1970), and a later example from Aberdeen has been published by Stones (1982).

69. According to Kaminska and Nahlik (1960), the horizontal loom was already in use in Poland by the tenth century.

70. An impressive example of this type of 'board' was sold recently by Christie's of London (*Antiquities, Works of Art and Important Renaissance Bronzes, Plaquettes and Limoges Enamels*, 8 July 1981, lot 23).

71. Similar items from Continental collections, however, are frequently interpreted as needle-cases: see examples from Altenwald (Waller 1957) and Wehden (Waller 1961) in Niedersachsen.

72. Graham-Campbell (1980), however, interprets a somewhat irregular gap in the rim of the original as an ingate.

73. The caskets illustrated on some West Highland sculptured monuments in Scotland are further pointers to a secular function (see Callander 1926).

74. I am grateful to Mrs Leslie Webster for allowing me to read the typescript of a paper delivered by her at a conference in Münster, in which this and other useful observations were made.

75. This is, in fact, the sulcus marking the fusion point between the third and fourth metatarsals in cattle.

Bibliography

Addyman, P.V. and Hill, D.H., 1969. 'Saxon Southampton: a review of the evidence. Part II', *Proceedings of the Hampshire Field Club and Archaeological Society* 26, 61-96.

Ahlén, I., 1965. 'Studies on the red deer, *Cervus elaphus* L., in Scandinavia I: history of distribution', *Viltrevy* 3, 1-88.

Akerman, J.V., 1855. *Remains of Pagan Saxondom* (London: Smith).

Alcock, L., 1963. *Dinas Powys. An Iron Age, Dark Age and Medieval Settlement in Glamorgan* (Cardiff: University of Wales).

—— 1970. 'Excavations at South Cadbury Castle, 1969: a summary report', *Antiquaries Journal* 50, 14-25.

—— 1972. '*By South Cadbury is that Camelot . . .*' (London: Thames and Hudson).

Alenus-Lecerf, J. and Dradon, M., 1967. 'Tombes mérovingiennes à Hollogne-aux-Pierres', *Archaeologia Belgica* 101, 5-33.

Alföldi, M.R., 1957. 'Knochengegenstände', in M.R. Alföldi et al., *Intercisa II (Dunapentele): Geschichte der Stadt in der Römerzeit* (Budapest: Archaeologia Hungarica new ser. 36), 477-95.

Alford, V., 1933. 'The Abbots Bromley horn dance', *Antiquity* 7, 203-9.

Allen, J.R., 1896. 'The primitive bone skate', *Reliquary and Illustrated Archaeologist* 2, 33-6.

Allen, J.R. and Anderson, J., 1903. *The Early Christian Monuments of Scotland* (Edinburgh: Society of Antiquaries of Scotland).

Allmer, A. and Dissard, P., 1888. *Trion. Antiquités découvertes en 1885, 1886 et Antérieurement* (Lyon: Association Typographique).

Allott, S., 1974. *Alcuin of York* (York: Sessions).

Ambrosiani, K., 1981. *Viking Age Combs, Comb Making and Comb Makers in the Light of Finds from Birka and Ribe* (Stockholm: Stockholm Studies in Archaeology 2).

Amsterdams Historisch Museum, 1977. *Opgravingen in Amsterdam* (Amsterdam: Dienst der Publieke Weerken/Amsterdams Historisch Museum).

Andersen, A., 1968. 'Mittelalterliche Kämme aus Ribe', *Res Mediaevales Ragnar Blomqvist kal. mai. Oblata (MCMLXVIII)* (Karlshamn: Archaeologica Lundensia 3), 25-42.

Andersen, H.H., Crabb, P.J. and Madsen, H.J., 1971. *Århus Søndervold: en Byarkaeologisk Undersøkelse* (Copenhagen: Jysk Arkaeologisk Selskabs Skrifter 9).

Anderson, J., 1872. 'Notes on the evidence of spinning and weaving in the brochs or Pictish towers . . .', *Proceedings of the Society of Antiquaries of Scotland* 9, 548-61.

—— 1881. *Scotland in Early Christian Times*, ser. 2 (Edinburgh: Douglas).

—— 1883. *Scotland in Pagan Times: the Iron Age* (Edinburgh: Douglas).

—— 1886. 'Notice of a casket of cetacean bone . . .', *Proceedings of the Society of Antiquaries of Scotland* 20, 390-6.

Andés, L.E., 1925. *Bearbeitung des Horns, Elfenbeins, Schildplatts, der Knochen und Perlmutter* (Leipzig and Vienna: Hartleben).

Arbman, H., 1943. *Birka 1: Die Gräber* (Stockholm: Kungliga Vitterhets Historie och Antikvitets Akademien).

Armitage, P.L., 1977. *The Mammalian Remains from the Tudor Site of Baynard's Castle, London: a Biometrical and Historical Analysis* (PhD thesis, University of London).

—— 1980. 'A preliminary description of British cattle from the late twelfth to the early sixteenth century', *Ark* 7, 405-12.

—— 1982. 'Studies on the remains of domestic livestock from Roman, medieval and early modern London: objectives and methods', in A.R. Hall and H.K. Kenward (eds.), *Environmental Archaeology in the Urban Context* (London: Council for British Archaeology Research Report 43), 94-106.

Armitage, P.L. and Goodall, J.A., 1977. 'Medieval horned and polled sheep: the archaeological and iconographical evidence', *Antiquaries Journal* 57, 73-89.

Armstrong, E.C.R, 1922, 'Irish bronze pins of the Christian period', *Archaeologia* 72, 71-86.

Armstrong, E.C.R. and Macalister, R.A.S., 1920. 'Wooden book with leaves indented and waxed found near Springmount Bog, Co. Antrim', *Journal of the Royal Society of Antiquaries of Ireland* ser. 6, 10, 160-6.

Armstrong, P., 1977. 'Excavations in Sewer Lane, Hull, 1974', *East Riding Archaeologist* 3, 1-77.

Arne, T.J., 1931. 'Skandinavische Holzkammergräber aus der Wikingerzeit in der Ukraine', *Acta Archaeologica* 2, 285-302.

Arthur, P., 1977. 'Eggs and pomegranates: an example of symbolism in Roman Britain', in J. Munby and M. Henig (eds.), *Roman Life and Art in Britain* (Oxford: British Archaeological Reports 41), 367-74.

Atkinson, D., 1916. *The Romano-British Site on Lowbury Hill in Berkshire* (Reading: University College, Reading).

Auden, G.A., 1909, 'Abstract of a paper on antiquities dating to the Danish occupation of York', *Saga-Book of the Viking Club* 6, 169-79.

Austin, R.G., 1935. 'Roman board games', *Greece and Rome* 4, 24-34, 76-82.

Bagshawe, T.W., 1949. 'Romano-British hoes or rakes', *Antiquaries Journal* 29, 86-7.

Baldwin, J.R., 1978. 'Norse influences in sheep husbandry on Foula, Shetland', in J.R. Baldwin (ed.), *Scandinavian Shetland: an ongoing Tradition?* (Edinburgh: Scottish Society for Northern Studies), 97-127.

Balfour, H., 1890. 'On the structure and affinities of the composite bow', *Journal of the Royal Anthropological Institute* 19, 220-50.

—— 1898a. 'Notes on the modern use of bone skates', *Reliquary and Illustrated Archaeologist* 4, 29-37.

—— 1898b. 'Sledges with bone runners in modern use', *Reliquary and Illustrated Archaeologist* 4, 242-54.

—— 1921. 'The archer's bow in the Homeric poems', *Journal of the Royal Anthropological Institute* 51, 289-309.

Bantelmann, A., 1955. *Tofting: eine vorgeschichtliche Warft an der Eidermundung* (Neumünster: Offa Bücher 12).

Barfield, L.H. *et al.*, 1968. 'Ein Burgus in Froitzheim, Kreis Düren', *Beiträge zur Archäologie des Römischen Rheinlands* (Düsseldorf: Rheinische Ausgrabungen 3).

Barnett, R.D., 1954. 'Fine ivory work', in C. Singer, E.J. Holmyard and A.R. Hall (eds.), *A History of Technology* 1 (Oxford: Clarendon Press), 663-83.

Barrett, J.H., 1969. 'A fipple flute or pipe from the site of Keynsham Abbey', *Galpin Society Journal* 22, 47-50.

Barrière-Flavy, M.C., 1901. *Les Arts Industriels des Peuples Barbares de la Gaule du Vme au VIIIme Siècle* (Toulouse and Paris: Privat and Picard).

Barthel, H.J., 1969. 'Schlittknochen oder Knochengeräte?', *Alt-Thüringen* 10, 205-27.

Bately, J. (ed.) 1980. *The Old English Orosius* (Oxford: Oxford University Press for the Early English Text Society).

Bately, J.M and Evison, V.I., 1961. 'The Derby bone piece', *Medieval Archaeology* 5, 301-5.

Bateman, T., 1861. *Ten Years Diggings in Celtic and Saxon Grave Hills* (London: Smith; Derby: Bemrose).

Bathurst, W.H., 1879. *Roman Antiquities at Lydney Park, Gloucestershire* (London: Longman Green).

Baume, P. la, 1967. *Das Fränkische Gräberfeld von Jünkersdorf bei Köln* (Berlin: Germanische Denkmäler der Völkerwanderungszeit ser. B, 3).

Beckwith, J., 1972. *Ivory Carvings in Early Medieval England* (London: Harvey Miller and Medcalf).

Behmer, E., 1939. *Das zweischneidige Schwert der germanischen Völkerwanderungszeit* (Stockholm).

Behn, F., 1938. 'Ein völkerwanderungszeitliches Frauengrab von Trebur, Starkenburg', *Germania* 22, 175-80.

Behrens, G. and Brenner, E., 1911. 'Ausgrabungen in Legionskastell zu Mainz während des Jahres 1910', *Mainzer Zeitschrift* 6, 53-120.

Bell, R.C., 1960. *Board and Table Games from many Civilisations* (London: Oxford University Press).

—— 1981. *Board and Table Games Antiques* (Aylesbury: Shire Publications).

Bellairs, A. de A. and Jenkin, C.R., 1960. 'The skeleton of birds', in A.J. Marshall (ed.),

Biology and Comparative Physiology of Birds 1 (New York and London: Academic Press), 241-300.

Bencard, M., 1975. 'Om et middelalderligt knivskaft fra Ribe', *Fra Ribe Amt* 19 (Festskrift til H.K. Kristensen) (Esbjerg), 36-61.

Bencard, M. and Hein, J., 1982. *Rosenborg: the Royal Danish Collections* (Copenhagen: Rosenborg Castle).

Benson, G., 1906. 'Notes on an excavation at the corner of Castlegate and Coppergate', *Annual Report of the Yorkshire Philosophical Society*, 72-6.

Beresford, G., 1975. *The Medieval Clay-Land Village: Excavations at Goltho and Barton Blount* (London: Society for Medieval Archaeology Monograph 6).

Berg, G., 1943. 'Isläggar och skridskor', *Fataburen*, 79-90.

—— 1955. 'A tool chest of the Viking age (the Mästermyr find in Gotland)', *Universitet i Bergen Arbok* 77-83.

—— 1971. 'Skates and punt sleds: some Scandinavian notes', in P.J. Meertens and H.W.M. Plettenburg (eds.), *Vriendenboek A.J. Bernet Kempers* (Arnhem: Vereniging Vrienden van het Nederlands Openluchtmuseum), 4-13.

Bergquist, H. and Lepiksaar, J., 1957. *Animal Skeletal Remains from Medieval Lund* (Lund: The Archaeology of Lund; Studies in the Lund Excavation Material 1).

Bergsåker, J., 1978. 'The keeping and milking of sheep in the old subsistence economy of Scandinavian Iceland and northern Europe', in J.R. Baldwin (ed.), *Scandinavian Shetland: an ongoing Tradition?* (Edinburgh: Scottish Society for Northern Studies), 85-96.

Beveridge, E., 1932. 'Earth-houses at Garry Iochdrach and Bac Mhic Connain in North Uist', *Proceedings of the Society of Antiquaries of Scotland* 66, 32-66.

Beveridge, E. and Callander, J.G., 1931. 'Excavation of an earth-house at Foshigarry, and a fort, Dun Thomaidh, in North Uist', *Proceedings of the Society of Antiquaries of Scotland* 65, 229-357.

Bicker, F.K., 1936. 'Germanisches Dorf des 3. u 4. Jahrhundert n.d.Z. bei Grossjena, Kr. Wissenfells (ehem. Kr. Naumburg)', *Nachrichtenblatt für Deutsche Vorzeit* 12, 294-5.

Bidder, H.F. and Morris, J., 1959. 'The Anglo-Saxon cemetery at Mitcham', *Surrey Archaeological Journal* 56, 51-131.

Biddle, M., 1970. 'Excavations at Winchester, 1969', *Antiquaries Journal* 50, 277-326.

Bidwell, P.T., 1979. *The Legionary Bath-House and Basilica and Forum at Exeter* (Exeter: Exeter Archaeological Reports 1).

Binding, G., 1968. *Die Spätkarolingische Burg Broich in Mülheim an der Ruhr* (Düsseldorf: Rheinische Ausgrabungen 4).

Bird, J. *et al.* (eds.), 1978. *Southwark Excavations 1972-1974* (London: London and Middlesex Archaeological Society and Surrey Archaeological Society Joint Publication 1).

Birley, R.E., 1963. 'Excavation of the Roman fortress at Carpow, Perthshire', *Proceedings of the Society of Antiquaries of Scotland* 96, 184-207.

—— 1977. *Vindolanda. A Roman Frontier Post on Hadrian's Wall* (London: Thames and Hudson).

Bjørn, A. and Shetelig, H., 1940. *Viking Antiquities in England* (H. Shetelig (ed.), Viking Antiquities in Great Britain and Ireland 4) (Oslo: Aschehoug).

Blomqvist, R., 1942. 'Kammar från Lunds medeltid', *Kulturen*, 133-62.

Blomqvist, R. and Mårtensson, A.W. 1963. *Thulegravningen 1961* (Lund: Archaeologica Lundensia 2).

Blümner, H., 1879. *Technologie and Terminologie der Gewerbe und Künste bei Griechen und Römern* 2 (Leipzig: Teubner).

Blurton, T.R., 1977. 'Excavations at Angel Court, Walbrook, 1974', *Transactions of the London and Middlesex Archaeological Society* 28, 14-100.

Boe, G. de, and Hubert, F., 1977. 'Une installation portuaire d'époque romaine a Pommerœul', *Archaeologia Belgica* 192, 1-57.

Bøe, J., 1940. *Norse Antiquities in Ireland* (H. Shetelig (ed.), Viking Antiquities in Great Britain and Ireland 3) (Oslo: Aschehoug).

Böhme, H.W., 1974. *Germanische Grabfunde des 4. bis 5. Jahrhunderts zwischen Unterer Elbe und Loire* (Munich: Münchner Beiträge zur Vor- und Frühgeschichte 19).

Böhner, K., 1950. 'Der fränkische Grabstein von Niederdollendorf am Rhein', *Germania* 28, 63-75.

—— 1958. *Die Fränkischen Altertümer des Trierer Landes* (Berlin: Germanische Denkmäler der Völkerwanderungszeit ser. B, 1).

Boeles, P.C.J.A., 1951. *Friesland tot de Elfde Eeuw* ('s-Gravenhage: Nijhoff).

Boon, G.C., 1962. 'The Roman sword from Caernarvon — Segontium', *Bulletin of the Board of Celtic Studies* 19, 85-9.

—— 1972. *Isca, the Roman Legionary Fortress at Caerleon, Mon.* (Cardiff: National Museum of Wales).

—— 1974. *Silchester, the Roman Town of Calleva* (Newton Abbot: David and Charles).

—— 1975. 'Segontium fifty years on: 1', *Archaeologia Cambrensis* 124, 52-67.

Bosanquet, R.C., 1948. 'A bone weaving-frame from South Shields in the Black Gate Museum', *Archaeologia Aeliana* ser. 4, 26, 89-97.

Bouchud, J., 1974. 'L'origine anatomique des matériaux osseux utilisés dans les industries préhistoriques', in H. Camps-Fabrer (ed.), *Premier Colloque International sur l'Industrie de l'Os dans la Préhistoire* (Aix-en-Provence: Université de Provence), 21-6.

Bourdillon, J. and Coy, J., 1980. 'The animal bones', in P. Holdsworth, *Excavations at Melbourne Street, Southampton, 1971-76* (London: Council for British Archaeology Research Report 33), 79-118.

Braat, W.C., 1967. 'Römische Schwerter und Dolche im Rijksmuseum van Oudheden', *Oudheidkundige Mededelingen* 48, 56-61.

Brade, C., 1975. *Die Mittelalterliche Kernspaltflöten Mittel- und Nordeuropas* (Göttingen: Göttinger Schriften zur Vor- und Frühgeschichte 14).

—— 1978. 'Knöcherne Kernspaltflöten aus Haithabu', in K. Schietzel (ed.), *Berichte über die Ausgrabungen in Haithabu* 12 (Neumünster), 24-35.

Bradley, R. and Hooper, B., 1975. 'Trial excavation on a Saxon site at Bonhunt, Essex, 1970-71', *Essex Journal*, 9, 38-56.

Branigan, K., 1971. *Latimer Belgic, Roman, Dark Age and Early Modern Farm* (Bristol: Chess Valley Archaeological and Historical Society).

Brears, P.C.D., 1971. *The English Country Pottery: its History and Techniques* (Newton Abbot: David and Charles).

Brent, J., 1865. 'Account of the Society's researches in the Anglo-Saxon cemetery at Sarr', *Archaeologia Cantiana* 6, 157-85.

—— 1868. 'Account of the Society's researches in the Anglo-Saxon cemetery at Sarr', *Archaeologia Cantiana* 7, 307-21.

Brewster, T.C.M., 1963. *The Excavation of Staple Howe* (Malton: East Riding Archaeological Research Committee).

Bridge, J.C., 1904. 'Horns', *Journal of the Architecture, Archaeology and History of Chester and North Wales* new ser. 11, 85-166.

Briscoe, T., 1979. 'Some Anglo-Saxon finds from Lakenheath and their place in the Lark Valley context', *Proceedings of the Suffolk Institute of Archaeology and History* 34, 161-9.

—— 1981. 'Anglo-Saxon pot stamps', *Anglo-Saxon Studies in Archaeology and History* 2 (Oxford: British Archaeological Report 92), 1-36.

British Museum, 1923. *A Guide to the Anglo-Saxon and Foreign Teutonic Antiquities* (London: British Museum).

—— 1964. *Guide to the Antiquities of Roman Britain* (London: British Museum).

Brodribb, A.C.C., Hands, A.R. and Walker, D.R., 1968. *Excavations at Shakenoak Farm, near Wilcote, Oxfordshire* 1 *Sites A and D* (Oxford: published privately).

—— 1971. *Excavations at Shakenoak Farm, near Wilcote, Oxfordshire* 2 *Sites B and H* (Oxford: published privately).

—— 1972. *Excavations at Shakenoak Farm, near Wilcote, Oxfordshire* 3 *Site F* (Oxford: published privately).

—— 1973. *Excavations at Shakenoak Farm, near Wilcote, Oxfordshire* 4 *Site C* (Oxford: published privately).

Brothwell, D.R., 1982. *Digging up Bones* 3rd edn, (London and Oxford: British Museum (Natural History)/Oxford University Press).

Brown, D., 1977. 'The significance of the Londesborough ring brooch', *Antiquaries Journal* 57, 95-9.

——, forthcoming. 'Writing equipment' and 'Gaming pieces' in M. Biddle and S. Keene (eds.), *Winchester Studies* 7 (Oxford: Clarendon Press).

Brown, G. Baldwin, 1915. *The Arts in Early England* 3 and 4 (London: Murray).

—— 1930. *The Arts in Early England* 6 (London: Murray).

Bruce, J.C. (ed.), 1880. *A Descriptive Catalogue of Antiquities, chiefly British, at Alnwick Castle* (Alnwick: published privately).

Bruce-Mitford, M. and Bruce-Mitford, R., 1974. 'The Sutton Hoo lyre, "Beowulf" and the origins of the frame harp', in R. Bruce-Mitford, *Aspects of Anglo-Saxon Archaeology* (London: Gollancz), 188-97.

Bruce-Mitford, R., 1975. *The Sutton Hoo Ship Burial* 1 (London: British Museum).

—— 1979. *The Sutton Hoo Ship Burial: a Handbook* 3rd edn, (London: British Museum).

Bruce-Mitford, R. and Luscombe, M.R., 1974. 'The Benty Grange helmet', in R. Bruce-Mitford, *Aspects of Anglo-Saxon Archaeology* (London: Gollancz), 223-42.

Bryant, G.F. and Steane, J.M., 1971. 'Excavations at the deserted medieval settlement at Lyveden: a third interim report', *Journal of the Northampton Museums and Art Gallery* 9, 3-94.

Bryant, G.F., Steane, J.M. and Adams, B.N., 1969. 'Excavations at the deserted medieval settlement at Lyveden: a second interim report', *Journal of the Northampton Museums and Art Gallery* 5, 3-50.

Bubenik, A.B., 1966. *Das Geweih* (Hamburg and Berlin: Parey).

Buckland, T., 1980. 'The reindeer antlers of the Abbots Bromley horn dance: a re-examination', *Lore and Language* 3 no. 2, pt. A, 1-8.

Budge, E.A. Wallis, 1930. *Amulets and Superstitions* (London: Milford).

Bulleid, A. and Gray, H. St G., 1917. *The Glastonbury Lake Village* 2 (Glastonbury: Glastonbury Antiquarian Society).

—— 1948. *The Meare Lake Village* 1 (Taunton: published privately).

Bushe-Fox, J.P., 1914. *Second Report on the Excavations on the Site of the Roman Town at Wroxeter, Shropshire, 1913* (London: Reports of the Research Committee of the Society of Antiquaries of London 2).

—— 1926. *First Report on the Excavation of the Roman Fort at Richborough, Kent* (London: Reports of the Research Committee of the Society of Antiquaries of London 6).

—— 1928. *Second Report on the Excavation of the Roman Fort at Richborough, Kent* (London: Reports of the Research Committee of the Society of Antiquaries of London 7).

—— 1932. *Third Report on the Excavation of the Roman Fort at Richborough, Kent* (London: Reports of the Research Committee of the Society of Antiquaries of London 10).

—— 1949. *Fourth Report on the Excavation of the Roman Fort at Richborough, Kent* (London: Reports of the Research Committee of the Society of Antiquaries of London 16).

Butler, L.A.S., 1974. 'Medieval finds from Castell-y-Bere, Merioneth', *Archaeologia Cambrensis* 123, 78-112.

Cabrol, F. and Leclercq, H., 1948. *Dictionnaire d'Archéologie Chrétienne et de Liturgie* 3 (Paris: Librairie Letouzey et Ané).

Callander, J.G., 1926. 'Notes on (1) a casket of cetacean bone, and (2) a highland brooch of silver', *Proceedings of the Society of Antiquaries of Scotland* 60, 105-22.

Capelle, T., 1970. 'Metallschmuck und Gussformen aus Haithabu (Ausgrabung 1963-1964)', in K. Schietzel (ed.), *Berichte über die Ausgrabungen in Haithabu* 4 (Neumünster), 9-23.

—— 1978. *Die Karolingischen Funde von Schouwen* (Amersfoort: Nederlandse Oudheden 7).

Capelle, T. and Vierck, H., 1971. 'Modeln der Merowinger- und Wikingerzeit', *Frühmittelalterliche Studien* 5, 42-100.

Casey, D.A., 1931. 'Lydney Castle', *Antiquaries Journal* 11, 240-61.

Catling, H., 1972. 'The evolution of spinning', in J.G. Jenkins (ed.), *The Wool Textile Industry in Great Britain* (London: Routledge and Kegan Paul), 101-16.

Chadwick, S.E., 1958. 'The Anglo-Saxon cemetery at Finglesham, Kent: a reconstruction', *Medieval Archaeology* 2, 1-71.

Chaillu, P.B. du, 1889. *The Viking Age* 2 (London: Murray).

Chambers, R.A., 1975. 'A Romano-British settlement site and seventh-century burial, Ducklington, Oxon., 1974', *Oxoniensia* 40, 171-200.

Chaplin, R.E., 1971. *The Study of Animal Bones from Archaeological Sites* (London and New York: Seminar Press).

Chapman, D.I., 1975. 'Antlers — bones of contention', *Mammal Review* 5, 121-72.

Chapman, D. and Chapman, N., 1975. *Fallow Deer* (Lavenham: Dalton).

Chapman, H., Coppack, G. and Drewett, P. 1975. *Excavations at the Bishops Palace, Lincoln, 1968-72* (Sleaford: Occasional Papers in Lincolnshire History and Archaeology 1).

Chatellier, P. du, and Pontois, L. le, 1909. 'A ship-burial in Britanny', *Saga-Book of the Viking Club* 6, 123-61.

Chatwin, P.B., 1934. 'Recent finds in Coventry', *Transactions of the Birmingham Archaeological Society* 58, 56-62.

Cherry, J., 1972. 'The seal matrix of Richard Cano', *Wiltshire Archaeological Magazine* 67, 162-3.

Chmielowska, A., 1971. *Grzebienie Starożytne i Średniowieczne z Ziem Polskich* (Łodz: Acta Archaeologica Łodziensia 20).

Christophersen, A., 1980a. *Håndverket i Forandring. Studier i Horn- og Beinhåndverkets Utvikling i Lund ca. 1000-1350* (Lund: Acta Archaeologica Lundensia 4° ser., 13).

—— 1980b. 'Raw material, resources and production capacity in early medieval comb manufacture in Lund', *Meddelanden från Lunds Universitets Historiska Museum* new ser. 3, 150-65.

Christlein, R., 1966. *Das Alamannische Reihegräberfeld von Marktoktoberdorf im Allgäu* (Kallmünz: Materialhefte zur Bayerischen Vorgeschichte 21).

Christy, P.M. and Coad, J.G., 1980. 'Excavations at Denny Abbey', *Archaeological Journal* 137, 138-279.

Clark, J.G.D., 1947. 'Whales as an economic factor in prehistoric Europe', *Antiquity* 21, 84-104.

—— 1963. 'Neolithic bows from Somerset, England, and the prehistory of archery in north-western Europe', *Proceedings of the Prehistoric Society* 29, 50-98.

Clarke, D.V., 1970. 'Bone dice and the Scottish Iron Age', *Proceedings of the Prehistoric Society* 36, 214-32.

Clarke, G., 1979. *The Roman Cemetery at Lankhills* (Oxford: Winchester studies 3, pt. 2).

Clarke, H. and Carter, A., 1977. *Excavations in King's Lynn 1963-1970* (London: Society for Medieval Archaeology Monograph 7).

Clarke, J., 1855. 'Remarks on the connection between archaeology and natural history', *Transactions of the Historical Society of Lancashire and Cheshire* 7, 210-35.

Clarke, R.R., 1952. 'An Ogham inscribed knife-handle from south-west Norfolk', *Antiquaries Journal* 32, 71-3.

Clason, A.T., 1967. *Animal and Man in Holland's Past* (Groningen: Palaeohistoria 13A).

—— 1978. 'Voorwerpen uit been en gewei', *Spiegel Historiael* 13, 294-7.

—— 1980. 'Worked bone and antler objects from Dorestad, Hoogstradt 1', *Excavations at Dorestad 1 The Harbour: Hoogstradt 1* (Amersfoort: Nederlandse Oudheden 9), 238-47.

Cnotliwy, E., 1956. 'Z badań nad rzemiosłem, zajmującym się obróbką rogu i kości na Pomorzu Zachodnim we wczesnym średniowieczu', *Materiały Zachodnio-Pomorskie* 2, 151-79.

—— 1958. 'Wczesnośredniowieczne przedmioty z rogu i kości z Wolina, ze stanowiska 4', *Materiały Zachodnio-Pomorskie* 4, 155-240.

—— 1969. 'Pracownia rogownicza z końca XIII i początku XIV wieku na zamku w Dobrej Nowogardzkiej, pow. Nowogard, woj. szczecińskie', *Kwartalnik Historii Kultury Materialnej* 17, 43-9.

—— 1970. 'Pracownie grzebiennicze na Srebrnym Wzgórzu w Wolinie', *Materiały Zachodnio-Pomorskie* 16, 209-87.

Coad, J.G. and Streeter, A.D.F., 1982. 'Excavations at Castle Acre Castle, Norfolk, 1972-1977', *Archaeological Journal* 139, 138-301.

Cobb, W.M., 1933. 'The dentition of the walrus, *Odobenus obesus*', *Proceedings of the Zoological Society of London*, 645-68.

Cocks, A.H., 1921. 'A Romano-British homestead, in the Hambledon Valley, Bucks.', *Archaeologia* 71, 141-98.

Coffey, G., 1909. *Guide to the Celtic Antiquities of the Christian Period preserved in the National Museum, Dublin* (Dublin).

Colgrave, B. and Mynors, R.A.B., 1969. *Bede's Ecclesiastical History of the English People* (Oxford: Clarendon Press).

Colardelle, R. and Colardelle, M., 1980. 'L'habitat médiéval immergé de Colletière a Charavines (Isère). Premier bilan des fouilles', *Archéologie Médiévale* 10, 167-269.

Collis, J., 1978. *Winchester Excavations 2 1949-*

60 (Winchester: City of Winchester).

Collis, J. and Kjølby-Biddle, B., 1979. 'Early medieval bone spoons from Winchester', *Antiquaries Journal* 59, 375-91.

Colyer, C. 1975. *Lincoln. The Archaeology of an Historic City* (Lincoln: Lincoln Archaeological Trust).

Como, J., 1925. 'Das Grab eines römischen Arztes in Bingen', *Germania* 9, 152-62.

Corbet, G.B., 1964. *The Identification of British Mammals* (London: British Museum).

Corder, P., 1948. 'Miscellaneous small objects from the Roman fort at Malton', *Antiquaries Journal* 28, 173-9.

Corder, P. and Kirk, J.L., 1932. *A Roman Villa at Langton, near Malton, E. Yorkshire* (Malton: Roman Malton and District Report 4).

Cornwall, I.W., 1974. *Bones for the Archaeologist* (London: Dent).

Cosson, Baron de, 1893. 'The crossbow of Ulrich V, Count of Wurtemberg, 1460, with remarks on its construction', *Archaeologia* 53, 445-64.

Cotton, M.A. and Gathercole, P.W., 1958. *Excavations at Clausentum, Southampton, 1951-1954* (Ministry of Works Archaeological Reports 2) (London: HMSO).

Cottrill, F., 1935. 'Bone trial piece found in Southwark', *Antiquaries Journal* 15, 69-71.

Coughtrey, M., 1872. 'Notes on materials found in a kitchen midden at Hillswick, Shetland, with special reference to long-handled combs', *Proceedings of the Society of Antiquaries of Scotland* 9, 118-51.

Cox, J.C., 1905. *The Royal Forests of England* (London: Methuen).

Cox, W.E., 1946, *Chinese Ivory Sculpture* (New York: Crown).

Cramp, R., 1964. 'An Anglo-Saxon pin from Birdoswald', *Transactions of the Cumberland and Westmorland Antiquarian and Archaeological Society* new ser. 64, 90-3.

—— 1967. *Anglian and Viking York* (York: Borthwick Papers 33).

Crane, F., 1972. *Extant Medieval Musical Instruments* (Iowa: University of Iowa Press).

Crawford, I.A., 1967. 'Whalebone artifacts and some recent finds in Berneray, Harris', *Scottish Studies* 11, 88-91.

Credland, A.G., 1980. 'Crossbow remains', *Journal of the Society of Archer-Antiquaries* 23, 12-19.

Crouch, K., 1976. 'The archaeology of Staines and the excavation at Elmsleigh House', *Transactions of the London and Middlesex Archaeological Society* 27, 71-134.

Crowfoot, E., 1966. 'Little Eriswell Anglo-Saxon cemetery: the textiles', *Proceedings of the Cambridge Antiquarium Society* 59, 29-32.

Crowfoot, G.M., 1939. 'The tablet-woven braids from the vestments of St Cuthbert at Durham', *Antiquaries Journal* 19, 57-80.

—— 1945. 'The bone "gouges" of Maiden Castle and other sites', *Antiquity* 19, 157-8.

—— 1950. 'Textiles of the Saxon period in the Museum of Archaeology and Ethnology', *Proceedings of the Cambridge Antiquarian Society* 45, 26-32.

—— 1952. 'Anglo-Saxon tablet weaving', *Antiquaries Journal* 32, 189-91.

Crummy, N., 1979. 'A chronology of Romano-British bone pins', *Britannia* 10, 157-63.

—— 1981. 'Bone-working at Colchester', *Britannia* 12, 277-85.

—— 1983. 'Crowder Terrace, Winchester, bone', in K.E. Qualmann (ed.), *Winchester Excavations since 1972* 1 *The Oram's Arbour Enclosure and the Western Suburb* (Winchester: City of Winchester).

Crummy, P., 1977. 'Colchester: the Roman fortress and the development of the colonia', *Britannia* 8, 65-105.

—— 1981. *Aspects of Anglo-Saxon and Norman Colchester* (London: Council for British Archaeology Research Report 39).

Cunliffe, B., 1964. *Winchester Excavations 1949-1960* 1 (Winchester: City of Winchester).

—— (ed.), 1968. *Fifth Report on the Excavation of the Roman Fort at Richborough, Kent* (London: Reports of the Research Committee of the Society of Antiquaries of London 23).

—— 1971. *Excavations at Fishbourne, 1961-1969* 2 (London: Reports of the Research Committee of the Society of Antiquaries of London 27).

—— 1975. *Excavations at Portchester Castle* 1 *Roman* (London: Reports of the Research Committee of the Society of Antiquaries of London 32).

—— 1976. *Excavations at Portchester Castle* 2 *Saxon* (London: Reports of the Research

Committee of the Society of Antiquaries of London 33).

Cunnington, M.E., 1923. *The Early Iron Age Inhabited Site at All Cannings Cross Farm, Wiltshire* (Devizes: Simpson).

Ćurčić, V., 1912. 'Die volkstümliche Fischerei in Bosnien und der Herzegowina', *Wissenschaftliche Mitteilungen aus Bosnien-Herzegowina* 12, 490-589.

Curle, A.O., 1939. 'A Viking settlement at Freswick, Caithness', *Proceedings of the Society of Antiquaries of Scotland* 73, 71-110.

Curle, A.O., Olsen, M. and Shetelig, H., 1954. *Civilisation of the Viking Settlers in Relation to their Old and New Countries* (H. Shetelig (ed.), Viking Antiquities in Great Britain and Ireland 6) (Oslo: Aschehoug).

Curle, C.L., 1982. *Pictish and Norse Finds from the Brough of Birsay 1934-74* (Edinburgh: Society of Antiquaries of Scotland Monograph Series 1).

Curle, J., 1911. *A Roman Frontier Post and its People* (Glasgow: Maclehose).

—— 1913a. 'Notes on some undescribed objects from the Roman Fort at Newstead, Melrose', *Proceedings of the Society of Antiquaries of Scotland* 47, 384-405.

—— 1913b. 'Roman and native remains in Caledonia', *Journal of Roman Studies* 3, 99-115.

Currey, J.D., 1970a. *Animal Skeletons* (London: Studies in Biology 22).

—— 1970b. 'The mechanical properties of bone', *Clinical Orthopaedics* 73, 210-31.

—— 1979. 'Mechanical properties of bone tissues with greatly differing functions', *Journal of Biomechanics* 12, 313-9.

Cursiter, J.W., 1886. 'Notice of a wood-carver's tool box, with Celtic ornamentation, recently discovered in a peat-moss in the Parish of Birsay, Orkney', *Proceedings of the Society of Antiquaries of Scotland* 20, 47-50.

Cust, A.M.E., 1902. *The Ivory Workers of the Middle Ages* (London).

Czerniak, L., Grygiel, R. and Tetzlaff, W., 1977. *Inventaria Archaeologia* 39 (Warsaw: Institut d'Histoire de l'Académie Polonaise des Sciences).

Dalton, O.M., 1909. *Catalogue of the Ivory Carvings of the Christian Period* (London: British Museum).

—— 1927. 'Early chessmen of whale's bone excavated in Dorset', *Archaeologia* 77, 77-86.

Danielsson, K., 1973. 'Bearbetat ben och benhorn', *Birka Svarta Jordens Hamnomrade. Arkeologisk Undersökning 1970-1971* (Stockholm: Riksantikvarieämbetet Rapport C1), 40-53.

Dannheimer, H., 1962a. *Die Germanischen Funde der späten Kaiserzeit und des frühen Mittelalters in Mittelfranken* (Frankfurt-am-Main: Germanische Denkmäler der Völkerwanderungszeit ser. A, 7).

—— 1962b. 'Zwei frühmittelalterliche Bronzegefässe aus Südbayern', *Germania* 40, 408-15.

Darling, F.F., 1937. *A Herd of Red Deer* (Oxford: Oxford University Press).

Dart, R.A., 1957. 'The osteodontokeratic culture of Australopithecus Prometheus', *Memoirs of the Transvaal Museum* 10, 1-105.

Davidan, O.I., 1962. 'Grebni Staroĭ Ladogi', *Arkheologicheskiĭ Sbornik* 4, 95-108.

—— 1970, 'Contacts between Staraja Ladoga and Scandinavia', *Varangian Problems* (Copenhagen: Scando-Slavica suppl. 1), 79-91.

—— 1977. 'K voporosu ob organizacii Kostoreznogo remesla v Dreveneĭ Ladoge', *Arkheologicheskiĭ Sbornik* 18, 101-9.

Dawkins, W. Boyd, 1869. 'On the distribution of the British post glacial mammals', *Quarterly Journal of the Geological Society of London* 25, 192-217.

Deonna, W., 1956. 'Talismans en bois de cerf', *Ogam* 8, 3-14.

Deringer, H., 1967a. 'Frühgeschichtliche Knochenkämme aus Oberösterreich', *Jahrbuch der Oberösterreichischen Musealvereines* 112, Abhandlungen 35-56.

—— 1967b. 'Provinzialrömische und germanische Knochenkämme aus Lauriacum', *Jahrbuch der Oberösterreichischen Musealvereines* 112, Abhandlungen 57-74.

Digby, B., 1926. *The Mammoth and Mammoth Hunting in North-east Siberia* (London: Witherby).

Diringer, D., 1953. *The Hand-Produced Book* (London and New York: Hutchinson).

Dobrowolska, A., 1968. 'Pierwiastki rodzime w kulturze ludowej Pomorza Zachodniego', *Materiały Zachodnio-Pomorskie* 14, 337-56.

Doppelfeld, O., 1964. 'Das fränkische Knabengrab unter dem Chor des Kölner Domes', *Germania* 42, 156-88.

Dornan, B., 1975. *Gaming in Pre- and Proto-*

historic Ireland (MA thesis, University College, Dublin).

Douglas, D.C. and Greenaway, G.E. (eds.), 1953. *English Historical Documents* 2 (London: Eyre Methuen).

Down, A., 1974. *Chichester Excavations* 2 (Chichester: Phillimore).

—— 1978. *Chichester Excavations* 3 (Chichester: Phillimore).

—— 1979. *Chichester Excavations* 4 (Chichester: Phillimore).

Drescher, H., 1975. 'Messerbeschläge aus Hanseschalenblech', *Zeitschrift für Archäologie des Mittelalters* 3, 57-68.

—— 1978. 'Untersuchungen und Versuche zum Blei- und Zinnguss in Formen aus Stein, Lehm, Holz, Geweih und Metall', *Frühmittelalterliche Studien* 12, 84-115.

Drew, J.H., 1965. 'The horn comb industry of Kenilworth', *Transactions and Proceedings of the Birmingham Archaeological Society* 82, 21-7.

Drexel, F., 1910. *Das Kastell Stockstadt* (Heidelberg: Der Obergermanisch-Raetische Limes des Roemerreiches 33).

Dryad, nd. *Tablet Weaving* (Leicester: Dryad Ltd).

Dümmler, E. (ed.), 1892. *Epistolae Merowingici et Karolini Aevi* 1 (Berlin: Monumenta Germaniae Historica Epist. 3).

Dunlevy, M.M. 1969. *Aspects of Toilet Combs found in Ireland (Prehistoric to the 17th Century)* (MA thesis, University College, Dublin).

—— 1972. 'Some comb forms of the fifteenth to eighteenth centuries', *North Munster Antiquarian Journal* 15, 22-7.

Dunning, G.C., 1932. 'Medieval finds in London', *Antiquaries Journal* 12, 177-8.

—— 1952. 'Anglo-Saxon discoveries at Harston', *Transactions of the Leicestershire Archaeological Society* 28, 48-54.

—— 1959. 'The Anglo-Saxon plane from Sarre', *Archaeologia Cantiana* 73, 196-7.

—— 1965. 'Heraldic and decorated metalwork and other finds from Rievaulx Abbey, Yorkshire', *Antiquaries Journal* 45, 57-63.

Durham, B., 1977. 'Archaeological investigations in St Aldates, Oxford', *Oxoniensia* 42, 83-203.

Dyer, J., 1974. 'The excavation of two barrows on Galley Hill, Streatley', *Bedfordshire Archaeological Journal* 9, 13-34.

Eckinger, R., 1933. 'Bogenversteifungen aus römischen Lagern', *Germania* 17, 289-90.

Eckinger, T., 1929. 'Knochenschnitzereien aus Gräbern von Vindonissa', *Anzeiger für Schweizerische Altertumskunde* new ser. 31, 241-56.

Edelstein, S.M. and Borghetty, H.C. (eds.), 1969. *The Plictho of Gioanventura Rosetti* (Cambridge, Mass. and London: MIT).

Edwards, B.J.N., 1978. 'Bone pins from Cuerdale', *Lancashire Archaeological Bulletin* 3, 129-30.

Ekman, J., 1973. *Early Medieval Lund: the Fauna and the Landscape* (Lund: Archaeologica Lundensia 5).

Ekwal, E., 1960. *Concise Oxford Dictionary of English Place Names* 4th edn, (Oxford: Clarendon Press).

Ellis, H., 1883. *A General Introduction to the Domesday Book* (London: Eyre and Spottiswoode).

Ellis Davidson, H.R., 1962. *The Sword in Anglo-Saxon England* (Oxford: Clarendon Press).

Ellmers, D., 1965. 'Zum Trinkgeschirr der Wikingerzeit', *Offa* 21-2, 21-43.

Elworthy, F.T., 1958. *The Evil Eye* (New York: Collier Macmillan).

Engelhardt, C., 1869. *Vimose Fundet* (Copenhagen: Fynske Mosefund 2).

Espérandieu, E., 1908. *Recueil Général des Bas-Reliefs de la Gaule Romaine* 2 (Paris: Imprimerie Nationale).

Evison, V.I., 1979. *A Corpus of Wheel-Thrown Pottery in Anglo-Saxon Graves* (London: Royal Archaeological Institute Monograph).

Faider-Feytmans, G., 1956. 'Talismans en bois de cerf trouvés dans les tombes mérovingiennes', *Revue Archéologique de l'Est et du Centre-Est* 7, 138-40.

Fairclough, C.J., 1979. *St Andrews Street 1976* (Plymouth: Plymouth Museum Archaeological Series 2).

Filipowiak, W., 1956. 'Port wczesnośredniowiecznego Wolina', *Materiały Zachodnio-Pomorskie* 2, 183-210.

Fingerlin, G., 1971. *Die Alamannischen Gräberfelder von Güttingen und Merdingen in Südbaden* (Berlin: Germanische Denkmäler der Völkerwanderungszeit ser. A, 12).

Floderus, E., 1934. 'Västergarn', *Fornvännen* 29, 65-83.

—— 1941. *Sigtuna, Sveriges äldsta Medel-*

tidsstad (Stockholm: Gebers).

Foote, P.G. and Wilson, D.M., 1970. *The Viking Achievement* (London: Sidgwick and Jackson).

Forbes, R.J., 1955. *Studies in Ancient Technology* 3 (Leiden: Brill).

Foster, W.K., 1884. 'Account of the excavation of an Anglo-Saxon cemetery at Barrington, Cambridgeshire', *Cambridge Antiquarian Communications* 5, 5-32.

Fox, A., 1955. 'Some evidence for a Dark Age trading site at Bantham, near Thurleston, South Devon', *Antiquaries Journal* 35, 55-67.

Fox, C., 1923. *The Archaeology of the Cambridge Region* (Cambridge: Cambridge University Press).

Franken, M., 1944. *Die Alamannen zwischen Iller und Lech* (Berlin: Germanische Denkmäler der Völkerwanderungszeit 5).

Freeman, W.H. and Bracegirdle, B., 1967. *An Atlas of Histology* 2nd edn, (London: Heinemann).

Fremersdorf, F., 1928. *Die Denkmäler des Römischen Köln* 1 (Berlin: de Gruyter).

—— 1940. 'Römische Scharnierbänder aus Bein', *Vjesnika Hrvatskoga Arheolškoga Društva* new ser. 18-21 (Serta Hoffilleriana), 321-37.

—— 1955. *Das Fränkische Reihengräberfeld Köln-Müngersdorf* (Berlin: Germanische Denkmäler der Völkerwanderungszeit 6).

Frere, S.S., 1972. *Verulamium Excavations* 1 (London: Reports of the Research Committee of the Society of Antiquaries of London 28).

Frost, H.M., 1967. *An Introduction to Biomechanics* (Springfield, Ill.: Thomas).

Fry, D.K., 1976. 'Anglo-Saxon lyre tuning pegs from Whitby', *Medieval Archaeology* 20, 137-9.

Gaborit-Chopin, D., 1978. *Ivoires du Moyen Age* (Fribourg: Office du Livre).

Gaitzsch, W., 1980. *Eiserne Römische Werkzeuge* (Oxford: British Archaeological Reports, International Series, 78).

Gaitzsch, W. and Matthäus, H., 1980. 'Schreinerwerkzeuge aus dem Kastell Altstadt bei Miltenberg', *Archäologisches Korrespondenzblatt* 10, 163-71.

Galloway, P., 1976. 'Notes on descriptions of bone and antler combs', *Medieval Archaeology* 20, 154-6.

Galloway, P. and Newcomer, M., 1981. 'The craft of comb-making: an experimental enquiry', *University of London Institute of Archaeology Bulletin* 18, 73-90.

Galster, G., 1961. 'En seiger fra Ålborg', *Kuml* (1961), 116-24.

Gardner, W. and Savory, H.N., 1964. *Dinorben: a Hill-Fort Occupied in Early Iron Age and Roman Times* (Cardiff: National Museum of Wales).

Garmonsway, G.N. (ed.), 1947. *Ælfric's Colloquy* 2nd edn, (London: Methuen).

Garscha, F., 1970. *Die Alamannen in Südbayern* (Frankfurt-am-Main: Germanische Denkmäler der Völkerwanderungszeit ser. A, 11).

Geijer, A., 1938. *Birka 3 Die Textilfunde* (Stockholm: Kungliga Vitterhets Historie och Antikvitets Akademien).

Gelling, P.S., 1958. 'Close-ny-Chollagh: an Iron Age fort at Scarlett, Isle of Man', *Proceedings of the Prehistoric Society* 24, 85-100.

Gilbert, J.M., 1976. 'Crossbows on Pictish stones', *Proceedings of the Society of Antiquaries of Scotland* 107, 316-17.

Glazema, P., 1950. 'Oudheidkundige opgravingen te Tiel', *Berichten van de Rijksdienst voor het Oudheidkundig Bodemonderzoek* 1, 23-5.

Goddard, E.H., 1896. 'Notes on a Roman cross-bow &c., found at Southgrove Farm, Burbage', *Wiltshire Archaeological and Natural History Magazine* 28, 87-90.

Goessler, P., 1932. 'Das frühchristliche Beinkästchen von Heilbronn', *Germania* 16, 294-9.

Goldschmidt, A., 1918. *Die Elfenbeinskulpturen aus der Zeit der Karolingischen und Sächsischen Kaiser* 2 (Berlin: Cassirer).

—— 1923. *Die Elfenbeinskulpturen aus der Romanischen Zeit* 3 (Berlin: Cassirer).

—— 1926. *Die Elfenbeinskulpturen aus der Romanischen Zeit* 4 (Berlin: Cassirer).

Goldstern, E., 1921. 'Hochgebirgsvolk in Savoyen und Graubünden 2: Beiträge zur Volkskunde des bündnerischen Münstertales (Schweiz)', *Wiener Zeitschrift für Volkskunde* 14, 59-114.

Gonzenbach, V. von, 1951. 'Zwei Typen figürlich verzierter Haarpfeile', *Gesellschaft pro Vindonissa Jahresbericht 1950-1951*, 3-19.

Gooder, E., Woodfield, C. and Chaplin, R.E.,

1964. 'The walls of Coventry', *Transactions and Proceedings of the Birmingham Archaeological Society* 81, 88-138.

Goodman, N. and Goodman, A., 1882. *Handbook of Fen Skating* (London).

Goodman, W.L., 1959. 'The Anglo-Saxon plane from Sarre', *Archaeologia Cantiana* 73, 198-201.

—— 1964. *The History of Woodworking Tools* (London: Bell).

Gordon, J.E., 1976. *The New Science of Strong Materials* (Harmondsworth: Penguin).

—— 1978. *Structures* (Harmondsworth: Penguin).

Götze, A., 1912. *Die Altthuringischen Funde von Weimar* (Berlin: Germanische Funde aus der Völkerwanderungszeit).

Gracie, H.S. and Price, E.G., 1979. 'Frocester Court Roman villa. Second report 1968-77: the courtyard', *Transactions of the Bristol and Gloucestershire Archaeological Society* 97, 9-64.

Graham-Campbell, J., 1973. 'The 9th-century Anglo-Saxon horn-mount from Burghead, Morayshire, Scotland', *Medieval Archaeology* 17, 43-51.

—— 1978. 'An Anglo-Scandinavian ornamented knife from Canterbury, Kent', *Medieval Archaeology* 22, 130-3.

—— 1980. *Viking Artefacts. A Select Catalogue* (London: British Museum Publications).

Graham-Campbell, J. and Kidd, D., 1980. *The Vikings* (London: British Museum Publications).

Grancsay, S.W., 1945. *American Engraved Powder Horns* (New York: Metropolitan Museum).

Grant, A., 1981. 'The significance of deer remains at occupation sites of the Iron Age to the Anglo-Saxon period', in M. Jones and G. Dimbleby (eds.), *The Environment of Man: the Iron Age to the Anglo-Saxon Period* (Oxford: British Archaeological Reports 87), 205-13.

Grassmann, A., 1980. 'Münzfunde aus der Lübecker Innenstadt', *Archäologie in Lübeck* (Lübeck: Hefte zur Kunst und Kulturgeschichte der Hansastadt Lübeck 3), 101-2.

Gray, H. St G., 1966. *The Meare Lake Village* 3, M.A. Cotton (ed.) (Taunton: published privately).

Gray, H. St G. and Bulleid, A., 1953. *The Meare Lake Village* 2 (Taunton: published privately).

Green, B., 1971. 'An Anglo-Saxon bone plaque from Larling, Norfolk', *Antiquaries Journal* 51, 321-3.

—— 1973. 'A Romanesque ivory object from Norwich', *Antiquaries Journal* 53, 287-9.

Green, C., 1964. 'Excavations on a medieval site at Water Newton, in the County of Huntingdon, in 1958', *Proceedings of the Cambridge Antiquarian Society* 56-7, 68-87.

Green, M., 1978. *Small Cult-Objects from the Military Areas of Roman Britain* (British Archaeological Report 52) (Oxford).

Greep, S., 1982. 'Two early Roman handles from the Walbrook, London', *Archaeological Journal* 139, 91-100.

Grieg, S., 1928. *Oseberg Fundet* 2 (Oslo: Universitetets Oldsaksamling).

—— 1933. *Middelalderske Byfund fra Bergen og Oslo* (Oslo: Norske Videnskaps-Akademi).

—— 1940. *Viking Antiquities in Scotland* (H. Shetelig (ed.), Viking Antiquities in Great Britain and Ireland 2) (Oslo: Aschehoug).

Griffin, A.H., nd. *The Story of Abbey Horn* (Kendal: Abbey Horn Works).

Griffith, A.F., 1914. 'An Anglo-Saxon cemetery at Alfriston, Sussex', *Sussex Archaeological Collections* 56, 16-53.

Grimm, P., 1930. 'Die Kammacherwerkstätte von Quenstedt', *Jahresschrift für die Vorgeschichte der Sächsisch-Türingischen Länder* 18.

Grohne, E., 1953. *Mahndorf: Frühgeschichte des Bremischen Raums* (Bremen-Horn: Dorn).

Groller, M. von, 1901. 'Römische Waffen', *Der Römische Limes in Österreich* 2, 85-132.

—— 1909. 'Die Grabungen in Carnuntum', *Der Römische Limes in Österreich* 10, 1-78.

Grove, L.R.A., 1940. 'A Viking bone trial piece from York Castle', *Antiquaries Journal* 20, 285-7.

Groves, S., 1973. *The History of Needleworking Tools and Accessories* (Newton Abbot: David and Charles).

Guðmundsson, F., 1965. *Orkneyinga Saga* (Islenzk Fornrit 34) (Reykjavik).

Guildhall Museum, 1908. *Catalogue of the Collection of London Antiquities in the Guildhall Museum* 2nd edn, (London: City of London).

Hagberg, U.E., 1976. 'Fundort und Fundgebiet der Modeln aus Torslunda', *Frühmittelalterliche Studien* 10, 323-49.

Hald, M., 1946. 'Ancient textile techniques in Egypt and Scandinavia', *Acta Archaeologica* 17, 49-98.

—— 1950. *Olddanske Tekstiler* (Copenhagen: Nordiske Fortidsminder 5).

Hall, R.A., 1975. 'An excavation at Hunter Street, Buckingham, 1974', *Records of Buckinghamshire* 20, 100-133.

—— 1976. *The Viking Kingdom of York* (York: Yorkshire Museum).

Halstead, L.B., 1974. *Vertebrate Hard Tissues* (London and Winchester: Wykeham).

Halstead, L.B. and Middleton, J., 1972. *Bare Bones: an Exploration in Art and Science* (Edinburgh: Oliver and Boyd).

Ham, A.W., 1965. *Histology* 5th edn, (Philadelphia and London: Lippincott).

Hamilton, J.R.C., 1956. *Excavations at Jarlshof, Shetland* (Edinburgh: HMSO).

—— 1968. *Excavations at Clickhimin, Shetland* (Edinburgh: HMSO).

Hancox, N.M., 1972. *Biology of Bone* (Cambridge: Cambridge University Press).

Hansmann, L. and Kriss-Rettenbeck, L., 1966. *Amulett und Talisman: Erscheinungsform und Geschichte* (Munich: Callwey).

Hardwick, P., 1981. *Discovering Horn* (Guildford: Lutterworth).

Harrison, A.C., 1972. 'Rochester east gate, 1969', *Archaeologia Cantiana* 87, 121-57.

Harrison, A.C. and Flight, C., 1968. 'The Roman and medieval defences of Rochester in the light of recent excavations', *Archaeologia Cantiana* 83, 55-104.

Harting, J.E., 1880. *British Animals Extinct within Historic Times* (London: Trübner).

Hartnett, P.J. and Eogan, G., 1964. 'Feltrim Hill, Co. Dublin: a Neolithic and Early Christian site', *Journal of the Royal Society of Antiquaries of Ireland* 94, 1-37.

Hassall, M. and Rhodes, J., 1974. 'Excavations at the new Market Hall, Gloucester, 1966-7', *Transactions of the Bristol and Gloucestershire Archaeological Society* 93, 15-100.

Hassall, M.W.C. and Tomlin, R.S.O., 1977, 'Roman Britain in 1976 II: inscriptions', *Britannia* 8, 426-9.

Hastings, E.A., 1977. 'Saleroom discoveries: an Anglo-Saxon seal matrix', *Burlington Magazine* 119, 308-9.

Hatt, E.D., 1942. 'Johan Turi og hvordan bogen "Muittalus samid Birra" blev til', *Fataburen*, 97-108.

Hatt, J.J., Parruzot, P. and Roes, A., 1955. 'Nouvelles contributions à l'étude des médaillons et pendentifs en corne de cerf', *Revue Archéologique de l'Est et du Centre-Est* 6, 249-54.

Haupt, D., 1970. 'Jakobwüllesheim', in 'Jahresbericht 1968', *Bonner Jahrbücher* 170, 381-91.

Hawkes, S.C. and Dunning, G.C., 1961. 'Soldiers and settlers in Britain, fourth to fifth century', *Medieval Archaeology* 5, 1-70.

Hawkes, S.C., Speake, G. and Northover, P., 1979. 'A seventh-century bronze metalworker's die from Rochester, Kent', *Frühmittelalterliche Studien* 13, 382-92.

Hawthorn, J.G. and Smith, C.S., 1963. *On Divers Arts: the Treatise of Theophilus* (Chicago: University of Chicago Press).

Hayward, J.F., 1957. *English Cutlery, Sixteenth to Eighteenth Century* (London: Victoria and Albert Museum).

Hebditch, M. and Mellor, J., 1973. 'The forum and basilica of Roman Leicester', *Britannia* 4, 1-83.

Heide, G.D. van de, 1956. 'Resten van middeleeuwse bewoning ten oosten van het voormalige eiland Schokland, Zuiderzeegebied', *Berichten van der Rijksdienst voor het Oudheidkundig Bodemonderzoek* 7, 111-32.

Hencken, H. O'N., 1937. 'Ballinderry Crannog No. 1', *Proceedings of the Royal Irish Academy* 43C, 103-239.

—— 1938. *Cahercommaun, a Stone Fort in County Clare* (Dublin: Royal Society of Antiquaries of Ireland).

—— 1942. 'Ballinderry Crannog No. 2', *Proceedings of the Royal Irish Academy* 47C, 1-76.

—— 1950. 'Lagore Crannog: an Irish royal residence of the 7th to 10th centuries A.D.', *Proceedings of the Royal Irish Academy* 53C, 1-247.

Henig, M., 1977. 'Death and the maiden: funerary symbolism in daily life', in J. Munby and M. Henig (eds.), *Roman Life and Art in Britain* (Oxford: British Archaeological Reports 41), 347-66.

Henshall, A.S., 1950. 'Textiles and weaving appliances in prehistoric Britain', *Proceed-*

ings of the Prehistoric Society 16, 130-62.

—— 1964. 'Five tablet-woven seal-tags', *Archaeological Journal* 121, 154-62.

Herman, O., 1902. 'Knochenschlittschuh, Knochenkufe, Knochenkeitel', *Mittheilungen der Anthropologischen Gesellschaft in Wien* 32, 217-38.

Herrmann, J., 1962. *Köpenick* (Berlin: Deutsche Akademie der Wissenschaften zu Berlin, Schriften der Sektion für Vor- und Frühgeschichte 12).

Herteig, A.E., 1969. *Kongers Havn og Handels Sete* (Oslo: Aschehoug).

Heslop, T.A., 1980. 'English seals from the mid-ninth century to 1100', *Journal of the British Archaeological Association* 133, 1-16.

Hilczerówna, Z., 1966. 'O grzebieniach ze Starej Ładogi', *Slavia Antiqua* 13, 451-7.

Hildyard, E.J.W., 1958. 'Cataractonium fort and town', *Yorkshire Archaeological Journal* 39, 224-65.

Hillgarth, J.N., 1962. 'Visigothic Spain and Early Christian Ireland', *Proceedings of the Royal Irish Academy* 62C, 167-94.

Hills, C., 1974. 'A runic pot from Spong Hill, North Elmham, Norfolk', *Antiquaries Journal* 54, 87-91.

—— 1981. 'Barred zoomorphic combs of the Migration Period', in V.I. Evison (ed.), *Angles, Saxons, and Jutes: Essays Presented to J.N.L. Myres* (Oxford: Oxford University Press), 96-111.

Hills, C. and Penn, K., 1981. 'The Anglo-Saxon cemetery at Spong Hill, North Elmham, part II', *East Anglian Archaeology* 11, 1-287.

Hodder, I. and Hedges, J.W., 1977. 'Weaving combs: their typology and distribution with some introductory remarks on date and function', in J. Collis (ed.), *The Iron Age in Britain: a Review* (Sheffield: University of Sheffield), 17-28.

Hodges, H., 1964. *Artifacts* (London: Baker).

Hoffmann, M., 1964. *The Warp-Weighted Loom* (Oslo: Studia Norvegica 14).

Holden, E.W., 1963. 'Excavations at the deserted medieval village of Hangleton, part 1', *Sussex Archaeological Collections*, 101, 54-181.

Holdsworth, P., 1976. 'Saxon Southampton: a new review', *Medieval Archaeology* 20, 26-61.

Holms, J., 1961. 'Broxbourne — Romano-British antler implement', *Transactions of the East Herts Archaeological Society* 14, 122.

Holwerda, J.H., 1930. 'Opgravingen an Dorestad', *Oudheidkundige Mededeelingen* 11, 32-93.

Hrubý, V., 1957. 'Slovanské kostěné předměty a jejich výroba na Moravě', *Památky Archeologicke* 48, 118-217.

Hucke, K., 1952. 'Frühgeschichtliche Geweih- und Knochengeräte von der Insel Olsborg im Grossen Plöner See in Holstein', *Zeitschrift für Morphologie und Antropologie* 44, 108-14.

Hübener, W., 1953. 'Keramik und Kämme in Dorestad', *Germania* 31, 177-89.

Huggins, P.J., 1969. 'Excavations at Sewardstone Street, Waltham Abbey, Essex, 1966', *Post-Medieval Archaeology* 3, 47-99.

—— 1972. 'Monastic close and outer grange excavations, Waltham Abbey, Essex, 1970-1972', *Transactions of the Essex Archaeological Society* ser. 3, 4, 39-127.

—— 1976. 'The excavation of an 11th-century Viking hall and 14th-century rooms at Waltham Abbey, Essex, 1969-71', *Medieval Archaeology* 20, 75-133.

Hughes, G.B., 1953. *Living Crafts* (London: Lutterworth).

Hughes, T.M. 1907. 'On the section seen and the objects found during excavations on the site of the old Bird Bolt Hotel', *Proceedings of the Cambridge Antiquarian Society* 11, 424-5.

Hull, M.R., 1958. *Roman Colchester* (London: Reports of the Research Committee of the Society of Antiquaries of London 20).

Hume, A., 1863. *Ancient Meols* (London: Smith).

Humphreys, H., 1953. 'The horn of the unicorn', *Antiquity* 27, 15-19.

Humphreys, J. *et al.*, 1923. 'An Anglo-Saxon cemetery at Bidford-on-Avon, Warwickshire', *Archaeologia* 73, 89-116.

Hunter, A.G. and Jope, E.M., 1951. 'Excavations on the city defences in New College, Oxford, 1949', *Oxoniensia* 16, 28-41.

Hunter, R. and Mynard, D., 1977. 'Excavations at Thorplands near Northampton, 1970 and 1974', *Northamptonshire Archaeology* 12, 97-154.

Hurst, J.G., 1965. 'Excavations at Barn Road, Norwich, 1954-55', *Norfolk Archaeology* 33, 131-79.

—— 1979. *Wharram. A Study of Settlement on the Yorkshire Wolds* (London: Society for Medieval Archaeology Monograph 8).

Hurst, J.G. and Colson, J., 1957. 'Excavations at St Benedict's Gates, Norwich, 1951 and 1953', *Norfolk Archaeology* 31, 5-112.

Hyltén-Cavallius, G.D., 1868. *Wärend och Wirdarne* 2 (Stockholm: Norstedt).

Ijzereef, G.F., 1974. 'A medieval jaw-sledge from Dordrecht', *Berichten van de Rijksdienst voor het Oudheidkundig Bodemonderzoek* 24, 181-4.

Iliffe, J.H., 1932. 'Excavations at Alchester, 1928', *Antiquaries Journal* 12, 35-67.

Ivy, G.S., 1958. 'The bibliography of the manuscript book', in F. Wormald and C.E. Wright (eds.), *The English Library before 1700* (London: Athlone Press), 32-65.

Jackson, D.A., 1980. 'Roman buildings at Ringstead, Northants.', *Northamptonshire Archaeology* 15, 12-34.

Jackson, D.A. and Ambrose, T.M., 1978. 'Excavations at Wakerley, Northants., 1972-75', *Britannia* 9, 115-242.

Jackson, D.A., Harding, D.W. and Myres, J.N.L., 1969. 'The Iron Age and Anglo-Saxon site at Upton, Northants.', *Antiquaries Journal* 49, 202-21.

Jacob, K.H., 1911. 'Zur Prähistorie Nordwest-Sachsens', *Abhandlungen der Kaiserlichen Leopoldnisch-Carolinischen Deutschen Akademie der Naturforscher* 94, 115-231.

Jacob-Friesen, K.H., 1974. *Einführung in Niedersachsens Urgeschichte* 3 *Eisenzeit* (Hildesheim: Veröffentlichen der Urgeschichtlichen Sammlungen des Landesmuseums zu Hannover 15).

Jacobi, L., 1909. *Das Kastell Zugmantel* (Heidelberg: Der Obergermanisch-Raetische Limes des Roemerreiches 32).

Jankuhn, H., 1943. *Die Ausgrabungen in Haithabu 1937-1939* (Berlin: Ahnenerbe-Stiftung Verlag).

—— 1944. 'Die Bedeutung der Gussformen von Haithabu', *Das Ahnenerbe* (Berlin: Berichte über die Kieler Tagung 1939), 226-37.

—— 1951. 'Ein Ulfberht -Schwert aus der Elbe bei Hamburg', in K. Kersten (ed.), *Festschrift für Gustav Schwantes* (Neumünster: Wachholtz), 212-33.

—— 1953. 'Die Kammshiene aus Terp Almenum', *Die Vrije Fries* 41, 37-45.

Janssen, W., 1972. *Issendorf: ein Urnenfriedhof der späten Kaiserzeit und der Völkerwanderungszeit* 1 (Hildesheim: Materialhefte zur Ur- und Frühgeschichte Niedersachsens 6).

Jennison, G., 1937. *Animals for Show and Pleasure in Ancient Rome* (Manchester: Publications of the University of Manchester 258).

Jessup, R., 1950. *Anglo-Saxon Jewellery* (London: Faber and Faber).

Johnson, A.E., 1974. 'A bone knife handle from the City of London', *Antiquaries Journal* 54, 278.

Johnson, S., 1978. 'Excavations at Hayton Roman fort, 1975', *Britannia* 9, 57-114.

Johnston, D.E., 1972. 'A Roman building at Chalk, near Gravesend', *Britannia* 3, 112-48.

Jones, D.M., 1980. *Excavations at Billingsgate Buildings 'Triangle', Lower Thames Street, 1974* (London: London and Middlesex Archaeological Society Special Paper 4).

Jones, L.W., 1946. 'Pricking manuscripts: the instruments and their significance', *Speculum* 21, 389-403.

Jones, M.U., 1975. 'Woolcomb warmers from Mucking, Essex', *Antiquaries Journal* 55, 411-3.

Jones, R., 1975. 'The Romano-British farmstead and its cemetery at Lynch Farm, near Peterborough', *Northamptonshire Archaeology* 10, 94-137.

Jope, E.M., 1958. 'The Clarendon Hotel, Oxford. Part 1. The Site', *Oxoniensia* 23, 1-83.

Kaminska, J. and Nahlik, A., 1960. 'Études sur l'industrie textile du haut moyen age en Pologne', *Archaeologia Polona* 3, 89-119.

Keller, E., 1971. *Die Spätrömische Grabfunde in Südbayern* (Munich: Münchner Beiträge zur Vor- und Frühgeschichte 14).

—— 1979. *Das Spätrömische Gräberfeld von Neuburg an der Donau* (Kallmünz: Materialhefte zur Bayerischen Vorgeschichte ser. A, 40).

Keller, M.L., 1906. *The Anglo-Saxon Weapon Names* (Heidelberg: Anglistiche Forschungen 15).

Kendrick, J., 1853. 'An account of excavations made at the Mote Hill, Warrington, Lancashire', *Proceedings and Papers of the Historical Society of Lancashire and Cheshire* 5, 59-68.

Kendrick, T.D., 1937. 'Ivory mounts from a casket', *Antiquaries Journal*, 17, 448.

—— 1941. 'Bone pins found with the Cuerdale treasure', *Antiquaries Journal* 21, 162-3.

Kennett, D.H., 1975. 'The Souldern burials', *Oxoniensia* 40, 201-10.

Kenward, H.K. *et al.*, 1978. 'The environment of Anglo-Scandinavian York', in R.A. Hall (ed.), *Viking Age York and the North* (London: Council for British Archaeology Research Report 27), 58-70.

Kenyon, K.M., 1948. *Excavations at the Jewry Wall Site, Leicester* (London: Reports of the Research Committee of the Society of Antiquaries of London 15).

—— 1959. *Excavations in Southwark 1945-1947* (Guildford: Research Papers of the Surrey Archaeological Society 5).

Ker, N.R., 1960. *English Manuscripts in the Century after the Norman Conquest* (Oxford: Clarendon Press).

Kielland, T., 1930. 'Sculpture sur l'os norvégienne et islandaise depuis l'antiquité jusq'aux temps modernes', *Acta Archaeologica* 1, 111-20.

King, J.E., 1964. *Seals of the World* (London: British Museum, Natural History).

Kirk, J.R. and Leeds, E.T., 1953. 'Three early Saxon graves from Dorchester, Oxon.', *Oxoniensia* 17-18, 63-76.

Kjellberg, S.T., 1940. 'Gnida, mangla och stryka', *Kulturen*, 68-91.

Kjellmark, K., 1939. ' "Fiskpuls" av rosenkrans fran hjorthorn', *Fornvännen* 34, 359-62.

Klindt-Jensen, O., 1951. 'Freds- og krigstid i Bornholms Jernalder', *Nationalmuseets Arbejdsmark* (1951), 15-23.

—— 1957. *Bornholm i Folkevandringstiden og Forudsaetningerne i tidlig Jernalder* (Copenhagen: Nationalmuseets Skrifter, større beretninger 2).

—— 1969, 'Scandinavians in the British Isles', *Medieval Scandinavia* 2, 163-207.

Kloiber, Ä., 1957. *Die Gräberfelder von Lauriacum. Das Ziegfeld* (Linz: Forschungen in Lauriacum 4/5).

Klumbach, H. and Moortgat-Correns, U., 1968. 'Orientalisches Rollsiegel vom Mainzer Legionslager', *Germania* 46, 36-40.

Knocker, G.M., 1960. 'Clare Castle excavations, 1955', *Proceedings of the Suffolk Institute of Archaeology* 28, 136-52.

—— 1969. 'Excavations at Red Castle, Thetford', *Norfolk Archaeology* 34, 119-86.

Koch, R., 1967. *Bodenfunde der Völkerwanderungszeit aus dem Main-Tauber Gebiet* (Berlin: Germanische Denkmäler der Völkerwanderungszeit ser. A, 8).

Koch, U., 1968. *Die Grabfunde der Merowingerzeit aus dem Donautal um Regensburg* (Berlin: Germanische Denkmäler der Völkerwanderungszeit ser. A, 10).

—— 1977. *Das Reihengräberfeld bei Schretzheim* (Berlin: Germanische Denkmäler der Völkerwanderungszeit ser. A, 13).

Koechlin, R., 1924. *Les Ivoires Gothiques Français* (Paris: Picard).

Kolchin, B.A., 1956. 'Topografiya, stratigrafiya i khronologiya Nerevskogo raskopa', in A.V. Artsikhovskii and B.A. Kolchin (eds.), *Trudy Novgorodskoi Arkheologicheskoi Expeditsii* 1 (Moscow: Materialy i Issledovaniya po Arkjeologii SSSR 55), 44-137.

Kossina, G., 1929. 'Die Griffe der Wikingschwerter', *Mannus* 21, 300-8.

Kostrzewski, J., 1949. *Les Origines de la Civilisation Polonaise* (Paris: Publications de l'Institut Occidental 1).

Kurnatowska, Z., 1977. 'Horn-working in mediæval Poland', in L. Gerevich (ed.), *La Formation et le Développement des Métiers au Moyen Age (V^e – XIVe Siècles)* (Budapest: Akademiai Kiadó), 121-5.

Labib, S.V., 1965. 'Handelsgeschichte ägyptens in Spätmittelalter', *Vierteljahrschrift für Sozial- und Wirtschaftsgeschichte* 46, 1-586.

Laidlay, J.W., 1870. 'Notice of an ancient structure and remains from a "kitchen midden" on an isolated rock near Seacliffe, East Lothian', *Proceedings of the Society of Antiquaries of Scotland* 8, 372-7.

Laing, L., 1973. 'People and pins in Dark Age Scotland', *Transactions of the Dumfriesshire and Galloway Natural History and Antiquarian Society* ser. 3, 50, 53-71.

—— 1975. *The Archaeology of Late Celtic Britain c. 400-1200 A.D.* (London: Methuen).

Lambrick, G. and Woods, H., 1976. 'Excavations on the second site of the Dominican priory, Oxford', *Oxoniensia* 41, 168-231.

Laser, R., 1965. *Die Brandgräber der Spätrömischen Kaiserzeit im Nördlichen Mitteldeutschland* 1 (Berlin: Forschungen zur Vor- und Frühgeschichte 7).

Lasko, P., 1956. 'The comb of St Cuthbert', in C.F. Battiscombe (ed.), *The Relics of St Cuthbert* (Durham: Dean and Chapter of Durham Cathedral), 336-55.

—— 1971. *The Kingdom of the Franks* (London: Thames and Hudson).

Laws, A., 1976. 'Excavations at Northumberland Wharf, Brentford', *Transactions of the London and Middlesex Archaeological Society* 27, 179-205.

Lawson, G., 1978a. 'The lyre from grave 22', in B. Green and A. Rogerson, *The Anglo-Saxon Cemetery at Bergh Apton, Norfolk* (East Anglian Archaeology 7), 87-97.

—— 1978b. 'Medieval tuning pegs from Whitby, N. Yorkshire', *Medieval Archaeology* 22, 139-41.

Layard, N.F., 1908. 'Bone skates and skating stakes', *East Anglian Miscellany* 2, 74.

Lebel, P., 1953. 'Amulettes ou manches de couteaux?', *Revue Archéologique de l'Est et du Centre-Est* 4, 334-40.

—— 1956. 'Note complémentaire' to G. Faider-Feytmans, 'Talismans en bois de cerf trouvés dans les tombes mérovingiennes', *Revue Archéologique de l'Est et du Centre-Est* 7, 140-3.

Leciejewicz, L. *et al.*, 1972. *La Ville de Szczecin des IXe – XIIIe Siècles* (Szczecin: Archaeologia Urbium 2).

Leeds, E.T., 1917. 'An Anglo-Saxon cemetery at Wheatley, Oxfordshire', *Proceedings of the Society of Antiquaries of London* ser. 2, 29, 48-65.

—— 1923. 'A Saxon village near Sutton Courtenay, Berkshire', *Archaeologia* 73, 147-92.

—— 1924. 'An Anglo-Saxon cremation burial of the seventh century in Asthall Barrow, Oxfordshire', *Antiquaries Journal* 4, 113-26.

—— 1927. 'A Saxon village at Sutton Courtenay, Berkshire: second report', *Archaeologia* 76, 59-80.

—— 1938. 'An Anglo-Saxon cemetery at Wallingford, Berkshire', *Berkshire Archaeological Journal* 42, 93-101.

—— 1940. 'Two Saxon cemeteries in north Oxfordshire', *Oxoniensia* 5, 21-30.

—— 1947. 'A Saxon village at Sutton Courtenay, Berkshire: third report', *Archaeologia* 92, 79-93.

Leeds, E.T. and Atkinson, R.J.C., 1944. 'An Anglo-Saxon cemetery at Nassington, Northants.', *Antiquaries Journal* 24, 100-28.

Leeds, E.T. and Harden D.B., 1936. *The Anglo-Saxon Cemetery at Abingdon, Berkshire* (Oxford: Ashmolean Museum).

Leeds, E.T. and Riley, M., 1942. 'Two early Saxon cemeteries at Cassington, Oxon.', *Oxoniensia* 7, 61-70.

Leeds, E.T. and Shortt, H. de S., 1953. *An Anglo-Saxon Cemetery at Petersfinger, near Salisbury, Wilts.* (Salisbury: Salisbury, South Wiltshire and Blackmore Museum).

Lefroy, J.H., 1870. 'On a bronze object bearing a runic inscription found at Greenmount, Castle Bellingham, Ireland', *Archaeological Journal* 27, 284-313.

Lepiksaar, J., 1975. 'Über die Tierknochenfunde aus den mittelalterlichen Siedlungen Südschwedens', in A.T. Clason (ed.), *Archaeozoological Studies* (Amsterdam, Oxford and New York: North Holland/American Elsevier), 230-9.

Lepiksaar, J. and Heinrich, D., 1977. 'Untersuchungen an Fischresten der frühmittelalterlichen Siedlung Haithabu', in K. Schietzel (ed.), *Berichte über die Ausgrabungen in Haithabu* 10 (Neumünster), 9-140.

Lethbridge, T.C., 1920. 'A burial of the "Viking Age" in Skye', *Archaeological Journal* 77, 135-6.

—— 1931. *Recent Excavations in Anglo-Saxon Cemeteries in Cambridgeshire and Suffolk* (Cambridge: Cambridge Antiquarian Society Quarto Publications, new ser. 3).

—— 1936. *A Cemetery at Shudy Camps, Cambridgeshire* (Cambridge: Cambridge Antiquarian Society Quarto Publications, new ser. 4).

—— 1951. *A Cemetery at Lackford, Suffolk* (Cambridge: Cambridge Antiquarian Society Quarto Publications, new ser. 6).

—— 1952. 'Excavations at Kilpheder, South Uist, and the problem of the brochs and wheelhouses', *Proceedings of the Prehistoric Society* 18, 176-93.

Lethbridge, T.C. and Carter, H.G., 1927. 'Excavations in the Anglo-Saxon cemetery at Little Wilbraham', *Proceedings of the Cambridge Antiquarian Society* 29, 95-104.

Levison, W., 1946. *England and the Continent in the Eighth Century* (Oxford: Oxford University Press).

Liebermann, F., 1903. *Die Gesetze der Angelsachsen* 2 (Halle: Niemeyer).

Lindahl, F., 1980. 'Spillelidenskab', *Hikuin* 6, 153-62.

Loë, A. de, 1939. *Belgique Ancienne 4 la Période Franque* (Brussels: Vromant).

Lombard, M., 1952. 'La route de la Meuse et les relations lointaines des pays mosans entre le VIIIᵉ et le XIᵉ siècle', in P. Francastel (ed.), *L'Art Mosan* (Paris: Bibliothèque General de l'École Pratique des Hautes Études, VIᵉ Section).

London Museum, 1940. *Medieval Catalogue* (reprinted 1954) (London: HMSO).

Long, C.D., 1975. 'Excavations in the medieval city of Trondheim, Norway', *Medieval Archaeology* 19, 1-32.

Longhurst, M.H., 1927. *Catalogue of Carvings in Ivory* (London: Victoria and Albert Museum).

—— 1929. *Catalogue of Carvings in Ivory* 2 (London: Victoria and Albert Museum).

Lorren, C., 1977. 'Le château de Rubercy (Calvados). Étude de la demeure principale (c. 1150-1204)', *Archéologie Médiévale* 7, 109-78.

Lowe, E.A., 1935. *Codices Latini Antiquores* 2 *Great Britain and Ireland* (Oxford: OUP).

Luff, R.M., 1982. *A Zooarchaeological Study of the Roman North-Western Provinces* (Oxford: British Archaeological Reports, International Series 137).

Lunde, O., 1977. *Trondheims Fortid i Bygrunnen* (Riksantikvarens Skrifter 2) (Trondheim).

Lutz, D., 1970. 'Wüstung Zimmern, Gemarkung Stebbach, Kr. Sinsheim, Nordbaden', *Nachrichtenblatt der Denkmalpflege in Baden-Württemberg* 13, 103-5.

Macalister R.A.S., 1940. 'The inscriptions and language of the Picts', in J. Ryan (ed.), *Essays Presented to Professor Eoin MacNiell* (Dublin: Three Candles), 184-224.

MacDonald, G., 1934. *The Roman Wall in Scotland* (Oxford: Clarendon Press).

Macewen, W., 1920. *The Growth and Shedding of the Antler of the Deer* (Glasgow: Maclehose).

MacGregor, A., 1974. 'The Broch of Burrian, North Ronaldsay, Orkney', *Proceedings of the Society of Antiquaries of Scotland* 105, 63-118.

—— 1975a. 'Barred combs of Frisian type in England', *Medieval Archaeology* 19, 195-8.

—— 1975b. 'Problems in the interpretation of microscopic wear patterns: the evidence from bone skates', *Journal of Archaeological Science* 2, 385-90.

—— 1976a. 'Bone skates: a review of the evidence', *Archaeological Journal* 133, 57-74.

—— 1976b. 'Finds from a Roman sewer system and an adjacent building in Church Street', in P.V. Addyman (ed.), *The Archaeology of York* 17 (London: Council for British Archaeology), 1-30.

—— 1976c. 'Two antler crossbow nuts and some notes on the early development of the crossbow', *Proceedings of the Society of Antiquaries of Scotland* 107, 317-21.

—— 1978a. 'Industry and commerce in Anglo-Scandinavian York', in R.A. Hall (ed.), *Viking Age York and the North* (London: Council for British Archaeology Research Report 27), 34-57.

—— 1978b. 'Roman finds from Skeldergate and Bishophill', in P.V. Addyman (ed.), *The Archaeology of York* 17 (London: Council for British Archaeology), 31-66.

—— 1980. 'A pre-Conquest mould of antler from medieval Southampton', *Medieval Archaeology* 24, 203-5.

—— 1982a. 'Anglo-Scandinavian finds from Lloyds Bank, Pavement, and other sites', in P.V. Addyman (ed.), *The Archaeology of York* 17 (London: Council for British Archaeology), 67-174.

—— 1982b. 'Bone, antler and ivory objects', in J.C. Murray (ed.), *Excavations in the Medieval Burgh of Aberdeen 1973-81* (Edinburgh: Society of Antiquaries of Scotland Monograph Series 2), 180-4.

—— 1983. 'Objects of bone, antler and ivory', in L.A.S. Butler and P. Mayes (eds.), *Sandal Castle Excavation: a Detailed Archaeological Report 1963-74* (Wakefield: Wakefield Historical Publications), 284.

—— forthcoming. Reports are in press on objects from the following:

Faccombe Netherton, in J. Fairbrother, *The Manor of Faccombe Netherton* (London: British Archaeological Reports).

Goltho, in G. Beresford, *Goltho: the Development of an Early Medieval Manor c. 850-1150* (Department of the Environment Archaeological Reports).

Ludgershall, in P.V. Addyman [Excavations at Ludgershall Castle].

Perth, in N.Q. Bogdan [Excavations in Perth].

South Witham, in P. Mayes [Excavations at South Witham].

York Minster, in A.D. Phillips [Excavations at York Minster].

MacGregor, A. and Currey, J., 1983. 'Mechanical properties as conditioning factors in the bone and antler industry of the 3rd to the 13th century AD', *Journal of Archaeological Science* 10, 71-7.

Maciejewski, F., Rajewski, Z. and Wokroj, F., 1954. 'Ślady osadnictwa kultury t.zw. Brzesko-Kujawskiej w Biskupinie, Pow. Żnin', *Wiadomości Archeologiczne* 20, 67-79.

Mackreth, D., 1978. 'Orton Hall Farm, Peterborough: a Roman and Saxon settlement', in M. Todd (ed.), *Studies in the Romano-British Villa* (Leicester: Leicester University Press), 209-23.

MacLaren, A., 1974. 'A Norse house on Drimore Machair, South Uist, *Journal of the Glasgow Archaeological Society* 3, 9-18.

Madden, F., 1832. 'Historical remarks on the introduction of the game of chess into Europe . . .', *Archaeologia* 24, 203-91.

Magie, D., 1960. *The Scriptores Historiae Augustae* 2 (London: Heinemann).

Magnus, O., 1555. *Historia de Gentibus Septentrionalibus* (Rome: de Viottis).

Maltby, M., 1979. *Faunal Studies on Urban Sites: the Animal Bones from Exeter 1971-1975* (Sheffield: Exeter Archaeological Reports 2).

Manby, T.G., 1966. 'Anglian objects from Wensleydale', *Yorkshire Archaeological Journal* 41, 340-4.

Mann, J., 1962. *Wallace Collection Catalogues: European Arms and Armour* 2 (London: Wallace Collection).

Mann, V.B., 1977. *Romanesque Ivory Tablemen* (PhD thesis, New York University).

Marangou, E.L.I., 1976. *Bone Carvings from Egypt 1 Graeco-Roman Period* (Tübingen: Wasmuth).

Marschallek, K.H., 1940. 'Die ostgermanische Siedlung von Kliestow bei Frankfurt (Oder)', *Praehistorische Zeitschrift* 30-1, 253-307.

Marsden, P.R.V., 1970. 'Some discoveries in the City of London 1954-9', *Transactions of the London and Middlesex Archaeological Society* 22, 32-42.

Mårtensson, A.W., 1961. 'Styli och vaxtavlor', *Kulturen*, 108-41

—— 1976. *Uppgrävt förflutet för PKbanken i Lund* (Lund: Archaeologica Lundensia 7).

Martin, M., 1976. *Das Fränkische Gräberfeld von Basel-Bernerring* (Basel: Baseler Beiträge zur Ur- und Frühgeschichte 1).

Maskell, A., 1872. *Description of the Ivories Ancient and Mediaeval in the South Kensington Museum* (London: Chapman and Hall).

—— 1905. *Ivories* (London: Methuen).

Matthews, C.L., 1962. 'The Anglo-Saxon cemetery at Marina Drive, Dunstable', *Bedfordshire Archaeological Journal* 1, 25-47.

Matthews, L.H., 1952. *British Mammals* (London: Collins).

Mayhew, N.J., 1975. 'A tumbrel at the Ashmolean', *Antiquaries Journal* 55, 394-6.

MacLean, F.C. and Urist, M.R., 1961. *Bone. An Introduction to the Physiology of Skeletal Tissue* (Chicago and London: University of Chicago Press).

Meaney, A.L., 1981. *Anglo-Saxon Amulets and Curing Stones* (Oxford: British Archaeological Reports 96).

Meaney, A.L. and Hawkes, S.C., 1970. *The Anglo-Saxon Cemeteries at Winnall, Winchester, Hampshire* (London: Society for Medieval Archaeology Monograph 4).

Mewgaw, J.V.S., 1960. 'Penny whistles and prehistory', *Antiquity* 34, 6-13.

—— 1961. 'An end-blown flute or flageolet from White Castle', *Medieval Archaeology* 5, 176-80.

—— 1968. 'Problems and non-problems in palaeo-organology: a musical miscellany', in J. Coles and D.D.A. Simpson (eds.), *Studies in Ancient Europe: Essays presented to Stuart Piggott* (Leicester: Leicester University Press), 333-58.

—— 1969. 'An end-blown flute from medieval Canterbury', *Medieval Archaeology* 12, 149-50.

Mellor, J.E. and Pearce, T., 1981. *The Austin Friars, Leicester* (London: Council for British Archaeology Research Report 35).

Mercklin, E. von, 1940. 'Römische Klappmessergriffe', *Vjesnika Hrvatskoga Arheološkoga Društva* new ser. 18-21, (Serta Hoffilleriana), 339-52.

Metcalf, D.M., 1977. 'The evidence of Scottish coin hoards for monetary history, 1100-1600', in D.M. Metcalf (ed.), *Coinage in Medieval Scotland (1100-1600)* (Oxford: British Archaeological Reports 45).

Meyer, O., 1979. *Archéologie Urbaine a Saint-Denis* (Saint-Denis: Maison des Jeunes et de la Culture).

Mickelthwaite, J.T., 1892. 'On the indoor games of schoolboys in the middle ages', *Archæological Journal* 49, 319-28.

Miles, A.E.W and Boyde, A., 1961. 'Observations on the structure of elephant ivory', *Journal of Anatomy* 95, 450.

Minorsky, V., 1942. *Sharaf Al-Zamān Ṭāhir Marvazī on China, the Turks and India* (London: Forlong Fund 22).

Mitchell, A., 1880. *The Past in the Present* (Edinburgh: Douglas).

Molaug, P.B., 1975. 'Oslo im Mittelalter. Ergebnisse der neuen archäologischen Ausgrabungen', *Zeitschrift für Archäologie des Mittelalters* 3, 217-60.

Moorhouse, S., 1971. 'Finds from Basing House, Hampshire (c. 1540-1645): part two', *Post-Medieval Archaeology* 5, 35-76.

—— 1972. 'Finds from excavations in the refectory at the Dominican friary, Boston', *Lincolnshire History and Archaeology* 7, 21-53.

Moosbrugger-Leu, R., 1967. *Die frühmittelalterlichen Gürtelbeschläge der Schweiz* (Basel: Monographien zur Ur- und Frühgeschichte der Schweiz 14).

Mortimer, J.R., 1905. *Forty Years' Researches in British and Saxon Burial Mounds of East Yorkshire* (London: Brown).

Morton, C. and Muntz, H., 1972. *The Carmen de Hastingae Proelio of Guy, Bishop of Amiens* (Oxford: Clarendon Press).

Moszyński, K., 1967. *Kultura Ludowa Słowian* 1 (Warsaw: Książka i Wiedza).

Müller, A. von, 1962. 'Völkerwanderungszeitliche Körpergräber und spätgermanische Siedlungsräume in der Mark Brandenburg', *Berliner Jahrbuch* 2, 105-89.

Müller-Using, D., 1953. 'Über die frühmittelalterlichen Geweihreste von Wollin', *Säugetierkundliche Mitteilungen* 1, 64-7.

Müller-Wille, M., 1978. 'Das Schiffsgrab von der Ile de Groix (Bretagne) — ein Excursus zum "Bootkammergrab von Haithabu" ', in K. Schietzel (ed.), *Berichte über die Ausgrabungen in Haithabu* 12 (Neumünster), 48-84.

Munro, R., 1879. 'Notice of the excavation of a crannog at Lochlee, Tarbolton, Ayrshire', *Proceedings of the Society of Antiquaries of Scotland* 13, 175-252.

—— 1882. *Ancient Scottish Lake Dwellings or Crannogs* (Edinburgh: Douglas).

—— 1890. *The Lake Dwellings of Europe* (London: Cassel).

—— 1897. *Prehistoric Problems* (Edinburgh and London: Blackwood).

Murray, D., 1904. *Museums, their History and their Use* (Glasgow: Maclehose).

Murray, H.J.R., 1913. *A History of Chess* (Oxford: Clarendon Press).

—— 1941. 'The medieval game of tables', *Medium Ævum* 10, 57-69.

—— 1952. *A History of Board Games other than Chess* (Oxford: Clarendon Press).

Musée Archéologique de Dijon, n.d. *Le Cycle de la Matière: l'Os* (Dijon: Musée Archéologique).

Musty, J., 1969. 'The excavation of two barrows, one of Saxon date, at Ford, Laverstock, near Salisbury, Wiltshire', *Antiquaries Journal* 49, 98-117.

Myres, J.N.L., 1969. *Anglo-Saxon Pottery and the Settlement of England* (Oxford: Clarendon Press).

Myres, J.N.L. and Green, B., 1973. *The Anglo-Saxon Cemeteries of Caistor-by-Norwich and Markshall, Norfolk* (London: Reports of the Research Committee of the Society of Antiquaries of London 30).

Myres, J.N.L. and Southern, W.H., 1973. *The Anglo-Saxon Cremation Cemetery at Sancton, East Yorkshire* (Hull: Hull Museum Publications 218).

Nash-Williams, V.E., 1932. 'The Roman legionary fortress at Caerleon in Monmouthshire', *Archaeologia Cambrensis* 87, 48-104.

National Museum of Ireland, 1973. *Viking and Medieval Dublin. National Museum Excavations 1962-1973* (Dublin: National Museum of Ireland).

Neal, D.S., 1974. *The Excavation of the Roman Villa in Gadebridge Park, Hemel Hempstead, 1963-8* (London: Reports of the Research Committee of the Society of Antiquaries of London 31).

Nenquin, J.A.E., 1953. *La Necropole de Furfooz* (Brugge: Dissertationes Archaeologicae Gandenses 1).

Nerman, B., 1935. *Die Völkerwanderungszeit Gotlands* (Stockholm: Kungliga Vitterhets Historie och Antikvitets Akademien).

Neville, R.C., 1855. 'Notices of certain shafts, containing remains of the Roman period, discovered at the Roman station at Chesterford, Essex', *Archaeological Journal* 12, 109-26.

Newstead, R., 1928. 'Report on the excavations on the site of the Roman fortress at the Deanery Field, Chester, no. 2', *Liverpool Annals of Archaeology and Anthropology* 15, 3-32.

Nichols, R.V., 1979. 'A Roman couch in Cambridge', *Archaeologia* 106, 1-32.

Nickel, E., 1964. *Der 'Alte Markt' in Magdeburg* (Berlin: Deutsche Akademie der Wissenschaften zu Berlin, Schrifter der Sektion für Vor- und Frühgeschichte 18).

Nierhaus, R., 1938. 'Grabungen in dem spätrömischen Kastell auf dem Münsterberg von Breisnach (Kr. Freiburg i. Br.) *Germania* 24, 37-46.

Noddle, B.A., 1975. 'A comparison of the animal bones from 8 medieval sites in southern Britain', in A.T. Clason (ed.), *Archaeozoological Studies* (Amsterdam, Oxford and New York: North Holland/ American Elesevier), 248-60.

Nørlund, P., 1948. *Trelleborg* (Copenhagen: Nordiske Fortidsminder 4).

Noss, A., 1976. *Før Strykejernet Slikjejake og Mangletre* (Oslo: Norsk Folkemuseum).

Okasha, E., 1971. *Hand-List of Anglo-Saxon Non-Runic Inscriptions* (Cambridge: Cambridge University Press).

Oldeberg, A., 1966. *Metallteknik under Vikingetid och Medeltid* (Stockholm: Kungliga Vitterhets Historie och Antikvitets Akademien).

Oldenstein, J., 1976. 'Zur Ausrüstung römischer Auxiliareinheiten', *Bericht der Römisch-Germanischen Kommission* 57, 49-284.

Oman, C.C., 1944. 'English medieval drinking horns', *Connoisseur* 13, 20-3, 60.

O'Meadhra, U., 1979. *Early Christian, Viking and Romanesque Art: Motif-Pieces from Ireland* (Stockholm: Theses and Papers in North European Archaeology 7).

Ó Ríordáin, B., 1971. 'Excavations at High Street and Winetavern Street, Dublin', *Medieval Archaeology* 15, 73-85.

—— 1976. 'The High Street excavations', in B. Almqvist and D. Greene (eds.), *Proceedings of the Seventh Viking Congress* (Dublin: Royal Irish Academy), 135-40.

Ó Ríordáin, S.P., 1949. 'Lough Gur excavations: Carraig Aille and the "Spectacles" ', *Proceedings of the Royal Irish Academy* 52C, 39-111.

Oswald, A., 1948. 'Finds from the Birmingham moat', *Transactions of the Birmingham Archaeological Society* 67, 79-80.

Owen, G.R., 1976. *Anglo-Saxon Costume. A Study of Secular, Civilian Clothing and Jewellery Fashions* (PhD thesis, University of Newcastle-upon-Tyne).

Owen, R., 1846. *A History of British Fossil Mammals and Birds* (London: van Voorst).

—— 1956. 'The ivory and teeth of commerce', *Journal of the Royal Society of Arts* 5, 65-71.

Ozanne, A., 1963. 'The Peak dwellers', *Medieval Archaeology* 5-7, 15-52.

Page, R., 1969. 'Old English *cyningstan*', *Leeds Studies in English* 3, 1-5.

—— 1973. *An Introduction to English Runes* (London: Methuen).

Palmer, N., 1980. 'A beaker burial and medieval tenements in The Hamel, Oxford', *Oxoniensia* 34, 124-225.

Párducz, M. and Korek, J., 1959. 'Eine Siedlung aus der Kaiserzeit in Ózd', *Acta Archaeologica Academiae Scientarium Hungaricae* 10, 159-207.

Parrington, M., 1976. 'Roman finds and animal bones from Kingston Hill Farm, Kingston Bagpuize, Oxon.', *Oxoniensia* 41, 65-9.

—— 1979. 'Excavations at Stert Street, Abingdon, Oxon.', *Oxoniensia* 44, 1-25.

Parrington, M. and Balkwill, C., 1975. 'Excavations at Broad Street, Abingdon', *Oxoniensia* 40, 5-58.

Patterson, R., 1956. 'Spinning and weaving', in C. Singer, E.J. Holmyard, A.R. Hall and T.I. Williams, *A History of Technology* 2 (Oxford: Clarendon Press), 191-220.

Paulsen, P., 1967. *Alamannische Adelsgräber von Niederstotzingen* (Stuttgart: Veröffentlichungen des Staatlichen Amtes für Denkamlpflege Stuttgart, Reihe A, 12/1).

Payne-Gallwey, R., 1903. *The Crossbow* (London: Longman Green).

Peers, C. and Radford, C.A.R., 1943. 'The Saxon monastery of Whitby', *Archaeologia* 89, 27-88.

Pelletier, R., 1971. 'Essai sur l'assemblage des elements de charnière en os gallo-romaine', *Revue Archéologique du Centre de la France* 10, 202-7.

Penn, W.S., 1957. 'The Romano-British settlement at Springhead. Excavation of the bakery, site A', *Archaeologia Cantiana* 71, 53-105.

—— 1968. 'Springhead: miscellaneous excavations', *Archaeologia Cantiana* 83, 163-92.

Penney, S.H., 1975. 'Rolled graver technique on a weaving comb', *Somerset Archaeology and Natural History* 119, 65-5.

Penniman, T.K., 1952. *Pictures of Ivory and other Animal Teeth, Bone and Antler* (Oxford: Pitt Rivers Occasional Papers on Technology 5).

Petersen, J., 1914. 'Bretspillet i Norge i forhistorisk tid', *Oldtiden* 4, 75-92.

—— 1919. *De Norske Vikingsverd. En Typologisk-Kronologisk Studie over Vikingetidens Vaaben* (Kristiania: Videnskapsselskapets Skrifter II. Hist.-Filos. Klasse 1919, 1).

—— 1940. *British Antiquities of the Viking Period found in Norway* (H. Shetelig (ed.), Viking Antiquities in Great Britain and Ireland 5) (Oslo: Aschehoug).

—— 1951. *Vikingetidens Redskaper* (Oslo: Norske Videnskaps-Akademi i Oslo II. Hist.-Filos. Klasse 1951, 4).

Philp, B., 1973. *Excavations in West Kent, 1960-1970* (Dover: Kent Archaeological Research Reports 2).

—— 1981. *The Excavation of the Roman Forts of the Classis Britannica at Dover, 1970-1977* (Dover: Kent Archaeological Research Reports 3).

Pietzsch, A., 1979. 'Nachbildung von Knochen- und Geweihkämmen aus der Römischen Kaiserzeit und der Völkerwanderungszeit', *Arbeits- und Forschungsberichte zur Sächsischen Bodendenkmalpflege* 23, 57-82.

Pinder-Wilson, R.H. and Brook, C.N.L., 1973. 'The reliquary of St Petroc and the ivories of Norman Sicily', *Archaeologia* 104, 261-305.

Pininska, M., 1974. 'Dawna kultura wyspy Wolin w świetle badań etnograficznych z 1970i 1971r', *Materiały Zachodnio-Pomorskie* 20, 395-432.

Pinto, E.H., 1952. 'Hand-made combs', *Connoisseur* 130, 170-6, 221.

—— 1969. *Treen and other Wooden Bygones* (London: Bell).

Pirling, R., 1966. *Das Römisch-Fränkische Gräberfeld von Krefeld-Gellep* (Germanische Denkmäler der Völkerwanderungszeit ser. B, 2) Berlin.

Pitt-Rivers, A., 1887. *Excavations in Cranborne Chase 1. Excavations in the Romano-British Village on Woodcuts Common and Romano-British Antiquities in Rushmore Park* (published privately).

Platt, C., 1976. *Archaeology in Medieval Southampton* (Southampton: Southampton Museums and Art Gallery).

Platt, C. and Coleman-Smith, R., 1975. *Excavations in Medieval Southampton 1953-1969 2 The Finds* (Leicester: Leicester University Press).

Plumier, C., 1749. *L'Art de Tourner . . . toutes sortes d'Ouvrages* (Lyons: Certe; Paris: Joubert).

Plummer, C. and Earle, J., 1892. *Two of the Saxon Chronicles Parallel* (Oxford: Clarendon Press).

Poel, J.M.G. van der, 1961. 'De landbouw in het verste verleden', *Berichte van de Rijksdienst voor het Oudheidkundig Bodemonderzoek* 10-11, 125-94.

Pommeranz-Liedtke, G., 1964. *Schachfiguren aus Zehn Jahrhunderten* (Frankfurt-am-Main: Insel Verlag).

Poplin, F., 1977a. 'Analyse de matière de quelques ivoires d'art', *Méthodologie Appliquée a l'Industrie de l'Os Préhistorique* (Paris: Colloques Internationaux du CNRS no. 568), 77-94.

—— 1977b. 'Utilisation des cavités naturelles osseuses et dentaires', *Méthodologie Appliquée a l'Industrie de l'Os Préhistorique* (Paris: Colloques Internationaux du CNRS no. 568), 111-18.

Porter, D.A., 1974. *Ivory Carving in Later Medieval England, 1200-1400* (PhD thesis, State University of New York at Binghamton).

Porter, E., 1969. 'Fen skating', *Folk Life* 7, 43-59.

Potter, T.W., 1979. *Romans in North-West England* (Kendal: Cumberland and Westmoreland Antiquarian and Archaeological Society Research Series 1).

Poulton, R., 1980. 'Cherchefelle and the origins of Reigate', *London Archaeologist* 3, 433-8.

Pritchard, J.J., 1956. 'General anatomy and histology of bone', in G.H. Bourne (ed.), *The Biochemistry and Physiology of Bone* (New York: Academic Press), 1-25.

Prummel, W., 1975. 'Some reflections on the faunal remains of the Roman castellum Valkenburg, excavation 1962', in A.T. Clason (ed.), *Archaeozoological Studies* (Amsterdam, Oxford and New York: North Holland/American Elsevier), 225-9.

—— 1978. 'Vlees, gevogelte en vis', *Spiegel Historiael* 13, 282-93.

—— 1982. 'The archaeozoological study of urban medieval sites in the Netherlands', in A.R. Hall and H.K. Kenward (eds.), *Environmental Archaeology in the Urban Context* (London: Council for British Archaeology Research Report 43), 117-22.

Rackham, D.J., forthcoming. 'Animal bones from Lloyds Bank and contemporary sites', in P.V. Addyman (ed.), *The Archaeology of York* 15 (London: Council for British Archaeology).

Rackham, O., 1980. *Ancient Woodland* (London: Arnold).

Radford, C.A.R., 1940. 'Small bronzes from St. Augustine's Abbey, Canterbury', *Antiquaries Journal* 20, 506-8.

Radley, J., 1971. 'Economic aspects of Anglo-Danish York', *Medieval Archaeology* 15, 37-57.

Raftery, J., 1960. *A Brief Guide to the Collection of Irish Antiquities* (Dublin: National Museum of Ireland).

Rahtz, P., 1970. 'Excavations at Glastonbury Tor, Somerset, 1964-6', *Archaeological Journal* 127, 1-81.

Rahtz, P. and Greenfield, E., 1977. *Excavations at Chew Valley Lake, Somerset* (London: Department of the Environment Archaeological Reports 8).

Rahtz, P. and Hirst, S., 1976. *Bordesley Abbey* (Oxford: British Archaeological Reports 23).

Randall, L.M.C., 1966. *Images in the Margins of Gothic Manuscripts* (Berkeley and Los Angeles: University of California Press).

Rausing, G., 1967. *The Bow: some Notes on its Origin and Development* (Lund: Acta Archaeologica Lundensia 8vo ser. 6).

Ray, J., 1738. *Travels through the Low Countries, Germany, Italy and France* (London: Walthoe).

Rees, S.E., 1979. *Agricultural Implements in Prehistoric and Roman Britain* (Oxford: British Archaeological Reports 69).

Regteren-Altena, H.H. van, 1970. 'De opgravingen in de Olofskapel te Amsterdam', *Jaarverslag van de Vereniging Hendrik de Keyser*, 29-41.

Reichstein, H., 1969. 'Untersuchungen von Geweihresten des Rothirsches (Cervus elaphus L.) aus der frühmittelalterlichen Siedlung Haithabu (Ausgrabung 1963-1964)', in K. Schietzel (ed.), *Berichte über die Ausgrabungen in Haithabu* 2 (Neumünster), 57-71.

Renn, D.F., 1960. 'The keep of Wareham Castle', *Medieval Archaeology* 4, 56-68.

Reynolds, P.J., 1972. 'Experimental archaeology', *Worcestershire Archaeological Newsletter* 9, 1-13.

Rhodes, M., 1980. 'A pair of late medieval spectacles from the Trig Lane site', *London Archaeologist* 4, 23-5.

—— 1982. 'A pair of fifteenth-century spectacle frames from the City of London', *Antiquaries Journal* 62, 57-73.

Richardson, K.M., 1959. 'Excavations in Hungate, York', *Archaeological Journal* 116, 51-114.

Richmond, I.A., 1947. 'The four *coloniae* of Roman Britain', *Archaeological Journal* 103, 57-84.

Rigold, S., 1971. 'Eynsford Castle and its excavation', *Archaeologia Cantiana* 86, 109-71.

Ritchie, A., 1977. 'Excavation of Pictish and Viking-age farmsteads at Buckquoy, Orkney', *Proceedings of the Society of Antiquaries of Scotland* 108, 174-227.

Ritchie, C.A.R., 1969. *Ivory Carving* (London: Barker).

Ritchie, J.N.G., 1967. 'Keil Cave, Southend, Argyll: a Late Iron Age cave occupation in Kintyre', *Proceedings of the Society of Antiquaries of Scotland* 99, 104-10.

—— 1971. 'Iron Age finds from Dùn an Fheurain, Gallanach, Argyll', *Proceedings of the Society of Antiquaries of Scotland* 103, 100-12.

Robertson, A., Scott, M. and Keppie, L., 1975. *Bar Hill: a Roman Fort and its Finds* (Oxford: British Archaeological Reports 16).

Robinson, J.A., 1923. *The Times of St. Dunstan* (Oxford: Clarendon Press).

Roe, H.M., 1945. 'A mediaeval bronze gaming

piece from Laoighis', *Journal of the Royal Society of Antiquaries of Ireland* 75, 156-9.

Roeren, R., 1960. 'Zur Archäologie und Geschichte sudwestdeutschlands in 3. bis 5. Jahrhundert n. Chr.', *Jahrbuch des Römisch-Germanischen Zentralmuseums Mainz* 7, 214-94.

Roes, A., 1956. 'Medaillons en corne de cerf et têtes de tauraux', *Revue Archéologique de l'Est et du Centre-Est* 7, 57-63.

—— 1958. 'Anneaux en bois de cerf', *Revue Archéologique de l'Est et du Centre-Est* 9, 323-5.

—— 1963. *Bone and Antler Objects from the Frisian Terp Mounds* (Haarlem: Tjeenk Willink).

—— 1965. *Vondsten van Dorestad* (Groningen: Archaeologica Traiectina 7).

Roesdahl, E., Graham-Campbell, J., Connor, P. and Pearson, K. (eds.), 1981. *The Vikings in England and in their Danish Homeland* (London: Anglo-Danish Viking Project).

Rogerson, A., 1977. 'Excavations at Scole, 1973', *East Anglian Archaeology* 5, 97-224.

Roth, H. Ling, 1950. *Studies in Primitive Looms* 3rd edn, (Halifax: Bankside Museum).

Roussell, A., 1941. *Farms and Churches in the Mediaeval Norse Settlements of Greenland* (Copenhagen: Meddelelser om Grønland 89).

Rulewicz, M., 1958. 'Wczesnośredniowieczne zabawki i przedmioty do gier z Pomorza Zachodniego', *Materiały Zachodnio-Pomorskie* 4, 303-54.

Ryder, M.L., 1968a. *Animal Bones in Archaeology* (Oxford: Blackwell).

—— 1968b. 'The origin of spinning', *Textile History* 1, 73-82.

—— 1970. 'The animal remains from Petergate, York, 1957-58', *Yorkshire Archaeological Journal* 42, 418-28.

Rygh, O., 1885. *Norske Oldsager* (Christiania: Cammermeyer).

Rynne, E., 1958. 'Three bone combs', *Journal of the Royal Society of Antiquaries of Ireland* 88, 150-2.

Sage, W., 1973. 'Gräber der älteren Merowingerzeit aus Altenerding, Ldkr. Erding (Oberbayern)', *Bericht der Römisch-Germanischen Kommission* 54, 212-89.

Salaman, R.A., 1975. *Dictionary of Tools used in the Woodworking and Allied Trades, c.* 1700-1970 (London: Allen and Unwin).

Salamon, A. and Erdelyi, I., 1971. *Das Völkerwanderungszeitliche Gräberfeld von Környe* (Budapest: Studia Archaeologica 5).

Salmen, W., 1970. 'Urgeschichtliche und mittelalterliche Musikinstrumente aus Schleswig-Holstein', *Offa* 27, 5-19.

Salin, E., 1959. *La Civilisation Mérovingienne d'après les Sépultures, les Textes et le Laboratoire* (Paris: Picard).

Salzman, L.F., 1964. *English Industries in the Middle Ages* (London: Pordes).

Sanders, H.W., 1910. 'On the use of the deer-horn pick in the mining operations of the ancients', *Archaeologia* 62, 101-24.

Sandys-Wunsch, T.V., n.d. *Ivory, Bone and Horn Cutting* (Toronto: Macmillan).

Sanford, E.C., 1973. *The Identification and the Working of Ivory* (Diploma in Conservation report, Institute of Archaeology, London).

Scapula, J., 1956. 'Habitats successifs sur la Butte d'Isle-Aumont (Aube) d'après les fouilles de 1954', *Revue Archéologique de l'Est et du Centre-Est* 7, 268-84.

Schietzel, K., 1970. 'Holzerne Kleinfunde aus Haithabu (Ausgrabung 1963-1964)', in K. Schietzel (ed.), *Berichte über die Ausgrabungen in Haithabu* 4 (Neumünster), 77-91.

Schlabow, K., 1978. 'Brettchenweberei', in H. Beck, H. Jankuhn, K. Ranke and R. Wenskus (eds.), *Reallexikon der Germanischen Altertumskunde* 3 (Berlin/New York: de Gruyter), 445-50.

Schmid, E., 1968. 'Beindrechsler, Hornschnitzer und Leimsieder im römischen Augst', in E. Schmid, L. Berger and P. Bürgin (eds.), *Provincialia. Festschrift für Rudolf Laur-Belart* (Basel: Schwabe), 185-97.

—— 1972. *Atlas of Animal Bones* (Amsterdam, London and New York: Elsevier).

Schmidt, B., 1967. 'Kammacherwerkstätten der spätrömischen Kaiserzeit', *Ausgrabungen und Funde* 12, 43-6.

—— 1970. *Die späte Völkerwanderungszeit in Mitteldeutschland* (Halle: Veröffentlichungen des Landesmuseums für Vorgeschichte in Halle 25).

Schmidt, P., 1969. 'Zum heidnischen und frühchristlichen Bestattungsbrauch auf dem frühmittelalterlichen Gräberfeld von Dunum, Ostfriesland', *Frühmittelalterliche*

Studien 3, 257-76.

Schönberger, H., 1978. *Kastell Oberstimm. Die Grabungen von 1968 bis 1971* (Munich and Berlin: Limesforschungen 18).

Schoknecht, U., 1977. *Menzlin. Ein frühgeschichtlicher Handelsplatz an der Peene* (Berlin: Beiträge zur Ur- und Frühgeschichte der Bezirke Rostock, Schwerin und Neubrandenburg 10).

Schoppa, H., 1953. 'Ein fränkisches Holzkästchen aus Weilbach', *Germania* 31, 44-50.

—— 1959. *Die fränkischen Friedhöfe von Weilbach, Maintaunuskreis* (Wiesbaden: Veröffentlichungen des Landesamtes für Kulturgeschichtliche Bodenaltertumer Wiesbaden 1).

—— 1974. *Aquae Mattiacae. Wiesbadens römische und alamannisch-merowingerische Vergangenheit* (Wiesbaden: Geschichte der Stadt Wiesbaden 1).

Schuette, M., 1956. 'Tablet weaving', *CIBA Review* 117, 2-29.

Schuldt, E., 1960. *Altslawisches Handwerk* (Schwerin: Museum für Ur- und Frühgeschichte).

—— 1978. *Burg und Siedlung von Gross Raden* (Schwerin: Museum für Ur- und Frühgeschichte).

—— 1980. *Handwerk und Gewerbe des 8. bis 12. Jahrhunderts in Mecklenburg* (Schwerin: Museum für Ur- und Frühgeschichte).

Schultz, H.A., 1965. 'Die Keramik der Burg Warberg im Elm, Kreis Helmstedt', *Neue Ausgrabungen und Forschungen in Niedersachsen* 2, 253-60.

Schumacher, K., 1895. *Das Kastell Osterburken* (Heidelberg: Der Obergermanisch-Raetische Limes der Roemerreiches 2).

Schwarz-Mackensen, G., 1976. 'Die Knochennadeln von Haithabu', in K. Schietzel (ed.), *Berichte über die Ausgrabungen in Haithabu* 9 (Neumünster), 1-94.

Scott, W.L., 1948. 'Gallo-British colonies: the aisled roundhouse culture in the north', *Proceedings of the Prehistoric Society* 14, 1-36.

Scullard, H.H., 1974. *The Elephant in the Greek and Roman World* (London: Thames and Hudson.

Sellstedt, H., 1966. 'Prehistoric bone material from Eketorp on Öland', *Acta Archaeologica* 37, 215-6.

Semenov, S.A., 1964. *Prehistoric Technology* (London: Cory, Adams and Mackay).

Sheldon, H., 1974. 'Excavations at Toppings and Sun Wharves, Southwark, 1970-72', *Transactions of the London and Middlesex Archaeological Society* 25, 1-116.

Sheppard, T., 1940. 'Narwhal tusks', *Naturalist* 782, 223-5.

Simonsen, P., 1953. 'Smedgraven fra Ytre Elgsnes', *Viking*, 17, 109-18.

Sissons, S., 1953. *The Anatomy of Domestic Animals* (Philadelphia: Saunders).

Sjøvold, T., 1971. 'Whale-bone tools in the Iron Age of North Norway', in J. Filip (ed.), *Actes du VIIe Congrès International des Sciences Préhistoriques et Protohistoriques, Prague 21-27 Août, 1966* (Prague: Institut d'Archéologie de l'Académie Tchécoslovaque des Sciences à Prague), 1200-4.

Skeat W.W., 1888, 'Ohthere's voyage', *Notes and Queries* ser. 7, 6, 44.

Smith, A.H., 1956. *English Place-Name Elements, Part 1* (Cambridge: English Place-Name Society 25).

Smith, C. Roach. 1856. *Inventorium Sepulchrale* (London: published privately).

—— 1859. *Illustrations of Roman London* (London: published privately).

Smith, D.J., 1968a. 'The archer's tombstone from Housesteads', *Archaeologia Aeliana*, ser. 4, 46, 284-91.

—— 1968b. 'Two unpublished rakes of deer-horn', *Archaeologia Aeliana* ser. 4, 46, 281-4.

Smith, G.H., 1979. 'The excavation of the Hospital of St Mary of Ospringe, commonly called Maison Dieu', *Archaeologia Cantiana* 95, 81-184.

Smith, J.A., 1870. 'Notice of remains of the reindeer, *Cervus tarandus*, found in Rossshire, Sutherland, and Caithness; with notes of its occurrence throughout Scotland', *Proceedings of the Society of Antiquaries of Scotland* 8, 186-222.

—— 1879a. 'Notice of the remains of the Great Auk, or Gare-Fowl (*Alca Impennis* Linn.) found in Caithness . . .', *Proceedings of the Society of Antiquaries of Scotland* 13, 76-105.

—— 1879b. 'Notice of the skull of a large bear (*Ursus Arctos* Linn.) found in a moss in Dumfriesshire . . .', *Proceedings of the Society of Antiquaries of Scotland* 13, 360-76.

Smith, R.A., 1902. 'Anglo-Saxon remains', in W. Ryland *et al* (eds.), *Victoria History of the Counties of England: Northamptonshire* (London), 223-56.

—— 1907. 'Anglo-Saxon remains', in W. Page (ed.), *Victoria History of the Counties of England: Leicester* 1 (London), 221-42.

—— 1909. 'Anglo-Saxon remains', in W. Page (ed.), *Victoria History of the Counties of England: London* 1 (London), 147-70.

Sowerby, A. de C., 1934. 'Chinese ivory carving, ancient and modern', *China Journal of Science and Arts* 21, 53-8.

Stade, K., 1933. 'Beinplatten für Bogenversteifung aus römischen Waffenplätzen', *Germania* 17, 110-4.

Stead, I.M., 1971. 'Beadlam Roman villa: an interim report', *Yorkshire Archaeological Journal* 43, 178-86.

—— 1976. *Excavations at Winterton Roman Villa and other Roman Sites in North Lincolnshire, 1958-1967* (London: Department of the Environment Archaeological Reports 9).

Steer, K. and Bannerman, J.W.M., 1977. *Late Medieval Monumental Sculpture in the West Highlands* (Edinburgh: HMSO).

Stein, F., 1967. *Adelsgräber des Achten Jahrhunderts in Deutschland* (Berlin: Germanische Denkmäler der Völkerwanderungszeit ser A, 9).

Stenberger, M., 1955. *Vallhager: a Migration Period Settlement on Gotland, Sweden* (Copenhagen: Munksgaard).

—— 1961. 'Das Gräberfeld bei Ihre im Kirchspiel Helvi auf Gotland', *Acta Archaeologica* 32, 18-20.

Stephan, H.-G., 1980. 'Archäologische Untersuchungen in der Hundestrasse zu Lübeck', *Archäologie in Lübeck* (Hefte zur Kunst und Kulturgeschichte der Hansestadt Lübeck 3) (Lübeck), 78-81.

Stevens, F., 1933a. 'An early chessman from Old Sarum', *Antiquaries Journal* 13, 308-10.

—— 1933b. 'A medieval chess piece found in Salisbury', *Antiquaries Journal* 13, 310-12.

Stevens, J., 1884. 'On the remains found in an Anglo-Saxon tumulus at Taplow, Bucks.', *Journal of the British Archaeological Association* 40, 61-71.

Stevenson, R.B.K., 1950. 'Romano-British hoes or rakes', *Antiquaries Journal* 30, 195.

—— 1952. 'Celtic carved box from Orkney', *Proceedings of the Society of Antiquaries of Scotland* 86, 187-90.

—— 1955a. 'Pins and the chronology of the brochs', *Proceedings of the Prehistoric Society* 21, 282-7.

—— 1955b. 'The chronology and relationships of some Irish and Scottish crosses', *Journal of the Royal Society of Antiquaries of Ireland* 85, 84-96.

Stoll, H., 1939. *Die Alamannengräber von Hailfingen in Württemberg* (Berlin: Germanische Denkmäler der Völkerwanderungszeit 4).

Stones, J.A., 1982. 'Wooden objects', in J.C. Murray (ed.), *Excavations in the Medieval Burgh of Aberdeen 1973-81* (Edinburgh: Society of Antiquaries of Scotland Monograph Series 2), 177-80.

Strutt, J., 1876. *The Sports and Pastimes of the People of England* (London: Chatto and Windus).

Süss, L., 1978. *Die frühmittelalterliche Saline von Bad Nauheim* (Frankfurt-am-Main: Materalien zur Vor- und Frühgeschichte von Hessen 3).

Sutcliffe, A.J., 1974. 'Similarity of bones and antlers gnawed by deer to human artifacts', *Deer* 3, 270-2.

—— 1977. 'Further notes on bones and antlers chewed by deer and other ungulates', *Deer* 4, 73-82.

Swanton, M.J., 1966. 'An Anglian cemetery at Londesborough, East Yorkshire', *Yorkshire Archaeological Journal* 41, 262-86.

—— 1969. 'A rune stone from Victoria Cave, Settle, Yorkshire', *Medieval Archaeology* 13, 211-4.

Sweetman, P.D., 1978. 'Archaeological investigations at Trim Castle, Co. Meath, 1971-74', *Proceedings of the Royal Irish Academy* 78C, 127-98.

Tatton-Brown, T., 1974. 'Excavations at the Custom House site, City of London, 1973', *Transactions of the London and Middlesex Archaeological Society* 25, 117-219.

Tauber, J., 1977. 'Beinschnitzer auf der Frohburg: ein Beitrag zur Geschichte eines Handwerks im Mittelalter', in L. Berger *et al.* (eds.), *Festschrift Elisabeth Schmid* (Basel: Geographisch-Ethnologische Gesellschaft), 214-25.

Tebbutt, C.F., 1961. 'A Roman knife handle from Croxton, Cambs.', *Proceedings of the*

Cambridge Antiquarian Society 55, 68.
—— 1966. 'St Neots priory', *Proceedings of the Cambridge Antiquarian Society* 49, 33-74.

Tebbutt, C.F., Rudd, G.T. and Moorhouse, S., 1971. 'Excavation of a moated site at Ellington, Huntingdonshire', *Proceedings of the Cambridge Antiquarian Society* 63, 31-73.

Tegner, H., 1951. *The Roe Deer* (London: Butterworth).

Tempel, W.-D., 1969. *Die Dreilagenkämme aus Haithabu: Studien zu den Kämmen der Wikingerzeit im Nordseekustengebiet und Skandinavien* (DPhil thesis, University of Göttingen).

—— 1970. 'Die Kämme aus Haithabu (Ausgrabung 1963-1964)', in K. Schietzel (ed.), *Berichte über die Ausgrabungen in Haithabu* 4 (Neumünster), 34-45.

—— 1972. 'Unterschiede zwischen der Formen der Dreilagenkämme in Skandinavien und auf den friesischen Wurten von 8. bis 10. Jahrhundert', *Archäologisches Korrespondenzblatt* 2, 57-9.

—— 1979. 'Die Kämme aus der frühgeschichtlichen Wurt Elisenhof', *Studien zur Küstenarchäologie Schleswig-Holsteins* ser. A., *Elisenhof* 3 (Frankfurt-am-Main), 149-74.

Tergast, Dr Med., 1879. *Die Heidnischen Alterthümer Ostfrieslands* (Emden: Haynel).

Theiltoft, R., 1977. 'Benmageres affaldskule', *Historisk Årbog fra Roskilde Amt*, 67-99.

Thomas, A.C., 1961. 'The animal art of the Scottish Iron Age and its origins', *Archaeological Journal* 118, 14-64.

Thomas, S., 1960. 'Studien zu den germanischen Kämmen der römischen Kaiserzeit', *Arbeits- und Forschungsberichte zur Sächsischen Bodenenkmalpflege* 8, 54-215.

Thompson, D.V., 1935. 'Trial index to some unpublished sources for the history of medieval craftsmanship', *Speculum* 10, 410-31.

Thompson, D.W., 1942. *On Growth and Form* 2 2nd edn, (Cambridge: Cambridge University Press).

Thompson E.M., 1912. *An Introduction to Greek and Roman Palaeography* (Oxford: Clarendon Press).

Thompson, F.H., 1954. 'A comb fragment from Caistor, Lincs.', *Antiquaries Journal* 34, 77-8.

Thorpe, B. (ed.), 1840. *Ancient Laws and Institutes of England* 2 (London: Commissioners on Public Records).

Thun, E., 1967. *Medieval Tommarp* (Lund: Acta Archaeologica Lundensia 8° ser., 5).

Todd, M., 1969. 'The Roman settlement at Margidunum: the excavations of 1966-68', *Transactions of the Thoroton Society of Nottinghamshire* 73, 7-104.

Togan, A. Zeki Validi, 1939. *Ibn Faḍlāns Reisebericht* (Leipzig: Abhandlungen für die Kunde des Morgenlandes 24, no. 3).

Tomes, C.S., 1923. *A Manual of Dental Anatomy, Human and Comparative* 8th edn. (eds. H.W. Marrett Timms and C. Bowdler Henry) (London: Churchill).

Toynbee, J.M.C., 1964. *Art in Britain under the Romans* (Oxford: Oxford University Press).

Treue, W. *et al.* (eds.), 1965. *Das Hausbuch der Mendelschen Zwölfbrüderstiftung zu Nürnberg* (Munich: Bruckmann).

Trimpe-Burger, J.A., 1966. 'Korte vondsberichten uit Aardenburg II', *Berichten van de Rijksdienst voor het Oudheidkundig Bodemonderzoek* 15-16, 211-9.

Trousdale, W., 1975. *The Long Sword Scabbard Slide in Asia* (Washington DC: Smithsonian Contributions to Anthropology 17).

Turner, D.J. and Orton, C.R., 1979. '199 Borough High Street, Southwark: excavations in 1962', in J.M. Harries (ed.), *Research Volume of the Surrey Archaeological Society* 7 (Guildford), 1-25.

Turner, G.J., 1899. *Select Pleas of the Forest* (London: Publications of the Selden Society 13).

Tylecote, R.F., 1972. 'A contribution to the metallurgy of 18th and 19th-century brass pins', *Post-Medieval Archaeology* 6, 183-90.

Ulbert, G., 1959. *Die römischen Donau-Kastelle Aislingen und Bürghöfe* (Berlin: Limesforschungen 1).

—— 1969. *Das frührömische Kastell Rheingönheim* (Berlin: Limesforschungen 9).

—— 1970. *Das römische Donau-Kastell Risstissen* (Stuttgart: Urkunden zur Vor- und Frühgeschichte aus Südwürttemberg-Hohenzollern 4).

Ulbricht, I., 1978. *Die Geweihverarbeitung in Haithabu* (Neumünster: Die Ausgrabungen in Haithabu 7).

——1980a. 'Knochen- und Geweihfunde aus

Alt-Scheswig—Aussagen zu Wirtschaft, Handel und Gesellschaft', *Lübecker Schriften zur Archäologie und Kulturgeschichte* 4, 211-14.

—— 1980b. 'Middelalderlig kamproduktion i Slesvig', *Hikuin* 6, 147-52.

Unverzagt, W. and Schuldt, E., 1963. *Teterow: ein slawischer Burgwall in Mecklenburg* (Berlin: Deutsche Akademie der Wissenschaften zu Berlin: Schriften der Sektion für Vor- und Frühgeschichte 13).

Unz, C., 1974. 'Römische Militärfunde aus Baden: ein Nachtrag', *Gesellschaft pro Vindonissa Jahresbericht 1974*, 85-91.

Vaughan, R. (ed.), 1958. 'The chronicle attributed to John of Wallingford', *Camden Miscellany* 21, 1-67.

Vebæk, C.L., 1965. 'An eleventh-century farmhouse in the Norse colonies in Greenland', in A. Small (ed.), *The Fourth Viking Congress* (Aberdeen: University of Aberdeen), 112-18.

Vertet, H., 1958. 'Médaillons en corne de cerf du Département de l'Allier', *Revue Archéologique de l'Est et du Centre-Est* 9, 241-4.

Vierck, H., 1972. 'Redwalds Asche', *Offa* 29, 20-49.

Vilppula, H., 1940. 'Luuluistimista', *Suomen Museo* 47, 51-8.

Vogt, E., 1960. 'Interpretation und museale Auswertung alamannischer Grabfunde', *Zeitschrift für Schweizerische Archäologie* 20, 70-90.

Volbach, W.F., 1952. *Elfenbeinarbeiten der Spätantike und des Frühen Mittelalters* (Mainz: Römisch-Germanischen Zentralmuseum Mainz Katalog 7).

Vollgraff, C.W. and van Hoorn, G., 1936. *Opgraving op het Domplein te Utrecht* 3 (Utrecht: Provinciael Utrechtsch Genootschap van Kunsten en Wetenschappen).

Wacher, J., 1975. *The Roman Towns of Britain* (London: Batsford).

Wachter, B., 1972. 'Bericht über die Probegrabung auf dem Weinberg in Hitzacker (Elbe) in den Jahren 1955/66', *Neue Ausgrabungen und Forschungen in Niedersachsen* 7, 241-82.

—— 1976. 'Mittelalterliche Knochenschnitzarbeiten von der Weinbergburg in Hitzacker (Elbe)', *Zeitschrift für Archäologie*

des *Mittelalters* 4, 123-30.

Wade-Martins, P., 1970. 'Excavations at North Elmham, 1969: an interim report', *Norfolk Archaeology* 35, 25-78.

Wahlöö, C., 1972. 'Läderstämpler', *Kulturen* 151-2.

Wainwright, G.J., 1967. *Coygan Camp* (Cardiff: Cambrian Archaeological Association).

Wainwright, S.A., Biggs, W.D., Currey, J.D. and Gosline, J.M., 1976. *Mechanical Design in Organisms* (London: Edward Arnold).

Walke, N., 1965. *Das Römische Donaukastell Straubing-Serviodunum* (Berlin: Limesforschungen 3).

Walker, F.G., 1908. 'Report on the excavations at Barton', *Proceedings of the Cambridge Antiquarian Society* 12, 296-313.

—— 1912. 'Roman and Saxon remains from Grange Road, Cambridge', *Proceedings of the Cambridge Antiquarian Society* 16, 122-32.

Wall, S.M., 1980. 'The animal bones from the excavation of the Hospital of St Mary of Ospringe', *Archaeologia Cantiana* 96, 227-66.

Wallace-Hadrill, J.M., 1962. *The Long-Haired Kings* (London: Methuen).

Waller, K., 1957. *Das Gräberfeld von Altenwalde, Kreis Land Hadeln* (Hamburg: Atlas der Urgeschichte, Beiheft 5).

—— 1959. *Die Gräberfelder von Hemmoor, Quelkhorn, Gudendorf und Duhnen-Wehberg in Niedersachsen* (Hamburg: Atlas der Urgeschichte, Beiheft 8).

—— 1961. *Der Urnenfriedhof in Wehden* (W.D. Asmus and C. Suchuchhardt (eds.), Die Urnenfriedhöfe in Niedersachsen 4), (Hildesheim: Lax).

Ward, R., 1928. *Records of Big Game* 9th edn, J.G. Dollman and J.B. Burlace (eds.) (London: Ward).

—— 1975. *Records of Big Game* 16th edn, Africa A.A. Best and W.G. Raw (eds.) (London: Ward).

Ward-Perkins, J.B., 1949. 'An eleventh-century bone stylus from York', *Antiquaries Journal* 29, 207-9.

Warncke, J., 1912. 'Mittelalterliche Schulgeräte im Museum zu Lübeck', *Zeitschrift für Geschichte, Erziehung und Unterricht* 2, 227-50.

Waterman, D.M., 1959. 'Late Saxon, Viking

and early medieval finds from York', *Archaeologia* 97, 59-105.

Waterman, R., 1970. *Ärtzliche Instrumente aus Novaesium* (Cologne: Hang).

Way, A., 1847. *Catalogue of Antiquities, Coins, Pictures and Miscellaneous Curiosities in the Possession of the Society of Antiquaries of London* (London: Society of Antiquaries).

—— 1849. 'Notice of a singular sculptured object, probably a chess-piece, found at Kirkstall Abbey', *Archaeological Journal* 6, 170-2.

—— 1855. 'Notice of a relique of old municipal ceremony, preserved at Chichester', *Archaeological Journal* 12, 374-6.

Webster, G., 1951. 'An Anglo-Saxon urnfield at South Elkington, Louth, Lincolnshire', *Archaeological Journal* 108, 25-64.

—— 1958. 'The Roman military advance under Ostorius Scapula', *Archaeological Journal* 115, 49-98.

Weidmann, S.W., 1967. *Dental Enamel: Rock or Tissue* (Leeds: Leeds University Press).

Weinmann, J.P. and Sicher, H., 1955. *Bone and Bones* 2nd edn, (St Louis: Mosby).

Wells, C., 1964. *Bones, Bodies and Disease* (London: Thames and Hudson).

Wenham, L.P., 1964. 'Hornpot Lane and the horners of York', *Annual Report of the Yorkshire Philosophical Society*, 23-56.

—— 1968. *The Romano-British Cemetery at Trentholme Drive, York* (London: Ministry of Public Building and Works Archaeological Report 5).

—— 1970. 'Discoveries at King's Square, York, 1963', *Yorkshire Archaeological Journal* 42, 165-8.

Werner, J., 1949. 'Eberzier von Monceau-le-Neuf (Dép. Aisne)', *Acta Archaeologica* 20, 248-57.

—— 1962. 'Ein reiches Leitengrab der Zeit um 400 n. Chr. aus Fécamp (Seine Maritime)', *Archaeologia Belgica* 61, 145-54.

—— 1964. 'Herkuleskeule und Donar-Amulett', *Jahrbuch des Römisch-Germanischen Zentralmuseums Mainz* 11, 176-97.

—— 1977. 'Zu den Knochenschnallen und der Reliquiarschnallen des 6 Jahrhunderts', in J. Werner (ed.), *Die Ausgrabungen in St. Ulrich und Afra in Augsburg 1961-1968* (Munich: Münchner Beiträge zur Vor- und Frühgeschichte 23).

West, B., 1982. 'A note on bone skates from London', *Transactions of the London and Middlesex Archaeological Society* 33, 303.

West, S.E., 1969. 'The Anglo-Saxon village of West Stow: an interim report of the excavations, 1965-8', *Medieval Archaeology* 13, 1-19.

West, S.E. and Plouviez, J., 1976. 'The Romano-British site at Icklingham', *East Anglian Archaeology* 3, 63-126.

Westwood, J.D., 1876. *A Descriptive Catalogue of the Fictile Ivories in the South Kensington Museum* (London: Eyre and Spottiswoode).

Wheeler, R.E.M., 1923. 'An insula of Roman Colchester', *Transactions of the Essex Archaeological Society* new ser. 16, 7-41.

—— 1927. *London and the Vikings* (London: London Museum Catalogue 1).

—— 1930. *London in Roman Times* (London: London Museum Catalogue 3).

—— 1935. *London and the Saxons* (London: London Museum Catalogue 6).

Wheeler, R.E.M. and Wheeler, T.V., 1926. 'The Roman amphitheatre at Caerleon, Monmouthshire', *Archaeologia* 78, 113-218.

—— 1932. *Report on the Excavation of the Prehistoric, Roman, and Post-Roman Site in Lydney Park, Gloucestershire* (London: Reports of the Research Committee of the Society of Antiquaries of London 9).

—— 1936. *Verulamium. A Belgic and two Roman Cities* (London: Reports of the Research Committee of the Society of Antiquaries of London 11).

White, D.P., 1977. 'The Birmingham button industry', *Post-Medieval Archaeology* 11, 67-79.

White, L., 1962. *Medieval Technology and Social Change* (Oxford: Clarendon Press).

Whitehead, G.K., 1964. *The Deer of Great Britain and Ireland* (London: Routledge and Kegan Paul).

—— 1972. *Deer of the World* (London: Constable).

Wiberg, C., 1977. 'Horn- og benmaterialet fra "Mindets tomt" ', in H.I. Høeg, *et al.*, *De Arkeologiske Utgravninger i Gamlebyen Oslo* 1 *Feltet 'Mindets Tomt'* (Oslo), 202-13.

Wichers, J. van Buttingha, 1888. *Schaatsenrijden* ('s Gravenhage: Cremer).

Wichmann, H. and Wichmann, S., 1964. *Chess. The Story of Chesspieces from Antiquity to Modern Time* (London: Hamlyn).

Wild, J.P., 1970a. *Textile Manufacture in the Northern Roman Provinces* (Cambridge: Cambridge University Press).

—— 1970b. 'Button and loop fasteners in the Roman provinces', *Britannia* 1, 137-55.

—— 1971. 'The South Shields heddle', *Archaeologia Aeliana* ser. 4, 54, 230-1.

Wilde, K.A., 1953. *Die Bedeutung der Grabung Wollin 1934* (Hamburg: Beiheft zum Atlas der Urgeschichte 1).

Wilde, W.R., 1863. *A Descriptive Catalogue of the Antiquities in the Museum of the Royal Irish Academy* 1 (Dublin: Royal Irish Academy).

Willems, J., 1973. 'Le quartier artisanal gallo-romain et mérovingien de "Batta" a Huy', *Archaeologia Belgica* 148, 5-61.

Williams, F., 1977. *Pleshey Castle, Essex (XII-XVI Century): Excavations in the Bailey, 1951-63* (Oxford: British Archaeological Reports 42).

—— 1979. 'Excavations at Marefair, Northampton, 1977', *Northamptonshire Archaeology* 14, 38-79.

Williams, J.H., 1979. *St. Peter's Street Northampton. Excavations 1973-1976* (Northampton: Northampton Development Corporation Archaeological Monograph 2).

Wilson, D.M., 1961. 'An Anglo-Saxon ivory comb', *British Museum Quarterly* 23, 17-19.

—— 1968. 'Anglo-Saxon carpenters' tools', in M. Claus, W. Haarnagel and K. Raddatz (eds.), *Studien zur Europäischen Vor- und Frühgeschichte* (Neumünster: Wachholtz), 143-50.

—— 1971. *The Anglo-Saxons* (Harmondsworth: Penguin).

—— 1976. 'Craft and industry', in D.M. Wilson (ed.), *The Archaeology of Anglo-Saxon England* (London: Methuen), 253-81.

Wilson, D.M. and Klindt-Jensen, O., 1966. *Viking Art* (London: Allen and Unwin).

Winkelmann, F., 1901. *Das Kastell Pfünz* (Heidelberg: Der Obergermanisch-Raetische Limes des Roemerreiches 14).

Winkelmann, W., 1977. 'Archäologische Zeugnisse zum frühmittelalterlichen Handwerk in Westfalen', *Frühmittelalterliche Studien* 11, 92-126.

Winter, F., 1906. *Die Kämme aller Zeiten* (Leipzig: Degener).

Wislocki, G.B., 1942. 'Studies on the growth of deer antlers I', *American Journal of Anatomy* 71, 371-415.

Woodall, D., 1959. *A Short History of the House of Kent* (London: published privately).

Woodfield, C., 1981. 'Finds from the Free Grammar School at the Whitefriars, Coventry, c. 1545-c. 1557/8', *Post-Medieval Archaeology* 15, 81-159.

Wrenn, C.L., 1962. 'Magic in an Anglo-Saxon cemetery', in N. Davis and C.L. Wrenn (eds.), *English and Medieval Studies Presented to J.R.R. Tolkien* (London: Allen and Unwin), 306-20.

Wright, R.P., 1946. 'Roman inscriptions on bone counters', *Proceedings of the Society of Antiquaries of Newcastle upon Tyne* ser. 4, 10, 16-18.

Young, A., 1956. 'Excavations at Dun Cuier, Isle of Barra, Outer Hebrides', *Proceedings of the Society of Antiquaries of Scotland* 89, 290-328.

Young, A. and Richardson, K.M., 1960. 'À Cheardach Mhor, Drimore, South Uist', *Proceedings of the Society of Antiquaries of Scotland* 93, 135-73.

Young, J.Z., 1957. *The Life of Mammals: their Anatomy and Physiology* (Oxford and New York: Oxford University Press).

Zachrisson, I., 1976. 'Medeltida ekorpillar?', *Fornvännen* 71, 117-20.

Żurowski, K., 1953. 'Uwagi na temat obróbki rogu w okresie wczesno-średniowiecznym', *Przeglad Archeologiczny* 9, 395-402.

—— 1973. 'Methoden zum Weichmachen von Geweih und Knochen in frühslawischen Werkstätten', *Berichten über den II Internationalen Kongress für Slawische Archäologie* (Berlin), 483-90.

—— 1974. 'Zmiękczanie poroży i kości stosowane przez wytwórców w starożytności i we wczesnym średniowieczu', *Acta Universitatis Nicolai Copernici*, Archaeologia 4 (Torun), 3-23.

Index

F = Figure; n = note; T = Table